G000160666

The Day Sasquatch Became Real For Me

Steve Isdahl

Contents

Forward

I have been a passionate outdoors person since the age of 5 or 6 due not only to my natural craving but as well a result of my grandfather and neighbors introducing camping and fishing to me. I was an accomplished angler and as well had become a successful self-taught bowhunter at an early age. Although I was taken on many a fishing and camping trip I did not grow up in a hunting family, so I had to learn myself by trial and error. I started hunting by myself and soon learned that to be a successful bowhunter, going alone would be key. Less scent, less movement and no one to want to go home early or when too wet on soggy days.

Wedge Mountains/Garibaldi Park B.C.

One evening while solo hunting for early Sept deer, the sun had disappeared bringing a late evening un successful hunt to an end. I was so stubborn and obsessed I would never quit early ever but would stick it out to the bitter end no matter how far the hike or how bad the weather. This meant a long hike out in the dark every time.

One particular evening with no previous knowledge or warning of any type, I had a face to face encounter with what could only be described as a large non-human being. It was terrifying. That moment was the moment Sasquatch became real for me. From that day forward I would find myself looking at life differently while the same time questioning basically everything. Why? because I now knew for certain we had been lied to, all of us, by the ones we are taught to look to for answers and guidance.

I went on to become a successful tradesman, contractor, a sportfishing as well big game hunting guide. During those 35 years in the outdoors, I would have one more visual encounter and numerous other related 'incidents' with these publicly unacknowledged beings. All but one experience I never intentionally sought out or asked to have in any way. Shape or form.

Let's face it, looking into the eyes of a menacing looking non human 800 lb plus 'humanoid' being which can have its way with you at any given moment, no matter what, isn't something to be craved. Not by me anyway.

That terrifying evening years back never actually gave me absolute proof of what I saw. I knew what I saw wasn't a man, I knew it but I never looked into its eyes as It was only a silhouette. Absolute confirmation of the existence of these beings came when I was 25 years old. My grandfather decided it was safe to share with me a face to face encounter he had years ago. He shared, but not until he could be certain no other family members could hear him tell me and as well after he made certain I believed in the existence of these beings.

This moment was 'IT' as in not a question about it. I immediately knew, without a doubt, what I saw WAS what I saw. I then wanted answers.

Fast forward, while making the public aware of my new outdoor knowledge filled apps, numerous people from around the world would harass me nonstop via emails, video comments and private social media messages while inquiring IF I had ever had a sasquatch encounter OR heard of any. At first, my reaction was, "I need to crack this open like I need a root canal". Only out of respect for my deceased grandfather did decide to come out publicly, and in a significant way. I made a YouTube video of my experience and his, and then the emails started to flood in.

At the time of this writing, I have close to 9000 emails from first-hand witnesses around the globe. Sadly, a high percentage of those people are troubled due to ridicule, being terrified and emotionally scarred from their experience wit nowhere or no one 'safe' to share with. These people need to be respected and heard. These people, as well as my grandfather, are who motivated me to write these honest experiences down and place them in this book, preserved and shared for all.

I thank you for buying this book and hope you can learn from its content's or at least bring comfort and confidence back to your lives which enables you to enjoy the natural world again. Please, once done reading this, pass it on to other's who may use it. We need honest knowledge shared again and from the people, not the ones who manipulate use and discard on a daily basis, the current global corrupt governments

Thank you again, be safe, be free and lose your fear.
Steve Isdahl

Chapter 1 - My First Encounter

I started running around the woods with a bow and arrow at around 12 or 13 years old near my mother's house. My parents had split up when I was in elementary school, and my mother, sadly left us to live rurally with her new partner, an abusive bully type alcoholic.

Her husband had earlier in life made a failed attempt to get into archery and had an old forgotten recurve bow in the storage room. I found it and instantly took to shooting the bow near the forest edge at the top of the road above their house. It was my escape from the home of 'misery' as well as the beginning of an adventure-filled lifetime.

The Sooke hills were basically across the driveway right next door to my mother's house. The moment I arrived every second Friday after school, I would grab the bow and hit the woods solo while chasing rabbits and learning how to hunt. Dark would come and to bed I went early. I remember making my mother set the alarm for ridiculous early times so I could be in the woods well before daylight while attempting my first eventual harvest which would be a rabbit. That poor woman, imagine your 12-year-old boy running out the door in the dark, alone into the forest, not knowing where he is and hoping he returns sometime after dark that evening time and time again.

Myself around 13 yrs. old near my mother's home.

One mention from those early days was the creepy feeling I would often get from the thick bush 50 yards from where I would shoot a target. There was a pile of topsoil in a vacant lot at the end of the road. Beyond that was raw woods a creek and power lines. I'll never forget feeling that time to time and wondering what may have been lurking in those dark shadows while I attempted to maintain focus on my shots. Not every time but often I would feel as though someone or something was watching me from a particular area of thick brush near the creek mouth coming from the timber. Admittedly, I never went in there to have a look, never intentionally stood and stared but would instead try to stay focussed on my shots while staying clear from that side of the lot. Now, years later, I often look back at those days, relive the feeling and wonder just how many times that 'something' was actually one of these beings. Now that I know what I know, I am confident I was being watched, not a doubt about it.

Fast forward to 1985, the time of year would be early Sept as I hiked solo yet again mid-week up to a hilltop at around 3 pm. I would be anticipating the evening to come as I sit and wait for last seeing light and possibly a chance to arrow a fine black tail buck as they fed into the open for the evening. By now, I had many deer harvested with my compound bow and was at the selective hunting stage, meaning I would allow much younger deer to live as I hoped for a large mature deer. I was patient, confident and loved every minute of it whether or not I had success. This time of year, was early September so the deer would only move at very last seeing light, all night and sometimes you would get lucky and catch them in the open and first light in the am. I was obsessed, stubborn and driven. I would stick it out until I could barely see after sun down no matter what the weather or how far the hike out in the dark to my old pick up.

I recall being reasonably troubled during numerous hikes into a certain evening spot while nearing the final high pass before I dropped down to an old logged off-shelf where I anticipated the deer to be. At the top, there was a stretch in the old deactivated road, which was narrow and closed in with thick underbrush consisting of thick willow followed by a deep salal patch and big timber. Both sides of the trail/road rose steep and were well covered with a screen of underbrush as well low light due to the big timber canopy above.

The hair on the back of my neck and arms would stand on end each time I had to walk through this particular stretch. I never understood why. The air would be deathly still, zero sounds, nothing heard as I silently slipped along with senses burning on fire like I was about to be pounced on or something. The feeling can only be described accurately as very vulnerable. I dreaded that stretch of my hike every single time, especially hiking back as the sun would be down and seeing the light to get out to the truck challenge. This was years before modern headlamps, and of course, I would never carry a flashlight.

This one particular evening, I had made it through the nerve-wracking stretch of my hike and was now rapidly descending the old gravel-covered washed out spur road. The dry gravel road under my trudging hiking boots was quite noisy as I dropped down steep and straight ahead. The need to be stealthy ended with the fading light. I would slip out of my spot quiet as possible to not disturb it too much, but once away and out of range, I would just noisily hike along as my only mission was to get home.

I came to a stretch the old dry gravel road dropped steeply down ahead of me, then shot straight right at the base of a rock face. The rock face went up from the old road main 25 ft. As I descended, the top of the rock would be at my eye level then switching to 'above me' as I made my way down.

I could barely see the ground I was walking on as it was near pitch-black however, the early sept deep blue sky was making the silhouette of the timber sharp against the skyline. This was something the being I was about to meet did not anticipate...or did it? As I hiked down the steep grade in the trail, I glanced up and couldn't help but notice a guy above me perched on top of the rock face looking down on me. It was undeniable we were looking directly at each other, although it was too dark to see facial features, only sharp silhouettes. It was basically 'in your face' obvious as this 'person' was just above me, maybe 12- or 15-yards tops.

Like anyone else would, I spoke out in a friendly tone with, "oh hey, any luck? "as I presumed it was another hunter sitting above the trail waiting for game himself. The moment the first sound came from my mouth, the 'person' went to defensive mode and slowly and very deliberately ducked down out of sight below the height of the rock top he was crouched down on.

Adrenaline was instant. Here I am, basically a teenage boy alone in the middle of nowhere, its pitch black all around me and this 'man' looked to be about to ambush me. Now I still have around a 45-minute pitch black hike to get out to safety. You want to freak a person out? Do what this dude did, it'll work guaranteed.

Why does this guy hide from me? Not say high back? Was he trying to kill me? He for sure knew I was coming not a doubt about it. What troubled me at first was the fact that seeing light for deer antlers had ended nearly an hour ago, why would he still be perched above the trail? He should have been on his way out easily an hour ago. Why would he be sitting in the dark alone above the path for an hour? Why no hello? Why was he waiting for me then?

Self-Preservation was in full effect. My adrenaline surged as I placed a razor-tipped arrow on my bowstring and kept it pointed between myself and the dark bush on the side of the road this 'man' was on. I then crept as slow as a snail, dead silent so I would be able to hear my assailant coming through the bush to attack and hopefully get my arrow into him before he caused me harm. The air was still, I could not hear anything, as in nothing. I remember I could hear my blood pumping between my ears. I had never felt so threatened in my life. That was the longest solo hour-long hike in my life as I slipped out silently in the pitch black to the safety of my old pick up. I couldn't run for it due to the fact I would make so much noise, and I would not hear the assailant coming behind me or running up past to ambush again. I had to stay silent, move intentionally and stay alert. It was agonizing not being able to run for my life. My steps slow, deliberate and silent as best I could all the while keeping that arrow pointed in the direction of who or whatever that was that appeared to be stalking me.

By the time I made it to my truck, I was so angry it was dizzying, let's face it, fear is actually anger. I thought, "WHY did this idiot do this to me? Who does he think he is? I'm going to wait for him at the beginning of this road and give it to him when he comes out". I drove to the beginning of the old dead-end road and waited ... and waited. I then drove to the main road, which was another 8 km out. Turned off my motor and listened for his engine, nothing. I soon realized there was nowhere else to park a vehicle out of sight, and the only previous tracks on the road were mine, none other. This was when I began to question exactly who or what was waiting for me upon that rock.

It was mid-week, and no one was out there but me. I had all my commercial fishing money in my bank account and no day job, so while my buddies either worked or went to school, I would be out hunting darned near full time. Weekend's would typically be busy with other hunters and not so busy during weekdays so that is when I would go. Now I was confused, how could some dude be out here with no vehicle or camp alone and mid week?

 The next day I brought a buddy with me, and we snuck a rifle with us (you had to be 19 to hunt alone with a rifle then, not a bow). I had my buddy go above me and sit where that dude was the night before. Upon seeing him and comparing, it was quite obvious the 'guy' on top of that rock was around three times the size of my friend. I am confident my eyes got pretty wide open at this moment.

Years would pass before I would figure out exactly who/what it was who was staring down on me that night.

High Above Birkenhead Lake B.C.

The Day Sasquatch Became Real For Me

Chapter 2 – Confirmation, My Grandfather's Share

My grandfather was a very accomplished outdoorsman. A passionate angler, geologist, government timber cruiser and eventually retired head of safety at the Victoria shipyards. Although he never hunted, he took my grandmother on endless camping trips filled with angling and gold panning activities. My grandmother would proudly bring out and show off her see-through pill containers filled with gold nuggets they found during their adventures. I'll never forget the times they took me along to camp at Cowichan lake staying in the old camper van at Bens Marina in Youbou. So much fun, so many memories.

I still have photocopies of my grandfather in uniform with Queen Elizabeth. During WW2, he was one of many brave men who climbed into a bomb filled sheet metal tube with wings and flew bravely to drop on the Germans to ensure we all would live the lives we do today, with no German accent or worse, death due to nationality. Imagine how terrifying that was? He was the sole original reason I finally came out publicly online to admit I had seen a Sasquatch.

For years, numerous people hounded me online non stop with, "any Bigfoot stories? You must have!" and, "come on, tell us if you saw them before, you had to," it was endless. It then struck me that my grandfather died scared of the same people he offered up his life overseas so many years back. Afraid of the ridicule he would have received had he come out openly about the being he had seen face to face broad daylight one faithful day on Vancouver Island. How I learned of his encounter is as follows.

Sometime around 1995, we were having Christmas dinner at my mother's house. I had previously bought my Grandfather a hard-covered book called "Mysteries of The World" as a Christmas gift. I was first to finish dinner, as usual and went straight for the living room to flip through the pages in the Sasquatch chapter. I wanted to see if there were any stories, I had not been familiar with. This was a long time before the internet.

My grandfather came in after me and sat next to me, looking at what I was reading. He then looked up to be sure no one was near or could hear and asked, "do you believe in these things, Stephen?". I replied, "yes, I do, I believe I saw one before and am certain of it." He then responded with, "well in that case, I have something I will share with you." As he scanned the other room to ensure privacy with me, I noticed he was dead serious with his demeanor. I recall feeling quite nervous or maybe excited? I don't know, but it was a very surreal moment, to say the least.

His story went like this.

"It was years ago I was timber cruising for the government near the head of the San Juan River on Fleet Creek. It was mid-July, noonish and quite hot out. I was headed to a creek through big first growth timber and neared the edge of the overhang above the creek bed below. I had to crawl over the root overhang, hit the gravel slope and slide down to the creek edge. Once I

stopped at the bottom, I looked down the creek to see a man in a fur coat looking back upstream at me. He rose, looked for a split second and abruptly took off up the bank and ran away". I then thought, "hmm, darn it; it's going to be a Port Renfrew hippy sighting report." He then said, "I thought it was a guy in a fur coat but soon realized that guy's fur coat was actually reddish hair growing from his naked body. He was covered in it except his face, the hair on his body was around 3 or 4 inches long."

I was speechless. Imagine my feelings as the man I trust the most on the planet just told me he saw and exchanged looks with a real live freaking sasquatch. All those years of knowing and not knowing what it was looking at me that night came to reality instantly. I was probably stuttering, trying to pick which of 50 questions to get out first. I immediately started the barrage:

How big was it?
"it was around 8 feet tall, maybe more".

What color was it?
"He looked to be around 8 ft tall or more."

Which way did it run?
"He took two leaping bounds up the bank and ran in the direction I had come. I could not believe how fast and how powerful he was as I had to climb up the bank to get back up where he simply leapt up with no effort. I recall his thighs were at least the circumference of my waist or more".

Were you scared?
"I was quite concerned for sure."

Who did you tell?
"I couldn't tell anyone as I would have been called insane and likely been fired from my job. I had to be credible with my findings".

Did you tell Grandma?
"Yes, I told your grandmother, and I believe she saw one as well years later."

Why didn't you ever tell me earlier?
"I felt if I told you I saw a naked 8 ft tall hairy man in the forest, you would not ever want to go fishing with me again and would think I was crazy."

Had you ever seen one since?
"No, it was the only time I saw one, and never really wanted to see another again."

Did you tell the authorities?
"No, I thought it best to keep that to myself."

So, there you go—confirmation with zero doubt. I then knew %100 these things were alive and

living right alongside us out there.
 Once you know, there is no going back. You will never be able to think the same or be relaxed the same in the woods ever again, or not question what we have been taught/lied to about ever again. I cannot speak for everyone else, but from that day on, I have pursued the answers to my questions about literally everything.

My number one question now is, "why have we been lied to.

Chapter 3 – Encounters And Questions

The Cabin Shook

I never met anyone who saw a Sasquatch during the immediate years after my grandfather shared his experience. Life was young yet, doors were opening, and my future adventure life was about to kick into overdrive. My circle of 'people' was small, and the internet hadn't been invented yet, the Sasquatch topic not popular at all.

My thirst for adventure was increasing rapidly as I found myself venturing into the forests of Vancouver Island, more often than not. I was becoming a seasoned bowhunter while consistently creating success time and time again. My true calling in life was becoming clearer by the day. During those times out in the wild, I still never stopped thinking of those beings I now knew lived in the very forests I hunted alone.

The year was around 1988, and I had rented a small old one-bedroom cabin on the outskirts of Sooke, B.C. The cabin was backed into the corner of the property with first-growth fir timber behind as well to one side. The underbrush was thick against the back house with maybe a 2ft path along the outside wall was about it. There were no curtains, no cable, only electricity and a small wood stove for heat.

I was alone reading a book lying on the couch, which was against the forest side of the room. The wood stove was behind me on the same side of the room, the forest side of the house. It was around 10 pm and very dark outside as there were no neighbors, no street lights, no nothing. There wasn't even an outside light on the cabin. Just me inside like a fish in a bowl for all outside to see easily during darkness. I cannot see out; anything can see in. One large window on the yard side of the house, one large window on the end of the room.

Imagine the jolt you experience as 'something' suddenly smacks or slaps the top of the cabin wall above you from the outside. Dead silence, no sounds, no wind, no storm, no rain, just you breathing while silently reading then BAM out of nowhere, the entire cabin shakes from the impact outside. The impacts were so hard. The cabin shook as well the stove and pipe up through the ceiling. WHAM! Again, and again. I haven't a clue how many times as the shock was something else. It was definitely a few times or more. The impact wasn't sharp as it would be from a stick or a rock; it was dull like from a large hand or some kind of padded flesh. It was deliberate, not a random accident. It was also above M.E. like who or whatever it was did it intentionally right where I was positioned in the cabin.

I haven't a clue why but I have never had 'panic' in me when it comes to situations. I have never run blindly, nor knee jerk reacted, thankfully. Once I realized my situation was completely out of my control (not even a phone to call for assistance), I calmly rose. I walked to the room to grab my old, 303 Le Enfield rifle, slid in the 10-shot magazine, racked one into the tube, then returned to the couch and continued to read. What else was I going to do? No outside light, no flashlight, no phone and definitely didn't need to meet what was beating on the wall in the pitch black, that was certain.

The slapping or banging stopped, whatever it was left; I was terrified. The power displayed was something else. I get goosebumps literally today as I type while thinking back, remembering what it felt like as I knew 'something' was watching me from the darkness outside those windows.

During daylight hours, the next day, I went for a look out back, loaded rifle in my hands. There was nothing between the house and those thick bushes, no stick, no log, no boulder and the ground too hard for any kind of prints. Who or what did that? I am certain I know the answer now as I did back then.

This experience happened maybe three years after my visual face to face encounter while bow hunting solo.

I Began To Ask Questions

Years later, maybe 1995, I headed to a local pub to meet up with a friend who was a Fisheries Officer, basically a cop on the water with a gun and badge. My friend skippered a patrol boat in the mid to north coastal waters of B.C. The vessel and crew would literally go on tour for 30 days straight, followed by 30 days onshore paid time off. Once to dock, phone calls and meet for beer plans made.

This one particular Friday eve, my friend called to invite me for beers with him and his crew. We met up, and there were 5 of them, one a biologist, the other officers as well a mechanic for the ship's power.

By this time, I was very inquisitive when meeting people who were employed in the wilds of B.C. (and other places). I would wait for the right moment then subtly but directly ask if anyone had ever seen anything odd during their travels in the remote coast or mountains. More often than not, people would laugh, shake their heads while questioning my sanity or seriousness of my topic. I found over the years that people who had seen one of these beings never shared willingly. They would keep it to themselves due to the reality of feeling ridicule from the community. But, I also soon learned that if you remained neutral, honest in delivery, looked all in the eye and never made fun, they would, in return, see you were seriously safe, and sharing would follow. Luckily, this happened that evening while I had beers with the Fisheries crew.

My friend took the initial lead with a loud, "Oh boy, here we go again, don't listen to this idiot" while laughing loudly and bringing his beer mug up for another sip. Me? I did not laugh but instead looked each crew member in the eye to see who was listening, who was looking for my reaction to tell seriousness or not. One of them knee-jerked with, "Ya, I SAW ONE and oh man, was it HUGE." He then looked around the table at his co-workers with the expression of "Whoops, did I just say that," then followed up with a delivery of "Oh well, this is what happened, and I don't care who believes me." His story went as follows.

Steve Isdahl   The Day Sasquatch Became Real For Me

"I was with a few friends having a few beers at Ma Millar's Pub, which was at the east end of Humpback road. We took the back road to head home to Sooke (Humpback Road). There were 4 of us in a small car. As we travelled along, suddenly, a large upright jet-black thing stepped out onto the road in front of us, ran along and veered off to the north side of the road disappearing into the darkness."

This road was a small winding road which went through big timber canopy nearly single wide lane with only a few houses at the west end near Sooke Road. The north side of the road was a no go zone due to the Victoria watershed. I used to bow hunt various areas just south of the road, and coincidentally, I first experienced the nasty smell of "death," which has commonly been associated with these beings. His next immediate words were, "It was HUGE, and we were scared to turn around." That statement confirmed they DID see what he described. Why?

The road was narrow, forest on both sides thick and dark. Turning the vehicle around would place your back to the darkness where the giant was, you would have to inch forward, backward about 3 times to fully turn the car around before speeding off. When picturing it, it made complete sense. Who would think of that detail if not true? Of course, it would be nerve-racking to have your back to that darkness while not being able to speed away right away. Imagine the panic from your passengers as they yell at you to "hurry up and get out of here."

Again, taking a chance and asking a group of strangers paid off. Soon it would be more common to receive a "Yes, I saw one" reply than not.

A Girlfriends Face To Face Encounter

Fast forward to around 2002. I found myself living in Pemberton, BC. Little did I know, I had moved literally to 'ground zero' for Sasquatch country and activity. The more people I met, the more stories I would hear firsthand from the local witness witnesses. I found it was more common to hear of a Sasquatch encounter than a cougar encounter within my community, and cougars were very plentiful.

I was dating a local girl who lived here for around ten years, originally from Edmonton, Alberta. The majority of the community at the time was First Nations and farmers.

We had just gotten back to my house one evening, and as I was walking into my bathroom, I glanced back to see her standing in front of my bookshelf where there were a few sasquatch books and a small plastic sasquatch figure which I thought she was looking at. As I walked into the bathroom, I said out loud, "Oh, that's just my Sasquatch roommate" or something random like that. I couldn't hear her clearly and only heard an "I know what I saw, bug me all you want." I kind of shook my head and said back, "Huh, what was that?" She replied with, "I know what a bear is, and it wasn't a bear I saw, bug me all you want, I don't care." Now my attention is %100 as I replied, "I just said that's my Sasquatch on the shelf, what are YOU talking about?" She then said, "Oh, I thought you knew about my sasquatch encounter and were about to tease me like everyone else." You know what I asked next.

After assuring her, I had no ridicule in me and as well had seen them before, she then began to tell me her incredible experience, it went as follows.

I was around 19 years old and was taking a road trip back to Edmonton with a girlfriend to visit family for Christmas. We were around an hour or two past Clearwater, B.C headed north on Highway 5 to Jasper. We probably shouldn't have been driving as it was late, dark, no traffic and basically started to white out (whiteout is when it's a blizzard, and you can't see past 20 ft ahead of you in the headlights during a winter storm). I was literally going at a snail pace as I said out loud to my girlfriend, I can't believe we were driving in this shit and looked toward her. What I saw was her wedged up against the passenger door, eyes bugging out of her head, speechless, staring in shock toward me but past me to my driver's side window. I turned my head to see what it was which had her frozen and there beside my face was an extremely large hair covered head and face looking right into my eyes from maybe 18 inches away. It was huge and was bent over running along right beside my car, looking into my window at us.

Now can you imagine that shock? Imagine not having a clue about these beings to only have one literally in your face living, breathing and real, and staring at YOU? What a wild random experience being shared with me right in my damned home!

I went on to ask her numerous questions:

Q: "What did it look like?"
A: *"It was huge, brown hair big square teeth, big dark eyes and a look on its face like it was rocking it out like it was amused."*

Q: "How much do you think it weighed?"
A: *"I haven't a clue, maybe 700 to 1000 lbs.?"* (she was a horse person, so she was somewhat familiar with large sized body mass).

Q: "Did it look angry?"
A: *"No, it looked amused, like it was thrilled to be looking at us, it was almost smiling and had teeth like ours, big square white teeth."*

Q: "How long did it run beside you?"
A: *"Not too long. I was trying to get focused on the road and saw the white line beside me on the opposite side of the highway. I had veered completely to the wrong side of the highway in the whiteout. I went to steer back to my lane, and it faded into the snowy darkness, and we never saw it again."*

She went on to tell me they then drove in silence to the next stop, which was Blue River husky Station. She as well mentioned the steep drop on the far side of the highway. I know this area well, and there is only one small section where there is any kind of steep uphill before Blue river. If you know this highway, you know where she was.

She added that once they arrived at the gas station, they ran inside, grabbed a table, a coffee and just sat waiting for daylight. She said they never spoke of the incident while sitting there, never spoke of it while driving to Edmonton, parted ways and never spoke again. Isn't it odd just how many people do this? React like this? I haven't a clue why it is, but many times you hear of two or more people sharing the same experience side-by-side and never speak of it. Why is that?

Alone With Two Of Them

A few years after my 'scare' in those meadows, I had volunteered my time and skills to deal with a local wolf population explosion. The wolves had realized how easy it was to kill pets in yards as well gruesomely pull calves out of beef cattle as they gave birth. Dealing with wolves takes a great deal of patience and determination as you cannot just go attempt it the odd weekend and expect results. You must stay focused, follow the wolves, learn their travel routes, nail the timing and locations, get it done and never quit until your goal is reached.

It was around mid-February late in the afternoon and very cold. It was -22 C (- 7.6 F) the air still no sounds at all but my own. I was up the Pemberton Valley following the tracks of a large travelling pack of timber wolves into a patch of first growth cedar trees which surrounded a swamp situated along the valley bottom up against the steep bluffs which shot up the mountain. It was the north side of the valley; south was the direction home.

I had worked my snowmobile around the west end of the timber patch, which surrounded the swamp and saw where the wolves had exited the timber as they headed straight west.

Snowshoes on, backpack on, loaded rifle and off I went into the dark timber patch to look for a bottleneck route of the wolves. When I found it, I would place my gear to catch them next time they came through.

I found a great spot after maybe 30 minutes snowshoeing along, took my pack off and started to ready my hardware. Due to the size of the trees, I would need to hammer in some long fencing staples into the large cedar tree to fasten my gear. My hammer was a metal shanked Estwing roofing style hammer, (hatchet one end, hammer other).

Now take note, after you have seen one of these wild beings, you never let your guard down while in the woods; ever! What I mean is, you cannot ever stop being alert to 'sounds' or shapes and shadows—you just can't stop yourself. Until you actually see or hear one of these beings, you may never clearly understand just how much you start to pay attention. I believe it's a survival thing built into us. Many people just don't go into the woods again after an experience with these beings and the ones that do? They never stop being alert; it's not possible.

The sound of my hammering was very loud in that valley bottom as the air was still and frozen. Pow, pow, pow as the hammer hit home on the steel staple. The final blow the loudest on the tree trunk. I then dropped the hammer, and as it hit the base of the tree. I 'thought' I had heard something but kept doing what I was doing while not pausing to look around, but I was now listening for more as I worked the gear out of my backpack. I was nailing in a second staple when the very clear, no mistake about it, POW of wood on wood echoed off the slope above me maybe 100 yards up. This instantly had my full attention.

I stood in silence as goosebumps instantly creep ed across my body. I was hoping it was hardwood bark popping but already knew it wasn't. A place in the interior of B.C. where I hunt late season mule deer would routinely create the frozen 'pop' of hardwood bark, it was normal – there. However, the timber before me was fir, cedar and hemlock. There wasn't bark popping here at home due to the freeze; this was an intentional sound. I was alone, and no other signs of humans were on the trail, just deep fresh powder snow with my tracks, nothing else. I stood, hoping it was tree bark and went to set another staple. I hit the tree with three swings, then a very loud wood on wood POW resonated above me again. Two seconds later, another wood on wood POW replied from my left maybe 200 yards and right above where my sled was parked. POW, another reply from the original position above me.

My potential worst nightmare was happening again. Not one but two of these beings had their attention on me, and it didn't feel so good. I instantly stopped what I was doing, loaded my gear into my pack, never looked up or around. Grabbed my rifle, loaded it, flipped the safety off and began my awkward trudge back through the deep snow, over fallen snow-covered logs, around the tops of bent willows and made my sled. I don't know if they popped the trees again as I hiked, I was breathing way too loud and making a lot of noise while snowshoeing back.

Once to my sled, it almost felt like you would as you were feet away from getting back into the shark cage while shark diving. You feel like something is going to grab you from behind, while you are focused on the security in front of you. I remember the stressed feeling while trying to turn my sled around on the unpacked deep snow. It's VERY easy to bog down and get temporarily stuck while doing this, and I didn't want that as one of these beings was above me for certain and very close. Back, forth, back, forth until I am facing OUT OF THERE.

Even while ripping down the mainline full-throttle on my 800 skidoo, I was stressed, why? Because a fellow big game hunting guide I know in Alberta had shared his experience of one of these beings pacing him in timber effortlessly as he sped away on his sled. He said the reddish-brown 9ft tallish 'thing' ran off to the side the same speed as him no problem as he raced to get out of there. Due to that story clear in my head, I never looked back, or to the side once, I just pinned the throttle and never let up until I was back to the mainline and eventually my truck.
I still to this day have never been back to that location, I just don't have the urge to tempt another face to face, I'm just not into it.

Chapter 4 - Why I Stopped Looking

I am fast-forwarding a handful of personal experiences and will share the one where I decided its best if I leave these beings alone. This book is not about 'me' but more about the people. I will share more personal experiences in book 2.

One year around 2009 or 2010, I quit guiding up north for a season. Normally I would leave home around July 15, head up to toad river B.C. and join the crew to get ready for three months straight of remote big game guiding. With my fall freed up, I decided I would once and for all put my skills to the test and find these local beings. In the previous few years, my interest grew as I intentionally began to ask any and all locals if they had, had an experience and where. After much input as well a few nervous moments myself, I chose my zone and would start early spring.

Early spring, I thought would be best as all the prey animals would be condensed to lower elevations and with no leaves on the undergrowth, visibility would be very good cover very sparse to hide a large being. This one particular intersection, as I referred to, would place me up the Pemberton Valley and between the drains of south Creek to the south side of the Lillooet River and North Creek to the north side. Due to the ongoing rec snowmobiling during the winter, I figured they must be travelling in timber only to avoid laying tracks on the ice fields above for all to see. If you look on Google Earth, you can see where a person could travel valley to valley through timbered connectors year-round.

One particular day I woke early. I grabbed my gear, camera tripod, 300 WM rifle and headed up the valley. I left my truck a kilometer back from my target area and began my slow, silent stalk into some hidden meadows. This day would be my first 'experience' in the area. Thick mature cottonwood trees surrounded the hidden meadows. The spring growth was picking up, and visibility was already limited with thick brush below the cottonwood canopy. I had a young guy who worked for me seasonally in Whistler BC as I was a contractor during the off-season between guiding. While we stood silent, looking, there was a sudden long, drawn outcall. It was a weird, unfamiliar sound, which still today I cannot mimic. We both heard it clearly as there was no wind, sun up, and it came from some thick timber only around 100 yards away.

The only way to describe it was it was low pitch, not high, three-toned, to long for human lungs and loud. Not car horn loud, but for a human voice. It was the length and loudness of the call that made it impossible to mimic. I can mimic basically any game animal, including wolves and quite effectively. There was no way I could mimic this one. It never did it again, and I immediately took it as a potential, "your busted" call. My hunter mind instantly decided, "look innocent, leave come back a few days later and pretend you didn't hear it."

I then decided to leave my truck a full mile back from the intersection and travel up the river edge instead of the logging road. Morning wind would be travelling downhill in my face, and the rushing water noise would cover my sound. I didn't feel uneasy, but as well didn't feel alone. I could somehow just feel they or someone was present in a way; I was right.

Soon I was in position again. The camera on the tripod rifle laying hidden in the grass. I had a good view of all three meadows from my position, so if something were to be in or cross a meadow, I would see it and for certain video it. I feel leaving a firearm behind would certainly pick up success with these beings; however, it was bear rutting season, and there was no shortage of grizzly as a well black bear sign.

Suddenly, in my front direction, 'something' swung through the underbrush and impacted the trunk of one of the large mature cottonwood trees. Not only once but a few times and very loud. To describe it clearly, to mimic it would mean to fasten a log to a backhoe boom and swing it very hard and rapidly into the tree trunk. The display of sheer power was unbelievable and the same and, at the time, intimidating. So intimidating, in fact, that I was literally frozen in my tracks.

I didn't think of the camera in front of me once. I had a serious surge to RUN from head to toe. I felt so vulnerable it was enough to make me feel sick. Whatever or whoever did that did it intentionally for me; it was that clear and obvious. If anything, or anyone wanted to tell you to go yourself without words, this was absolutely effective. I knew instantly I didn't want to have anything to do what sent that direct message. I'll admit it, I was terrified, and my only thought was, "get me outta here." I grabbed my rifle, grabbed my tripod/camera, looked down and marched my ass out to the mainline logging road and hastily made my retreat down the road to my truck. I nearly received whiplash from looking behind me every second step as that mile walk was a long and stressful one.

I never went back to that place, but a few years later would have yet another similar encounter with two of them while trapping wolves. I will save that and other personal experiences to share in the next book as it is time to hear from the people in the following chapters.

And yes, that was the last time I intentionally sought out these beings. From that day on, my mind would repeat, "I know you are here; you know I am here, let's not ruin this for each other.."Chapter 6 - Prints, Proof and People

I believe I have mentioned more than a few times publicly that I really do not have much interest in the sign of Sasquatch beings. I mean, really, why would I? These beings are travelling literally, maybe 300 yards out behind the house routinely. I have seen them first hand more than once (possibly four times) to date and heard them more than a half dozen times. At the same time, I have no urge to attempt to prove their existence to the world. Let's face it; there have been more than enough pictures, thousands of tracks, dozens of videos, tens of thousands of first-hand witnesses already so the proof is in. What would change if I were to seek out and photograph or cast footprints of tree breaks? Nothing. The fact our modern governments refuse to public knowledge and inform the people is %100 the reason I am writing this book. The government needs the support of the people; the people do not need government support.

The next pages of this book are from the people for the people. Each experience is no more important than the next or last and has not been placed in any significant order. Read carefully, take knowledge from each experience and secure it in your own database. Learn from these experiences and share the knowledge with friends, family and future generations.

I find it almost a crime we are not fairly informed. Why does a family man or woman currently have no choice of where they may potentially bring their children for a safe, pleasurable weekend while camping, hiking or fishing? Did a person or persons get chased away from a 9 ft tall hair covered being exactly where an unsuspecting family is about to go camping? Where may they be going camping the very next day? That is a crime that is currently repeating and must be stopped.

The scientific community has been presented with over 130 DNA samples and refuses to acknowledge; it's just not going to happen through 'them.' For a more in-depth read on that/those fact, be sure to read Scott Carpenter's book "Truth Denied The Sasquatch DNA Study."

The fact our modern governments refuse to acknowledge and inform the people publicly is one hundred percent the reason I am writing this book. The honest facts need to be shared with the public. No human has the right to keep knowledge from another; we are all in this together.

The government needs the support of the people. The people do not need the support of the government. People need to support each other, and that is what we are doing here.

Chapter 5- The People, My Motivation

Years later and maybe a dozen or more experiences with these beings, including a second sighting, I seemed to have created a bit of a following online while promoting outdoor knowledge. Now and again, a subscriber would ask publicly, email and private message me questions of whether or not I had any Sasquatch stories or encounters. I ignored the topic openly for the most part. A few years prior, I was outspoken on a hunting forum after someone created a thread on the topic, but that was about it.

Once I decided to share my own and my grandfather's story, the public reaction was off the chart. People started messaging me as well as emailing me with significant relief as they finally had someone, they could share their experience with.

I soon realized there were a significant number of troubled souls out there who as well had experiences and were not having such a good time dealing with it. These people needed support and a safe place to share. I reached out on the camera via my YouTube channel and urged the audience to email me their encounter story if it would help them. I created a new email address with my domain called 'tellmystory@howtohunt.com'. It didn't take long for the first story to come in, then another and another, then a dozen, a dozen more, a hundred, a hundred more, then thousands and to date has not stopped.

While reading out loud and sharing these numerous encounters, I soon realized there were many individuals and groups attempting to quiet these people by shaming and ridicule. All I see is good, hardworking, honest people being shit upon by numerous bully dirtbag types. Me being a natural protector/defender decided it was time to stand up and fight back. In honor of my grandfather and many more, I felt and still do that one of my purposes here is to fight for the good, the truth and that is exactly what I am doing here today.

The following shared factual stories are from people around the globe. Innocent, honest, hardworking people who need support and the respect they deserve. Support to help deal with the fall out received due to their experiences they never asked for once. In this first book, I deliver the factual encounters, word for word by the people who had them.

Read and learn.

Chapter 6 – The Encounters

A Bald Sasquatch

Hello Steve,

My name is James, and I really enjoy your channel I respect the hell out of you, not only as an extremely experienced hunter and bushman but for what you are doing about this subject and what you are doing for those who are just looking for answers for what they have experienced and not have to worry about the repercussions of ridicule and disbelief. I have my own theories on what these beings are, but I generally yield to folks like you who have had so many experiences and have rubbed shoulders with others who have actually gone out with boots on the ground and have done their own research. However, I would say the biggest reason I respect your point of view is that you put the first nations people's histories and knowledge at the top of the list of people to listen to about this. I think people scoff at the Natives' beliefs, oral history, and experiences are ignorant, small-minded, and so full of themselves that they wouldn't know whether to scratch their watch or wind their ass when it comes to these things. I truly believe that all Native tribes had a better handle on their surroundings then we could even fathom.

Let's see... should I listen to some jackass who goes out running around whooping and banging sticks on trees and claim they caught a glimpse of one, so therefor they know more, or the guy whose people thrived in some of the most inhospitable territories known to man with sticks and rocks for thousands of years? Places that still claim the lives of people who have gone out with modern equipment to this day.

Anyway, I digress for now, and I will finally share my story. I am the Program Manager at a group home for at-risk teenage boys here in Utah. I know when someone is lying to me, and I am very good at sifting through the bull shit and recognizing the truth when or if it arrives. Teenagers are like wild animals; just don't turn your back to them because they will eat you.

I was born and raised in Jackson, Wyoming and spent my youth running around the woods and mountains from the southern end of Yellowstone through Grand Teton National Park and the surrounding mountains of Jackson itself. My ancestors settled Jackson and the surrounding areas, and they fought for every bit of what they had, and I was raised the same way. You take care of you and yours and help those in need and if it's broken, then fix it, and when you give your word, then you honor it. Back home, we call that cowboy logic. It's the only way I know how to do things, so when I told this story to someone, I thought I trusted and who I thought would help me out. Instead, he said what I saw was impossible and would never happen. WHAT IN

THE F*CK! So, I just kept my mouth shut about it for a long time until I found "How to Hunt", and I slowly started to trust my memories again.

When I was around ten years old, back in 1990, I had a friend who lived down the street from me who got a horse for his birthday. So, I saddled up my horse, and we hit the trail. Back then, kids like us could take off for a few days before anyone started worrying. I think I remember that we rode those poor horses all over that country for three days. The second and third day, we went way up this canyon called Cache Creek Canyon to see how far we could make it. We got to this place where they had put a covert in way back when they were still logging the area. The covert was sticking out of the rode and had holes in it, and it looked pretty gnarly, and we found that our horses would jump over it so we must have ran them back and forth over that d*mn thing for an hour until the horses were all lathered up. We decided to unsaddle and let them cool off. I remember clearly that my horse had his ears pinned forward and would give a little sort now and again concerned about something off in the timber, but I couldn't see anything. Then I smelled something awful, a rotting flesh mixed with a wet dog smell. The first thing that came to my mind was it must be a dead elk because that canyon is a migration route for elk in the fall and spring. I told my buddy that I was going to go check it out to see if I could acquire some ivory.

I went up to the base of this cliff that was about 60 feet tall. The trees blocked the area between my friend and the horses and me. As I was scanning the area, I looked over to my right, and this giant black man was standing right at the base of the cliff. The evening sun was behind me, and the way the shadow played off the base of the cliff, I could only see the top half of this man. Now, normally that would be cause for concern, I suppose, but in my mind, it was another mountain man who decided to quit civilization and live off the land like in the old days. I had been with my dad and grandpa when we had met other men who would come down to stock up on supplies and then head right back up into the mountains, so I really just thought he was one of them. Yes, he was huge! But again, I was an ignorant little country boy who up to that point never met a black person before. The only thing I did know was what I saw on T.V. when we watched the Packers play, and all I knew is that those black folks were bigger than white folks and usually better at sports than us. LOL, so in my mind I that's what I was seeing. The man was enormous, with long dreaded black hair and a fairly long beard that was silver up the middle of it. This is where it gets weird. He was bald on the very top of his head, and

I remember that it looked raw and possibly cut up or something, and I was thinking man that looks like it hurts. Another thing I noticed was his head was fairly pointed as well. He was wearing what I thought was a black bearskin coat because it was pitch black hair covering his upper body, but I could see his massive shoulder muscles and biceps moving under the hair. I'll near forget the look he gave me; it was a look of annoyance. I knew the look well because I was a really annoying kid back then. But he was more concerned about something else up the ridge because he would look up the ridge and study it for a bit then back at me like I was in the way or something. I don't remember how long the encounter lasted, but it seemed to be a couple of minutes, maybe a little more. He then lifted his arm and grabbed a ledge on the cliff wall, and kind of leaned against it. Then my buddy called out to me, and he snapped his head over, and so did I and when I looked back at him, he just pulled himself up the cliff and grabbed another ledge with his other hand and repeated it like two more times until he was at the top and disappeared from view. I yelled to my friend, 'did you see him?' As he walked up to me, he asked: 'who was that?' Several years later, I tried talking about it with him, and he claimed he didn't see anything or anyone. I was sure he saw him, though.

Anyway, a couple of years later, we were taking a pack trip to a place called Turquoise Lake. I remember I was 12 because that spring, my cousin and I were taught how to train our first colts and rode them on that pack trip. We got up to that same covert, which was even gnarlier then before, and our colts wouldn't cross over it. As the rest of the group went on ahead, we stayed behind, trying everything to get them fillies to go over that covert. After a while, we had to take a rest, so we just sat and talked for a bit. I was on my horse when I realized that I was standing right next to that cliff, and was eye level with the ledge where that man had put his hand on. Let me repeat that, I was on my horse and I was eye level with where his hand was. That was about 9 feet from the ground. I then proceeded to tell my cousin the story and what I saw, but he immediately blew me off, saying there was no way I saw a man that tall climb that cliff only using his arms.

Even then, I hadn't thought much about it. It wasn't until 2007 that I started getting into Bigfoot, and I saw a drawing of one that some guy had drawn after he had an encounter. I thought my mind was going to quit me. I scrambled to find paper and pencil. I went to town frantically drawing; my hands were shaking so bad. When I was done, I stepped back and just stared at it. There he was the man I had seen so long ago, and all I did was make the creature the other guy drew bald and with a beard, and it was exactly what I remembered. Now, say what you will, but I swear I believe I may have seen a Bigfoot that day. The only thing that doesn't make sense is the fear people, and you have described. I didn't experience that, maybe I was too dumb or innocent or both to have even thought to be scared, I don't know, but in my mind, these beings are a lot like us. They will get mean and aggressive if they feel like they or their family are being threatened; I can only imagine how scary that would be. In most cases, they just slip away further into the woods.

I don't want to downplay what you and others have experienced, but I really believe they normally wouldn't want to harm us as long as we're far enough away. But then, of course, there's probably some dick heads out there too just like we have in our species, so caution must be taken at any rate.

I don't give a rip if you use my name or if you want to share this. I'm too old and tired to give a shit what some pricks think of me, and I can tell that you are telling the truth about what you saw and I know you are an honorable man who wants to help people and anymore I've learned that you're the kind of person to float the river with. So, keep it up man, you are doing a good thing!

All the best – James

Jim's First Email To Me

Good day,

I hope you are doing well. Feel free to use my story, or part of it, as it runs a little long.

It was late Fall, early winter of 1980 in the rural mountains of N.C., near the Va./Tn border in an area called Roans Creek. I was 14. I had spent the majority of those years hunting and fishing. In my 14 years, I was never over a 2-minute walk from the woods. Living in a rural setting without siblings left me two options, 1) sit on my ass or 2) get out in the woods! I loved the outdoors and spent every hour I could hunting or fishing. I had NO FEAR of the woods. I would walk 45 minutes in total darkness to my deer stand, hunt all day and return home after I could no longer see 10 feet in front of me. I never gave it a second thought. The woods were my private Heaven...little did I know, they would soon become my worst nightmare.

I came home from school with time to grab the Beagle, Hunting vest and my trusty .410 single shot. I ran across the road, down my Great Uncles driveway, turned left up to the old Sawmill landing. I released Katie. She started her "Z" pattern, nose to the ground with an occasional "oohhllpp" to assure me where she was. Katie was trained to circle the rabbit and push it back to the hunter, unlike many dogs that you have to follow. I climbed up on a pile of old slabs to secure a better view. Probably 4-5 feet high. She was cutting back and forth through Mature White Pines, between 30-40 feet high. They had been planted in nice straight rows after the depression ended; roughly 1933? I mention the straight rows so you can picture how the setting sun's light would light up the open areas.

I could see Katie crossing back and forth, and occasional "oohhllpp"...so very relaxing. Then out of nowhere, Katie yelped as if she was being hurt. We've all heard dogs in pain and scared, a long continuous crying yelp. I focused my sight in her area, about 80 yards out. NOTHING...then her cries became further away. As she ran away; cries that went out of ear shot...crying out the entire time, until I could no longer hear her.

My eyes never left the tall pines. I then saw something moving through the rows. The sun was at an angle to my right. I could only see its 'shadow' as it came closer. Bear? Horse? Uncle

Rex??? 70 yards...60...50. The landing of the old sawmill was about 30 yards long, circled with 4-5-foot-high slab piles. I last saw 'IT' to my right at about 40 yards. I climbed off the slabs to my left. This allowed me to see up the rows, as the slabs blocked the sun to my right. I eased along the slabs, moving closer to where I had seen 'IT.' I swung out wider, so I could see around the slabs at the end...Then my world changed forever.

The next 20 seconds takes 10 minutes to explain. Time moved in slow motion, as I can recall every step I took and each eye blink. A horrid smell engulfed the area. Almost like a musk; warm, yet piercing. I'm sure you know what I mean by musk. if that makes sense?

Every hair on my neck stood up, my senses were in overdrive, I wanted to throw up, I knew I was being watched, and I knew 'IT' was close. I turned to my right, and just on the other side of the slabs was Bigfoot. 15 yards away. I could see him from his waist up. His head was semi pointed. No hair on forehead, cheeks or nose. Wide nose, thin lips, square teeth, with deep dark eyes. His shoulders were freakin' huge, the size of basketballs, the chest was defined, and any body-builder arms went past his knees, and they were 27-29" thick...he had some "guns." The hair color was dark, kind of grey/brown.

I froze, I told myself, 'there's no such thing as Bigfoot!!' I looked down, rubbed my eyes when I looked back up... he was still there. I rubbed my eyes again and dipped my head down and to an angle...STILL THERE...At this moment I turned and ran maybe 10 yards...again I said, 'NO SUCH THING!!!' I stopped, turned around...He had stepped up on the slab pile.... My God! It was 10 feet tall...shoulders 4-foot-wide, thighs 38-40" thick... I'd say it weighed 700-800 lbs. That's it; it is real! I threw my gun to my shoulder...then thought; I will only make this thing MAD... I lowered the .410 to my waist, keep in mind, I was looking this creature in his eyes. When I lowered my gun, time stood still. I could hear him breathing. This may sound crazy, but I never felt threatened. The eyes were firm, but I didn't see 'EVIL.'

I leaned hard to my right so the setting sun would be hidden behind a large Pine Tree behind him. He leaned his head to the other side and gave a light exhale; GAME OVER! When he moved, I turned and ran through the thorn bushes, down the hill, jumped halfway over the creek, landing in the middle, I tripped coming out the other side, falling on my rear...just in time to see HIM following me down the bank. I could see my house, 100 yards to go. I began screaming....MOM >>>MOM!! I jumped over the barbed wire fence, catching my boot...just on the tip, just enough to trip me up, just enough to turn my head and see HIM stopped at the creek.

My mother had heard my screams and was on the porch at the top of the stairs. I came flying up the steps. My jacket torn to shreds by the bushes. My face covered in scratches. Mom said, 'you are white as a ghost, what happened?' About the time she asked, this creature began a blood curling scream as it paced back and forth along the creek, just in the shadows of the Pine trees. 10-15 minutes of pacing and screaming. It stayed there until well past dark. Mom kept asking, 'what did you do? What did you make mad?' Needless to say, I didn't sleep that night.

Next day...I come home. My mother says, 'get your gun and get up there and find Katie; she never came home. You need to get back on the horse. It was probably a wild Bore, and if you don't go back in the woods today, you will let fear win and never go back. I grabbed my .410 and out the door I went. I didn't make it four steps down...BLOOD CURLING DEATH SCREAM!!!! Mom even said, 'STOP, Get back in here!' You could see the shadow of this creature strutting back and forth...About 20 feet back under the Pine trees...After about 5 minutes my Great Uncle called the house, mom answered, he asked what the hell was wrong with me and what was I yelling and screaming about?? She informed him of what was occurring, and he left it at that. That creature paced back and forth until dark...he would only 'YELL' when I came out.

This went on for the next two days, but only when I was there. Finally, Saturday came. I was looking forward to catching up on lost sleep.... NOPE! A little after sunrise, a knock on the door; in walked my Uncle, my grandfather along with his 2 brothers. One of which owned the old sawmill. The same great Uncle that had called earlier in the week. 'We need you to come with us...Why in the HELL did you tear up the sawmill? Uncle Rex is good to you, and you repay him by throwing sh*t everywhere?' We went together to see the sawmill. There were slabs all over the place! The entire landing area was covered. I got one more ass-chewing until I pointed out the 20" bare footprints, the 300lbs chunks of stumps thrown around, and the 22-foot Steel I beam guide for the mill tossed on its side. They looked at each other, walked around with hands-on-hips, and then across their chests, then came back. 'Dick, we think it's best if you stay outta the woods for a while.' No argument from me!

Over the next couple of weeks, My Great Uncles would drive to the old sawmill about 30 minutes before dark, and I noticed their truck lights would come on from time to time throughout the night. I never heard the 'scream' again! Well, not from the sawmill and not for 38 years. I'll never know why it screamed, why it paced, or why it came back that week? If it had wanted to 'get' me; it had me at the sawmill. It never ran after me. It just followed me. END OF STORY---

What are your thoughts?? Your personal story stands the hair up on my neck. I think there are some of us who 'believe' we are attached to nature; have our 6th sense working, whereas most people have had it bred out of them. I know when I'm being watched. I know what I smell. I have no doubt that these Beings know 'who' can see them...or sense them. I have had numerous 'tree knocks' ...too many to remember. I've had 6-7 rocks thrown near me (different times)...and even had a rock tossed at me in my tree stand! I think rock-throwing is just a warning. Not to hit us, maybe even sometimes, just playing. I feel these beings around me. I feel no threat from 99% of the time, but every now and then, I get the feeling of GET THE HELL OUTTA HERE... as if some of these creatures might not be as 'forgiving' if we walk up on them.

I could go on for hours. My wife and I live in Rural NC Mtns about a mile from Tn. on a hundred acres, mostly wooded. We respect all wildlife. We only kill what we are going to eat and try to see that the animals have food during the winter. I think 'THEY' know our hearts...'they' know we're never going to shoot at them, or bring in News Crews to try and film them...etc.

I'm sure you have 100's of stories also...not all encounters last 3 minutes. Most are just simple

Tree Knocks, rocks, smells and the KNOWING they are watching; that uneasy feeling. I don't expect you to read this novel. Maybe you'll like the 'MAIN' story. I have some PICS also, just got to find where I put em. I send you another email with the pics. Sorry so long-winded, I ease up on the next report.

PS. Can't believe you didn't leave that Meth Head under some stump for Grizzly bait...what a scumbag!

Best Wishes Richard

Jim's Second Email To Me

Good evening Steve,

I hope all is well. After watching your video about the man fearing for his children as the Sas' seems focused on his kids' play area, I have decided to tell you about the evening that changed my Love of the outdoors.

It was deer season, December of 1982. I still lived at the same house, where two years earlier, I had my Face to Face encounter with a Sasquatch. Since that encounter, I had pretty much stayed out of the woods except for hunting with my brother or Uncle, NEVER alone.

I had just turned 16 and picked up my first vehicle, a 1974 CJ5 4x4—a Remington 30-06 pump-action (no more single shot 410 for me). Needless to say, I felt as 'BIG' n Tough as anything on the planet !...and at that time, the 30-06 might as well have been a cannon in my mind...(ah, the joy of a foolish youth) OK, back to it.

Feeling confident, I began deer hunting again. I still didn't like the dark, but I knew that my 30-06 could take care of any animal out there. I had purchased a Male Doberman (Butch) shortly after my first run-in with the Sas,' and had spent two years with Butch by my side, and he even slept right beside me. Needless to say, Butch was my best friend and never a day passed that we didn't wrestle, play fetch and run the fields. Butch was over-attentive. When I went deer hunting, he would sit with me in blinds or lay at the base of the tree where I had my stand. He became a problem after I shot a little six pointer...his first 'kill.' After I hit the deer with a double lung shot, the deer made his way off a steep hill about 60 yards.

After finding the deer, I began dragging it out with the 90 lb. Doby pulling against me! Finally made it to the top of the hill, only to have 1/2 mile straight back down to my house.

During the pull downhill, I slipped, the deer came on top of me, and Butch LOST HIS MIND, attacking the dead deer which he felt was attacking me...long story short, after this, Butch hated deer and wouldn't allow me to hunt without chasing the deer as they approached !! Butch was now left at home to await my return during deer season.

I had finished lunch and started my 2-mile hike to a favorite isolated field surrounded by hardwoods and Persimmon trees. I arrived in time to sit for a couple of hours, watching a few Do's browse and hoping for Ole Mossy Horns to step out. About 30 minutes before dark, I heard something coming, hard and fast. I readied myself for the huge buck to step into range; there was Butch. He paid no attention to the browsing does. He circled me while whining and bumped me repeatedly. This kept up for about 10 minutes. The Doe's ran off, and He refused to lay down or obey commands. I got so mad, so fed up, I got up and proceeded back towards home. Keep in mind; Butch was still whining and acting crazy while we walked.

We made it about a half-mile to a hard curve in the old logging road. I could bare left, walk up the mountain, hit the ridge and save 30 minutes by walking through the woods or continue the logging road. It was 10 minutes before dark. Just enough light to get up the hill hit the fence line and walk home in the open woods by moonlight. I turned left and began up the hill. At that very moment, the air turned thick, that smell of rotting flesh mixed with feces and piss filled my nose. It came flashing back at 1000 mph. Again, time stood still, and a loud low grunt-yelp drew my attention to a fallen tree stump 40 yards straight up hill. Just enough light to see a two-legged figure at the stump...no running this time! I had 90 lbs. of teeth and a 30-06. I yelled, 'SICK HIM BUTCH!!'

Butch tore up the hill; and as quickly as he went up, he came down, yelping like a scared puppy He flew past me. I had a 30-06, I took a few steps towards this Being, I raised my rifle. At that moment, I felt something pulling my leg, BUTCH had sunk his teeth into my Camo's and was pulling with everything in him, still whining, he would let go only long enough to 'BARK-CRY' at the THING above us. Butch was terrified, and his bark was of terror. I looked back up, raised my rifle, trying to remain balanced while Butch yanked at me. Then this creature yanked the stump outta the ground and HURLED it in my direction. The stump was bigger than me, and it crashed and rolled within 10 yards of me. I know this sounds crazy, but I felt then, and still today, he didn't intend the stump to hit me. As the stump stopped, this creature let out a YELL straight out of the bowels of hell...at that moment, my 30-06 felt like a B.B. gun. This 10-foot creature stood with his arms in a 'COME AND GET SOME' stance. He began a Growling-Chant-Yelp.

Butch was now running. I heard him go out of sight down the logging road.." YELP<YELP<YELP...GONE! Now, there I stood alone, 30 yards from 'IT'. I lowered my rifle and began backing up, never letting 'IT' out of my sight. I felt the old road under my feet and began walking towards home. Watching as this 'THING' shadowed my steps. The entire time knowing I only had maybe 10 minutes of light left. I had over a mile and a half to go. 3/4 of this would be on the old abandoned logging road, surrounded by 30-40 trees.

From the time I smelled the air turn bad to where I now stood had taken maybe 15-20 seconds, though it seemed to be 15 minutes. No one can imagine how time slows to a millisecond crawl as if a camera running 30,000 FPS is put in slow motion. As I kept walking, I began shaking, almost uncontrollable, I could hear him breath. I heard him chatter his freakin' teeth!! At this point, HE knows he's got me, and I'm doing exactly what he wants. I am in 100% panic mode, and every sound, every grunt, tree snap is meant to increase my fear. Five minutes pass, I know I'm closing in on an intersection near the old weigh station. The intersection will bring another logging road from his direction.

I feel he will hit that old roadbed and come straight at me. We come to the old weigh station. I can barely see it now. He steps out onto the roadbed, I can see his dark figure standing in the middle, his shoulder damn near as wide as the road!! At that moment I decide, when he comes at me, I will empty my 220 grain Brush Busters in his chest. I stop, take a deep breath and try to control the shaking. I bring the rifle to half raised, just touch my shoulder. I have to close my eyes, trying to force myself to adjust to the last minute of light, trying to see the figure 30 yards away. HE steps into the woods and comes back up beside me. We begin the walk again. This time, there is no seeing him. It is dark, and the moon is too low to break through the tall trees. I'm 200 yards from the State Road. I know the Right of Way will be wider, and the road runs dead East. I will have moonlight to at least see where I'm walking, and maybe a car will travel my way.

I make it to the State Road. HE is right beside me, 20-30 yards. If I stop, HE stops, when I move, he moves. I pick up my pace. I never run! I don't dare make enough noise that I can't still hear him walking. My Uncle was a Sniper in Nam and had spent five years teaching me to STALK, teaching me little tricks, always telling me to be quiet and 'use your ears, as much as your eyes.' It's amazing what goes through your head. The Grunts and yelps have become almost zero. He was still breaking limbs and right beside me. I can just see my Great Uncle's house and can see the T.V. flashes in his window. Another 200 yards and the woods will end. It opens up to grazing land for the Cattle. My eyes have adjusted, the moon has risen quietly a bit over the past hour. I can see the open field, and YES, the cattle are grazing along the fence at the edge of the steep bank above my head. I can make out their shadows in the moonlight.

At last, the woods end, and it's an open field from here on out. Surely, he will stay in the woods. Just ten more minutes! NOPE! I notice the cattle become nervous, then they turn and flat out run! That damn thing is walking in the field, just to my left and behind me, probably 20 feet above the road, up a steep bank. I can't see him. The twilight is in front of me so, I'm sure I stick out brightly to HIM. One hundred yards, I can see our kitchen light bouncing off the leaves. I stop and turn in HIS direction; he keeps coming, black as night, stinking, grunting. I raise my rifle. He stops and starts the teeth chatter.

By now, the tears are flowing, and I'm shaking again. I called him a MO-FO in a voice that was probably only loud enough for me to hear, but it was all I could muster up. I turn towards home, and I feel the gravel of our driveway under my feet. I'm shaking so bad I can hardly walk up the steps. I get to the door in time to hear that blood-curdling yell about 50 yards away, directly behind the house. He had followed me to the fucking door! As I walked in, my mother said, 'NOT AGAIN?' She sees by my tears and deathly white complexion along with uncontrollable jerking, the answer is YES, AGAIN!

As I calmed down, my mother said, 'I was just getting ready to come look for you.'...there is something wrong with Butch, and he won't come out from under the steps. Bigfoot or not, I headed outside to check on my best friend. He was under the porch, in the back corner, in a space not big enough for a good size cat...he is in a ball, shaking and whimpering. I crawled towards him, to get him out. He snapped at me. My friend was scared. It took a few days before he came out, but he was never the same dog. He didn't live a month.

The next day my Great-Uncle gave me an ass chewing for running his cattle at night. What the hell was I doing? What was I thinking? I had caused one of his cattle to fall, and I needed to come over and help him remove her from the field. As we pulled up on the scene, the steer was torn, and an entire Ham was missing. He looked at me and said, 'must be a damn Panther, I heard one YELL last night.' I just said, 'wasn't no cat. We moved a couple of months later, and it would be three years before my next meeting with Ole Stinky.

I truly believe there is NO HUNTING these creatures...they HUNT you, and they are well advanced. This creature knew what he was doing, and he could have snapped me right up at any moment. We are in their playground, in their homes. They are in control when we are in the woods. I had a different view of the mighty 30-06 after that day.

Back pack hunting in north central remote B.C.

Camping Alone

My name is Joel,

I had a couple of really unique experiences in my life. I'm now 35, but the first time I realized these things where real, I was just a kid, and I was out camping with my dad and his friends and some of the other kids. Myself and one of the other boys were sharing a tent, and the other person with me started shining his light around right near when the sun went down, and suddenly we saw this shadow of something right outside our tent. At first, we thought it was one of our dads trying to scare us, but we tried to ask them who it was and there was no response, the unusual thing about the outline was that it had a pointy head we thought his dad was wearing a beanie or something. Wake up the next day, and we ask our dads why they were outside our tent, and they have no idea what we are talking about, we ask them where the hat is, and there was no hat it was the middle of summer, and no one had a beanie or anything that could make that shape we even looked through his dad's stuff. It turns out my friend's dad, who was a farmer, had seen one of these creatures before and he told us about it and what it looked like.

That experience always sat in the back of my head even up until I was an adult, but I didn't know what to think about it. I had done a lot of fishing in my early 20s, and where I grew up is a place in eastern Washington state called Walla Walla and specifically the Blue Mountains and that's where this all occurred. Looking up and researching fishing and hiking spots, I started to stumble on the occasional Bigfoot story. It turns out a famous researcher by the name of Paul Freeman had been in my area during most of the 80s and 90s and had a pretty sizable following in the Bigfoot community because he had been a forest ranger and ran into one and nearly spent his life searching for proof. I read a lot of the subject and about Paul and others because I thought it was interesting, but I thought, well this is so rare I may never get near one. A local newspaper reporter named Vance Orchard had written a book on the topic, and I read it all the way through. One of the interesting things about reading this book was it had listed all sorts of places I was well aware of and grew up near my entire life, so they were only a short drive away, I filed these in the back of my mind.

I spent maybe 3 or 4 years going out into the Blue Mountains every chance I got. Now there is some federal land way out there called the Wenaha Tucannon Wilderness Area, and it has some prime Elk hunting I had heard, but I hadn't been out there. The upper reaches of these mountains, especially a decade ago, were covered with snow most of the year, and this particular year was the summer of 2008. I drove up one day to see where the snow line was with a friend, and we hit deep snow, so we didn't get to go out very far. I wanted to go to this campground I had heard of called Squaw Springs then (skyline campground now) and camp out a night or two. It was also mentioned in the books, and I had been to most of the other places in the book, so this was kind of the unexplored territory for me but interesting nonetheless. I had hiked everywhere I could and not seen anything in the last few years, so I expected this trip to be the same. I contacted the rangers about a week later, and it turns out the snow had melted pretty quickly, and now the pass was clear, but this time my friend couldn't go with me. No big deal I was just going to camp out a night or two and go home.

I drove up to this campground about noon or so. It's August, a hot day, and my car has been having trouble overheating from time to time. I get out to look around. I hear a kind of growling noise I initially thought was my car. A low guttural almost gurgling sound that happens for a few seconds stops and then I hear it again a minute or two later again. At first, I thought it was my overheating car because of the regular intervals at which it was happening. The way it resonated almost sounded like a drain, and I have never heard anything like it before or since

Steve Isdahl   The Day Sasquatch Became Real For Me   Copyright© 2020

and I've camped out at this same spot just last year (trust me it still creeps me out 11 years later). There was one other person who had gotten there before me, but this was an out of the way spot, and I thought well there must be some explanation for the noise.

I started setting up my tent for a while and got everything situated, and I had a mallet in my car to hammer down my tent poles. I hear something hit behind me. Like a large rock or something hit the ground but I didn't see what it was. Now at this point, I hear the growling noises again every few minutes but also slaps like wood hitting wood, and this is really confusing. Bigfooter's call this "wood knocking," but I had no idea at the time what it even was or if it was a common noise, something made until I started asking people and heard some similar stories about it related to Bigfoot. I'm still setting up my tent, and at one point, it almost sounded like this wood hitting wood noise was mimicking me smacking tent posts into the ground. This was starting to get odd. I go back to my car and grab my camcorder (smartphones where not much of a thing in 2008) I hear something moving in the brush, so I think, this is it whatever the fuck this thing is I'm going to get it on camera. Start recording and I go toward where I hear some rustling, all that was there was a deer. "Whew," I thought, it was nothing, all in my mind. Go back to the car and then noises are gone, so I decide maybe I should take a hike to a spot a mile or two away down the trail.

I hike for ways and start seeing thin outlines of feet, and at this point, I think my imagination is getting the best of me, I have no idea what to think or how to process this. I go over a few small hills, and then I get to this point where there is a side of a grade and a narrow spot between two hills that go further down towards the Wenaha river and the lower part of the area. Well low and behold on the side of this hill in a clearing in perfect mud, I see the biggest footprint I've ever seen in my life. I had about a foot and a half long five very clear toes, a heel and I just sat there and stared at it and stared at it. Look where I came from and look back down at it, just wondering what the hell I have come across. There were no claws to be found in this print, and more prints are coming up to this point and going down into the lower area. I feel a creature at some point had used this spot for getting down into the valley and back up to the high point I was at.

Things start winding down, I hike a bit more, and I go back to camp, the other people who were there have left, and I begin to get things settled in my tent. It's nice and cooler now and feels good because it has been so hot. I start to settle in, and all of a sudden, I hear the growling noises again. I ignore it. Maybe it'll go away. I keep hearing it every minute or two. Now I start to think back, oh shit, my car has been off for hours now. Now I feel paranoid. The noises keep going and going, and it's just past dark. It starts to sound closer. It sounds like whatever it is is growling right at me. I have never been scared of hiking or camping in the woods, but this had me absolutely terrified. Finally, I can't take it anymore. I don't even collapse my tent; I get my flashlight and throw everything in the back of the car as fast as I can. I didn't even look back, and sometimes I wonder just how close this thing was from me. I went back into town, and I was so scared I started pacing back and forth down the main street in Walla Walla to calm my nerves, and I ran into this girl I knew, and she even commented right away how visibly shaken I looked. I didn't even know what to say to her.

Steve Isdahl   The Day Sasquatch Became Real For Me   Copyright© 2020

And that was the end of it; I will forever wonder about that night. That was the turning point when I knew these things were real, and I think about it every once in a while, and wonder what these things are. I have dreams about seeing one even all these years later; it haunts me.

I live in Seattle now, but I still go back to visit my old favorite part of the woods in Walla Walla. I love the Blue Mountains. It feels like home to me despite that crazy thing that happened. But it is quite a mystery to me. I will always go to my spots, but it's been 11 years and nothing like that has happened again. I like that you are so bold about this because no one believes me when I tell this story. It just seems so far outside of their reality to them. You seem like a really stand-up guy. If you are ever in the Seattle area, let me know I'd like to buy you a beer and shake your hand some time. The world is a lot wilder than I think people realize, and that sense of adventure really speaks to me. I don't think I'll ever stop just wanting to be out there in the middle of the woods, enjoying every minute of it.

Thanks for reading my story
Joel

Steam Rose From It

Thanks for putting all of this together. I had an experience years ago and except for a very few people, 6 to be exact, I don't mention it much. When I was young, I didn't want to be made fun of or thought too odd. I wanted to fit in. But now that I'm much older than 58, I don't give a crap what people think. And to hear your experiences brought it all back to me, and I remember it like it was last week. So here you go.

I was 14 and living in Ogden, Utah. I was with a church group, and we were playing games in a cabin close to the Snowbasin ski resort. It was early spring, so there was still some patchy snow on the ground. We were in this cabin playing musical chairs. It was down to 2 players—Rick Patterson and me. The music stopped, and Rick had won the game. As he went to sit down, I pulled the chair out from under him, and I sat down, and he went to the floor. It was a good prank and got a lot of laughs, but he got up and started chasing me.

I was pretty fast back then, but I needed room to run so outside I went with him on my tail. I took off running down this groomed trail that was about 15 feet wide and left him in the dirt. He went back in, and I stood there about 100 years from the cabin. It was dark, a bit chilly, but a full moon lit my way. As I stood there catching my breath, I got that hair raising feeling I was not alone. I turned around that there 20 yards away was something standing in the trail that wasn't there before. I was staring at it, trying to wrap my mind around what I was seeing. It was big and broad shoulders, although I couldn't see arms or legs, so I was thinking maybe a tree or bush in the trail. Then I noticed it was hairy and with the moonlight, I could see steam was coming off the head and shoulders. Then it exhaled, and I saw that steam coming out of the face area.

That's when I knew it was alive, and it scared the shit out of me. I took off running back to the cabin and looked over my shoulder to see if it was following me, but it was gone. My next thought was it was going to cut me off before I made it back. It didn't. When I ran back into the cabin, I must have had the look of death on my face. All the leaders came running over to see what was wrong. They said I was white as a ghost and looked terrified. They were right, but I never told them what I saw. I hadn't spoken of it to anyone for maybe 30 years. I used to think, how does something that big sneak up and leave without ever being heard.

After spending many years in the hunting woods, I've seen the same thing with big elk and moose. All I know is that he was too big to be a man, and it was not a bear. I don't care if I ever see one again; in fact, I'd rather not. I'm even getting goosebumps talking about it this many years later. Well, anyway, that's my story so share it if you want. And thanks again for getting this page started.

It Was 9 To 11 Feet Tall

Hi Steve, I hope you are doing well. I just want to thank you for the very entertaining personal touch you add to your videos, and the offer to share others experiences. Of course, I heard of Sasquatch and dad took me to see the Paterson film as a kid, but never really believed or even thought much about the subject till I had my encounter.

It all happened back in the summer of 2002, but I remember it like yesterday. One day while picking up my pay in the war room at Ft. Indian Town Gap, I overheard news that my National Guard unit was about to get orders to deploy as part of Operation Enduring Freedom. At that time, I was a rifleman with Co. C 111th Infantry 56 Stryker brigade, out of Kutztown, Pa. I had currently volunteered for state active duty as part of Operation Noble Eagle guarding the Limerick Generating Station. I was carrying full combat load on that detail for almost a year when I asked to be relieved. At the time I wanted to deploy with my unit, you know that whole Band of Brothers thing, plus the retirement points and veterans' benefits increase if you're deployed in combat. I guess you have to be a grunt to get it because my civilian friends thought I was out of my mind.

A forty-two-year-old infantryman and wanting to be sent to an area of hostel fire. Hahaha, now that I look back, I guess I was a little nut. It was then when a friend offered to take me on a weekend camping trip to a little pay campsite along the banks of West Branch of the Susquehanna just west of Williamsport, Pa. It was meant to be a relaxing trip before I deployed, and while there, we would drink a few beers, look for Indian arrowheads in the nearby fields, and he was also going to give me a flint knapping lesson. We soon got bored with the area walking after only finding a few broken projectile points and some chippings. There was an excellent flowing feeder stream emptying into the river just downstream called Big Run, and I wanted to explore it.

I have been hunting arrowheads for many years and have found that almost every stream and spring in Pa. has a small Native American hunting camp at the head where the water first pops up out of the ground. It was scorching that day, and my friend got tired after a mile or so, and he wanted to turn back. I however, was determined to find a camp and went on alone. I followed the stream for another mile or two when eventually it got so thick with rhododendron it became nearly impossible to follow. At that point, I started to hear the sound of a highway way off in the distance and found a crushed soda can in the stream. From the can I came to the concussion that the head of the stream was somewhere on the other side of the highway, and farther away, then I was prepared to travel.

At the bottom of the mountain, I remembered seeing an old logging road that ran up the gorge to the left of the stream. I decided that would be the easiest and quickest way back down to the river. After fighting my way through the thick undergrowth, I finally found the old logging path that was about 200 yards to the left of the stream. As soon as I located the trail, I found a nice flat spot that had a push pile from making the road, so I decided to scratch around in a pile to see if I could find any traces of flint chips in the soil. I have discovered whole arrowheads in these topsoil piles in the past at other locations. All I found in a pile that day was a few small Northern Ring-necked snakes. It was getting even hotter, and I was almost out of the water, so I decided to pack up my scratcher and head back down the mountain. Not two steps into my journey home standing about 60 yards in front of me was the most terrifying experience in my life. Honestly, I would like to think that I'm a reasonably brave man, but I was not prepared for this encounter at all. Being an experienced infantry soldier and an avid big game hunter, it takes a lot to rattle me.

What I saw standing in front of me shook me to my very core, and I instantly froze. A flood of thoughts went through my mind in a second. I wanted it to be a bear in the worst way, just like I have seen many times before, but it just wasn't a bear. When I realized what it was, overwhelming fear hit me, and I felt like I was going to vomit. When it turned and started running toward the stream, where I just came from, I couldn't believe the speed it achieved in such a short time. I could clearly see these two massive muscular legs running because the deer had everything browsed off as high as they could reach. The legs alone had to be as tall as me. I'm 5'6, so this thing was probably almost 6 feet just to the waist.

Being a long-time bear hunter, I think this creature had to weigh anywhere from 800 to 1200 pounds minimum and stood approximately 9 to 11 feet tall. The legs were thick and muscular and reminded me of hair covered telephone poles. The hair appeared to be very dark brown or maybe black, and I'm thinking no more than 4 inches long. It sounded like a bulldozer busting through the rhododendron snapping branches as thick as my ankles. I remember thinking there is no way I can outrun this thing, and if it wanted to, it could easily catch me.

Being unarmed at the time didn't help with the fear factor, and at that point, I knew if I survived that day, I would never venture into the woods unarmed again. Like I said before, a flood of overwhelming thoughts in seconds. I knew to get back to camp; I had to go toward where this thing was just standing a second before. I remember thinking the sounds I heard earlier that I thought were deer must have been this creature following me. When I made that left uphill to get out of the rhododendron, I must have inadvertently flanked it. My thoughts were that this thing was stalking me. That's when the almost 20 years of infantry training kicked in. You see, in an ambush situation, you always charge into the contact, and never go any other direction because that's where the real trap is. Sounds crazy, but at that point, I just bolted in the direction of where I first saw it.

To tell you the truth, I didn't know that I could even run that fast. I never also looked back because I was in full panic mode, but I knew if I didn't slow down a little, I would eventually fall because it was rocky and downhill. I remember thinking If I fell, I would inevitably be injured severely and in bigger trouble. Somehow, I gained my composure and slowed myself down a little but kept running for what felt like three miles till I came to the river. Funny, I never told my buddy that took me on the trip about it. I'm not even sure why I kept it to myself. Now that I think about it, I'm not sure if I got a look at its face at all, or if I did, I must have somehow blocked it out of my memory because I was so scared. I think I may have gone into a slight shock because I felt sick instantly.

I know it saw me first. As soon as I started heading down the logging path towards it, I heard it move, and I looked up. At the same time, it turned to its right and took off like a bat of hell. It busted through that rhododendron at amazing speed. What would have taken me 15 minutes to climb and weave through, it plowed through in seconds. I think the sound of the snapping branches made it even worse knowing the power that it would take to snap those thick branches. I have had nightmares about this big guy, and in them it's face looked more human than not, and the head was shaped kind of like a coconut still in the outer shell.

In the dreams, it's never aggressive, but it still scares the hell out of me with its enormous size. I know one thing If I would have had a camera, I would never have had the time to take a picture, nor would I have tried. It was too close, and it all happened so fast. I hope I never see another, at least not that close. I have heard that they are supposed to smell bad, but I didn't smell anything out of the ordinary.

The hair was not as long as I have heard in other reports, either. Maybe by early summer, the hair is shorter, I don't know. I often get a feeling that perhaps that area is part of a migration route, but I have no idea where that idea even came from, weird, I know. I think that's why I couldn't find Indian hunting camps along that stream, maybe the Indians knew and stayed away. I know If I had a topo map of that quadrangle, I could pinpoint the exact location due to the terrain features. Even to this day, every time I go hunting or into the woods, it's in the back of my mind.

I swear to God, this is 100% true to the best of my recollection.
-Jeff

A remote fly lake northern Yukon Territories

To The Point

So one night, I took my little brother night fishing in an attempt to get him off his video game and get him to do something outside. Well, we began hearing footsteps and a grunt or two off in the woods, now we live in Georgia. We're in a swampy area, so we figured that the steps were just hogs, so we decided to get into our tents (we were in two separate tents, by the way, due to space and comfort) and then all of a sudden, I hear gunshots. Hence, I rush out my tent only to see my little brother white as snow in the face with tears running down his face. He said that it reached inside of his tent and drug him halfway out it. He was scared enough that he had slept in the tent with me for the rest of the night. When we woke up in the morning, our fishing stringer was gone, and we had a yeti cooler which seemed to have been ripped open and tossed around or something throughout the night. To this day, he refuses to go into woods alone and without a weapon.

East Arkansas

Hi Steve, I am from East Arkansas and have lived here for most of my life.

My story is from when I was about 6-8 years old around that time frame; it was the early 2000s. I was at my grandparents in Shirley, Arkansas, for a couple of weeks to go to Greer's ferry lake and go cliff diving and ride the innertube.

It was the second night I was there along with my cousins, and we were sitting out on the deck looking at Sugarloaf Mountain, which is on Greer's Ferry lake BC when the sun starts to set. It's just a very nice and relaxing place to be, but that's beside the point. After a while, my grandparents, and all my cousins decided to go back in because it was almost dark but not dark enough to where you couldn't see anything.

In front of their house, they have a considerable yard very open and have two large cattle pastures that belong to the neighbors directly across the way and from the deck you can see just about see everything that's in both fields without problem even when it's getting dark, I looked down that way to see if any cows were walking around. I looked left of the neighbors' house, and there were two figures running upright on two legs VERY fast there. I saw them start almost from the neighbors' house; both looked way too big to be human and way to quick. Now let me stress to you the pasture is HUGE the one they were running in. I still have no clue if it even was what I think I saw. It took those things less than 5 seconds to be out of sight and out of the pasture and also, there is a barbed-wire fence that went above my head when I was around that age. There are thick brush and trees in the direction they were running to I saw both basically take one leg and step over it like it was just a crack in the sidewalk.

It was many years ago I'm going to be 22 tomorrow.
-Jacob

It Left Me Feeling Isolated

First of all, I just want to thank you for coming out and talking about Sasquatch. You have nothing to gain and a lot to lose talking about this subject, and you are doing a lot of good helping people who have had a Sasquatch experience and simply can't talk about it without social consequences.

I live in Minnesota, and I am 30 years old. I've been hunting, fishing, camping and recreating in the outdoors my whole life. My main passion, though, was coyote hunting. I enjoyed the fact that it gave me something to do in the dead of winter, and It helped farmers. I mention this to help you understand that I am a person who is quite comfortable being alone, at night, calling in predators. I've been doing it since I was a kid. I don't get creeped out by it, and I have made several solo hunting trips over the years in the wilderness of northern Minnesota.

Never gave Sasquatch much thought. I saw all the typical Bigfoot stuff growing up but never gave it much of an opinion either way. All I knew was I had never seen one.

Then in June of 2016, I, along with my girlfriend and her family, went on a six-day camping and ATV trip in the foothills state forest in northern Minnesota. We got there on a Friday, and it was a fairly busy weekend, but Sunday night, all the other groups of campers had gone home, leaving my group to be the only ones there. All the camping spots are along the forest road, and they were all empty by 4 pm Sunday. We planned to stay until Wednesday and get a few days of the trails all to ourselves.

Tuesday night, we had a fire. The barred owls were hooting. Crickets and frogs were singing. About half the group had gone to bed, leaving me and three others still sitting there. When all of a sudden, something vocalized about 100 yards into the woods loud. Like louder than any wolf, coyote, fox, you name it. It was powerful and unlike anything I've ever heard in my entire life, very primate-like but way bigger than me. It lasted for about 20 seconds straight, and when it stopped, everything was dead silent. No more owls, crickets or frogs, just nothing but dead air. My Australian cattle dog, who is a coyote decoy dog and not afraid of shit, crawled under my chair and laid down. Everyone is looking at me for answers while my mind is racing trying to figure out what I just heard. All I could say is, "I have no fucking idea." A wave of fear came over me, and not normal fear, I'm talking primal fear. Like I just wanted to go into my tent and hide in my sleeping bag. And I did. I went to my tent, and that was it for me for the night. Everyone followed suit after me, and we packed up and left the next day.

I went on the DNR website the next day and got a list of every known animal in Minnesota and started listening to an audio of their vocalizations, and I was coming up empty. Then I decided to go down the Sasquatch hole. I didn't want to, but I wasn't finding anything. I found a recording from 2003 in northern California of an almost identical vocalization, and it was titled as a Bigfoot vocal. I have shown the vocalization to many people I trust, asking them what animal makes that sound and none of them know, they just say it sounds like an ape or something like that.

It fucked with me for a while, and I do go back in the woods still now that I know these things are real. I've seen your videos for years, and when you posted that first Sasquatch video in April, it was quite a surprise, and they helped me come to grips with the whole thing. It's a hard thing to get through, coming to terms with something that isn't supposed to be real, and it's laughed at, is indeed real. It makes you feel isolated, and you have to bottle it in. Seeing these videos puts it into perspective, and knowing there are other hunters and outdoorsmen that have experienced these things lets me know I'm not crazy or alone in this whole thing.
So once again, thank you for everything.

It Had Greyish Red Hair

Just want to share an encounter I had when I was younger, this experience changed everything. I grew up on the north end of Vancouver Island. The encounter happened when fishing a river near Georgie lake; the area is about a 45-minute drive from Port Hardy on a logging road. I was with my friend and his father. Unfortunately, the fish and wildlife were busy asking my friend's father questions regarding the area we were fishing. When this was happening, we walked along the shore of the river to an area with a large sandbank. We started throwing rocks at this bank; it was causing the sand to slide down the middle of the bank. In between throwing rocks, sand began to slide down from the top of the bank. We both looked up at the same time, and we locked eyes with a large Sasquatch that was leaning over a stump. This creature had greyish mixed with dark reddish-brown hair covering every portion of his body that we could see other than areas of his face. He looked similar to the light brown creature on Todd Standing's video, but not so youthful. It stared at us until shock kicked in, and we ran back to the truck. I've been very fascinated with these creatures ever since that encounter and now plan some of our camping trips to Sasquatch hotspots. There's no doubt in my mind that what we saw was a Sasquatch. Keep up the awesome work getting all these stories out. Please let me know if you know of any other stories near Port Hardy.

Thanks, Liam

Haida Gwaii Included

Hi Steve,

I have had a couple of incidents and one sighting. I do not tell people about my experiences anymore because they just do not believe or want to hear about it.

These all happened between the mid-1970s to early 1980s on Haida Gwaii (Queen Charlotte Islands back then).

I used to love going for walks to the beach with my dog (Shepherd/Collie cross) and my radio to sit on a log, listen to music and watch the waves on the beach and just be in my own little world. This was about the 3rd time my dog and I had gone to the beach (known as Cemetery Beach). On this day everything was peaceful, a beautiful day. I was enjoying my relaxing time, and the dog was asleep beside me. All of a sudden, she bolted awake and started whimpering and whining, looking towards the bush to the left of the way we had to go to get back home. She was acting strange. My gut was telling me she wanted us to get out of here and now. She had been on many overnight camping and hunting trips with my dad and brother and never acted like this. She would bark at bears and deer. I listened to my gut and the dog and headed home. As we left the beach and entered into the bush on the dirt road, I had a strange creepy feeling of being watched. We walked back to town at a pretty good pace. (I have never been a runner). I am not 100% sure if it was a Sasquatch that made the dog act like that but the process of elimination as to what it could have been, leads me to believe it very well could have been.

A few months later, there was a big beach part out at the same beach. I had forgotten about the previous experience. I went to parties and beach parties just to hang out with friends. If I drank, it was just pop. I did not like not having my wits about me when I am not home. Anyway, it was getting late (around 11:00 pm) to head back. As I was trying to catch up to my sister and her friend, I lost sight of them. It was a moonlight night where you could see things pretty good; I was looking down watching where I was walking so not to trip on a log When I looked up, I had turned a little of course to the right from the direction of the road, clear as day I saw a very tall hairy being walking upright on two legs. (I am terrible at judging distance) The best guess would be about 30 feet away) It was walking fast, taking big strides and arms were swinging back and forth with each stride. I stopped in my tracks and did not make a sound. It turned its head and looked straight at me. When it turned its head back forward and was out of sight, I turned tail and ran back to the fire. I am not sure how fast I was running (remember previously, I do not run), but when I tripped on something, I remember seeing the sky go by twice. When I got back to the fire, my best friend (who is First Nations, and I am White) said, "Holy shit, for a White girl, you sure are white." By the time I calmed down, there was a crowd around me. When I told them what I saw, some believed me and others said it was just a cow. I explained cows do now walk on their hind legs like that.

A few years later, a bunch of us were out at Pure Lake, which is South of Cemetery Beach about a half an hour drive. We were talking about wanting to camp there sometime. One of the guys says watch this (more like listen to this). He whistled really loud. We all stood there super quiet listening then across the lake (thick bush and brush) we heard what sounded like a very loud whack on a tree ahead and to the right a little. Then a few seconds later, another very loud whack ahead and to the left of us. The guy whistled again, but this time there was no sound back. So much for camping. We all high tailed it out of there.

I have not told those stories in many years, but remember it all like it was yesterday.

I do not mind if you want to share the store but anonymously, please.

Oh, what the hell, like you say, who gives a crap what other people think. Use my name if you want.

Thank you very much for sharing your stories. It helps me to realize there are more people that are experiencing the same things with sights and ridicule.

Have a great day,
K

It Caught The Wild Pig Easily

Hello buddy, I started watching your videos about a year ago. Damn, you're a badass storyteller. I wish I had that ability. I'm a big hunter and fly fisher and have seen everything there is to see out there, and it would make my stories a lot more interesting if I could talk like that. I just want to say, before this encounter, since I was a kid, I've always thought that Bigfoot was as real as Santa or the Easter bunny. All the media I've seen and the bullshit stories and pictures I've heard and seen beat it into my head that those things are made up stories to get publicity.

Anyhow, I'm from West Virginia, and I've hunted with my grandpa on his property since I could walk pretty much. This was about six years ago, and I just started hunting on my own, so I was 16. It was archery season, and the rut was just kicking in for the whitetails (early November). I was hunting 300 yards away from my grandpa in a ladder stand. I didn't see anything and returned to the house and got a call from my grandpa. He had shot and wounded a decent 8 point that we had been getting on camera since July. He was in a stand we call "old faithful" and took a 40-yard shot at last light. He needed help tracking, so I grabbed a flashlight and my knife out of my hunting clothes, and I grouped up with him. We had followed the blood trail for an hour or so, and it was becoming reduced to a drop every ten feet or so.

He had to work early the next morning and had to get to bed, so I told him I would stay out and track until I couldn't see any more signs. It's probably 9:30 at night, and I'm alone in an old open hardwood forest on what's left of this trail with my flashlight. I noticed the woods started to thicken a bit, and that meant I'm coming up on the property line of a farm that neighbors my grandpa's property. I wasn't afraid of the dark, but I always got severe anxiety crossing into this section of woods/brush. This is a massive farm that has dairy cows, pigs, and its own butcher shop.

Anyhow, I was just crossing the property line, and I heard a pig let out this blood-curling squeal from about a mile away. Scared the hell out of me, but I calmed down and figured the pigs got out and either the farmer was trying to get its ass back to the farm, or a coyote got a hold of it.

I walked/crawled about 20 more yards through some brush, and I heard something take a step. Before I even had to lift my head or flashlight. That pig let out another scream this time about 30 yards from me. I fell on my ass, scared shitless and raised my flashlight over a brush pile that was between me and the sound of the pig. That's when I saw whatever was standing there clear as could be staring at me. It had to be 8-foot-tall, light brown/gray. I heard something run from where it was standing, but the thing didn't move.

I thought there was another one, and it was running to come to get me, but I guess it was the pig trying to getaway. I shined my light back at the creature, and it let out this growl that cut right through me, unlike anything that I've ever heard. I'm not afraid of black bears and know that you're supposed to stand your ground and make noise to scare it off. That's what it was doing to me, and it meant business. I wanted to get up and run away, but I froze and didn't want to turn my back to it. I didn't even have time to think about the buck knife on my belt, not that I could fend this thing off with it anyhow. The only way I could describe the way it looked is if you could imagine a less hairy, pissed off Chewbacca. I think it knew I was pissing my pants, and it looked in the direction of what I assume was the pig that ran off and took three steps and was out of sight.

I got up and sprinted the two or three miles back to my grandpa's house.   The next day I told him that I lost the blood trail and never found the deer. I did tell him about the pig squealing in the woods and that afternoon. We went over to the farm to talk to the farmer. He said he was missing one pig and that there was no way that it should've been able to get out. We're talking about a 150-pound pig in a pen that has 4-5-foot-tall sheets of tin that make up the walls and no door. The farmer lowers a latter into the pen to get in and out. My grandpa suggested maybe a kid messing around, let it out to screw with him, and that was the end of it.
To this day, I've never told him or anyone, what I saw or what happened to that poor pig. It just blows my mind how fast that thing had to be going to carry or chase that pig as quickly as it did. I've done research online and read about archeological digs in Native American mounds in my area. A big topic is giant skeletons being dug out of these mounds and never being released to the public. I've since grown interested in Native American history but in no way want to cross paths with that thing ever again. The emotional scar that thing has left me with makes me not want to be out in the woods and do what I do.

Sounded Like Pipe Organs

I live in northern Indiana, and I have a true story I would like to share with you. We have a cabin about 300 miles NNW of Thunder Bay, Ontario. We drive till the road stops then take a floatplane into our cabin. My Dad built our cabin in 1968, and we go up three times a year. The end of May, mid-July and early Sept. One fall trip maybe 15 or 20 years ago now, we wanted to portage to a different lake. In the spring and fall, if the weather were cool, we would go after some Lake Trout.

If I had to take a guess, I have been on that lake 30 to 40 times now. We are the only cabin on our lake, and there are no cabins on Lake Trout lake. We have three small boats we just leave on that lake because we go there so often. We had six men in 3 Boats that day. We all kind of went our own way and started fishing. It was maybe 4 hours later (around 2 or 3 pm) all three boats met back up in the middle of the lake, and we all killed our engines and started to eat our lunch. It was a beautiful sunny day with no clouds, and the lake went completely flat, no wind at all. Ok, now this is the part where you are going to think I'm nuts, so here I go. The first sound came from our north, that's the way we have to go to get back to our lake. The best way I can describe it was like someone holding a note on a freaking pipe organ. The notes were perfect, not flat or anything like that. The notes would last maybe 5 to 8 seconds, that's a long time to hold a perfect note.

When one would die out, another would start from a different shore at a higher or lower note but all just perfect and sounded like a pipe organ. All the sounds were just single notes; we never heard two different notes at the same time. This lasted for maybe 15 or 20 min. We all six were hearing 20 + pipe organs play single notes around a lake with no cabins in the Canadian wilderness. The notes were loud and with no wind and land no more than 200 to 400 yards away in any direction; the notes would echo around a bit. My brother did not want to make the portage, so he stayed in our lake with one of my uncles.

Later back in our cabin, we all were telling my uncle and brother what we heard. They both said they could also hear the notes from our direction but not as loud as we could. We never saw a thing and man we were all looking very hard. Nothing in the trees, on the ground or in the water, just the beautiful Canadian wilderness playing freaking pipe organ notes. I don't know what was making the notes. About the only thing I do know is there are no pipe organs around that lake.

Over the years, we have been back to that many times and nothing. Over the years, we have asked State biologists; they look at me like I'm nuts. I even have asked a First Nation friend from that area. At least he gave me a kind answer. Are you ready, I sure was. He said some things in nature are best left unknown. Lol, what that is your answer, I was so prepared to find out, and that's what I got. I'm the last one of the eight people still alive who heard the pipe organ notes around a lake in the Canadian wilderness. I have been watching your videos and just thought maybe you with countless hours of being in the woods maybe you have heard freaking pipe organ notes. I know you are out in BC but figured I would ask anyway.
Thank you,
Greg

It Didn't Want To Get Shot

Ok this is the second time I've told this and was hesitant about telling it now but if you can tell your story I can to in 2016 my brother and I decided to go hunting so we planned on the following weekend I'd come pick him up and we would go so Saturday morning I was up got ready and went to the truck I had to recheck my straps on my ATV I had loaded the day before I remember it was a cold Kentucky morning the straps had ice buildup on them everything was god so I went picked up my brother and headed to where we was going to hunt we have hunted there many times there's a big strip where they had cut Cole from the rock cliff when you get to the top you have a big holler to your left a big open bottom then the cliff that stretches all the way around the bottom so I dropped my brother off a half mile up the road he wanted to be on the cliff watching this bottom as I rode my ATV up the other side so I was given him time to get to his spot before I started up the old road In case I jumped one but he shot way before getting to the cliffs he had got a deer I didn't know that at the time so I was expecting him to be sitting on top as I rod by so I start up the hill and stop when I got half way up like I do all the time to load my rifle I had a savage 30-06 that has a strap on it.

I had it in my lap as I entered the bottom I was looking for my brother witch he was heading back to the truck with his deer when I saw this thing run out from the holler about 40 yards in front of me and was heading to the cliffs I freaked pulled my gun up and shot didn't know if I'd hit it or not I never even look in the scope so this thing keeps running and went straight to the corner of this bottom between the cliffs it had nowhere to go at this time trying to figure out what I was looking at it sit behind this little Bush and was looking at me I'm 5-8 and this thing was probably just a little taller than me I'm shaking so I jumped off my ATV put my gun up and was going to shoot this thing and as I looked through the scope it had its arms up like you and I would do if something was going to hit you to protect your face it was trying to protect its face and looked like a scared kid shaking and jumping at every little sound I couldn't take the shot it was scared just as much as I was I lowered the gun and said you're alright I'm not going to hurt you and got back on my ATV and started back off the hill watching behind me the whole way back i told my brother about what had happened when I returned he just said I was full of shit and didn't believe me but we have hunted there many times after that and I've never seen it again in a way I hope I never do but I would like to video it to prove to my brother I'm not crazy but after my encounter I started taking a camera with me on all my hunting trips but that was my story take care.

They Won't Leave My Home Alone

Hello Steve,

Your page, along with others such as Mr. Scott Carpenter, has inspired me to write about my situation that is ongoing at this time. I'd also like to bring awareness to this creature, and it's a desire to observe my children. Even to the point of being captured on video, shot at twice, navigating 19 game cams and six security cameras, just to watch my kids. I believe my location is important because people in my general area need to be informed.

I moved to the Antlers-Atoka area of SE, Oklahoma, about four years ago. If you had asked me if I believed in Bigfoot while I was living in the Armpit of Arkansas (Pine Bluff), I would've said naw. A month or two after moving to a 40-acre ranch outside of Antlers. My wife fell asleep on the couch and woke up to what she said was someone jiggling the front doorknob, she jumped up to lock it, and said when she turned around, there was a shadow outside the side window of a figure with a big head, long hair and was gone in a flash. She said she could've imagined it. I blew it off.

My son was three at the time and got him a battery go-kart, and his mother heard him say, " They can't catch me now." When she asked him what he meant, he said, "the man who lives in the woods, he stands at my window at night and watches me sleep, he can't catch me now". I now have a two-year-old daughter who used to throw fits to be outside till one day she ran inside, slammed the open front door and was crying. I've noticed before she goes outside, she will poke her head out the door and look around for a min before going outside. Rarely will play on the playhouse that is close to the tree line. About a year ago, I was lying in bed, not fully asleep and heard a melodic whistle kind of chatter, and I sat up because it sounded like it was coming from near the woods outside my bedroom. My dogs started immediately howling, not barking and wouldn't come off the porch and usually are aggressive. One of my dogs bit the mail lady, UPS man, and the neighbor. She didn't leave the porch that night. I heard the same kind of whistle chatter but slightly different about 3 min after the first whistle. That really stuck with me. I googled what I could best describe as the sound I heard, and Bigfoot talk kept coming up. Well, the other day (Nov 11, 2019), my son came running into our bedroom and said "daddy, there is a bear outside, it has a white face, and it was looking at me." I had recently watched "missing 411" and remember a kid describing what I believe was a Bigfoot as a bear that could talk or something like that...I grabbed my rifle and ran outside to where he said he saw it and didn't see anything. Now I'm wondering if my kids have seen something.

A few days later (Dec 3, 2019), I recorded a shadow that appeared to be on two feet approaching my house. So far, all of my recordings you can just easily blow off, I've heard some whoops on some of my recordings and what sounded like wood knocks and strange behavior from my dogs. This was the first time that I had proof that something was coming up to my house. Shortly after everything got quiet, TVs were off all lights were off, and we were going to bed.

The night of the video of The Shadow, I was watching a live video feed from my phone because the dogs were acting weird. I saw what appeared to be a shadow on two feet. Approaching the corner of my house, I immediately grabbed my gun. The two bumps that you hear in the video are me going through my bathroom and out the other door to warn my wife that I was fixing to open up the front door and shoot off a couple of warning shots. Now I have three sleeping children. At this time, I have my disabled father next door. It is approximately 11:30 p.m. I do not want to be busting off shots out of my front door, but I felt like I needed to try to scare this thing away. As soon as this happened, I shut the front door. I called nine-one-one told him I had an intruder in my yard and requested a deputy.

The next morning, I went to the sheriff's office to add to my report a link to the video on YouTube because I had since uploaded it so they would have access to it and had a conversation with a couple of the deputies up there. One deputy named Branson followed me outside and said he wanted to talk to me outside for a minute. He said that he knew that they were out there that they get numerous reports this time of year. A lot of people approach him directly with pictures or footage for him to review because they do not want an official police report or people from their Church finding out or to have people contacting them or coming on their land. He gave me his personal number and told me if I had any more problems to contact him directly. I feel comfortable sharing his name and what he said to me because he did not ask me to keep this just between ourselves; he just didn't want to speak of it in front of the other deputies. I was surprised when he contacted me the next morning at about 8 a.m. He was curious about how my night went if I had any more disturbances, and I told him no that it was a very quiet night. It didn't last.

I put up more wireless security cameras can we catch numerous Limbs breaking sounds of something of large Mass pushing through the brush.

My main dog came up missing. He was the one that alerted me that they were close.

I started by putting up six-game cameras and a bait station. I never recorded anything related to what I was trying to record. December 25th at about 9 p.m., I pulled up my camera's live feed. I have bipedal footsteps running in short bursts, stopping and running again, and I caught a flash of eyeshine on camera so close that I could see the slots of the eyes and I could see the pupils. I grabbed my gun and went outside with a flashlight but didn't see anything.

The next night on December 26th at approximately 7 p.m., I turned on my camera to the live feed. I saw a pair of eyes standing next to one of the pine trees in my front yard near my kids' playhouse. Now, this is where it's going to get interesting. This was also when I realized just how much I'd underestimated the intelligence and instant reaction these things possess.

Grab my big flashlight am I Kimber 45 crimson. I head outside, shining my light looking for the figure that I saw on camera. I walked between the pine trees and my kids' playhouse shining my light out into the pasture. I didn't see anything, so I went back inside. About 20 minutes later, I pulled up my camera's live feed, and something had put an object in front of my camera. grab the flashlight, grab the gun and went back outside. I was standing approximately 15 feet from my kids' playhouse area, shining my light on the playhouse. While keeping my flashlight on the playhouse, I reached down with my right-hand gun to unholster my pistol, cocked the hammer and proceeded to look around. I didn't see or hear anything yet again. I was reviewing my video footage that was recorded while I was outside after I went back to the house.

Upon review of the video, I just recorded. The camera on the playhouse that picked up the eyeshine. Had also picked up a shadow that was cast onto my horse cover by my flashlight. What I didn't realize, when I was focused on unholstering my pistol and cocking the hammer, this thing was hidden behind my playhouse. It stood up and relocated to another area of the playhouse for more cover in the few seconds that I was looking down at my gun. It saw me looking down at my gun and instantly took advantage of that moment to stand up and relocate, and crossed right in front of my flashlight beam. and I never heard it.

I went back to review the video of the first time that I went outside and can see it cast a Shadow the first time. It was a juvenile, and I think I was so focused on looking for a 9 to 10-foot

Sasquatch that I never saw a small juvenile.

Well, the third time, I didn't even bother going outside. Grabbed my AR-15 with a night vision scope, had the wife throw open the front door, and I already had my gun pointed at the playhouse area. Through my night vision scope, I could see it standing behind the playhouse, looking at me through the slats on the railing. Right when I pulled the trigger, it darted to the right and was gone. But believe it or not, it actually came back that same night.

The next day December 27th, a total of 19 game cameras were installed around the perimeter and upgraded to a total of six wireless security cameras. That night about 7 p.m., what am I game cameras recorded a figure walking behind the playhouse. I started wondering why the focus is on the playhouse. We had a lot of company, my nieces and nephews on December 23rd and 24th. The focus of their activities was on the playhouse area. I was going through some of my recordings from then. I had a few videos that were set off by the motion of my horses. I noticed that the horses were moving away at a brisk pace from the tree line. I zoomed in on this area and in four videos taken on December 24th at 10:30 a.m., I can see two large adult-sized Sasquatches that are taking turns observing the children from an observation point behind a leaning tree. I had this video footage recorded for four days before he even realizes what it was. I believe this to be the mother and the father of the juvenile that approached the playhouse on December 25th and 26th.

I believe that they are just curious.

What bothered me about the whole situation was, I was told the majority of the time when they become aware that you're aware of them, they usually move on. They are very persistent, installing all the game cameras and security cameras only changed how they approach my house. Shooting four shots after the first shadow figure on December 3rd is shooting at the juvenile standing behind my playhouse on December 26th didn't deter them one bit. I became concerned because her focus was on the children. I made a hard decision and took my kids out of school while they were still on Christmas break and relocated them and my wife to her mother's house in Arkansas until I could figure out a solution.

When my wife and children were gone for two weeks, the activity began to stop. So, I brought the kids back to the house for the weekend. They arrived on a Friday, Saturday night I was reviewing footage from the day and lo and behold there he is standing behind the same leaning tree again. This was very disturbing to me because they had to be close enough to my house to hear the children. At this time, my wife and children visit but are still in Arkansas. I installed numerous infrared lights. I've cut back to brush in the woods surrounding my house. When my children are outside, I patrol the tree line with a semi-automatic tactical shotgun loaded with black magic Magnum slugs. Our situation is improving, but it is ongoing.

Even In England
Great channel! Great honesty!

Steve Isdahl   The Day Sasquatch Became Real For Me   Copyright© 2020

Despite being English, I also 100% appreciate the no BS approach... Doing a great job of putting some thought-provoking n paradigm challenges out there for the YouTube muppets!

Anyways, I do have a story. I have told this to about three people; I am 37 now, this occurred when I was around 14. My friends, which I have confided in, are relatively open-minded, so I know it was a safe place to share. Other guys, not so much. Not a thrilling story but potentially of interest because of location. I was always open to paranormal, supernatural, aka anything we are not spoon-fed!

I was in Bere Forest, Hampshire (an ancient though now v small, comparatively) I was about 14, which made the Yr. 1996ish. Time and days escape me. But the memory does not. I was too young to be out fooling around with a guy! So, who can blame a girl for not being proud to tell the story! We were fooling around in the car, which was parked in a small clearing about 40 yards from a quiet back road from Denmead to Portsmouth. We were kind of absorbed at that moment as many teens may be. An instinct interrupted both our thoughts. We both jumped away from one another, looked up and out of a foggy car window.

Sauntering by with seemingly no ill intention but certainly, a tangible presence was a figure I can only describe as 'non-human'—too big, too tall n moving in a way that had my transfixed and terrified. I leapt into the passenger seat and begged to get out of there. Everything happened very quickly. The figure moved around from the back of the car, circled to the left, in an unnecessarily wide manner. I could feel we were being watched. This was a place I knew well as a child and a teen. Not just a one-off. My boyfriend was shaken. He sped us away quickly. The creature had already passed in a semi-circle type trajectory by the time we sped off. I grew up there. It is a woodland. Nothing, a spec compared to the wilds of this world. I have since looked at UK Channels on YouTube. Heard some more similar encounters. I don't know what to make of it. But it is very much a case of 'I know what I saw.'

I wanted to ask also if you had heard of n what you thought of the work of the late 'Lloyd Pye' - everything you know is wrong. I feel it has merit, but I find the confines of barely sidestepping evolution probably inadequate.

Thank you for your time, if you have been able to read this!

Kind regards from England,
Katherine

Straight To The Goods

Hi Steve,

I live in SW Washington and do most of my hunting in the high cascades. Currently, 63 years old, and I have been fishing and hunting my whole life. Mostly archery, so tracking and reading signs is what I do.

I first found footprints back in '74 but wasn't until the late '90s in my hunting camp that things started to happen. I have been camping in the same spot since 1990, and to this day, I still spend the archery season there. The first encounter I had up there, the thing came in and peed on the front and back door of my army tent at 3 in the morning. Since then, every encounter aside from seeing the damn thing has happened.

Tree knocks so loud they wake you up, pushing trees over, hoots, rocks placed on my kitchenette, rocks stacked behind camp, trees jammed into the ground upside down, and occasionally the hairs on the back of the neck area alert me, something isn't right. One night we packed an elk out and got back to camp a little after 3 in the morning. Twenty minutes later, we heard the craziest language right outside the tent, which ended with a growl. So far, I have found tracks up there three times, one of which was about 20".

From what I have witnessed, there is NO doubt of its existence. I think I will write a book, 'I Hate Sasquatch.

Thanks for listening,
Mike

Yes, Loggers See Them

Hi Steve,

I'm a loyal follower of black tail Hunter. I admire your passion, honesty, and enjoy your hunt stories. Also, your hunting tips are spot on! They mirror many tactics I've learned in the 50 years I've been hunting black tails. I live in Washington State in the Pacific Northwest. I hunt the triangle between Mt.Saint Helens, Mt.Adams and Mt.Rainier. I've been a timber cutter for 40years. In the last 15 years, I've been cutting danger trees for the forest service, and mostly in the national parks.

Mount Currie B.C.

4 years ago, I was cutting some old growth in the mountains about 30 miles from the town of Packwood. It was the middle of June. Due to the hot weather and humidity, we had to stop cutting around noon. So, we would start most mornings around 3:30/4:00 am. One morning I was working on a tree that had fallen the previous day. The first rays of light were starting to shine through in front of me. I was about halfway through my first cut of a chest-high Douglas fir when a chill came over me. This happened a few times in my life. Happened while in big timber, either working or hunting. Every time I've gotten this chill, I stop and check my surroundings. The feeling either goes away, or I get the hell out of the woods.

This time I kept working and tried to ignore the feeling of being watched. But I couldn't. I also started surveying my surroundings, first looking over each shoulder, then to my sides. It was still too dark to see more than 30 feet. I looked in front of me towards the light coming in from the road and saw what I felt was watching me. It was about 50 yards away standing facing me. All I could see was the huge silhouette, no face, just the black form with the light behind it. Even at 50 yards, I was looking up at it, and we were on level ground. I didn't panic and somehow continued to saw the log, not wanting it to know I saw it. I continued to look for what seemed like minutes but was only seconds. I had to look again when I did; it was gone. I instantly pulled my saw from the tree, kept it running and headed for the crummy, at a 45-degree angle away from where it stood. I came out of the timber, slid down the bank to the road, and into the crummy. I honked the horn until my partner came out to see what the hell, I was carrying on about. I told what I saw and said I was done for the day. He turned white and jumped in the crummy, leaving his saw in the woods saying, "let's go, let's go!" I asked if he saw it too? He said no, but it, seen him. He said when he was fueling his saw, he got a feeling something was watching him. Tried to ignore it. But, when he heard my saw moving through the woods towards the road, he dropped his; and headed towards the road as well. When I honked, he started running—feeling like he was being chased. We drove up the road to a turnaround and drove down past where we were working. It was the only way out. When we passed the spot, I was cutting; the adrenaline was high in both of us.

We couldn't talk, and I almost got sick to my stomach. We both took three days off. I went back the following Monday to retrieve our stuff. Never finishing bucking the trees we had down there. Still, across the Pacific Northwest trail, hikers have to climb over or go around them. I know what I saw, and nobody can tell me otherwise. I have a whole different attitude when I'm in the timber now 75% of me is focused on what I'm doing, and the other 25% is watching my back—never wanting to have that cold feeling again! The mountains and big timber are such a big part of me. I can't stay away from them. I just have to accept I'm not the alpha male. My cutting partner gave up cutting and lives somewhere in California now. I know he's a believer like me. Keep up the good work.

Sincerely,
Rick

While I Dragged My Deer

Hi Steve,

I had a sighting dragging a buck out of state game area in Roscommon county Michigan 4th day gun season 2013. I've been hunting for 45 years, spent a lot of time in the woods,3 to 4 weeks a season camping. We hunt a flooding area roughly a 6000-acre lot. A swamp with islands, some nice oaks on them. The DNR plants a few rye fields back there also, where I shot a nice 8 point that evening. Two days previous to this, we had bad storms blow through the area with a lot of rain on the 17th. Raised water levels in the flooding a lot, we have to cross an area that has a big culvert for draining mud lake to a swampy area. On the way out that afternoon the 19th, we noticed a lot of dead fish washed up onshore. Well anyway shot a buck that evening in the farthest rye field a way from camp maybe a mile. Forgot the deer cart back at camp, so we took the slings off our rifles to drag it out. Took a shortcut, a little piece of high ground next to the swamp. Come out to the trail that leads back to camp. Standing there taking a rest, no wind temp about 24 degrees. You can see your breath going straight up in your headlamps. It was dead quiet. Roughly 150 yards in front of us sounded like a bowling pin hit a dead cedar. There was another tree knock-in between us and the rye field where I shot and gutted the buck, the third tree knock was between us and camp. Still had roughly 1/4 mile down the trail back to camp. Got to the edge mud lake, and I told my son wait here, and I'll go get the deer cart for the last 300 yards instead dragging it. As I got across the little dam, water is roaring from the rain two days earlier. I heard splashing next to shore just past the dam. I thought what in the hell is that splashing and I can hear over the roaring of dam. Got closer to the sound and turned my headlamp up looking down in the tags I was on a slight elevation. This thing slowly looked up at me at about 15 yards away its eye was as big as around as a bottom of a pop can, brilliant blue. Its head was very wide; we locked eyes for a few seconds. It was standing in 2 feet of muck, and the tags were about 5 feet tall. Its head was about 1 foot above the tags. When it took off through that shit, it was as fast as a bolt of lightning. It was dark but could see its silhouette, looked to be maybe 4-foot-wide at the shoulders. I yelled at it as it was hitting the other bank; I'll get you son of a bitch. Had the scope on it out of instinct. Two rounds left in the 06. Almost let one go over that things head to send it on its way. I either carry a 350-rem mag or a 450 marlin now.

-Tony

Penned Up For 40 Years

My name Is Eric, and as a young man at the age of 16 in the late fall of 1979, I was followed by Bigfoot.

A friend and I decided to share our profits from running two different trap lines while still in school. My friend ran a muskrat & mink line, and I would run a fox, coon & opossum line. My buddy had five lakes and a creek that was about 2 miles of mostly open terrain. I had a four-mile run, all woods except a little stretch of a pasture field. We both got up early before school to check our lines and also in the evenings after we got our homework done. The pelts were sold before Xmas, so we were able to purchase presents for our families.

One morning before school, I got up and dressed to check my line. I would carry a small wooden club and a hunting knife on my side. It was dark out when I would leave and had a headlamp and a stronger flashlight I would carry in my backpack. I had an English Springer Spaniel that always went with me on my morning and evening runs. About halfway on my run, I had two coons in my backpack, but I felt I was being watched. As I stopped to look and listen, I heard my dog growling very low, and she was looking behind us. I felt the hair on the back of my neck standing up. The dog just confirmed what my six senses were telling me. I scanned the woods with my headlamp behind us for movement, nothing. I continued to check my trap line, but as I started, my dog was walking backwards and growling very low. This was a behavior I've never seen in her. We travelled another 200 yards with me stopping periodically to light up the area behind us, nothing.

Although I would hear footsteps stop after I stopped, we went another 100 yards with her still walking backwards and starting to growl louder. The noise behind us was closing in on both of us. I stopped and pulled my brighter flashlight out of my backpack. By now, my dogs' growl was much louder. I scanned once with my headlamp and then turned on my flashlight. As I swung the flashlight from left to right, I saw two human-like figures at a distance of 75yards. I knew then I had a serious problem, but I never stopped swinging the flashlight, I didn't want them to know they'd been spotted.

As I continued to swing the flashlight, my light hit an old tree stump with no bark on it. Although, this trunk has what looked like fur growing off of it. Also, at about 10 feet up this broken off dead tree, I saw steam in the air. As I continued swinging my light to the right, never stopping, I saw the reddish reflection of an eye. This third one had closed to within 50 yards. I had 30 yards to go before I could get to the open pasture field. My dog, by this time, had also seen what I had seen glancing down at her. She was now turned around and her eyes looked like they were pleading with me to please run. I took her advice; with a full out sprint we were both heading toward the open field. I believe, at one point in the sprint, I was leading her. We hit the open field, but there was a fence to cross, which my dog made short work of by going underneath.

I threw my backpack over and followed her lead by diving and rolling underneath the fence, all the while thinking it would grab my leg as I was trying to get under. I knew by the sound of the leaves it was right behind me. As I scooped my backpack up, I swung the flashlight behind me. All I could see was fur; the smell in the air was like something sweet and repugnant. It was huge, and as my flashlight hit its face, which was pointed up at a 45-degree angle, it let out a scream that felt like it reverberated through my soul. This thing could have easily ended my life. To this day, I try to figure out why it didn't.

Three things never happened again after that morning. One, I never checked my trap line without my father's 348 strapped on my shoulder. Two, my dog never went with me to recheck my trap line. Three, the most important of all, is I never again questioned my sixth sense.

Thank you for giving me the opportunity to release this experience, which has been penned up inside me for 40 years. -Eric

It Happened Here

Dear Steve,
I thank you for what you are doing, and I want you to know you have my utmost respect. I like the way you say it like it is. We have very few brothers in that respect, and you are teaching me things all the time. With that said, I will try to make good paragraph breaks for you.

My name is Jeremy; I live in Montana. I've been an outdoorsman for my whole life. I've been tracked and followed by cougars, been in close unseen proximity to bears, yadda yadda.

My encounter happened when I was contracted to paint the interior of a new house being built in a place that was remote but not so remote, I would ever have thought this would happen (Bull Mountains). I noticed on my drive into this build that there were more turkeys than I had ever seen. It was early elk season when I started, so I had all my gear in hopes that I could sneak off and bag an elk.

I was a new Dad, and the mortgage bubble had just hit, so I was working alone, having had to lay off my crew because there was virtually no work to be had. I drove a long way to get to this job. I intended to work late and spend the night every night. Upon my arrival, the general contractor left me in charge and left. Sweet I thought.

Night one: I worked until around ten at night. I went outside and jumped in my truck, exhausted. I'm 6'0 tall. Sleeping in a truck cab just doesn't fit, but I was tired and wanted to crash. The nearest farm was about a mile away. I just lied down across the front seat (2001 Dodge 4x4 with topper full of tools extra cab) and crashed. I slept like shit. I felt like I was being watched. Odd for me as I like resting and relaxing in the woods. I woke up, made coffee and thought, what a weird night. Why did I feel like that?

Night two: I couldn't shake the feeling of being watched the night before. I was alone all day, and frankly, I obsessed over it. That night I took a masking machine, with paper and masking tape, and masked off the windows to my truck from the inside. Who would notice I thought, out here in the middle of nowhere? If it makes me feel better and sleep, I'm doing it. Screw what my tough guy buddies would say.

That night in the middle of who knows what time I awoke to my truck rocking pretty hard. I thought," pretty good wind. It's going to snow and get cold. Well, I got to piss. So I get out of the truck, and it's so dark you can't see your hand in front of you, and walk a few steps and start to piss. It's at this moment I realize that it is a beautiful night, warm and calm, no wind whatsoever. There are no sounds in the woods. Odd. But half asleep to deal with it. Why was my truck rocking like it was in a windstorm? Spider-sense now on full heightened alert. What is going on? I get in the truck and go back to sleep.

Night three: I can't take sleeping in the truck anymore. I must stretch out. I set up a Thermarest sleeping bag in the bottom room of the unsecured (not even doorknobs) house. I don't feel good about it. But I must sleep. I don't think I slept at all that night. If I did nod off, it was in abject fear. I had an idea of what was going on. I just didn't want to admit it to myself. I felt watched all night! I couldn't find any sign inside or out the next morning.
  The next day the general contractor showed up, was happy with my progress and left me in charge again—this time with permission to use his R.V. parked 50 yards down the hill off to the side. SWEET I thought. Let me inform you that I had two halogen lights. One I left by the garage door to allow me light to get tools from my truck and one that I moved around with me to light my work area. The job site was an absolute horror show of a mess. Hard to get around.

So, I left my truck backed up to the garage, and the driver door opened all day long this day. I would periodically go out and smoke a cigarette and check my phone. I only had cell service or radio reception during the day for whatever reason. All normal until the end of the day.

Night four: At the end of the workday (around ten again), I walked out to the truck and stood right next to the open driver's door. I could hear a clicking sound about 30 yards straight below me.

I stood, smoked a cig and, in the open light of the halogen light, simply listened to the noise below me. I was in a canyon with rimrocks to my back, a creek bottom below me, and a slight slope with tree cover to the top of the hill on my opposite side. The road paralleled the creek at the bottom of the hill.

The noise was a wood knocking sound that was quiet but regular. It was nothing like the "researchers " do. It was actually very quiet: about the same volume as knocking something off a wooden spoon into a pan. Maybe even slightly less loud. It took a little thinking to sort it out. At first, I thought it was a rancher opening a gate, but no lights, no dog, no truck or ATV, etc. Weird I thought. It was like no natural sounds of the woods I knew of that were not man-made. However, there was no way a man was doing anything out in the middle of nowhere, in the complete dark without at least a flashlight. I listened for about a minute (remember this is about thirty yards away) > It was pitch dark down there. I finally reached into the back seat of my truck into my elk hunting pack and broke out my call and let out a few crappy sleazy cow calls.

This is when the shit hit the fan. I heard the stick get dropped and bounce end to end as it settled. I heard this entity run to my left around fifty yards. It then jumped the fence, crossed the road and ran up behind me around 150 yards or more. It climbed the rims behind me and ended up on the top edge and stopped. It paused for around a second. It performed this evasion/climb in a matter of time that was truly amazingly fast. I wouldn't even guess a time. Too fast is all I could think. After it stopped, it screamed at me in a "voice/matter," which I could only describe as aggressive, territorial, and terrifying. It was unlike anything I have ever heard. Very low (like bass) to very high (like a hawk) with all ranges in between. It lasted just a few seconds. The volume was insanely loud. It terrified me! I knew what it was. This area was dry compacted dirt covered in pine needles with a little dry grass here and there. No tracks left I could find. In the time I heard it run, I can say it was bipedal. The sound of a man running. Nothing like the sound of a horse/cow/bear/elk running. If a person can't hear that distinction, I submit they must live in the city or whatever. We country kids know.

I never saw this entity. I know I was within 15 or fewer yards from it multiple times. The thought of me peeing while it stood behind my truck right next to me scares me to near death. For the rest of the job, I would have to finish for the day, shut off all the lights and then walk to the R.V. in the dark. Not too far but around 50 yards in the total dark. I was terrified every night. I walked with a pistol in one hand and a hunting knife in the other while wearing a headlamp. The funny thing is that I knew they would do me absolutely no well. We do what we can, I guess. I never had any more interactions that contained details that were of any interest or note other than the simple fact that I could feel this entity around me at night. The feeling of being watched gave me Goosebumps. It lasted for just under a month until the job was done for me.

Interesting note: When I brought it up to the old (brash, tough guy) contractor, he had nothing to say about it other than the odd, uncomfortable pause. His younger brother quit the job while they were framing. He wouldn't tell me why.

I've thought about the question you pose about why these beings are covered up by those who are in the know. I think it is for the same reason all the skeletons of giants reported in newspapers throughout the 1800s were collected and hidden by the Smithsonian. I know you are not a Christian. However, I am. I think this line of thought would be helpful in your endeavor of understanding why this information is kept under wraps. It is the same reason why evolution is propped up at all costs. Ever wonder why all the animals on cave walls from 10,0000 years ago are the same as today? Shouldn't they have evolved at least a little bit since then?

I have multiple friends (including a first nations game warden) who have had encounters. I have had two. Interestingly enough, just like my friends. Just as you said: " when they know you know about them; it seems they take pleasure in taunting you" or something like that.

I have difficulty in the woods now. I wish I had your strength. I can't say I'm not scared of anything as you do. I feel pathetic and robbed of what I love. I will send you more things I know in the future. Thank you for what you are doing. I did not understand why I started typing this, but now I feel like it was some sort of simple venting. Thank you! I needed this. I just didn't know it.

Sincerely and with respect,
Jeremy

No Shortage Of Rock Throwing

Hey, man, first I'd like to say I'm a huge fan of what you do on your channel. Thank you for being there for those of us who don't feel comfortable doing so. I'll keep my encounter short because I know you're on a time crunch, but if you have any questions, feel free to ask.

I'm from a small town in the hills of Kentucky. Around here, not much is said about these beings. I was 15 when I had my encounter, a friend of mine, and I was hiking in the woods behind my grandparents' house. It's hundreds of acres of trees, but in the very back, there's an old abandoned strip mine pit. We would always grab sticks, rocks or anything to throw off the high wall, which was 80ft straight down to the water. As we were finding things to toss in, I found this huge rock somewhat buried and probably 250lbs+. I called my friend over to help me pick it up, but even with both of us couldn't budge it.
We lost interest eventually and went on hiking. As we got probably 200 yards away from the spot with the rock, I heard this big KADOSH! We went back over there to see what sounded like someone jumped off the cliff, that's when we saw that the massive rock was gone. No drag marks, not that it had been rolled because it was about 40 feet from the edge. Nothing but the indentation where it once was. It looked like it had just been plucked from the ground and thrown in. We never saw or heard anything, but we got the hell out of there, and I haven't been back since. I can't say it was or wasn't a bigfoot, but what else could've sat there and watched us struggle with it, and after we leave, just toss it in like a pebble. I've always wondered if it was just trying to show its dominance because it knew 2 of us couldn't pick it up. Anyways once again, thank you for your time and your no-bullshit policy. Please don't use my name.

He Saw 4 Of Them

Hi Steve,

My friend was missing chickens, thought maybe it was raccoons. But he was shocked at what he found behind his chicken house. Less than a mile from the Costco store in Smokey Point near Everett Washington. It's real because I have had many encounters with these. My friend is now freaked out.

I was hunting with my walker hounds one night, and my dogs were on a scent, so I sat down on a log to wait and hear which way they were going all of a sudden, I heard a branch break and it was my dogs laying behind me shaking. I thought, what the hell is this my dogs would fight a bear. Then I heard voices saying I am five miles from the nearest house on a moonlight night at 2 am. I had no flashlight on just sitting there.

Next thing I saw 4 of these. 2 males 10 to 12 feet tall one female 8 feet tall and the child about 5 to 6 feet tall the young one was walking in front of the three that were walking side by side. They got about 30 feet from me, and the tallest one stopped lifted his head and took a big sniff of air, and they all stopped and pinned me. I was so scared I was going to die that night. The largest one took one step towards me, and the one next to the female grabbed its shoulder and spoke in its ear and said something to it. I think it saw my rifle. They veered off into the brush. I do believe it was my gun that saved my life; otherwise, I think I would be dead now because I got the drop on them.

I have had several encounters in Washington State hunting One in Oregon bass fishing a huge rock was thrown at my boat off a cliff right before dark, and One time in Idaho bass fishing at night there were 2 of them calling each other one each side of the lake we were fishing.

Last year my son and I were hunting over in Oroville at my brothers' property along the Canadian border. I put apples in the tree about 10 feet high. I set up a trail camera night before opening day of deer season next morning they were gone I looking up the tree and son says what's this a circle 2 feet around 1 inch wide of deer hair freaked us out no pictures on the camera and both are cell phone was dead.
This is all true. Use my name if you want too.

Thanks, Steve,
Rick Alexander

A Female And Baby

Steve,

My name is Jeff McComas. I am from the very southern tip of Ohio. I am an honorably discharged Navy veteran I served during the Persian Gulf conflict. If you were to talk to anyone who knows me, they'd tell you that I do not lie about anything. In 1986 I had gone deer hunting in an old coal strip mine area that is now part of the Wayne national forest in Gallia County, Ohio. There have been many encounters with these things reported since the early 1800s in and around Gallia county.

Well, this is what happened to me it was bow season 1986 I'm not for sure of the exact date.

Still, I had scouted this area since early September and had built a few of the old-fashioned deer stands in a patch of woods that probably spanned two miles in each direction there were a few old strip mine roads and two old strip mine ponds. I tried to alternate between the tree stands going to a different one each day that I hunted on this particular day I decided to go to the stand that was maybe 40-50 yards away from one of the old ponds. I got to the tree stand around 5:00 am it was still dark, cold, and foggy when the sun finally started to break. The fog started rolling back.

I started hearing a buzzing sound, and I thought to myself there can't be any bees nest in this tree, especially as cold as it was all of a sudden, I caught a glimpse of something out of the corner of my eye. I first thought it was a black bear. Still, as it broke through the fog, I made out what it really was SHE was maybe 6'-7' tall. SHE was carrying a baby one, and the whole time she was humming and looking at the baby one, I don't know if it was a newly born baby or if it was sick. Still, she walked to the edge of the pond, got a scoop of water in her hand and either gave it to the baby or wiped him off, but as quickly as she appeared, she turned and walked away through the thickest briar patch. After that, I didn't hear the buzzing or humming anymore. I feel like that she was so into taking care of the baby one that she didn't notice me setting up in the tree stand.

This is probably one of the most uneventful encounters that have been sent to you. Still, it's absolutely true they do exist, and I know it to be fact again my name is Jeff McComas I'm 53 years old I have 12 grandchildren been married to the same gal for 30 years and a truly honest individual feel free to use my name and to tell my story thanks!

When I Walked, It Walked

Steve: I sent an earlier experience to you about when I was a Marine, stationed at Camp Lejeune NC regarding at least four bigfoots that scared the living shit out of myself and four other Marines while fishing on the backside of the base. Now I would like to tell you about another experience that I had when hunting near Mt. Saint Helens, WA, after I got out of the service.

I again wish to thank you before starting my encounter experience with you for what you are doing to bring the facts to the light of day regarding Bigfoot and the people who are trying to keep this a secret or make people think if it is real, that it is a harmless APE. This narrative is simply bullshit.

I know that it is not an APE and want to share my experience with you and hope that you know for a fact that many of us have experienced these beings that would like to help you in any way possible, you must bring the truth out in the open where it belongs.

There are far too many people that go blindly into the woods thinking that there is nothing out there and if it is out there, that it is a big furry, friendly creature that means them no harm. To that, I say bullshit. So, for someone like you to step up. Try to get the facts out there that may keep someone safe; you're doing a great job. We need your help in getting to the bottom of this

Steve Isdahl   The Day Sasquatch Became Real For Me   Copyright© 2020

conspiracy, or whatever it is that keeps these mindless money-grubbing, fake researchers going in circles like dogs chasing their tails.

This experience happened to me in 1978, shortly before Mt. Saint Helens blew its top. I was on the South Side of the Mountain, where I had hunted for years before going into the service. This was my first trip back to do some Elk hunting, and I was so excited to be back home and able to go hunting, which I love so much.

My hunting partner was not able to go with me on this trip, so I was going to make a solo trip, which I had done many times before. I knew the area very well and was prepared for what the area would present. I always take at least three days' worth of provisions when hunting as well as survival gear in the way of extra clothing, poncho, matches, Firestarter and other essential items in a backpack that I carry. I know that many do not take such precautions when hunting, but I do because once while hunting, I got turned around so bad that I spent three days in the woods wishing I had something with me other than my gun, knife, and what I was wearing on my back.

On this trip, I was going to hunt a power transmission line right of way, that allowed me to park on the logging road and walk about a mile to where I would sit on top of a ridge where I would be able to watch both sides of a hogback on top of the ridge. It allowed me to be able to have a clear shot for over 400 yards in either direction. I had taken several elk in this same location, on various seasons, over the years before entering the service.

I walked in before the light and reached the spot where I intended to hunt before the sun came up. I was there all day and did not see a thing. This was highly unusual as every other time I had chosen this location to hunt from, I always saw something—deer, elk, even a black bear on several occasions. Maybe the things I would see on those hunting trips were not what I was looking to hunt for, but on this day, nothing seemed to be around, not even a rabbit. It was also quieter than I remembered. For some reason, I also had the feeling of being watched but thought it was nothing.

It was getting later about an hour before dark, close to when I would have to leave. I started to hear movement across the right of way in the woods; it was not the usual sounds you hear from an animal. More like someone walking in the woods. I thought that maybe someone else was hunting in this area and took careful note to be careful not to shoot in that direction should an elk walkout. I had never seen anyone else but me in this hunting area before. I had spent a lot of time gone while in the service and thought maybe someone else had found that this was a great location too.

I continued watching both sides of the hogback but kept having that feeling I was being watched, call it, sixth sense or whatever, it was just a feeling I could not shake. I started to hear more movement in the woods across the right of way, from, and it sounded like it was someone walking towards me. I felt that as late as it was, it was time to leave and walk back to my car. Knowing that someone was on the other side of the right of way and might shoot in my direction when I got up to leave, I yelled over and said I am coming out, for god sake, don't shoot—more as a joke than anything.

No one said anything, and there was no more movement from that direction, I once again yelled a little louder, I came out, please don't shoot. I got up and started walking towards the dirt road that ran down almost the center of the right of way and wandered back and forth between the transmission power towers.

I thought it funny that whoever it was didn't call back to say that they had heard me and had said it was ok. Once I got to the dirt road, I started back to my car, thinking that whoever it was didn't want to make any noise to scare any animals as it was not quite dark enough to stop hunting, but for me, I felt the urge to leave.

As I moved towards my car, the sound of walking in the woods started again off to my right. Just inside the tree line. I thought that maybe whoever it was, had decided to walk out with me. But whoever it did not come out of the woods but just kept paralleling me. I stopped; they stopped. This was beginning to creep me out, so I asked them to come out where I could see them. There was no reply. I again, in a louder voice said, enough is enough no more games, get your ass out here so I can see you. Still, there was no reply. I took my gun off my shoulder and jacked around in the chamber. Keeping the gun pointed in the direction of the area where I heard the walking, I had my safety on. I continued to walk to my car.

When I walked, it walked, when I stopped it stopped, as it was getting darker, I became worried, maybe this was not a human, remembering my experience when I was in the Marines at Camp Lejeune, I began to think perhaps this might be a bigfoot. I was also aware that maybe there might be another one on the left side of me, I started to watch not only my right side but the left as well as watching my back trail closely. After all, I would rather be safe than sorry.

I still had quite a way to go to get to my car and knew it would be dark by the time I got there if I didn't hurry, so I started to jog back so I could get there before it was dark. The thing to my right started keeping pace with me. I could hear it breaking limbs and what sounded like small trees as it kept pace with me. It was at this time I knew it was not a human being and was almost sure it was a bigfoot.

I made it to my car without ever seeing what it was, but I wasted no time in putting things away neatly, I simply threw my stuff in the car and got out of there as fast as I could. Even without seeing it, I can tell you it was not a bear, not a cougar, bobcat or anything else that I have experienced in the woods. I cannot say it was for sure a bigfoot, but I would bet all that I have that it was. Needless to say, I have never hunted in that area again.

I want to thank you for reading my encounter and want everyone to know that they should be extra observant when in the woods as well as armed. I am cautious when in or near the woods. I carry a 44 magnum in a chest holster as well as my rifle, which is a 300 Win Mag. I am very proficient with either weapon. I forgot to mention. I was a Sniper for the Marines during my tours in Vietnam; As well as a marksmanship instructor before that. I can hit just about anything that I can see, but in the case of Bigfoot, unless it was genuinely trying to hurt me or someone else with me, I don't think I could shoot one. The one that I did see at Camp Lejeune looks far too much like a human to kill one. Not that I wouldn't shoot if it were necessary, just that I would not want to kill one just to say that I did when they had done nothing wrong.

It is just my thought, but I think that sometimes, the Bigfoot creatures are a little too curious for their own good, other times they just want you out of their territory and do what they can to get you to leave, other times, they may have own intentions and that is why I am always armed when in the woods. If they are human-like, there are good and bad humans making me think, maybe they are a lot like us. I don't trust easily, and I believe that is how we should treat these creatures.

Keep up the great work, Steve and may you be successful in your endeavors. Feel free to use my name.
Sincerely,

Dennis Coplin

Gold Bridge B.C.

Steve, I want to start by thanking you for all you do with regards to the topic of Bigfoot. You've changed my life and made me feel that it's ok to talk about this after 30 years. I've briefly told you about my encounter over your YouTube channel, but I thought I'd give you a bit more detail. It was 1991, and I was hunting California bighorns in the alpine Mountains around Gold Bridge BC. I had hunted this area for years, but this trip was to be very different. I was a week into my three-week hunt and had a beautiful little camp spot at the base of an alpine bowl just in the tree line at a creek. For a week, I felt right at home as I always do in the wilderness, but one night after I ate my freeze-dried Salisbury steak dinner, a terrible feeling came over. I felt very uneasy and as though I was being watched. I never slept that night as I was sure it was wolves, grizzly or something near my camp. I spent the next day glassing an adjacent bowl for sheep, and as the afternoon came, I saw nothing, not even a deer, which was strange as hell for this area. As I was looking around at the bottom of the bowl, I noticed something move slightly and thought immediately it was a grizzly, by its color, shape and size. It was about 300yds from me, so I put my binoculars on it to take a look. Just as I got on it, it stood, and I knew immediately what it was, it was NOT a grizzly...

The creature began to walk to the right towards the jack pines taking 7-8 strides. I dropped my binos and grabbed my 300-win mag, just out of instinct. I went prone and put the crosshairs directly on the creature. Its arms were swinging, and its hands down almost to its knees. I could honestly see the muscles flexing as it walked. At first, it took my breath away, and my heart was pounding so hard that my scope was jumping. Just before the creature reached the timber, without stopping, it turned and looked DIRECTLY at me. Not only in my direction, Steve, but it also looked right into my scope and into my eyes. The image of this creature's face and expression as I looked Right in his eyes through my scope.

The expression on its face will be etched forever in my memory. It looked so old and weathered, dark leathery, wrinkled skin and its eyes deep in its head but visible. Oddly, I felt no threat or fear at the time. It felt like the encounter lasted minutes, but I know it was seconded, and I was in the trees and gone. I'm 6'3" and 230 lbs., and I would guess this creature to have been 7'6" easily and probably 400lbs. Its shoulders had to be 4' across and the thickness of its chest 3'. The muscle mass was incredible, and I could see all its muscles flexing as it walked, much like a giant bear or wolverine that is solid muscle. That creature KNEW I was there, and I honestly believe it was watching me the entire time.

Two years later, within a few miles of this spot, I was deer hunting in late November and was hiking up a valley. Something screamed/roared at me that still sends shivers up my spine to this day. I was fucking terrified, and I turned around and ran/walked for 3 hrs. back to my truck and left. This bloody creature was pissed that I was there, and it warned me to fuck off right now and trust me, I wasted no time. I've heard a bear's death roar, I've listened to cougars scream, and that day in that valley, I heard a Sasquatch screaming at me to get the hell out of its area!!! I only ever told a few people about my encounter until I found you and your channel. Most people laughed at me except a native friend of mine who simply said you were lucky, be careful out there. The other person I told was a friend who was a CO at the time, and I was shocked by his reaction of " oh ya, where'd ya see him"! Right there on the spot, I felt the need not to tell him the truth, so I made up a different area far from where I was. I think this guy knew, a lot of them know they exist, they just won't admit to it or tell us. Anyways Steve, thanks again for all you do; you're making a difference in many lives. Keep up the good work, keep it wild, and, most of all, BE SAFE!

-D. Clark Project Superintendent

Even The Game Wardens

My name is Doug Erickson. I'm a retired Minnesota Game Warden/ pilot. My patrol area was in the northeastern part of the state, which is mostly wilderness. Feel free to use my name because, like you, I don't take crap from people either.

In the 1980's I was patrolling a vast lake in my patrol area on a very nice day. I decided to tie the boat up on shore and walk across a peninsula to observe any fishing activity in the next bay. I spotted a man still fishing in a boat about a hundred yards out from me. I concealed myself and sat down. He did not move once. I put my binoculars on him to see what was up. Within a moment, he started fidgeting and looking all around. He had his back to me and turned and looked directly at me. I was completely hidden, so he did not hear or see me. He started his boat and came to shore about 30 yards down the hill from me and started looking around underbrush and behind trees. I thought that he must have a hidden pile of fish somewhere and decided to let him pick it up before I picked him up. He looked from side to side, back to where I was, and all around. After a few moments of this, I realized that he was looking for me. I was startled by this but also very curious. As he walked around and started to get further away, I mentally told him to come back, and he did so each time until he walked up to the brush in front of me, spread it apart and looked me right in the eye. I said, "how ya doing", and he said, "I knew someone watching me." I said, have a seat and let's talk. We soon discovered that we were both army vets, and he said that he found he had that skill while in Vietnam, and it saved his ass many times. I have felt this sixth sense many times when working and always took it as a warning, get the hell away and find another route. What this guy did was terrific. He knew I was not dangerous. I forgot to check his fishing license. After a feat like that, a handshake was more in order.

Jump ahead 30 years or so. A group of us outdoor types shot sporting clays, and we were sitting on the deck of the clubhouse, and the subject of Bigfoot came up. I mentioned that I had doubts about any primate(?) living in the wild in Minnesota in the winter because they lose body heat too fast, and the calories needed would not be obtainable. We do get -60f and colder here. My teammate spoke up and said he had seen one. He managed a mining supply company and was travelling between towns and had to take a leak. He pulled off on a side road close to where his hunting shack is and stopped by a power line. As he was doing his thing, he looked down the hill to a small swamp and saw a huge figure pulling cattails out. After a moment, the figure stopped, turned around and looked at him. It then ran to a poplar tree, hid behind it and looked at him from side to side. Not realizing that its shoulders were four times the width of the tree. Nobody in the group said a word. Three of us were retired law enforcement, and some were loggers or miners and log cabin builders—all outdoorsmen. I broke the silence and asked where he was exactly when this happened. He said right near Eveleth Mn. Close to me and one of our coldest towns.

I have never seen or found a sign of a Bigfoot during my working years, and if I had, I would have kept my mouth shut until retirement. My friend said that it spooked him, and he told no one except his wife and hunting shack partner. I believe my friend.

High Level Security And Still Saw One

Hi Steve, my name is John Blatt, and I have a very odd story to share with you. I am 48 years old, a single father, military veteran, and have held three top-secret clearances doing security for the military and government contractors. I chose to do that type of work no longer, but I share this because the story that I am about to tell is hard to believe, and I need to share that I am a no-nonsense, truthful person that is trustworthy. The military and the government would not have granted me the level of security clearances that I had if it was otherwise.

I have had several encounters with Sasquatch beings over the years, but it was my first encounter that had the greatest impact on my life. This first encounter happened to me over 40 years ago at the young and tender age of seven. For the first eight years of my life, I grew up in a distant suburb of Chicago called Park Forest and went to Dogwood Elementary School, which was a short walk from my home. It was during a 2nd-grade field trip to the Des Plaines Dolomite Prairies Land and Water Reserve that I had the encounter that would dramatically affect my life forever. I honestly do not remember a lot about that field trip except seeing wildlife and going on walks around the Reserve with my classmates. At that age, everything is wondrous and new, and I don't believe I had ever been on a nature walk in the wild before. As can be expected, we were all in fascination and excited to be on such a great exploration of those wetlands. I remember it being a magical experience, that is until I had my encounter.

I distinctly remember walking on a dirt path or trail through woodlands and walking in the back of the line of kids. Looking back, I am surprised an adult was not in the back over watching the children, but it was the 70s and life was much simpler and not as fearful back then. Taking everything in the back of the line, I had noticed a small turtle on the ground to the right of the trail and stopping to examine it. It was amazing to me because I had never seen a real turtle before, and it was just beautiful. I had stopped, squatted down, and after examining it for a while, I picked it up and just was enthralled with this little creature. So much so that I was completely oblivious that the rest of the class. Adults had continued down the trail and had been gone for quite some time. I believe it must have been at least several minutes of being engrossed with my new little friend when I slowly realized that I was completely alone in the woods. I don't remember being frightened at all by this realization. But I know I had put the turtle back down on the earth where it was, and as I did so, I remember hearing a noise coming from my left in the direction of the woods. I turned, and before me was something I did not understand. It was a hairy giant. Something that looked similar to Chewbacca from Star Wars was standing about 20 feet from me, but it did not make me feel safe or comforted. It must have come up from behind me when I was alone looking at the turtle.

My initial instinctual impression slowly changed from stunned astonishment to this growing fear as I realized that what was before me was a monster, and I was completely alone with it. It stood there just looking at me. Its long brown hair came down and mostly covered its face. I don't remember being able to see its eyes. After a few moments of being still, it slowly started to sway back and forth while it was looking down at me. I don't remember ever having a fight or flight experience or having a desire to run. Although I was becoming more and more terrified by the moment, I never thought of fleeing. Why I just don't know.

What happened next is something I've been trying to understand and cope with for the rest of my life. It let out this incredible moan or cry that made my whole body vibrate. It was so deafening. As it was making this cry, something happened to me. I could not move. I tried to scream, but I could not open my mouth, and I could not move my body at all. It wasn't that I was just paralyzed with fear, but I was locked in place. I believed I would have just fainted out of sheer terror, but it never happened. It was like it had somehow connected with my brain and was overriding my mental, bodily commands. That's the only way that I can describe it. I was standing there unable to move for what seemed like hours, but I am sure it was only moments. This giant started walking towards me, came right up to me only a couple of feet away, squatted down, gently grabbed me under my armpits and stood up with me in its hands. My face was only a couple of feet away from its face.

It was at this point that I realized that I was no longer looking through my own eyes, but I was outside my body looking at myself being held by this creature. Now, as an adult, I understand

Steve Isdahl   The Day Sasquatch Became Real For Me   Copyright© 2020

that what I was experiencing was an Out-of-body experience, but at the time, it was like a dream. I no longer had any fear but was watching this like I would watch a TV show. I don't know if this creature was causing this to happen to me or if my fright was so bad that I ended up leaving my body. My intuition tells me that it was the Sasquatch being that was causing this to happen to me. While I was in this state, I did not have any fear or anxiety but remember being very peaceful all the while looking at myself being held many feet off the ground by a giant hairy monster.

The next thing I remember was being carried down the path, not by the creature but by one of my teachers. The creature, of course, was gone, and I was much further down the trail. My teacher was very upset with me because they were trying to find me for quite some time. All the other students were already on the buses and were waiting for me. I was frantically trying to explain that I had seen a giant hairy monster, and I was crying and sobbing. All the adults and the kids were angry with me because, to them, I had run off and caused the rest of the field trip to be cut short because I was missing. I don't know how long I had been gone, but as best as I can recall, it must have been at least an hour. What made it worse was that I had thoroughly soiled myself during the encounter, and the adults were furious with me and the rest of my schoolmates being spiteful and teasing me. I didn't care about that at that moment. I just wanted someone to listen to me and help me with what I had just gone through. No one, of course, believed me, and I just remember shutting down mentally after that. I just don't remember much after that. I know I just wanted it all to be over and forgotten as soon as possible. I do remember my mom having to go to school the next day and meeting with the principal and my teacher and feeling like I had done something wrong. I kept thinking to myself that they must have heard the cry that thing made. It was so loud. Yet there was never mention on it at all from them.

Shortly after, this is when the nightmares began. Night after night, I would have these terrible night-terrors of what I called the "Siren monster" because its moan sounded like an ambulance siren, and I had no other frame of reference to call it anything else. Terrible night sweats and waking up running into my parents' room to try to sleep with them. I remember at night lying in my bed just petrified when I would hear ambulance sirens in the distance thinking that it was the siren monster coming to get me and that it was going to come walking up the stairs into my room in the middle of the night. It was horrible! My little life was turned upside down, filled with fear and monsters. I tried and tried to explain to my mom what had happened to me. But I feel that she thought I must have just taken a nap during the field trip and dreamt the whole thing. That was one of the worst parts of this entire experience, not having anyone who you trust to believe you and those who should have been my protectors and comforters were my punishers.

After having these nightmares for weeks, my mom sat me down and said that sometimes when you are afraid and have deep-seated fears that the best thing to do was to face those fears and a lot of time those fears will go away. So that is exactly what I did. Right at that time, my mom had bought me one of those Readers Digest books on unexplained mysteries (I think it was called Strange Stories Amazing Facts?) I believe within that book was a sketch that someone drew of the creature they had seen that looked identical to what I had encountered. That was it! It helped me to know that I wasn't crazy but also that this "monster" was called a Bigfoot or a

Sasquatch. So, at the age of seven, I set out to try to face my fears, understand what had happened to me, and try to learn everything I could about these beings called Bigfoot. This opened my mind at that young age to a life full of mystery, wonders, and of course, very frightening things. While my friends were learning baseball and getting into sports, I was watching monster movies and reading all I could get my hands-on regarding Bigfoot and other mysterious things. Don't get me wrong I still played baseball and had a relatively normal childhood. But I was more interested in mysteries and scary movies than anybody else I knew.

One of the lasting effects of this encounter that I had as a child was, for lack of better terminology, psychic abilities. I would just know things that I had no way of knowing. I would have visions and spiritual experiences that no one else around me would have a frame of reference for. I could sense things, see dead people and communicate with spirits, know whether someone was good or bad, and even have conversations with trees. Actually, I thought all of these things were quite normal until I would share them with other kids, and I quickly realized that this wasn't a normal thing that everyone experienced. I remember telling a teacher about seeing a dead person standing in the corner of the classroom after I was distracted, continuously looking at this person. During recess, she took me aside and asked me why I was ignoring her and just staring into the corner? She looked at me like I was crazy, and that started a series of psychological evaluations. I remember overhearing the conversation between my mom and the psychiatrist that I was perfectly normal and healthy. Just a little... odd. After that, I learned to keep my mouth shut.

In 1982 the films Poltergeist and The Entity came out (and yes, my parents let me watch just about everything), and within those films were scientists who studied the paranormal and psychic phenomena which were called Parapsychologists. This gave me another frame of reference, and I began to study parapsychology at the age of twelve. I ended up reading every book on parapsychology, Bigfoot, ufos, ghosts, psychic phenomena, and anything else that falls into the category of "the unexplained." I exhausted all of the books at the city library as well as our school's libraries.

I do not know whether or not my first encounter with Sasquatch was responsible for opening these psychic experiences in my life, whether it was just sheer coincidence, or that my encounter happened because I had these sensitivities in the first place? I do not know what had happened to me during the time I was missing and that I could not remember. Why didn't the Sasquatch just walk off with me never to be seen again? Why don't I remember anything after it picked me up? I still have many questions that are left unanswered.

Since that first encounter, I have had at least four other encounters with these intelligent beings. I do not believe that they are monsters or an unclassified ape. They are clearly of intelligence that is higher than ours and has abilities that we just do not understand. Each one of my proceeding encounters has had some level of psychic aspect to them. During each encounter that I have had, I was in a vulnerable position and could have easily ended with great harm coming to me. But that never happened. They could have easily hurt me or ended my life. But chose not to harm me and not to frighten me as well overly. Did my first encounter mark me in some way? It feels that way sometimes. It's strange; when they are near, I can feel them even when there is no physical rationale why I could know that. No wood knocking. No smell. Just an overpowering sensation. Not fearful but an intensity that is hard to explain. I have had it when they come close to where I used to live (near the foothills of the North Cascades) I would suddenly wake up in the middle of the night and know they were close. Like they were just stopping by to say hi or something. One night I woke straight up out of deep sleep and without any thought I looked out my window, and two enormous glowing amber eyes are looking at me, and I watched as it turned away into the night and I was like "Oh it's just a sasquatch" and laid back down and went to sleep. Who does that? Hahaha.

If you are interested, I would be happy to share my other encounters with you. They are nowhere as intense as my first encounter. But I think they are all interesting all the same. I've never gone looking for them or have ever wanted this in my life, especially as a child. I continued to have infrequent nightmares with Sasquatch up until my mid-30s. There came a moment where I began to acknowledge this strange connection with them. With deep sincerity, I laid down all my desire to try to prove to other people that they were real or to try to acquire evidence of their existence for science to acknowledge them. I gave up trying to have a name for myself in the Sasquatch Community.

I stopped trying to "find" them and trying to get evidence. I stopped researching them like they were a pet project of mine. I let them go. It was only after I did this that my nightmares ended. The night after I let them go, I had a powerful dream with a Sasquatch in which this being came up to me while standing on a bridge. It knew that I had given up my pursuit of them and had let them go in my life. The Sasquatch then transformed into a human in front of me, smiled and said, "Thank you." I felt sincere gratitude from it, and it turned and walked away. By turning into a human, it showed me that he wasn't a monster; he was an intelligent living being just like a human. He was a person. I still have dreams with them in it, but they are never scary or intimidating. If anything, the dreams with them in it are very pleasant, deep, and powerful. I have made peace with them and am grateful for the experiences that they have given me.

I consider their connection in my life as a very interesting blessing, full of mystery and wonder. Yes, I have done my research and have read probably hundreds of books about them over the years, but I no longer consider myself a researcher or desire to be considered an "expert." With as crazy and narcissistic as the Sasquatch and Cryptid Community is, I found out early on that it is better to stand back in the shadows and not participate in the toxic drama and egocentric personalities and groups. People who are "Sasquatch Hunters" or who are in Bigfoot Groups and do field expeditions and research wonder why they don't have any meaningful encounters with them. I mean, *I* don't want to have any meaningful encounters with them, so why would these super intelligent and psychic beings want to either? Just a thought anyway.

Thank you for taking the time to read my story (or at least a part of it). Feel free to use my name or to edit it where I might not be as clear if you chose to share this with others. If you don't want to share, this that is ok too. I just truly respect you and like you as a person. You seem genuine and real to me and are not a part of "The Community." You might want to know that this is the very first time I have ever shared all the details of my first encounter with anyone.

Yes, I had shared before that I had a face to face encounter when I was seven, but never the stranger details. I don't honestly care if others don't believe it or not. That is not my concern. I just think it is important to share ALL the information to the world, instead of trying to sanitize it to fit some agenda or ideology (like Sasquatch being an Ape). We should no longer be afraid to share the stranger details in our encounters just so that we don't offend someone or just to make our encounter easier for others to believe you. We shouldn't have to fear what other people think. If anything, I hope others will feel freer to share all the weird and strange details that are held back due to fear of ridicule. That time needs to come to an end, and I feel you are helping others, like myself, to share openly without the fear of negative backlash.

Thank you again for the work you are doing. May you be blessed in all that you do!

John Blatt

Montana And Up Close

Hello Steve, my name is Justin Myhre (pronounced Myer). I'm 45 now, born & raised in Wyoming and am an avid outdoorsman. I am standing with you 150% and with others who encounter these creatures. I have several stories, including finding a nest to be followed home one night. But my 1st encounter, man, it's like it was yesterday & still gives me the chills, not to mention bad dreams. I was living in Billings, MT. For my first three years there, the people I met would tell me, my brother and parents, not to venture alone in this particular wooded area south of town known as Riverfront Park, that something creepy was there.

Well, in 1993, I decided to go fishing at the main pond one early April morning at around 7 AM. I got to a favorite spot just past the only bridge there. I sat under this line tree, no one else there, I had the pond all to myself. Well, I was sitting on the north side, and to my left, across the pond at around 7:30, I heard a bunch of splashing. It was too cold for swimmers, so I thought maybe a couple of dogs, I heard it again, so I looked over, and I about shit myself. This thing, covered in auburn hair, massive in size (bigger and taller than Shaq and The Big Show, Paul Wight, who I've met both) stood up out of the water and took a step into the shore. I moved back in shock. It was about 75 feet from, turned and looked straight at me.

Ugly, horrific, and right down scary. We made eye contact just for maybe 15 seconds, then it turned away and walked off into the woods. I stood up, watched it and heard it crash through the brush and break off tree limbs, I instantly gathered my stuff, walking backwards to the parking lot, and this other guy just showed up and was sitting in his pick up, and I asked if he had also seen it. His reply was yes, and that he had seen it before. Well, I instantly knew that it was a sasquatch. The flat face, the bipedal walk, the sheer size, the cone-shaped head. Of course, no one believed me, but I did get my brother and a friend to go back with me the next day, and it ended up that our friend, who was 6'7 had to stand in a stump and raise his hand to measure how tall this sasquatch was. We then measured it to 9 feet. Its shoulders are about 4 feet across. That gave all 3 of us the chills. I never saw it again, but I never went alone either after that.

Footprints would be seen from time to time. I'd hear other people mention it. Now in 1996, I saw another one and a nest, but that's another story/account. I don't go alone into the woods, my senses are heightened, and I don't sleep if I camp out. I do go armed, but I do go armed!!! I've come close moose and grizzlies, but the sasquatch are the ones that I fear the most. I stand with you, Steve. Keep up the good work!

Changed My Hunting Forever

Hello Steve, I'm going to tell you the events that changed my hunting passion, I couldn't wait till the season came to I sold my best coonhound because it wasn't fair for her to be penned up. It all started when I was about 14. I was coon hunting with my grandfather and uncle. We were walking on a river island, and my grandpa's dog started barking. Upon getting to her, she was not barking hard. Not upon the tree like she normally would be.

About the same time my uncle's dog came to check-in, he started staring at the area Sally (my grandpa's dog), was barking. He commenced growling, and all the hair on his body was standing straight up. Limbs broke beyond Sally, and her reaction was the same as Joe, (my uncle's dog). My grandfather was a hard man, and at the time, I didn't understand when he called the dogs off, and we leashed them and walked back casually back to the pickup truck. I asked what the dogs run, and my grandfather played it off, saying it was a slick tree. He wouldn't answer at the time what was causing them to start growling like they were fixing to fight for their life. No matter how much I asked.

Fast forward three years. It was the opening night for coon season. The date was October 15th. I had my walker hound, Bonnie and Bluetick Buck. Mind you, I was approximately 5 miles from the spot I was at with my grandfather. I unloaded the dogs and started my journey up an old road that went to the base of the mountain where the inclined started around a two-mile walk. I had got about a half-mile or so. The dogs were out hunting, coming back every 10-15 minutes to check in as I call it, and they'd go back out hunting. At about this point, I could faintly hear something walking behind me. At first, I thought it was one of the dogs, so I didn't pay it any mind. I was nearly a half-mile from the end of the road where the mountain started to incline that I noticed whatever was walking behind me was matching me step for step.

They were close, but as I cast my light threw the big timber, I couldn't see a thing. I had heard of bobcats being nosey critters, and I played it off again. Figuring I'd have a good chase on my hands if the dogs caught the cat's scent, I was going to try and scare it off. I started walking but decided after about ten steps I was going to turn quickly and cast my walk light on this cat and scare it off. Well, after I turned and threw my light up, I didn't see a cat. I saw a bear; I saw it staring at me from an old-growth poplar tree. I quickly loaded my single shot 22lr and was about to shoot and scare it off when this big hairy thing, every bit of 7 feet tall and 40 inches wide, walked out from behind that poplar and proceeded to walk past me on my right.

I was scared shitless. Couldn't move, much less pop a round at this thing. About that time, my dogs came back and caught sight of it. It started running ahead of me the direction I intended to go. Was I ever so glad when my dogs gave chase. I knew I had a chance to get the hell to the truck.

I literally broke out running as fast as I could. I knew the mile and half would take roughly 10 minutes, but I was glad to get the shit out of there. About two minutes into my run back to the vehicle, I could hear the dogs chasing parallel to me, but they were on top of the ridge, and I was in the hollow. Another minute of running and they were ahead of me in the direction I was heading. I knew I had to get out of there; this thing was circling me. I ran faster than I ever had. Clearing blowdowns that I'd generally walk around.

I was parked beside an open field where the dirt road I was travelling passed. About 300 yards from my truck, I heard the most intense roar I'd ever heard in my life. The dogs had shut up. I didn't have a clue what was going on, but I knew I was getting in my truck. When I reached the gravel road, my truck was roughly 50 yards parked beside the fence that went around the field. As I got near my truck, the fence flattened as a tree had fallen on top of it. But nothing was there. The screams continued. I looked, and my hounds had crawled under my truck. I opened the door, and they jumped inside, and I wasn't going to waste time putting them on the rear box.

You can say I made record time getting home that night. I lived with my grandfather. Upon walking in the house after tying up my dogs, I was asked by grandpa if I had caught a coon. Hell, no was my answer as I caught myself speaking to him like that. He looked at me and said, boy, you're pale. You look like getting sick. I told him no that I saw something, and I sat down and explained what I saw and what happened. His first words where wou were up on the mountain by the old dynamite shed. I asked him immediately how he knew. The only thing he said after that was don't go back in the woods that I had a lot of other good hunting lands.

I never questioned my grandfather that night. In fact, I never coon hunted again. In 2005 as my grandpa was pretty much housebound. Not able to get out and walk, with that night still on my mind and him knowing where I was without anyone knowing I had to ask to get some type of closure.

He said Bill when I was your age we went to look for a guy in that very spot that had gone hunting but never came home, we found him. He had shot himself. I asked, do you think it was his ghost, his spirit? He said you're not getting it. This guy was built like a mule, could beat any man that he knew of, and he was too religious to commit suicide for no reason. I said, do you think he was murdered?" He looked at me and said I'll never repeat this. The guy we found had two broken legs. He was scared of killing himself. I've seen them several times day and night, hunting or cutting timber. But the ones up there will kill you. I encountered one once drilling ore in that very spot. I asked what was said of the man's legs. It wasn't reported. It was the early 1900s. We kept it to ourselves but figured he was tortured and committed suicide to get it over. I then asked what he saw when up in their drilling ore, and he looked at me and said the conversation ends here. I have a feeling he had an encounter like me.

I'm in my forties, and I drive by the same field; I parked that night, but I always look straight ahead until I'm past the spot. Its many things in life people will do for a dollar. I wouldn't walk that two-mile journey back in those woods for a million.

If I had the money, I'd pay to know what I witnessed!!! Thank you for letting me tell someone. Other than my grandfather, who took this with him to his grave, you're the first person I've told Steve!

This took place in Augusta County, Virginia. In the Shenandoah Valley.

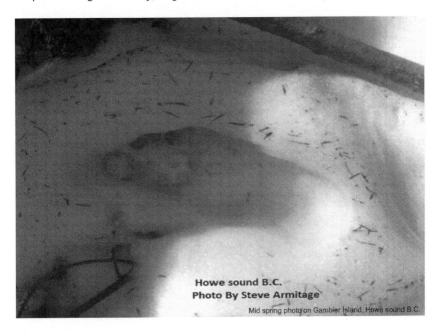

Howe sound B.C.
Photo By Steve Armitage
Mid spring photo on Gambier Island, Howe sound B.C.

Illinois Cop Tells All

Steve,

I felt compelled to send you an email to let you know what you are doing is very much appreciated by so many people. I watch your YouTube channel whenever there is a new video posted. It takes courage, true grit and big balls to stand up against those who are knowingly misleading the public to further their own fake agenda.

I consider myself to be an honest man. I am a retired police officer living just East of St. Louis, MO in Illinois.

I have zero field experience when it comes to any form of research, and I have never hunted in my life. My father, who is 96, never allowed any toy guns around the house, so I never even owned and fired one until I was 20. Fighting in WWII must have instilled in my dad a strong dislike for all guns. Anyway, I have read so many books on Sasquatch. I've learned the best way to get more educated on this subject is to keep my mouth shut and use my ears to listen and learn. I have had an interest in this subject since I was a child old enough to read and certainly have been laughed at by distant family members. In the police academy, an old school state trooper told me a very important thing to do while you are out patrolling. He looked me in the eyes and said if you take the time always to pay attention to your surroundings, remember that you WILL SEE more odd things out there if you regularly look into your rear-view mirror! I have read of so many accounts of law enforcement officers who reported seeing a large hairy bipedal creature walk across the road right after they drove by! I have been taught to follow the evidence, and in my opinion, it is overwhelming!

I WANTED YOU TO KNOW THAT ALL OF YOUR HARD WORK, STANDING UP TO THE HATERS, LIARS AND INTERNET TROLLS IS SO MUCH APPRECIATED!

This subject is like a huge dam holding backwater, but over many decades some holes and cracks just keep getting bigger and letting more water leak through. The truth about this creature is just the same as all that water. By the way, Melba Ketchum is one of my heroes, and what they did to her is terrible.

God Bless You and Continue to Fight the Fight!!!
Sincerely,
Mitchel

Haven't Hunted The Family Farm Since

Hey Steve,
I have been listening to your YouTube channel for months. Finally got the courage to message you about one of many encounters.

I'm a young 29-year old I've hunted pretty much everything you can hunt in the state of Pennsylvania. Small game squirrel, rabbit, pheasant, turkey, goose, duck, large game deer, bear and coyote. I'm 5'11 and 240 pounds. And pretty much there's nothing that scares me. When I was a child, my dad made up some crazy story about these things called molly guardians. He said these things come out at night, and if I didn't come in at dusk, they're known to take children. As a kid, I just thought it was something to scare us children and listen when it got dark to come in and settle down for the night. I'll get back to the molly guardians later, but keep that in mind.

On a beautiful late October day in 2016, I was hunting for gray squirrels on my family's 270-acre farmland in Pennsylvania. There was not much wind at all that day, and I was successful in my hunt that day with already four squirrels. So, I sat alongside a hill where a path went alongside it. I sat on a stump with my squirrel carrying a bag alongside it, and I was there for a good 40 mins. I was taking in the beauty of that day when everything slowly went silent. Then a few minutes later, I heard deer running down the hill a good 45 yards away. I got startled and had no clue I watched on that side of the hill. I was very still, and they ran out the area one behind another like a bat out of hell, hulling ass like something scared them. I wasn't sure what it was.

Not a moment later, I saw something my eyes weren't prepared to see and to this day strikes fear and terrier within me that I haven't hunted squirrels in years because of it. I saw an 8-foot hairy bipedal being following where the deer went. I sat there and grabbed my gun when I moved the thing looked in my direction. Armed with only my marlin 22, I sat there feeling of dread feeling hopeless. Had no visible neck almost, but what I can tell you it had black orangish brownish hair. Seeing its face, dark eyes see the skin on the face and mouth area that was dark too. And we sat there looking at each other for what felt like a lifetime. I was so terrified I pissed my pants. Watching its every move. But, to my surprise, this thing did not feel threatened by my presence.

As scared as I was, I got up slowly and had my 22 facing drawn downward the ground in a non-violent manner relaxed as I could be. It let off this violent roar like a woman screaming and like that the thing ran the way that the deer ran as I watched it run through the woods with no hesitation in movement. It's like watching a marathon runner jumping over obstacles. It was fast and agile and moved with no problem through and over and down into a ravine. I quickly got out of that area and forgot my squirrel carrying the bag by the stump.

After that incident, I have not hunted over at my family's farm since. I spent the night at my family's farm, and the next day, my squirrel carrying a pack was put on one of the gate posts to one of the pens for the many farm animals. There was no squirrel, but I had my bag back. I got to my dad's, and my dad asked me if I had any luck. I said yes, I did, but something took my squirrel. Curious as my father was, he kept praying, asking me what happened, so I told him. He said oh, so you finally saw a molly guardian. I said no, dad, it was a bigfoot sasquatch looking thing. He said yea that's a molly guardian. I asked him how the hell he ever came to call it something like that. He said your grandfather saw one once, then I did, and my dad called them that on the account you don't want to be called crazy or some nut case. We gave it that name because it sounds scary and the way they rawr the sound is so terrifying like a woman screaming. So, when we talked about bigfoot, we were talking about molly guardians.

I asked my dad if he had ever been hurt. He said no, but he has heard of people's dogs that have cooped up disappearing. Caught one before in the woods with someone's dog, dragging the dog by the back legs. My family has had their fair share of bigfoot or what we call them molly guardians.

North Carolina

Hey Steve,

My name is Mary. I grew up on a farm in rural NC. I have been in and out of the woods my whole life. When I was 8, I got my first gun. I have a CCW in 4 states. I am no stranger to the outdoors. When I was around 12, I was just on a walk-behind our house on my family's property. I was sitting by a creek and heard something walking downstream. I thought it was my dad but saw quickly that it was not. It was something covered in blackish-brown fur and stood about 6ft tall. I stood completely still. It caught me staring, and when I looked in its eyes, I dropped down and rolled up in a ball. You know I've always heard if you come across a bear, that's what you should do. I heard it walking away, but I stayed in that ball for over an hour, maybe more. When it started getting dark, I decided it was time to go. I got up and ran to my parent's house, which was at least a mile away. My daddy was home when I got there. I told him what I saw, and he told me they were wood boogers. He told me not to tell a soul what I had seen, and I never did. At that time, I didn't stop doing things that involved going out alone or hunting. I really didn't think about it.

Fast forward to the age of 33. I got my dream job working for the Florida Department of Game and Fish. Whenever they acquire new tracks of land to make it a WMA, they do control hunts to the public. At that time, my job was to manage the area while the hunts were to happen. We had a shed out in the middle of nowhere that would be my office and a four-wheeler. I weighed and tagged animals, as well as took samples of blood for each one. This area was on the banks of the St. Johns River. I had a hunter who wasn't out of the area, and it was time to close the gate. I went to look for them on the four-wheeler.

I came to the bank of the river and standing on the other side was the same thing that I saw when I was 12. But, much, much bigger. This time I got a good look at it. It had a human face, and it had red hair instead of black. And its hair was matted. I reached for my gun, and when I did, it screamed. It was almost like the roar of a lion; it was so deep and loud. I backed that machine up and turned around and got the hell out of there. Thank God, my hunter was waiting at the shed when I got back! I was almost going to leave him. I shook when writing down the stats of that hog. I never went back to the woods again. I told my dad I didn't want any of the land that I was supposed to inherit because I would never live there. Just because of them. Whatever they are. I now live in a very urban area in Florida. About six months ago, I started seeing your posts about your own experiences and experiences of others. It interests me. I've researched as much as I can without actually being alone in the woods.

Something strange is happening around my house at night. Weird noises, my dogs were barking at all hours of the night. Stuff that a year ago wasn't happening. I've even had someone look under my house for the source of the strange noise. Whatever it is, I've never heard before in my life. I've heard some of the things Scott Carpenter talks about, and read up some on Nephilim. Maybe that's the reason I never told anyone. Another reason I didn't say anything was the fact that both times I saw this thing, my hair stood up. I got chills. That has never happened to me, ever. Keep the stories coming. Thank you for your time.

Sincerely, Mary

It Charged At Us Roaring

Dear Mr. Isdahl,

I recently discovered your site on Facebook and have begun looking at your videos. I'm writing to you to tell you how much I appreciate your voice on the subject of Bigfoot/Sasquatch. I had an up-close encounter myself at the age of 7. I estimate that the creature was about 75 feet directly in front of me. There were four of us, my mom, grandma, my brother and myself. It charged us from the wood line and was roaring the whole time. It is the only thing I can say that EVER truly terrified me in my life, and I'm 52 now. This was in Florida, by the way, in the seventies.

I grew up on a farm and lived in an area that was either farmland or woods. I thought I knew all the animals out there until that day of my encounter. However, I can't really call this creature only an animal because it had human-like facial features and hands and feet. Just on a massive scale that would've made Arnold Schwarzenegger look small. It was reddish-brown and approximately 8 feet in height, and about 600 plus pounds.

You KNOW what you've seen can't be explained and yet can't be more real. I'm a knower!! Like you!! So, I'm just here to sincerely Thank you for coming to the front and defending those that are mistreated by so many ugly people out there. Fortunately, I'm a very strong-willed redhead and speak what I feel to be real truth. However brutal it might be. That's what you get from me. I see that character trait in you and appreciate it. Thank you. Sincerely for your voice and experience!!!

-Elizabeth

It Was Trying to Get In The Door

Hey Steve,

I'm an ex combat vet who served five tours in Iraq and Afghanistan and was wounded twice! It Has been almost 14 years.

When I came home back in 2011, I was stationed at Ft. Leavenworth one night in January 2012. I was on guard detail at a medium-sized perimeter station concrete walls 2 feet thick and a solid steel blast door a foot thick just about a half-mile from the Missouri River. My comrade stepped out to smoke. This was around midnight and in a snow storm. He started bagging on the door within a minute of being outside. I opened the door, and like wtf, you just went out there? He's like there's something out there, and it's not a man, and it's not an animal. He heard it screaming at him, but he couldn't see it. So, I stepped out with him. We could hear something big, very big, just into the woods about 100 feet away. Then we heard a screaming roar. We both went back inside and locked the door. Within minutes the thing started banging on the door with such force. Took me back to combat, ready in a flash! We looked at each other and the monitors in the station, and we could see only the top of its head. Long story short, we finally opened the door after it took off—found dents in the solid metal door. Yes it still freaks me out! We also found footprints in the snow 21 inches long. They led over the perimeter fence, which is 15 feet high with razor wire, headed towards the river.

Photo By Randy Brisson, B.C.

Golden Ears Provincial Park, Randy Brisson photo

I'm a very rational person, don't take shit, and keep to myself. But I had to share this. I have never told anyone except my comrade who was on duty with me that night. It changed both of us to this day. Thanks for all you do brother! Keep posting this stuff we need to know what we are dealing with.

Thanks again for a release with no shame that night will always be with me just like being wounded has. -Michael

You Have Given Me Strength

Hi Steve,

My name is Roger. I am in my mid 40's. I had an incident as a little kid that has never left me. I still look over my shoulder and go slowly, taking in everything around me before I move forward when I am in the woods or fishing at a lake. I love the forests and wooded areas, especially when there is a mountain stream running through them. I have spent most of my life, hunting and fishing. My dad tells me I caught my first bluefish at six months old...haha...off the coast of

Maryland.

My mother always told me I came out with a rifle in one hand and a fishing pole in the other. There is literally nothing better than that experience of being at peace with nature. I am telling you this so you can understand why what I am about to tell you isn't natural in any way that I can understand.

Granted, I was young, under 10, but I can still remember the paralyzing fear. That feeling has never left me. Anyway, I will get into it.

I was living in Maine at the time, around Lisbon Center. We had a post office, a corner store, and there were no gas stations or grocery stores. It was a one-horse town. We lived at the dead end of a road that emptied into the great forests of Maine. Just for some perspective, my back yard started with giant pine trees that, as a child, seemed to reach into the sky. I remember being up in those trees looking down at my brother on the ground. He looked like a little ant from up there. I spent most of my childhood hunting those forests and fishing those streams and rivers. It was about a year before I moved to Michigan that it happened. I was walking with my cousin down a well-made trail, probably 5 or 6 feet wide—about a half-mile from my house. Our heads were mostly down and glancing at each other as we quietly talked and walked along. For some reason, we both froze in mid-step and couldn't move.

I could barely raise my head to look mostly forward. I heard no sound, but for some reason, we both froze. I remember the feeling because it scares the hell out of me even thinking about it— something I will never forget. My body was paralyzed in place except being able to raise my head slightly. I was struck with the fear of death in my entire body. I don't know why. My eyes looked forward, and it was like a foot in front of me. If I wasn't paralyzed, i could have punched it. It was that close. It didn't make any sound, it didn't even move, but for some unknown reason I couldn't move and the fear I had never felt before or since in me.

I saw the two human-like arms going down its side, the reddish long flowing hair that slightly moved in the almost still wind. That moment has been etched in my mind, and I have never been able to let it go. Then it was as if the paralysis started lifting. I could feel my head turning to my cousin and his to me, but it was like watching a blurry moving picture. The image I saw looking at him was distorted, and I could only imagine mine was to him. It was like our heads were stretched, and mouths opened too far to be real. We started turning and ran as fast as we could until we got back to the house.

I never seen its face. It was too close to me, and I couldn't look up. I have never doubted myself as to what I saw. I knew, and I still know. Nothing will ever change that. I tried to tell my story of what happened when I was young, but the few that believed me said I probably saw a bear. It wasn't a bear. I was laughed at and ridiculed as a kid. My cousin said he never remembers being in the woods with me when I told them he was with me. He won't admit what happened, but I will. Whatever this creature was, it had the power to emit overwhelming fear to the point of paralysis. It never even did anything that would make you think it was aggressive. It did nothing scary. To this day, I have never felt anything like it. I have been on the ground 30 yards from a black bear that wasn't sure what it wanted to do. I was scared but not that kind of fear. I know what I saw and what happened, and nobody will ever tell me any different. I have always had a feeling that if I had been alone that day, I wouldn't be alive. I don't know why I have always felt that way. It was an instinct in my gut.

In hindsight, hearing of all the missing children and clothes found in the wrong places, I know if I were alone that day, my name would be among those. I quit telling my story over 30 years ago. Nobody believed me, but that paralyzed fear and that image of seeing that hairy beast with arms, only a few inches from my face, has never left me. The stories I hear you talk about with the missing children makes me wonder if that almost happened to me.

I hope this helps somebody. Or might help to understand what may have happened to their missing child. You have given me the strength to speak out. Thank you.
-Roger.

It Happened To Us Elk Hunting

Hi Steve,

I hope this is the right email to send you the story of my and my best friends' encounter with one of these beings.

My buddy and I became close in the marine corps. We have been deployed twice together. And we have been in some serious shit together too. Nothing that we've been through in Iraq has even been close to what happened to us elk hunting that day.

My buddy is from the south and during our years in the service, I used to go on and on about hunting stories from my childhood, besides the occasional whitetail buck he had never shot any big game, so I promised to take him elk hunting. Well, the opportunity came, and I took him into a very remote location in southeast Idaho. It is a very rough country and remote, so you either hike in or take a pack string in. We took out trusty steeds. On the first day, we rode about 12 miles in and made camp. The first day/night was kind of unnerving, and the two horses and mule were acting very on edge, and I just chalked it up and the first day jitters. We decided in the morning we would ride over the next ridge that overlooks good drainage that should give us good shots if the elk are out feeding.

The ridge we rode to was about another 3 miles away from camp. We hunted all morning and didn't see anything and ate lunch and the whole time we felt as if we were being watched, my buddy kept saying that he came out here to relax and instead he can't help but feel like shit is about to go down. I would play off his comments like he wasn't used to the backcountry even though I knew something didn't feel right. Getting close to dusk, we headed back for camp. As we headed for camp, I noticed how quiet the forest became. Our horses got really spooked, and snorty and I could smell this nasty musty piss smell. For a split second, I thought perfect we found some elk. (smelled nothing like elk) and then almost like a fire hydrant this god-awful scream erupted our horses both reared up and damn near came over backwards my buddy and I both fell off and there our horses go thundering off though the timber toward camp.

So there, my buddy and I are standing in the middle of a horse trail scared shitless. I had my 06 slung across my back, so when I got dumped, my rifle came with me, and my buddy had his semi-auto 10mm. It was damn near dark, and we didn't really know what to do. Here are two seasons combat vets that are so frightened they don't dare venture into the darkness back to camp. So, we did what we had done before when we were cut off, we sat on the ground back to back arms ready to fight our way out. We sat there in the middle of the trail back to back the whole night! During the night, we heard various whoops and hollers mixed with strange vocals anywhere from 100 yards and 75 yards away. Way too damn close, that's all I know.

We heard towards camp some loud noises, and all I could think is whatever this is has Killed our horses, I wasn't too concerned about the mule she is nasty mean and would probably kill a wolf pack if given a chance. Finally, after one of the most miserable nights, daylight finally came, and we got the hell back to camp. What we found was the mule still tied up, but the horses were nowhere to be found, but the hoof tracks were headed in the right direction for the trailer. We packed camp up and, on the mule, and walked the 12 miles out. When we got back to the trailer, there were our horses standing there. Not a scuff on them and all our gear in place. It is amazing to me at camp 3 miles from these bastards our horses knew they were there.

That was one crazy 48 hours, and I have to say I am glad my brother was there by my side. We have fought for each other before, and we were both ready to do it again that night. I hope we get some truth about these things. It would do them and us justice. Thank you so much for what you do.

We Shot It

When I was thirteen, I had an encounter that I will never forget. I grew up in the country and have hunted everything possible in my area. I was in the woods every chance I could get all year around. Here's what happened. My parents' neighbor has hundreds of forest acreages. My brother and I were friends with his son. We hunted his father's land constantly. The neighbor's son and my brother asked if we could build a log cabin back in the woods. The father said no problem. So about 5 of us teenagers built a small cabin several miles back in the woods. It was roughly about 12ft x 15ft with a tin roof. And a temporary plywood door that was too small, there was about an 8-inch gap at the top of it. If we weren't in school, we stayed in that cabin all year round. Hunting and being kids having fun.

The cabin wasn't finished by any means but was pretty good for kids building it. Between the logs, we hadn't chinked it but had used rolled up feed bags to close the gaps until we could chink it properly. Inside the cabin (northeast corner), we had in the corner a bunk bed, and next to it, we had a bed that hung from the north wall. West wall was a table. The south wall was the door in the center of the wall. The southeast corner was a small wood stove. And in the rafters was one skinny plywood plank bed. One night my brother, the neighbor and some city friends and I stayed in the cabin. We had played penny poker until about 1 am and we decided it was time to bunk out. My brother and I decided to share a bunk because we didn't have enough blanks. The city boys were on the top bunk and one in the rafter bed. The neighbor was on the wall bunk. About 30 minutes after we bunked down, something started hitting the northeast corner of the cabin. That's the corner where the bunk bed was. It sounded like an axe chopping at the logs. It didn't scare us at first because we constantly had people show up to stay in the cabin. And we thought one of our friends had shown up and was trying to scare us. And yes, people would show up late at night. They would come up after work. Anyway, my brother hollered out to whomever it was asking who it was. He got no reply other than the chopping kept going on. He and the neighbor followed up by whoever is out there needs to tell us who it is because we have guns, and if you don't reply, you could get shot. No reply again. So, they signaled me to chamber my pump shotgun, which I did. It was done to get the point across to whomever it was. No reply, just chop chop-chop.

Close up brightened photo courtesy Randy Brisson

At that time, we became scared. Who's not afraid of a shotgun? We started asking each other if we knew any of our friends that said they were going to come up. We came to no one that we knew of. My brother hollered out to whatever it was he was going to shoot if they didn't answer in the count of three. He stuck his rifle barrel between the logs on that corner and counted. After three, he fired one shot. No answer and the chopping stopped. We listened for maybe 30 minutes or so in silence and heard nothing. So, we decided to go back to sleep. Not long after, the chopping started again. At that time, we became upset and threatened to fire again. My brother stuck his rifle back out and fired several shots after counting to three. This time we heard something for sure. It started walking along the north wall going west and then down the west wall leading to the south end of the cabin where the door was. When we heard the first steps, we became terrified. It was very heavy and was two steps, not four-legged. When it turned the corner and went south toward the door end of the cabin, we all jumped from our beds and loaded our guns. And what I see next, I still can see in my mind to this day.

It leaned over from the west side of the door and looked through the 8-inch gap at the top of the door. All of us paused for maybe about 3 seconds and then began firing at the door. The door seemed to disappear almost; it was riddled. When everyone was reloading, it apparently moved to the east side of the cabin, and it smashed down the tin roof. It hit it. We unloaded on that wall. We reloaded and listened to the best we could and didn't hear anything. Especially after shooting in a small place. We were terrified and huddled in the center of the cabin, wondering what to do. We stood there for a couple of minutes and decided we needed to leave and get out of there. The only problem was that we only had one 4wheeler with us, and two of us walked up to the cabin. We couldn't get all of us on the one 4wheeler. We voted, and my brother and I were to go out jump on it and ride like a bad out of hell back to the neighbors' house and get his father to come and get the other two. So, we slowly opened the door and spotlighted what we could to see if we saw anything.

We looked at the ground to see if we saw blood, and there was none. We slowly creeped out, looking as we went in every direction while making our way to the 4wheeler. Once we got on it, we rode faster than seemed possible. We made it to the house and told his father what had happened, and he grabbed his gun, and we jumped in his truck. There is a jeep trail that leads up to the cabin. When we got there, the others came running out, and we told his dad just take us off the hill, don't hang around. And he drove us off the hill.

This happened about 30 years ago, and to my knowledge, none ever went back up to the cabin again. Not even my neighbor's dad. The face I saw looking at us wasn't a bear as I've hunted bears and know what they look like. It was covered in short dark hair that laid close to the skin. The eyes were big—heavy brow. I Don't care if anyone believes me or not. I know what I see, and so do the other people that were there. I've heard several years later screams and other things coming from the woods behind my parents' home. One of the other neighbors had their cabin hit, and stuff carried off from their place at night. Tree knocks have also been heard by several people. The screams I've heard sound Identical to some I've listened to on TV from other people's recordings. VERY loud and bizarre-sounding.

I've only been back on those hills a handful of times since my encounter, and it's not a very comfortable feeling. I've told this as best I can and hope it's understandable.
- Heath

I was 95 Yards From It

Hi Steve,

I recently discovered your Channel on YouTube as we just got Netflix on our Smart TV; otherwise, I'm not socially connected at all, so this is a whole new thing for me. I'm hooked on your channel, and I appreciate your straightforward, honest approach to dealing with issues and people. A little background on me: I'm 57 and have had a lifelong passion for deer hunting, trapping and fishing. I've spent hundreds of hours camping, scouting and hunting the western states pursuing my passion. I spent 11 years in the USMC Recon, most of which as a scout sniper. I was involved in many missions all over the Middle East and Africa and Serbia and saw a lot of combat and horrible things. I can handle myself in the woods or anywhere else.

My son is also a very passionate Outdoorsman. A hunter found you on YouTube and convinced me that I needed to write to you and tell you my story. He's one of only a few people I've ever told, but he knows my word is the only thing that matters to me, so if I said it, it happened. I watched some of the TV shows and heard some broadcasters and personalities who all seem to think this is some sort of joke. I wonder how much time they spent in the woods? Or how much time they spent with mortars going off around them and .762 AK-47 rounds were flying by their face. I wonder why their words would be more honest than mine? Douche bags.

It was 2006. I was hunting in Central Oregon on the east side of the Cascade Range, trying to kill a big black tail I had my base camp set up at about 4000 feet in a small clearing about four miles from any road. I had spent the first two days scouting and found a buck that I wanted to try for, so on the third morning, I set off an hour before sunrise and started heading up the slope to a good spot where I could easily see a couple of Meadows at first light. I got set up, leaned my rifle against the tree and started wiping the dew off my binoculars and opened up a power bar. It was still a little too dark to see. So, I started turning my eyes into the meadow while I ate my breakfast. I had made at least 20 DIY hunts in the Western States in my life. But never to this particular area as I have never killed a big black tail and this was supposed to be a good area. Not having the funding for an outfitter/guide, I always went by myself on public land and had a good time. So, first light comes, and I start glassing the meadow I heard some noise off to my left the West it sounded like something was coming up the ridge it was going to come out in a small neck down that fed into the meadow. I turned and got my rifle up, assuming it was a deer. I can see movement in the brush about a hundred yards to my West, but the brush was thick enough I couldn't make it out but could tell it was not a deer.

Eventually, I could make out that it was upright, so I assumed it was another hunter. He got to the edge of the meadow and stood there kind of crouching behind some bushes. I'm getting a little pissed off as someone else's got in the same area I was in. I hadn't seen a soul in the two days. I scouted for any human tracks. I rose up slowly and whistled at the guy waving my right arm over my head. Letting him know "hey there's a hunter here go somewhere else... " he immediately wheeled to his right to face me directly when he did that I could see he was immense across the shoulders I thought holy Christ I'm 6 '2" 220 he made me look like a child. As soon as he saw me even though it was dimly lit, I could tell we were looking at each other, and he ducked down in the bushes. I thought, what the hell? So, I set my rifle back against the tree and stepped out into the meadow so he could get a clear look at me.

I started walking towards him. I want to hunt this area. I want him to go somewhere else. There was plenty of time for him to leave and do that. I took about five steps, and he stood up again, this time I could tell it was not a man it was just too damn big and covered in hair. He started grunting at me and shaking the bushes in front of it. My rifle was still leaning against the tree where I had originally sat. I raised my Zeiss up and looked at his face. I can't tell you a ton of details. I was totally startled, but he had dark hair certainly all over what I could see. Except for the face, there was a lot of flesh, a broad forehead, broad nose, big lips, a huge set of shoulders and chest. I couldn't see his legs very well because of the brush. But I have sent spent countless hours looking through binoculars and a rifle scope. I know exactly what I'm looking at when I'm looking. This was no man, and it was no ape, and it was no joke. It was a no dumbass in a ghillie suit.

The whole instant only took a matter of minutes, but it never stopped grunting, growling and shaking the bushes at me. Though it never came out in the clearing or towards me any further, it certainly made me feel like it did not want me there, and I was in danger. He was downhill from me, so it was hard for me to get a judge his height, but the bushes were clearly four to five feet tall, and it was well above those I'm going to guess it a good seven or eight feet tall with shoulders a good 4ft across with massive arms and head were also massive in proportion to a human.

I was within 95 yards of this thing with a clean line of sight looking through quality Optics. I've never seen anything like it before or since and I do not ever want to see another one. It was a truly a spooky deal I instinctively backed up I picked up my rifle shouldered it and centered the crosshairs on his face. It stared at me intently and very menacing it would have been an easy shot. Still, something told me inside not to shoot. Something told me it was absolutely the wrong thing to do. So, I held my rifle up with my right hand and raised my left hand over my head and looked at him in a submission.

I didn't know what else to do. I slung my rifle, picked up my backpack and headed back down the trail to Camp. Never looking back. I never heard him or saw him again.

I got back to my tent and packed up everything headed down to the truck, went to town. I stayed the night in town. In the morning, I drove to a new hunting area 35 miles to the north to finish out my trip. I didn't want to waste my tag or waste my Bible vacation time, so I tried my best play. I ended up unsuccessful in filling my tag. That season and yes, I was rattled the whole time.

I've only told my family and a few close friends, my story. My son believes me; I don't know if anyone else does or doesn't. I don't really give a shit. I've got nothing to prove to anybody. I know what I saw and as I said, a man's word should be enough. Thanks for hearing me out I really appreciate what you were doing it's nice to have a sounding board to get this off my chest it's been almost 14 years. I relive it every single day. I cannot get it out of my mind. Everything that goes bump in the night what makes a sound in the woods gets my immediate attention isn't that crazy question mark, especially after what I've been through. What a world we live in, huh Steve? Be careful, my friend and God bless. Feel free to contact me anytime you can share my story with others if you want.

Semper Fi
Kurt Johnson

Across Canada

Steve,

The first thing that happened THAT I CAN REMEMBER was in 1961. I was 13. I lived in Little Southwest Miramichi River, New Brunswick.

I don't know what I saw, but the experience has stayed with me for almost 60 years. Later, when the Patterson Gimlin tape came out, I didn't want to believe that what I had seen had anything to do with Bigfoot. Though, I have never doubted the veracity of the Patterson incident. I just didn't want to believe that it had happened to me. There are many things I have been in denial about. But, I'm old and time's almost up. Must get to the bottom of this shit!

Here's what happened. I grew up in a small town. The forest began less than a block from my house, and I used to go exploring and hunting beginning when I was very young. It was a large forest that stretched about 100 miles to the ocean. I played in those woods often, and as I got older, I fished and hunted there as well.

My Dad was raised on a farm on the Miramichi N.B. He and I drove over there to visit my uncle and to do some hunting. In those days, it took about 4 hours to make the journey. Dad and my uncle had planned a private hunting excursion and my cousin and I were going to spend the day hunting in the forest just above their 100-acre farm. Blake was the same age as me, but he had pretty poor eyesight and wasn't a great hunter. So, he took the 12 gauge, and I had the 303. The plan was that if we saw grouse, he would shoot, and if we saw deer, I would.

We left the house before daybreak and walked up the field to the forest. We opened the gate and pushed through about 20 feet of alders to get to an old logging road. It was grown over, but passable so we headed east into the rising sun.

We walked for some time, and it started to warm up. I couldn't get Blake to stop talking. A little grouse walked out onto the trail ahead. I pointed it out to Blake and told him to shoot it. He wore coke bottle lenses for eyeglasses. So, I don't know if he even saw the stupid little bird, but he didn't fire. I kept urging him to shoot, but he just stood there. I couldn't believe it! Finally, I raised my rifle and picked the dumb little bird's head clean off. (I had lots of training and practice.)

Well, Blake went wild, jumping up and down and going on about how that little bird didn't have a head. Lol. He was making so much noise that I figured we'd never get a deer. So, when he said he wanted to show his mother how the bird lost its head, I encouraged him to go immediately. I said I would be back at dark, hoping that he wouldn't return. And he didn't! Whew!

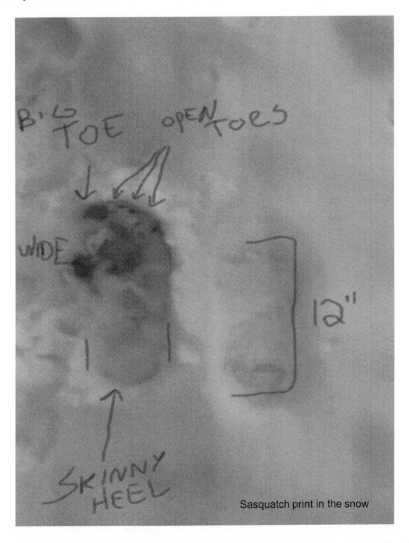

Sasquatch print in the snow

I spent most of that day heading east and looking for signs. Then I turned around to head back. I started to feel uneasy. I loved the woods, and I usually had no fear, but I had a very strange feeling all the way back. I felt like someone was watching me. I picked up my pace, and it took an hour or so to reach the entrance to the farm.

It was just sunset when I arrived. I had to push through the alders to get to the gate. Just as I was stepping into them, a black figure passed in front of me from East to West. Not more than 10 feet from me. It was huge and fast, and except for a swooshing sound as it brushed the bushes, it was silent. My first thought was, "It's a bear." But I knew it couldn't be. The thought persisted. "it's a bear." But it was too tall! And the hair was too long.

Whatever it was must have been following me, but it didn't expect me to turn off the road just where I did. So, as I headed towards it, it made a dash in front of me and disappeared. I froze for a few seconds- or hours. Then I decided to get out of there. I needed to digress for a bit.

When I was very young, some really bad things happened. I don't remember what they were because I had decided that I never wanted to remember them ever again. So, as a small child, I created a space in my head that I called my "forgettery." I know I've dumped a pile of shit into that big black hole, and to this day, I can't remember what's in there. And that's what I tried to do that day. But the memory kept popping back up. It just would not stay down!

The only other time I ever felt so terrified was in Alberta when I stepped off a well-beaten trail and was stopped dead in my tracks by a very large wolf. It growled and showed its teeth but didn't attack. It stared at me with the fiercest eyes I've ever seen as if to say, "get out of here. This is private property". I backed away and left- shaking for hours.

I didn't see the head of that beast in N.B, but I got a quick look at a muscular shoulder and jet-black hair. The shoulder was well above eye level. Too high for any animal indigenous to N.B. It terrified me, but I kept telling myself that it was just a bear. I couldn't figure out how it could be so damn quiet. I then thought that it might have been some kind of cat. They can be very quiet. I know! Crazy, right! But I just couldn't sort it out. What the hell was that thing?

By the time I got back to the house, I had convinced myself that it was only a black bear. They don't bother people unless you get between a mother and its cubs. So, I did my best to ignore the fear. But I couldn't get it stuffed into the forgettery. So, ever since that day, I have always been much more alert in the forest. And that's probably a good thing, - given that I've had quite a few other scares. One in an area that you are familiar with - Sayward,- 4 or 5 years ago. I'll get to that.

Most of my beast experiences were just noise and extreme discomfort. Who knows what those events were? I don't. But I also had other experiences that had nothing to do with animals but that I now know are connected. Once in Oregon in 86 and two others in N.B.

I also had some strange things happen in northern Alberta. They all had to do with orbs or UFOs or whatever. No one believes me, - though on two occasions there were other people with me.

There are other encounters that I won't go into right now. But I want to tell you about an event in August 2013 in Fredericton NB and another in Sayward in 2015. I am telling you about this is because you did a video with a recording of a sasquatch. Thank you for that! I had heard that exact sound in both places.

I was living on the edge of a wooded park. It was quite large- may be a section, and at the top of the woods, there was a commercial street then the highway and then the woods, which goes on for miles. It was about 3 AM, and I woke up. I went outside to have a smoke, and while I was enjoying the summer air and the quiet, suddenly, a loud sound could be heard. It was EXTREMELY loud. It sounded almost exactly like the recording you posted. (Also, the same sound I heard in Sayward in 2015.) But at the time, I thought the high-pitched portion of the sound was the blade of a D9 Cat scraping over a solid stone. And that the low-pitched sound was the engine running. But it was so loud that I decided to go see if I could find it. It had to be very close. I jumped on my motorbike and raced up the hill to where I thought it came from. Then I turned off into the park and stopped. I heard it again but now coming from down the hill. So, I raced back down and entered the park at the lower entrance. It was clearly coming from inside the park. There is no possible way that heavy machinery could be in there. I was baffled. Then the noise stopped. I looked through the park the next day, and no excavation projects were going on. It wasn't until I found your video that I understood what I had heard. It wasn't machinery! It was that damned creature in the middle of the city!

I now live in a fairly remote village in Cambodia. I've been studying the Bible and learning what I can about all of the damn lies. I don't care much about anything else. I'm only interested in the truth. I'll be dead soon, and whatever I can share with people like you who have a heart for REALITY, I want to share. I had two more experiences here. No one ever believes me.

Once I saw a triangular-shaped object come out of the sky at night and go underwater on the Mekong River. Another time I saw a 3½ foot tall rabbit hop through my camp near the border of Vietnam in the Northeast jungle. "Nonsense," they say. But so what? I know what I saw. And no drugs or booze involved.

I know that the world is completely deceived about many things. And I think I know why. You and Scott have scratched the surface of the Titanic iceberg. But it's going to sink the ship. I want to buy his books but haven't found a way to pay for them, yet. Everybody needs to pull together and learn. There is only one way to resolve the situation, and that's by knowing the truth. You are doing your part. But there is much more that we all need to know. I hope we can share something of value together. As far as I can tell, this is all leading up to something big, and people need to be warned.

As for the warning I mentioned, - in May this year, I believe that we are going to begin hearing of more and more abductions and killings by these transhuman beings. This comes from Bible prophecy, something everyone says we can't know. So, what is it? Is God an idiot? Did He go to all the trouble of giving prediction just to confound us? I know better. People don't want to know the TRUTH. But ignorance is going to prove very costly. I hope you are more open-minded than 99.9999% of people.
-Blessings Brother

Outside Bellingham

Hi Steve,

I enjoy your no bs YouTube channel. I have had a couple of encounters with these beasts I would like to share with you. First, let me explain, I grew up in the woods hunting and fishing and hiking, etc. And I know what the animals are out there. In other words, I know what a bear is and what it's not. I was born and raised in Bellingham, WA, which is where these two stories took place. And I've spent a lot of time fishing in B.C, in the Cariboo. So, I am quite familiar with your area.

Anyway, the first "encounter" took place in a small neighborhood near where I grew up. Granted it was a long time ago, I was nine years old at the time, and I'm 57 now. I remember it like it was last night. My brother and I were staying at a friend's house and sitting on his front porch. We could hear some dogs barking in the distance, which were getting closer and closer to us. Before long, there was this hairy manlike thing running across the lawns of the houses across the street from us with about 5 or 6 dogs chasing it. It appeared to be about 7 or 8 feet tall and was covered in hair from top to bottom. It was running very fast on two legs with its arms kind of stiff down to its sides. It didn't fit the "normal" description of bigfoot as it was kind of slender looking. Maybe a juvenile? That was on the outskirts of Bellingham, where there were a lot of woods around at the time.

The second occurrence was four years later when my brother and I were together on a deer hunting trip up the north fork of the Nooksack River. This area, incidentally, is known for some sightings. My brother and I met up in some green timber. It was snowing pretty heavily at the time with big, heavy, wet flakes that were accumulating at a fairly rapid pace on the ground. We came upon some tracks that looked like human barefoot tracks, but they were about 15 to 17 inches long. As I said, it was snowing pretty good at the time, and there was no snow in the tracks, so this thing was there just ahead of us. The snow was heavy and wet, so the tracks were as perfect as they could be. We could clearly make out each toe, ball of the foot, heel, etc. Unfortunately, it was way before everyone carried cell phones, so no pics. We followed the tracks for a couple of hundred yards into some denser brush and decided that we should turn around and head back to the pickup, as it was getting to be dusk.

-Jim

Louisiana

Hello Steve,

My name is Kelly. I am a 50 yr. old dad of 2 teenagers. I own and operate an auto repair shop. I have been in business in Metairie, Louisiana, for 25 years. I was in the Navy Reserve for eight years. I am not a good writer, as you will see. This is a short story of what happened to me in the fall of 2014.

I had recently gotten interested in motorcycle riding. I had just hired a mechanic who owned a bike. He would let me ride it and found out immediately. I really liked the feeling of freedom and complete independence. So, I began to look for a bike. I ended up with a used Kawasaki Vulcan 800, not a hog by a long shot, but fine enough for me. My wife didn't like the idea, but so be it. After Hurricane Katrina my parents who lived in New Orleans all their lives moved to Albany Louisiana, a small town I guess 75 miles or so from New Orleans. Metairie, where I live, is only 10mins from New Orleans. One weekend I decided to ride the bike to their house in Albany. I was not used to the traffic on interstate 10 and 55, the two Highways I had to take to get to their house. People do not care that you are on a bike, believe me! Anyway, I made it to their home in Albany.

Upon arriving, though, I hit the front brake and slid in their gravel driveway and tumbled onto their carport. My mother was worried at first. But started laughing so hard she had to go inside, my dad was already laughing. I wasn't hurt, just embarrassed! My wife and kids were coming up in the car, so they didn't see it thank God! The reason I told you all of this is that I decided to take another route home, it is safer for a less experienced rider. My dad, mother, wife, and both kids agreed! We ate dinner and visited with them till about 10 pm. So, I left on my way home to Metairie. The alternate route is Highway 51. It's a two-lane highway that runs parallel to Interstate 55, which is raised. 51 runs right through the Maurepas Swamp wildlife management Area. The interstate Is raised up above it. I was about 6miles into my ride on highway 51, and I really had to go pee really really bad! So, I pulled over, shut off the bike and walked a little off to the side of the Highway. It's pitch black, no street lights at all. You can hear the interstate above you but other than that pure seclusion. While I was walking to the side of the road, I could smell what I thought was dead fish, pretty common in the swamp where people fish and leave guts on the side of the road. The minute that took me to go, I was staring into the darkness, and what I thought was a willow tree until it moved! Not from the breeze which did not exist but on its own power! I have to say; instead of pissing, I suddenly felt the urge to crap! I was paralyzed in fear.

This thing was only 20 feet in front of me when it ran across the road. It was at least 9 feet tall and 4 feet wide. It was not a man; it wasn't any type of anything I have ever seen! The very strange thing was it made a kind of Fart noise when it passed me and a loud awful grunt! I really think this thing was doing its business, and I pulled up on it to do mine! The smell as it "farted" and ran with two steps across the road into the swamp was nauseating! I could feel the concrete below make a shake as it hit the road and ran away. The noise it made was as if it was straining or irritated. From what I could see through the moonlight. There was an outline of a head-on top of long hair; that's all. It scared me so bad I never rode that way again on my bike.

I didn't tell a soul till now after I found your channel. I plan on telling my wife and kids, so share if you want. I like that you do not make fun of any story, no matter how crazy it sounds. Please tell me what you think, it's haunted me since it happened. I fish and hunt a lot down here. It is ALWAYS on my mind!

Thank you, Steve!
-Kelly Mainly

Louisiana Again

Hello, my name is Thomas. I'm 53 years old and grew up hunting in the swamps of Louisiana and fishing inshore and offshore. Back when I was 19, a friend of mine, Rob and I used to go out shining deer and Hogs. Yeah, I know it was against the law, but we still went out there and did it anyway. It's an excellent way to get some quick meat for the freezer. One night we were hunting behind the Stennis Space Center. An area known as the Honey Island Swamp, right across the state line in Mississippi. We would park on the road and walk down swamp on both sides. We can usually snipe a hog or a deer crossing the roads. This one night, we parked the car like we typically do an old piece of shit Pinto hatchback. We Both had 12-gauge shotguns and big ass lights on our heads—mag lights tape to the shotgun barrels. As we were walking down the road one night all of a sudden, something started matching our steps off the tree line in the swamp. It was kind of crazy to start walking.

I would hear Splish Splash, Splish Splash, Splish Splash, two feet walking through the swamp. We would shine the light in the swamp to see where the noise was coming from. It was inside the tree line out of our range of sight, even with the big fucking light on our heads and the two Maglites tape to the shotgun barrels. We always had the plugs out of our shotguns shooting 3in double-ought Buck magnums. With an additional couple of boxes of stuff in our pockets. If whatever it was would have walked on the road, or we would have seen it would have got the shit knocked out of it. Down the road about a mile and a half, we stopped at a big turnaround.
Just staring in the swamp with our lights on trying to figure out what the fuck was in there. It was pacing back and forth in front of us. We could not see what it was, and we didn't want to waste ammo blind shooting. About this time, my fear started getting the best of me, and I started farting my ass off. May sound funny, but when you were getting the shit scared out of you, you start farting your f*cking a*s off!!!!!!!!!!!!

Whatever it was never made a sound, never made a Roar, never made a growl, never made a noise. Just heard footsteps; Splish, splash. At this point, we both said f*ck this sh*t! We started walking back towards the car with this f*cker still pacing Us in the swamp Splish Splash, splish splash, splish splash. We got maybe two hundred yards from the car, then the Splish Splash stopped.

As luck would have it as we were turning the Pinto around, it got stuck in a ditch. We had to get Jack out one of those old steel bumper jacks put it and the bank of the ditch, Jack, on the bumper pushing the front end out of the ditch. We had to do this a few times to get it out. Must have taken a half an hour, maybe longer. The whole time we were waiting for something to pop out the swamp and gobbler our ass up. We never went back to that part of the swamp again. I brought this up with my partner Rob a couple of weeks ago, and he still remembers it like it was yesterday. I told him it was Bigfoot; he says to me I'm crazy!

I am now 53, and as I said, have six kids a wife very hectic job running a towing operation out the City of New Orleans dealing with assholes all day long. If anybody wants to believe the story, they can believe it. Anybody that doesn't want to believe it doesn't have to. I don't care, I just wanted to share the story with you.

Steve Isdahl   The Day Sasquatch Became Real For Me   Copyright© 2020

Still hunting the woods, not scared, I do more fishing now than hunting offshore in my boat out of Venice, Louisiana. If you ever come down to New Orleans hit me up, I'll take you out of my Glacier Bay and catch some tuna.

Yours Truly,
Thomas

Fingers On The Tent

Steve,
A couple of years ago, my best friend and I went camping in Arkansas and had one of the eeriest and scariest experiences ever, at least up to that point. Our last night in the mountains, we had heard some bizarre "calls." Something we had never heard before. I had my two dogs with me, and one is a terrier, afraid of NOTHING!

I woke up around 3 in the morning to a HUGE set of fingertips lightly brushing against the tent. I don't know what woke me because my dogs never barked, nothing was rustling, nothing specific, just a "sixth sense." It was the absolute worst time to get the urge to go pee! I was so scared that I literally considered peeing in my sleeping bag!
My friend wakes up and asks me if I am awake. I whispered that I was but didn't say a word about what just happened and what I saw. I didn't want her to think I was crazy!

She tells me she has to go pee and doesn't want to go alone. I grabbed my flashlight, and my gun told her to grab her gun, and we would go. All the while, I was trying to convince myself that I had just dreamt about what happened. I knew I hadn't, but I couldn't rationalize the situation.
I got out of the tent, called my dogs, and they were frozen in the tent. She had to push them out of the tent literally! Big red flag, but I kept telling myself I was overreacting. My dogs were both shaking and why I thought it was a good idea to walk around in the dark is beyond me. Not like the tent would have protected us from anything or anyone.
We didn't discuss how strange it was for a couple of weeks. It came up in conversation one day, and we both knew that something was very off and very wrong. We just didn't want to say anything out of fear the other person would think we were crazy.

Now I am not saying that Bigfoot was the culprit, but there was NO one else around, and we never saw anything. My dogs were just as freaked out like us, though, and that should have been a HUGE red flag. I guess something inside of us said something was very wrong.

I thought it was a once in a lifetime experience UNTIL we went to Colorado the following year and had an experience that was beyond terrifying. That's a story for another time. This is not something I share, EVER, because I know how people react when others tell their story.

Thanks for being a safe place for those of us who had nowhere else to share our experience(s).

I think some people attract these things more than others, or some of us are just more self-aware.

Thanks for your time,
BJ Russell

Vancouver Island, The Boys Saw It

Hello Steve,
How are you doing? I watched a few of your videos. Welcome to the club, just kidding. So, you've seen a sasquatch? So, have I, and it wasn't out in the great north. I saw and felt the presents of one in 1976/77 was about 14 years old. It has changed me quite a bit. When I looked at it, it woke me up.

I lived a bit out in the woods before seeing it on Vancouver Island. And my brother used to take a shortcut on a path along the tree line. It was weird that we would be walking, then we came to this point that I called the invisible line in the forest. Then all of a sudden, the hair on the back of the neck would stand on end and fear took us over. My brother was a faster runner than I, and he would always say the last one through is going to get caught by the town drunkard, the troll, every time we would go through, he would call it something different. It was winter then, so it got dark early. We got out of school at five, so by the time we got to that area, it was dark, so we would always take a long way home. It wasn't till spring break that my brother and I took my go-cart up to the three hills, where houses were being built. We were having a great time; it was starting to get dark when my brother asked if I wanted to go down the hills before it got dark, I said yea. We were close to the top of the second hill, and we both looked up, and halfway up the third hill, this gigantic creature took three steps to cross the 32' roadway. The hair went up just like in the pathway, and terror sank in. Don't ever remember that go-cart going so fast as my brother was pushing it. Two or three years passed before I saw the Patterson footage and realized what it was.
A year or so after seeing that footage, I started asking natives and hunters about the subject. Some of the natives told me stories about their grandfathers seeing one, but some of them believed in them. They were told not to talk about them as they would be told they were crazy. The majority of the hunters would laugh at me. They would go on about being in the woods most of their lives and never seen anything as crazy as that. They would also accuse me of drinking or doing drugs. Since I have moved down island to Nanaimo, I am still talking and asking mainly local natives and have collected many sittings. I wouldn't call myself a researcher; but, I have found some structures and a few other interesting happenings regarding areas I have left apples and walnuts etc. So just to let you know they are living well on Vancouver Island. I also believe they are very intelligent, and the ones I have had happenings with are not evil like those that want to shoot one. Also, I think they aren't all evil and have heard many interesting happenings regarding these grand beings. I know you are a busy man, a reply that you received my Email would be nice even if it takes a while to receive: a believer and a knower.
-Dave

They Saw It While Hunting

Hello there. I Just wanted to reach out and share my story. I've been following and listening to you on YouTube. I appreciate what you do. With no further, here is my story. Please feel free to use my name if you choose to share it with the public. Most certainly hard to do myself.

My name is Darrel. I'm 29 years old, married with a seven-year-old son. I currently serve in the U.S. Army and have for the last ten years. My encounter took place when I was 18 years old on a hunting trip with my uncle and cousin in California. South of Lake Tahoe, north of Lake Mono, and just west of the town of Bridgeport, to an area we know as Buckeye creek. It is a creek that runs from the snow-covered mountain tops to the Bridgeport Reservoir some miles to the east.

In California, in order to get certain hunting zones, you have to put in a wish list of your top three places you want to hunt, and the zones are picked in a drawing from the Department of Fish and Game. This year my father, two brothers and I got the desert zone d12, one of our favorites, and my uncle and cousins got x12, another one of our family's favorites. And because the zones are so distant from one another, they are broken up by months due to the environments they are in, so the season dates are different. For example, X12 is in October, and D12 is in November. My family would always put the same areas to hunt on our wish list as my uncle and cousins. That way, we made family hunting trips every year. I did so since I was a baby.

Dad and uncle did long before us kids. But because my uncle and cousins got a different zone this year, they asked if I want to tag along due to my younger cousin not going because of school. The older of the two cousins and I are only a week apart, and we were very close. Every hunting trip, he and I would always go out together because we always travelled in pairs while out hunting. So they asked me to come. Not to brag but I was the eagle eye when it came to deer hunting, I always spotted them before everyone else. My cousin made a joke and told me I was only coming to guide him and get him a buck. We laughed, but honestly, I made it my mission. He has never harvested a deer, and I was determined. So we set out on our journey, travelling from southern California to about mid to northern California, an 8-hour drive. But the drive is beautiful, and we never cared about the length of the ride. Driving through the Sierra Nevada's was breathtaking. But fast-forwarding to the opening day of hunting season. Our trip was planned for five days.

On the first morning, it was very cold. I remember the temperature being displayed in my uncle's truck at 9° C. Because it was so cold, my uncle didn't want us walking around the snow-covered mountains and hillsides, so we took to the roads and drove around the majority of the first two days. By the 3rd day, it was much warmer at about 30°C; even then, he didn't want us doing much walking unless we spotted deer and had to make a stock. By the afternoon on the 3rd day, it was sunny and warm at about 40°C, and he wanted to make the short drive across the 395 highway to a place he and my dad called Buckeye creek because he knew there were tons of deer in that area, just had to hike a little bit. I remember turning onto buckeye road and getting this nervous, excited feeling because we knew this area was a good one. Driving down the road he asked where we wanted to stop because he needed a nap due to all the driving, he has done for the last couple days, naps were a common thing for our old men during hunting seasons.

About 15 minutes down the dirt road, we spotted some does' jumping a ridge and decided to give chase. With my uncle staying at the truck, and my cousin and I gearing up to do the steep climb, we stepped off at about noon, give or take an hour. My cousin was carrying his 243 and his backpack with snacks, ammo, deer tag, water, etc. All I had was my dad's gun belt; he made me take it, so I wasn't unarmed, because he knew there were bears and mountain lions in this area that we were hunting. On the gun belt, I had his 357 mag, a buck knife, an ammo pouch and a canteen with water. We did the climb that took us maybe 30 minutes because we were 18 and unstoppable. We reached the top and made a short descent to a little knob on top of a hillside to sit and glass the area. After a few minutes, we spotted 15 to 20 deer, unfortunately, no bucks.

We sat and watched for 2 or 3 hours, hoping something would stand up from a spot we couldn't see. Nothing. So, we eventually made our way down the hillside heading towards the deer but going right, across the hill, so we didn't spook them. We sat and glassed another hillside for about 30 minutes before deciding we should head back because darkness would fall in about an hour. Between us and the hillside we were glassing was a deep ravine that headed back towards the road, so instead of going back the way we came, we took the ravine route. What a MISTAKE that was! We started down the hill to the ravine, where we were in between two steep hillsides, but we knew if we jumped anything, we would certainly see it running up a hillside. About 10 minutes into our walk down, we heard the sound of something running in the grass/bushes, so we stopped to listen. Shortly after we stopped, we spotted deer trotting down from the direction we just came, passing us within 20 feet. One deer stopped and looked back, as they often do when being chased or startled. So, my instinct was to look in the direction she was and saw nothing.

The deer continued their quick descent, and my cousin and I looked at each other with a weird eye, almost like what we just saw was strange. Because we were in the open and they paid us no attention. Shortly after they disappeared from our view, they came blowing back by us faster than I've seen deer run before, not in a line like they normally travel either; they were dispersed across this ravine as if something was given chase. They were scared. I remember seeing a doe as it ran by us at about 10 feet, as if I made eye contact with her, I can see the white in her eyes when normally all you see is black as if her eyes were wide open like she was scared.

After the deer passed us, my cousin looked at me and whispered WTF. But he used the actual words. I looked at him and asked, that was the same deer, wasn't it? He said it had to be. I remember him saying to me, I don't like this, and I smiled at him and said to myself either, but let's get out of here before it gets dark. And at that moment, time stopped. A sudden fear came rushing over me as I stared at something running behind some tall grass/brush. I grabbed my cousin's arm, as he was slightly ahead of me and told him to stand still. I whispered to him; there is a bear right in front of us behind that brush. A second or two went by, then he saw it too. After turning around to make sure nothing was behind us, so if we had to, we could backtrack our way out of there. We turned back in the direction of the so-called bear, and saw something huge, WALKING, like a man, quickly behind a massive pine tree. (I didn't see a face, because I was looking at its legs.) Out of sight of this thing, he asked me what the hell was that? I said I have no idea.

I remember pulling my dad's 357 out of the holster with my right hand, hammer back, and grabbed my buck knife with my left, gripping both very tightly. My cousin loaded a round into his rifle, and removed his safety switch, ready to shoot. We moved about 10 feet forward in the direction we were going, towards the road, and I stopped him again, speechless this time, I couldn't move. I could see my cousin looking at me out of the corner of my eye as he was slightly to my left, the direction of which I was staring. Minutes have gone by, and neither of us has moved. The image I was looking at, to this day, raises the hair on my neck and gives me goosebumps all over my body. I was terrified like never before. I've been to war, and nothing scared me as this thing did.

I was staring at the backside of what I now know was a Bigfoot. At the time, I was clueless, and in disbelief. I stared at this thing for what seemed like a lifetime, but it was really only a few minutes. When I came to, I looked at my cousins and told him to kneel down, so we did, I told him something was standing over there. I don't think he realized what I was saying when I said standing. When I told him to look, we slowly stood up and looked over to where it was standing, and it was gone. At that moment, I knew it was time to go. We rushed down that hill, never looking back until we reached the brush-covered hillside. Once in the wide-open terrain, we looked back and saw nothing. So, we continued to the truck and spoked nothing about it. Not for years. To describe what I was looking at, behind a tree STOOD on two FEET, a man-like being. The tree was easily 5 feet wide. This thing was leaning against it with one shoulder, quartering away from where I stood. But from where we were before we moved 10 feet, I wouldn't have seen it. I could see two legs, the waste, the back, right shoulder, and the top of its head. It seemed to be looking down as it hid. I stand 5'9 tall. My cousin is a couple of inches taller than I. This thing was easily 3 to 4 feet taller than I. Making it 8 to 9 ft tall. Maybe 3 1/2 feet wide. Brown hair covered its body but almost seemed patchy. Like some hairs were longer than others. If that makes sense? The brown looked like the same color the deer were, maybe slightly darker.

To this day, I've spoken about this maybe five times. Only my wife has heard the entire story like this, but I even think she doesn't believe me. She says she does, but she often jokes about it. I asked my cousin a couple of years back what he thinks we saw, and he says he doesn't know. But he said he doesn't think he saw what I saw because our angles were different. I asked him if he thinks it could have been a bigfoot, and he was shocked and said maybe. Around that same time, I asked my older if he thought Bigfoot was real, and he told me it was very possible. And I told him I think I saw one, and he said you probably did. And the fact is I know I did. They are real. I tried to tell some buddies at work once, and they turned it into a joke almost instantly, so I never again mentioned it at work. I am a man of faith, and I'm telling you I saw one.

It is hard to talk to people about it because I know most frown upon people that come out and report sightings. This is the first time I wrote this down, and I can feel the fear I had that day, and how little I felt in the woods. To this day, anytime I'm in the forest, I'm on constant lookout and armed. I continue to hunt but due to work not as often. But any chance I get, I'm doing so as afraid as I am. I guess I'm just curious to know more. I would like to see one again, but maybe from my vehicle. Not 15 feet away without anything being us. I guess I failed to mention how close we were to this creature. No more than 15ft. Maybe even less. So, I know my description is accurate. I don't remember a smell like most do, but I can say if I had to guess or make an assumption, the thing was caught off guard by us and was trying to hide. And when I said it disappeared and was gone, if I had to guess, it probably just moved around that tree so we couldn't see it anymore. Like when we moved, it moved. Freaky. And it did not go up, because we looked. And the tree it was behind was in the open with the nearest tree at about 20 yards. There was no sound of it running off or climbing. No vocalizations. Nothing. Just silence.

That's my story, my encounter, so do what you want with it. I'm sorry if I rambled. But I would like to give a shout out to your listeners by saying, "You are not alone. We know they are real." I appreciate what you do for people like me. God bless. And I hope you get the chance to see one. Stay safe out there.

Prints Leading To Kneeling

Hey, I know you get a lot of sasquatch stories coming in from other listeners. But I felt the need to tell you I never was a believer until my mother found footprints. So, I grew up on a small hobby farm in Michigan. And my mother still owns the property. She likes to snowshoe around the property with her boyfriend when he comes over. And they both think sasquatch is a joke as did I at the time. But one day I went over to visit my mother and Both her and the boyfriend started telling me this story of how they went snowshoeing the day before.

As they were walking, they came across large size 12 or 13 footprints in the hard-crusty snow, and it was a barefoot... could see toes and all. It's like 12 to 20 degrees out. Being in the area we live in is a big thing with all the low lives, so they instantly thought some guy on drugs went for a midnight walk. Barefoot in the snow. They ended up following the tracks, and within the first 300 yards of following these prints, my mom's boyfriend noticed these tracks acted like it was hunting. It would be very erratic back and forth, running up hills and down kneeling next to trees. And he used to run dogs in PA for coyotes, so it reminded him of the erratic back and forth of a dog looking for a scent. They followed the tracks for miles until they gave up, but she took pictures of these prints, and you can tell the toes curled while walking up hills, so it wasn't a fake print someone strapped to their feet.

And another odd thing is some of the shit it walked through. They said it walked through brier patches and never cut its feet on thorns or the hard-crusty snow due to no blood on the ground. But I figured I'd share this with you. I'm a believer now, but as long as I never see one, I'll be able to go in the woods as I always have. So, I hope I never see one of whatever it is.

Steve Isdahl   The Day Sasquatch Became Real For Me   Copyright© 2020

The Boy Saw Glowing Orange Eyes

Hey Steve,

I appreciate you taking the time to read this and all the work you do on this subject.

I am 23 years old and have grown up most of my life in southern South Dakota. My family lives on a creek bottom of a ranch near the border of Nebraska. The ranch is in the middle of nowhere, and the closest town is 25 miles away. The terrain is pretty rugged and full of buttes formed from the river breaks leading to the Keya Paha River just 3 miles south. The trees in the creek bottom are the most trees you'll find in much of the prairie until you reach the Keya Paha river, where it's dense with cedars.

This was years ago when I was in the 5th grade: It was mid-summer and had woken up to a big storm north of us about 15 miles at 1:30 am. I was terrified of storms at the time is not a year before we had baseball size hail. I went to my parents' room, which sits on the back of the house overlooking the creek bottom. It is about 20 yards from their room until it drops off into dense woods. As I was trying to wake my parents to see if the storm was coming, I began to hear leaves crunch outside. Their window was open and other than the distant thunder; it was dead quiet. I look up, thinking maybe it's one of the three dogs outside. There was no dog. I saw these two orange/red eyes with slits in the middle looking at me while whatever it was walked. I could see nobody just hear the footsteps. It turned back to look away and walked down into the bottom of the drop-off. I was terrified. My parents were asleep. I told them what I saw, but they brushed it off to bring a cow out or something. I've seen animals' eyes reflect in the dark, and this was not that. I get chills still thinking about it, and all the times I've been out early morning in those woods bow hunting.

I went back and saw no tracks, and what is interesting is the dogs didn't bark when usually they bark at everything in the night. Whatever it was, was only maybe six or maybe seven feet at the most, though.

That's the only experience I've had and would like to have. My father has a few experiences he could share too, which is interesting as if seeing them is a genetic "gift" handed down.

You can share my first name by the way and the locations if you ever want to read this.

Thanks for your time.
- Austin

Saw A Sasquatch Stalked By A Cougar

Steve,

I used to live in eastern Kentucky (born and raised). I'm a big, outdoors person. I used to dig ginseng every season. I wanted to not only share my bigfoot experience but try to let people see the contrast between three different predators. Digging roots, I encountered several black bears, and every time it was the same. As soon as they spotted me, they were gone like a shot! One day while digging on the border of Daniel Boone National Forest (a place I've been many times), I noticed the lack of birds that day, and although I thought it strange, didn't think much about it and started my day. About an hour into digging, I felt something watching me, and the feeling was overwhelming. I looked around and behind a tree about 20 yards away was a Sasquatch behind a tree watching me! It wasn't a huge one, but it scared the piss out of me nonetheless! I immediately got up, announced out loud I was leaving and literally walked backwards all the way out of the holler. Armed with nothing, but a machete! It didn't attempt to follow me that I could notice, and I'm certainly glad I didn't think about the fact that these things travel in groups at the time because I probably would have done something stupid like run. Anyway, the incident was over, and I never dug that area again.

Now the kicker! A few years later, I moved West to Arizona and was visiting New Mexico in the Alamogordo area in the mountains (I never venture into the woods without a firearm anymore btw). I was walking through this clear-cut power line right of way when I felt that same feeling again of being watched. I looked to my left and caught a glimpse of a mountain lion creeping low and for sure stalking me just off to my left in the wood line! I immediately drew my pistol and started walking backwards, yelling at the cat to get out of here, but it kept matching me step for step! I had to walk backwards nearly 200 yards back to the cabin, and this damn cat stalked me the entire way! The ordeal ended without further incident, and we finished our little vacation just fine.

Anyway, I guess my point is what I thought was the most dangerous critters in the woods (bears and Bigfoot) turned out to just be critters that need to be respected. In my opinion, mountain lions are probably the biggest danger in the woods. Of course, I've not been in a grizzly country, nor do I have any desire to hang out there, but I thought if you get to read this, maybe you could relay the message to folks so they can feel a little better about Bigfoot and black bears.

Thanks for all you do! Feel free to use my name and locations.
-Gene G

If You Don't Share Your Friend Will

Dear Steve,

A friend told me this story several years ago, and I have been fascinated by it ever since. He is a very serious and hard-working family man, and I'm quite sure he has never told this story to anyone else except his family. They are very private like, and he only told me of it after I had hunted with him for three years or so. I hunt in Minnesota for whitetail deer and turkey and am an avid outdoorsman for most of my life since my teens, I myself have never seen one of these creatures. I have always thought that I would see one someday. I found your YouTube stories about hunting and sasquatch to be really great as I am very interested in these subjects.

So here goes. My friend was about 18 or 19 at the time. He lived on a farm in northern Minnesota, about 35 miles west of Duluth. This would have been about 1975 or '76. The surrounding area has occasional small farms and hay-fields but is mostly wooded with large areas of timber and swampland. Logging for the paper mills and an occasional gravel pit are around as well.

My friend had finished working on haying the fields and evening chores around the farm. He was taking a sauna at the end of the day. That was custom for many of the Finnish people in the area. The sauna was located in the back of one of the 40-acre parcels that the family-owned. It was near a stream. My friend was sitting just outside the sauna naked and cooling off. Usually, he would do a few sessions of heating up and cooling off. The area was not visible from the road as it was in a lower elevation and could not be seen, so they had privacy. He said he had an eerie feeling come over him that someone was looking at him, and he turned to look behind him toward the sauna. He said he saw the head and shoulders of someone looking at him from over the eve of the sauna. He immediately said, " I see you (yells brother's name)." Then he realized it was definitely not his brother. It was dark, hairy and tall. He felt an instant fear as his mind registered "bear." Then in a second, he thought, a bear could not be that tall. The eave of the sauna was about six and a half feet high, and this being whatever it was, was 2 or 3 feet taller than the sauna roofline at the eave. It was evening, and the light was just turning to twilight, but he could still see details fairly well.

Now he was terrified, and the being went back, and the head and shoulders disappeared from view behind the sauna shack. Then it reappeared again in seconds. This time, he was looking at him from above the other eave. He didn't know what to do and was frozen in fear as he was naked and felt vulnerable. He did not know what this thing or animal was. Then in a few seconds, it went back and disappeared from sight. Behind the sauna roofline altogether.

He thought about rushing back to the sauna to get his clothes and get out of there. But didn't want to go TOWARDS the creature. Finally, he ran back inside the little changing room in front of the sauna and got his clothes on as fast as he could. He felt like it was staring at him through the small window, and he didn't want to look at it. He ran back to the road and jumped into his truck and sped to the farmhouse about three-quarters of a mile west on the same road. He got his dad and two brothers, and they grabbed lanterns and flashlights and shotguns and sped back to the sauna to see if they could see anything. It was just now dark, and they didn't see any sign of it. They looked for tracks, but the area was grassy, and all there were areas of flattened grass, no footprints. They never saw anything again. It remains a mystery.

My friend did say that he remembered for a short time in his school, that in early fall, the school bus driver would occasionally see something big and tall and dark, walking upright across the rural gravel roads on his route. One time he remembered he sped up to the spot where he thought it went into the woods, and he flung the bus doors open to listen, and they heard something crashing away into the timber.

So that's it. I have always since wondered, what exactly did he see? I have always been interested in his story and other sightings, similar to what he saw. I found your YouTube site and have listened to almost all of your Sasquatch recollections. This seems like one of them.

I have many questions about Bigfoot, like what are they, the female DNA unknown male DNA, (I am currently reading the book by Scott Carpenter)how many are there? How do they reproduce and rear their young? How do they survive the harsh winters? The Nephilim connection, the baby Bigfoot carried by the female, what do they see when they say it was a female, breasts curved hips?? Many other thoughts, how do they communicate? Language intelligence etc.? The common bad smell, and on and on.

Anyway, thank you for all the posts, and I hope this mystery will come to light so people can be informed of the truth, for safety reasons and post-traumatic stress issues and just general knowledge of the beings. I love the outdoors and cherish the times and memories I have from spending time out in the woods. I hope you will find the answers and the truth on this subject.

Best regards. I am always searching for the truth.

-Dean T

Sometimes It Is Short, But It Happens

My name is Justin. I'm a long way away from you, but I have a story I would like to share.

My wife and I had recently moved to Atlantic Beach. We were exploring the Croatan forest and just happened to be riding around one Saturday night and came across a new trail that we had not yet explored. We parked at the entrance to the new path. We sat there looking around and talking. My wife was talking to me, and I went silent. She asked me what was wrong and could clearly see a look of shock or overwhelming distress on my face; I was speechless. She asked me 3 or 4 times what was wrong? My only reply was, " I just saw bigfoot." She immediately started asking questions and the only way I could ever describe the creature was over 7 ft tall and was extremely hairy.

The gate in front of us was about 20 ft across, and whatever I had just seen made two steps and cleared the path and was gone from the headlights view of the truck. I immediately got out of the truck, only equipped with a Glock 19 with a light. After I got the nerve, I got out and went to the gate and just listened and heard nothing, no birds, no wind, nothing just silence. As we were walking back to the truck, which was about 10 yards away, I heard a crack from a breaking limb in the woods. I jumped back in the truck and just sat there to see if I could see whatever I had just seen again with no prevail. After about 20 minutes, we left and went back home. I haven't told anyone this story until now. To this day, I don't feel comfortable even riding through the Croatan at night.

We both love watching your videos on YouTube and watch every video. Thanks for letting and giving people a chance to tell their stories without judgement. And again, your videos are fantastic and keep up the great work.

On The Deck Looking Into The House

Hi Steve,

I absolutely love your channel and your support, as well as messaging on this topic. It's fantastic that you are giving people a vehicle to share their experiences and get the truth out there. The reality is this. There is definitely something out there. I cannot explain what I saw as an eight-year-old child in the late 70's. But it forever has creeped me out about being in the woods. I have friends that are avid hunters here in BC, and I think you may know some of my friends. When they head out, I am always "yay, good for you" but left feeling uneasy.

Here is my story!
When I was 7-8 years old, my parents divorced, and my dad ended up building my parents' dream home deep in the woods of Ft. Assiniboine, Alberta. (Near Swan Hills, AB). My mom and I lived in Barrhead, about an hour or so away. The dream home was in the woods. The deck was built onto a large hillside with forest all around. The main living area of the house faced the hill, and the Assiniboine River, which had beautiful views, was all glass. It was the main floor where decks all around the house on this level circled the kitchen, living room and my bedroom. This detail is important, so bear with the floor plan LOL.

We used to visit my dad every second weekend or so as part of the divorce agreement. This was a late fall weekend visit. My dad was told that there were several grizzly bears in the area recently. We had horses as well as chickens on this property. We always woke up to bear tracks on the lower driveway and yard. So, we were fairly bear aware and cautious.

Here is the encounter. It was about 11:30 at night, and everyone had gone to bed. I remember hearing CTV news at 11, and then I fell asleep. A short while later, I could hear very loud banging, thumping and the rustling of trees at the front room with large glass windows. The banging got louder, so I got out of bed. I kid you not, the next part sounds like a movie, but it was very real, I assure you.

I went down the hall, and I was about 15 feet or so back from the large open concept living room. I could see something very large and hunched over on the deck at the window. My dad has his bedroom in an open loft area above the living room. He came out onto the balcony. He turned on the lights to light up the area. I swear to God Steve, what stood up from a crouched position was not a bear. It just wasn't. I knew what a bear looks like, and there was no bear. It was very, very tall, covered in hair, but did not have bear paws when it stood and balanced just like a human. My dad started yelling for me to get back to my room, and when I looked up at him, he had a shotgun pointed at the large floor to ceiling window and was prepared to blow that window out to shoot whatever was on the deck. That was no bear. As a child remembering this. I thought it was a gorilla honestly because, in a kid's mind, that was my point of reference. All of this happened so fast. No shots were fired because the creature was up, over the railing, and up the hill to the ridge, so fast it made your head spin. A bear could not have done that. The railing was fairly flush with the hillside. We used to climb over it all the time to get onto the deck.

The next day my dad was very agitated. I kept asking what that was, and he was pretty pissed off at me for persisting. He kept saying bear, but he was on the phone. It was an early Saturday morning talking to friends around the property and in town about what was on the deck the night before. Even he had no idea for sure but did drop the sasquatch word. The rest of that day, we had his buddies on the property looking for footprints, walking up the ridge from the deck and driving the roads around us with shotguns. Driving around with guns was pretty typical for a late 70's afternoon in Alberta LOL.

People said it was probably a Sasquatch. I had never heard of this before, and my dad said not to talk about it. My mom said it was kooky to think it was anything other than a bear. I was kind of made fun of as a kid for sharing the story, so I stopped. As I got older, I thought that these creatures didn't exist in Alberta, so it was probably a bear. As I hear your stories, it brings the memories back, and people are 1000% correct. Once you see one, there is no going back! Even for a young kid who was only turning 8. It was very profound.

The house was fairly new in that part of the woods, and it was one of the first times I had been there. I wonder if maybe the sound of little girls running and playing in the woods drew the creature out? Or we were also throwing rotten chicken eggs at trees further up the ridge. (We got in supreme shit for that too). Maybe that smell, along with the laughing, drew it out. I have no idea. Thank you for all you do.

-Michele

Saw It Through My Scope At 40 Yards

The incident I'm sharing took place during the Christmas Holidays when I was 14 years old. Forgive me if it's long, but I'm trying to be detailed.

I was one of the lucky ones. My family had 4600+ acres for me to roam and hunt on anytime I wanted. It was my Grandfather's Ranch. He raised black Angus cattle. The property was sold after my grandfather's passing to a developer in 1988, then parceled out for 3-5-acre homesites.

I knew every trail, tree, creek and bog on the place. I'd do overnight solo campouts from the age of ten. Never feared anything. I was very comfortable in my grandfather's woods. I'd have my .22 and Bob.

That day in December, I hunted the high pasture in the morning and had seen several deer but only one scrawny buck.

I returned to the house around 10:00 am looking forward to Nana's cowboy breakfast. As I neared the house, my grandfather came out of the barn carrying a feed bucket. Didn't hear any shots... did you see anything, he asked. Before I could answer, he asked when I had left out this morning and if I had seen Bob.

Bob was a 6-year-old Blackmouth Cur. He was scared and grizzled with tattered ears. Bob was grandpa's constant companion unless I was there or he saw or smelled a skunk, then he'd charge off after that skunk and wouldn't return until he had caught and killed it and then he would deposit it on the front porch. His trophy!

That day I watched my grandfather work around the outside of the house and barn. Several times he'd stop and turn. He'd look into post oaks and briars for a moment, sometimes calling for Bob. Sometimes he wouldn't.

As the afternoon came around, I picked up my possible bag and my .243. Walking out to the yard between the house and barn, I met and told my grandfather I was going to hunt the bottom, between the creeks. He shook his head "no" and said; why don't you try the high pasture one more time. I really wanted to hunt the bottom. It was rich with life: deer, turkey, vermin and the occasional hog.

I agreed to hunt the high pasture, but as soon as grandpa entered the house, I turned and headed toward the old tree stand between the creeks.

The way to the stand was through trees and brambles so thick it sometimes blocked out the light and the air was always still. The sandy loam ground was always moist. It made for quiet walking. You had to cross Lil Sandy using a game trail. Then a couple of hundred yards through the thicket. I knew the way like the back of my hand. The stand had been built long before I began to hunt. The platform was some 16-18' up in an old hackberry tree. Grandpa had killed the ranch record buck out of it four years before. I climbed and settled in—my back against the tree, sitting on a recently added bucket. The original bench had rotted.

Sitting there, I could see the canopied trail I had used to get there. To my left, Big Sandy Creek snaked through the bottomland. A long shot from that blind was 90 yards, with most being 50-60 yards. The ground below me was cut with dozens of game trails.

After about an hour or so, I caught movement to my left. There standing on the high bank was a doe. I didn't move. She was only some forty yards away, and the steep bank was just 8-9 feet below my blind height. I had been busted by deer on the high bank before.

This doe looked right at me and then turned her gaze back to the thicket in front of me. She whistled and stomped her foot. Then she would lower her head then raise it again. Repeating this several times. Whistle, stomp and head bob.

I tensed up and slowly readied my rifle. I was sure some ol' buck had caught her attention. I then caught movement in the thicket. The doe whistled, spun in her tracks, hauled ass!

Focusing on the movement, I tried to make out a shape.

It slowly and only partially became visible. Dang it, I said. That's a cow, just lying there in the shadows, black as pitch. I turned my head away and scanned the area. A few minutes passed, and I decided to raise my rifle, look through the scope and see if I could find and read the cow's ear tag. I needed to let grandpa know where it was.

The hair was all wrong, black and grey and long! I thought to myself that's a huge hog, maybe seven feet long. I continued to look, trying to find a place for my crosshairs to settle. Then it happened. A hand reached up and placed itself flat against the fallen post oak in front of it. This THING was only some 40 - 50 yards away. The 4X scope was clear, and I could see long fingers and black nails, but the brush blocked much of its body.

I became nauseous with anxiety. Fear covered me like a heavy quilt, and I felt my strength leave me. I was terrified. There was a gorilla in the thicket!

My gaze never left it, but suddenly it was gone. That terrified me even more. Where had it gone? With only 30 minutes or so of light left, I summoned all my courage and climbed down. No way I was staying up there; gorillas can climb! There was also no way I was returning home through the thicket, so I crossed the Big Sandy and climbed the bank. I followed the bank to the old abandoned homestead. Crossed over a few fences, then it was open pasture to the house.

Once I hit that pasture, I ran like a gazelle.

I could see the compound in the distance, and every light was on. The house and barn were lit up like an airport. I was so happy I may have begun to cry.

I burst through the side door, cutting through the laundry room into the kitchen. Nana and Grandpa, we're sitting at the table. GORILLA, I blurted out. There's a gorilla in the thicket. I saw it.

My grandmother rose and wrapped her arms around me. I'm sure I was shaking. Howard, she said. My grandfather sat there staring off with pursed lips but said nothing. Howard, she repeated. He said nothing. I figured he was mad at me for lying about where I was going to hunt.

Nana told me to go clean up and eat dinner. She followed me into the bathroom and pulled the window curtains closed. That was strange, I thought. There wasn't another person to see in for miles. Besides, the bathroom window was at least 7 feet from the ground.

After I showered, I came into the kitchen and noticed all the drapes were closed. I asked grandpa if he wanted us (because there was no way I'd go alone) ... to go out to the pole and kill the floodlights. He said no. It's not going to hurt anything to leave them on tonight.

Now my grandfather was a big hunter. He'd hunted Africa at least four times. Taking elephant, lion, Cape buffalo and many others. He'd hunted Alaska, British Columbia, Manitoba, Saskatchewan, Oregon, Montana, Wyoming, Colorado and Idaho. He was a student of ballistics and owned dozens of rifles. He was also one of the coolest men under pressure I'd ever seen.

Once when I was about 7, we were at the bottom looking for Turkey. Papa was carrying a Savage combination gun. It had a 30-30 top barrel and a 12 Gauge bottom. As we neared the bog, a group of piglets began to squeal and ran in all directions. Then we heard grunting and crashing as a large hog charged. Grandpa pushed me behind him, raised the gun, switched barrels, aimed and fired. He had never moved a step. When I came from behind him, I took three steps and touched the dead hogs' nose. There was a single hole almost between the eyes.

I only mention his courage and understanding of game vs. ballistics because, after dinner, I went into the living room to join him watching TV. There lying on the floor next to his recliner was his big flashlight and his Wesley Richards 450/400 double rifle. I knew better than to ask. So I drank hot cocoa, and grandpa sipped black coffee and smoked his pipe.

When I finally went to sleep, it was fitful. I woke early. The sun was just breaking the horizon. I thought no one else was up. I opened the front door, and the stink assaulted my nose. I pushed the screen door open to see Bob standing over a dead skunk and by the smell, it had given quite a fight. My grandfather came walking from the right of the wrap around porch with a shovel; it startled me. He handed it to me and said, take that skunk to the burn pile before your Nana gets up. He turned toward the porch bench where there was an ashtray, a thermos of coffee, his big light and the double rifle leaning against the wall. He'd been up all night.
My parents arrived that afternoon to take me home. I couldn't wait to tell them what had happened but, grandpa made me swear to say nothing.

The memory is never far from me. Like some traumatic event, I can recall it in detail.

I did eventually share it only to be laughed at and called spooky. Maybe you can share it or not. Please don't use my name.

I would never venture into the bottom again without a slug loaded shotgun. And you could kiss camping out there good-bye. It just wasn't fun anymore.

As I said, I don't know what I saw. Your channel is partially dedicated to bigfoot, and I've never heard of any in Central Texas. Maybe it was a gorilla.

It Spoke In A Deep Voice

First of all, thank you for all you are doing. It makes a difference for those that have had experiences. A friend sent me a link to your YouTube because of a conversation I had with him.

I have had 2 1/2 experiences.

I was one of the biggest bigfoot naysayers until I wasn't.

I have spent a fair amount of time in the woods. My dad was an avid outdoorsman and took his family. I never saw anything as a child, though.

My first experience with a group of about 7 to 8 people was camping in Tucannon in Dayton, Washington. It was morel mushroom season, and we always went mushroom picking at the end of May. This year in 2012, we got to the end of the road. Hiked in about 3 miles, then up the side of the mountain about a 1/4 of a mile. We were picking mushrooms, and I smelled the foulest, pungent, rotten smell. Remember, I didn't believe it before this! I started looking around for an explanation, then we heard rocks being hit together, not a rock on the ground being hit by another, but a rock in each hand being hit together three times. We all went quiet, and the hair on the back of our necks started standing up. We started picking mushrooms, and it happened again three rock smacks now it has our attention, and we were on alert, we were all looking at each other wondering what to do. When we didn't leave, it started charging down the mountain towards us breaking large branches, and to me, it sounded like a freight train. We all started running down the mountain. We were quiet all the way back to camp; this isn't the end either. When we woke up in the morning all around our campsite, it smelled like condensed urine. Needless to say, I haven't been back to those mountains.

The next year we started going to little Naches in Washington state. The first year we had no experience; however, the next year 2014, a few of us were exploring new areas to pick mushrooms. We wandered into this area of the woods. The first thing I noticed is how silent it is, no birds, chipmunks, no insects making noise NOTHING!!! This had me on alert. Then a friend told me the handheld GPS is messed up, and it said we were going east when we were going west. We thought that was strange also, but we kept alert, and I kept hearing bird calls and branches breaking behind me, nothing was there. Then a friend saw something about 4 foot quickly walk behind the trees, at that moment he freaked out and fired two shots into a stump to scare it away. He looked at me and said let's get out of here, were walking down the side of the mountain and came across a thicket we couldn't get through so we would have to walk around it, once we turned and then from behind us we heard a deep voice say BOOM BOOM (mimicking the gunshots from earlier) my friend said, "what did you say?" I said I didn't say anything. I believe we were in between a mother and a child, that's a scary place to be! That was the quietest ride home ever. I should mention this encounter happened in the middle of the day, just afternoon.

My 1/2 experience happened when we were hiking and just hanging out in the woods, out of nowhere for no reason the hair on the back of our neck stood up. Five minutes later, it sounded like someone pulled a large tree out of the ground and toppled it over, breaking it to pieces. It was then time to leave, we started down the mountain and got halfway down, and my friend said maybe we should tree knock, he got a branch and knocked three times, and two came back. The whole way down the mountain, it felt like we were being followed.

Please feel free to use my name, I know I didn't see one face to face, but the experiences were real. I have told my story, and it made others feel free to share theirs, others try to discredit what they do not understand.

Thank you for all you do,
Charlotte Dallas
Touched

Tore The Cabin Up

In 1967 I was ten years old and had gone trapping with my grandfather on the Groundhog river in Northern Ontario. He had built a couple of cabins along the river to serve as stopovers as he made his rounds. We arrived at the cabin, which was deepest in the bush. Only to find our cabin completely ransacked by what we, at least I thought (not having heard of Squash at this time), were bears.

For years I put off the strange things I saw that day as merely the incredible abilities of a hungry and curious bear, but today armed with the knowledge of sasquatch in retrospect, it could have only been Sasquatch.

Trailing into untouched wilderness for 90 days, B.C.

I should have guessed by the puzzled look and awkward silence from my grandfather, that this was no ordinary bear b&e. The door had been ripped off and was found in a clearing a couple of hundred yards down the trail. The woodstove, a cookstove that took three men to move, was found five hundred feet up the trail. What was even stranger is that there were no drag marks anywhere between where it originally sat and the clearing where it was found.

Every jar lid, every container, every box had been opened, a case of wooden matches with twenty smaller boxes in it had been opened, and every little box had also been opened.

The two cot beds were never found, mattresses and all. Fortunately, the bunks had been left intact. One of the windows had a loose steel mesh over it with the squares being approx. one inch. It looked as if something had put its hand or paw in it and squeezed all the metal to the center.

The list goes on, things a bear could never do, but I was too young to realize. I never thought to look for tracks, but I am certain my grandfather did (being a master woodsman), which is probably why he did not mention it. That was the last year my grandfather was trapped, often wondering if it was because of an encounter or simply old age?

Another interesting story, I'm certain you have never heard.
In 1994 was working in a healing center in Australia where they often had Shamans, psychics come and do presentations, etc....

A woman psychic had come, and as part of her presentation, she had asked a couple of the staff to put some pictures in unmarked envelopes so she could guess what they were. As one of the pictures, I put a sketch of a bigfoot. That evening, as she successfully guessed her way through the envelope, she came to my envelope. Immediately her face went completely deadpan dropping the envelope on the floor she said in a terrified voice, "someone must stop these beings, they are working with the ET's and disappearing people." She was very upset and refused to touch that envelope again. Sure enough, it was my Bigfoot pic.
Make of that what you may.
-Dan.

A Brave Navy Man Shares His Experience

Hello Steve,

My name is Dave. I'm closing in on 60 years old and have lived a pretty interesting life.

I've been a hunter since I was old enough to know what end of the gun points downrange. I trapped the streams, marshes and fields of Western Pa until I graduated high school in 78. I've always preferred being outdoors and have hunters (not killers) respect for wildlife.

After high school, I joined the US Navy and started my electronics career. Being athletic, loving guns and knowing how to use them, and loving the rush of a natural high- the Navy was interesting. I quickly realized I didn't want to be on board ships so much, so I looked into the UDT/ SEAL program. UDT was dropped in the 80s and became SDV (SEAL Delivery Vehicle- small manned subs). Because I'd signed up for advanced electronics on a 6 yr. hitch, I was not eligible for the SEAL program as they required me to give them my six years in electronics as it was considered an advanced (6 yr.) hitch. After six years, I could pursue what I wanted. So, three years into my 6-year hitch, I volunteered and was selected to work alongside SEALS in the small special warfare boat units - now known as SWCC (special warfare combat craft). What a rush. I'd found my place.

We trained with them, drank with them, attended some intense training on weapons, attended the SERE training program (survival, evasion, resistance, escape). Being a hunter, shooter, country boy, I excelled on the gun range. M16 open sight 200-yard qualifications I received the highest you could get- an expert - twice. A sharpshooter a 3rd time (must have been an off day).

I was a man in a young man's body. Certified as a diver through PADI by my LT Commander, who was a career SEAL- I learned from the best.

I tell you my background because it's important for what happened to me. I was alert, paid attention to detail, always able to take care of myself. I'm not crazy, on drugs, drunk or lying. It's not my nature, and anybody who knows me will tell you that. I honestly consider myself one of the good guys. Modest and not wanting any limelight in anything I did. Although when you do things well, shit just sticks to you.

Fast forward to June 2010. I was just turning 50 then. As an avid ATV rider, I invited my best friend, one who joined the Navy with me out of high school. I wanted to ride some groomed trails in the PA forest known as the Allegheny National Forest (ANF). It's a beautiful area of NW Pa- all forest. Many whitetails, black bear, some Puma, all sorts of small game, and an Elk herd just East of the area. It claims to be the least inhabited area of its size- east of the Mississippi River. I wanted to take Paul there because he wanted to buy one of my ATVs, I was moving up into bigger equipment, and the two-trail system of the Marienville and the Timberline trails join together for about an 80-mile loop- a good half-day of riding at least. In one area it gets kind of boring, so you can open them up a bit.

That's where we were when an event happened to me that changed my life. We were a few hours into riding, heading back north towards the trailhead where my truck and trailer were parked. We were on the boring part of the trail where it was logging roads and an old gravel road for a few miles. I told my buddy Paul that I'd meet him ahead, where the trail turns back into the forest. By now, he was familiar with the arrow signs that show you where the legal trail is. I usually don't separate when riding, but my ATV was a 500 (at that time) and hauled pretty good. I wanted to fly, and Paul was content just riding mellow- taking in the views which were new to him. I knew we were both safe, so I hauled butt northward on the boring gravel road part of the trail system. When I reached where the trail turned right- back into the brush and vegetation of the trail and finally off the gravel road, I pulled over probably 50 yards into the forest. The trail here was through a small forest field. The left was a steep hill. To the right, there was maybe 30 feet from the forest tree line of 2-3-foot-tall grasses and small, sparse brush. No trees until the forest line some 30 ft perpendicular to the trail. It was like that for maybe 70-100 yards. Then the trail was right back amongst the trees. In that small field, I brought my ATV to a stop off the left side of the trail but turned toward the right a bit so that I could watch for Paul. From my parked location, I could see any ATV traffic on that gravel road, and if Paul missed the trail turnoff, I could turn around and go back for him.

At this point, let me make this perfectly clear. I was NOT a sasquatch enthusiast and could care less for conversations about cryptids. I had seen the Patterson Gimlin footage from Oct '67 as a 7-year-old, and I'm sure I thought a monster existed wherever California was. But that's it! I didn't give the subject any thought, but I was confident that a breeding population surely didn't exist. After all- I'd hunted, camped and rode trails all over PA, Ohio and West VA and never had a reason to think otherwise.

The 2nd week of June 2010, here I was in the middle of the old forest of Pa-The ANF, riding ATV's with my buddy and enjoying the day. The trails still had mud, and mud holes and the tree leaves were still dripping because it poured rain all the night before and up to about 10 am. But the sun came out, and it was a perfect riding day. I was happy- in my own space. So, I was pulled over, waiting for Paul to catch up. I just parked it, took off my helmet and slung my left leg over the seat so I could grab water from my bag, lean against the seat and enjoy the moment. This was seconds from pulling in and stopping. Then ping a rock somewhat smaller than my fist bounced off from somewhere on the right front of my ATV, the fender, wheel or wheel well. It didn't register for a second because rocks often hit the ATV when riding. It was like a slightly delayed reaction, but it occurred to me that I was parked. Rocks shouldn't be hitting my ATV. Within 10 seconds, another rock came in. It was either that one or a third one that I caught its movement flying through the air out of the corner of my eyes, to my right and behind me. Basically, where I had just driven through, now, this forest had no cabins or camps or human habitation for miles, except the sparse primitive tent camping throughout the forest. But nothing and nobody near where I was at.

So, I caught sight of this rock coming in and turned quickly to my right. Fully expecting some idiot standing there throwing rocks, about to be shot. My eyes were quickly moving to my right looking for wherever these air rocks were coming from and about the time my eyes made it to this spot, that in my peripheral vision, I thought was a stump or fallen tree, this creature sprang straight up. Steve, this was daylight about 4 pm, and instantly I knew what this creature wasn't. It was no bear- not even close. I know they have to ask that question in an interview, but really? It was no man - it had no clothes. But it resembled a man more than a wild creature. This thing was 70-90 feet away - some 30 long paces, in the open, no obstructions between us, standing up in 2-3 ft tall mountain grasses. The grasses came up to just under its knees. It was square to me, staring right at me. It bent its right arm at the waist and froze. I looked for rocks in its gigantic hands. The fingers moved, no rocks. I had to have driven right past it. What the hell was I looking at? It was covered with dark black hair, almost bluish from the wet or oily hair. But it looked groomed - not a mess all covered in mud and knotted up. It was actually beautiful once you get past the sheer panic of the unknown and the size of the thing. I had nothing to judge size except the 2- 3 ft tall grasses. I wasn't thinking about measuring its size at the moment. I'm not sure what I was thinking. But I'm probably close to 7.5 to 8 ft tall. Its arms were extremely long, and I did notice that the upper arm seemed massive. The lower arm seemed longer from the elbow down. It had 3-5 inch very black hair and massive shoulders. It was wide, very wide. It had no neck, just like witnesses say.

I thought it was bent over slightly because the arm length, the head seemingly without a neck and the top of its head was different. Conical? I'm not sure, but it seemed bent forward. The face was black as well, but I could tell it wasn't hair. I assumed black skin. Its eyes? I'll never forget those huge black sockets; no whites- just black eyes. I now think it must have been shaded out from the brow ridge and deep-set eyes. I couldn't see great detail in the face, but I could see its lips were closed and went from one side of its face to the other. Thin lips. Flatter nose but again, not great detail from 80 ft or so.

Steve- I've never felt like this ever. It never gave me a reason to fear it and thankfully, I just froze too. I had my phone camera and a .45 in my fender bag and NEVER thought about either one. The stare down lasted maybe 15 seconds, and it was occurring to me what the hell I was witnessing. I've been deployed with SEAL Team 4 and never felt this anxious. Let's call it anxious. In the military, although it may suck and you pray it never happens, when you end up in shitty places, you know its part of the job. This day- what I was experiencing wasn't part of anything. A fear came over me and about the time that was happening, this thing took 3-4 steps straight back into the forest- gone. It never took its eyes off me. Never turned around. I never got to see its profile or backside.

When it slowly moved, I lost it. I was on that ATV hauling ass skipping sideways up the trail. As the trail came closer to the thick tree cover, I just kept envisioning this friggin thing running out of the forest and taking me off the ATV. I couldn't go fast enough. But I never saw it again. I rode about a mile or two up trails to where a big mud hole was where other riders were hanging out mudding. I stopped my ATV looking behind me when I realized " shit- I need to go back for Paul." Luckily, I didn't have to as he was pulling up within seconds. I now believe this thing heard him coming, and that's why it stepped back.

I never mentioned it to my buddy until 3 or 4 years later, and he said I was acting weird and wanting to load up and head home more than I usually do when riding.

So even though I wasn't hunting (it was June), I never went into the woods with a rifle after that year. I got my 2010 license but never used them and never renewed my license after. I don't know why. I still camp, still ride ATVs, and since then, I've been researching areas near there. Not as much lately, but the point is, I still go in the woods (not alone anymore). Every year as the Fall gets here and I smell it in the sir, I think of being hunting. I guess I'm still hunting, just differently.

People expect me to know about these creatures since I saw one, but I know nothing. Who does? I often say this. I'm dumber now since I've had that encounter because before that, I never had questions. Now my questions are endless. Like how in the hell don't we know about these things. They get huge. I don't blame folks for their skepticism. That was me once. It took that slap in the face to wake me up.

Folks also tell me, " Dave- I'd love to have that sighting." All I can say is watch what you wish for. It becomes a responsibility. I didn't ask for this to happen. I wasn't out looking for sasquatch. But there it was, and I can't take it back. It's embedded in my life, and I'm not so sure I enjoy living with the knowledge that they absolutely exist.

The artist Sybilla Irwin asked to do a witness sketch. I agreed, and what I'm sending you is what I signed off on. The body shot she added to a photo of the ANF- almost exactly like the area it happened at. The hair on the head wasn't all combed back, but I couldn't place every hair. The one word I used was "groomed" because it had no mud on it. I suspect it cleaned off rubbing along the wet foliage in the forest that day.

Steve Isdahl   The Day Sasquatch Became Real For Me   Copyright© 2020

It's funny to me because when I've been asked to tell my encounter, there's always that one "expert" who says Sasquatch doesn't do that. They don't give away their position. I now assume it drew my attention to it because I was too close to young ones, but my response to those so-called experts is " someone forgot to send that SOP to this one because that's exactly what it did. "

Thanks for your time, and thank you for your interest in the subject. I appreciate your no BS approach. I'm new to your videos, but they are awesome. I'll be subscribing soon for sure. Keep up the support. These damn things are out there, and now I owe it to folks to tell them what I saw. I don't care what anyone thinks. It is what it is, and I can't give it back. Peace!

Sincerely,
Dave Groves

UK Diplomat Watches A Sasquatch

Hi Steve,

Now please don't use my name as my employment may be affected.
It was in the late 1970s I was working as a bodyguard to a very influential man. We were on a business trip to the states. We had a couple of days off between meetings. The person that we were staying with had arranged for us to go out into the high country with a 1st nation guide to see the wildlife. It's so different from the stuff we have here in the UK.

All went well we drove so far up and walked about a mile to this mountain meadow I being the bodyguard had been given a 12 gauge with slugs just in case a bear or the like got too friendly. We were standing in the woodland right on the edge of the meadow. The wildlife was out and about doing their own thing. Truly stunning to see and listen to. Neither my boss or I had cameras. Just being there was magical.

Our first nation's guide, a really nice and very knowledgeable man, was telling us what each thing was and what it ate. When suddenly, he just went silent, and his eyes wandered into the distance. We both followed his gaze and saw what he was looking at. It was about seven and a half feet tall, slight stooped shoulders, and had grey-brown hair all over going into silver on the head and shoulders.

I immediately slid the gun off my shoulder and went to raise it when our guide said in a quiet voice, don't; put it down. So, I lowered it but kept it ready. By this time, I can tell it made my pooper pucker. My boss just stood transfixed, never a sound or movement out of him.

By this time, it was only a 100ft away from us. When it looked around and saw us three, it stopped and stared at us. The guide stepped two paces forward and raised his hand and spoke to it in his native tongue. It just looked at him and then walked away across the meadow and into the high timber. Our guide then told us that it was an elder, and we were in no danger and to please not tell anyone what we had witnessed or where we were.

I hope you stay safe and hunt well.

It Vanished Into Thin Air

Hello Steve,

I've watched all your videos, and I appreciate your mission. To be honest, six years ago, I would be the guy that rolled his eyes in disbelief if I stumbled across your channel. But after my first experience, I can't play that - superiority card anymore.

I live in southeastern Kansas, at Toronto Lake. We have rolling hills and thick black oak forests, with great whitetail deer and turkey hunting. In the summer of 2015, it was around 10 PM, and I was sitting in my living room reading when I heard a loud tree branch snap just outside the house. My dogs started frantically barking. I got up to take a look. I turned the porch light on and opened the front door of my small self-built cabin. The dogs were twenty feet from me, just off the porch. They were looking up and barking at what I assumed was a raccoon in the tree. I yelled at them, and they didn't respond, which is unusual because my dogs are very disciplined - I train K9s for veterans with PTSD. This struck me as unusual, so I took two steps onto the porch to see this raccoon. Instead saw a nine-foot-tall, 700-pound monster staring right at me. Steve, this creature was exactly twenty-five feet away. I was frozen in fear. All I felt was an overwhelming sense of dread. I still suffer a sense of fear when I think about it. Only my wife knows about my encounter until now, if you are reading this email.

Maybe I'm projecting things into the experience, but I don't think so. I felt like this thing knew I was in the house, and it wanted me to see it. I can't shake that thought. It stood just a couple of feet beyond the direct light of the porch, but it was a cloudless full moon night, and I could see it was covered in very dark hair. I'm a big man at 6'7" and 385 lbs. I haven't been scared since I was eight years old. This thing could have ripped me to pieces.
*I'm reluctant to share this part, but here it goes...It stared at me for maybe five seconds and turned away and took four steps, crossing a path that leads to my art studio. There was a tall white metal privacy fence one hundred feet beyond that, that enabled me to see its silhouette as it walked away and into the dark. I don't mean out of view. I mean, this freaking thing on its fifth step vanished into thin air! When that happened, I was so terrified I ran into the house, locked the door and grabbed my 12-gauge shotgun and loaded it with slugs. I was in full panic mode. I didn't sleep well for days.

Over the past five-plus years, I have set up cameras and lights all over my five-acre lake property. This monster encounter has changed my life and most of what I believe. For me, Bigfoot is not from here. It has to be an alien species because physical objects don't disappear into thin air.

Steve Isdahl   The Day Sasquatch Became Real For Me   Copyright© 2020

The rest of you can chase big monkeys in the woods, I know better. These things are ten-thousand years more advanced than us.

I wish you the best. You are a blessed man to live and hunt in such a beautiful part of Canada. I haven't a clue why you still go into the mountains.

-John Lipscomb

It Spoke with Its Mind

Hey Steve,

Here's another one for you. Feel free to share it, but keep in mind there is some very controversial content. Not that that's going to dissuade you, but other people might not be able to comprehend it.

I live off the grid in Oregon. My family has had numerous experiences with these beings since we repurchased the property in 1988. I grew up hunting and know the woods and have sharpened my 6th sense more than the average person. Anyone who spends the majority of their time in the woods is able to sharpen that sense. I've hunted cougars and everything in this part of the continent. (Never with a guide), always on my own.

Anyway, in the last five years, these beings have been coming to the upper canyon of our property and staying from late summer/early fall and then leaving when winter hits. Except for this year, it seems they have stayed and have made it their sanctuary. I've seen so many signs over the years; it's not even a question that they are here.

The way we produce electricity is with a hydro plant, and we have 2 miles of PVC pipe running up and tapped into the creek where we draw the water from. The other day I hiked up to clean the debris from the pipes so the power would turn back on and all of a sudden, I felt that predatory vibe lasered in on me. My dog was shaking and couldn't wait to get the fuck out of there. He's a Rhodesian ridgeback and weighs 114 lbs. He isn't scared of much, although he is cautious after the encounters we have had.

I stood up while I was still in the creek and saw a tree being shook. This tree is a decent size Ash, and I saw this thing behind it shaking it with such force I couldn't believe it. Not only that, but I heard him communicate telepathically that he and his family are pissed off that we are diverting water from the creek.

I've grown up around American Indians my whole life and have heard the stories of how these beings "mind speak" as a way of communication. I really have debated with myself telling you this story. I know you're open-minded and speak the truth, but I've told a few friends what has been going on, and all I get is ridicule. It's such bullshit. There's really no point in trying to convince them. You're the only person outside my family that I trust to tell. So, thank you for allowing people a means to share their experiences. I figured you would want to hear about the telepathy these things have. It was the first time anything like that ever happened.

I've called these damn things in with a fox pro predator call when I was going after a cougar that had killed one of our young horses. At 2 am I heard it give out a very deep growl, not even 30 yards behind me. I wasn't able to see it at that time, which has always bothered me. Not sure if it crawled into the call and was laying down or if they have the ability to not be seen. Also, for the record, no, it was not a bear or cougar lol. Bears will run right up to the call, and I know what Cougars can sound like. Anyway, there it is.

Keep up the good work and thanks again for your no-bullshit demeanor and for speaking the truth. Take care and be careful out there.

I meant to describe this being in my first email. You know what they look like. 8 to 9 ft tall, 4 to 5 ft across the shoulders and this one had a reddish-brown color. His hands were what stood out the most when I saw him gripping/shaking the ash tree. The size of dinner plates comes to mind. His fingers didn't have hair, and I could clearly see his yellowish fingernails. Very human-looking. I've heard first nations talk about how they are another tribe of humans. It's no coincidence that EVERY tribe in North America describes the same thing and the same abilities. Not sure what they are, but I believe it is highly plausible that they are interdimensional. If people were to say that 20 years ago, you would be laughed at and ridiculed for the rest of your life! So there it is.

Thanks, Steve.

Minnesota And Pacing Me

Hello Steve,

My name is Russ, and I'm from northern Minnesota. I had my experience in December of 2012. I had several other things take place that year during the early bow season that all led up to my encounter. I had heard several loud moans and howls around late September, early October. My ex-wife and I found a huge turd in the middle of the trail. When I say huge, it's a complete understatement. It was close to two feet long and about as round as coke can and jet black. If this was a person, I would like to shake their hand and buy them a trophy.

All joking aside, it was the morning of December 7th. It was cold and frosty that morning, but we had a surprisingly warm winter so far with no snow on the ground. I parted ways with my brother and proceeded back through the thick woods where I parked my wheeler. My brother had about another 15 minutes to ride to where he parked, although we were only around 350-400 yards apart. I shut off my machine, grabbed my bow, turned on my headlamp and flashlight and headed down my trail towards my deer stand. I only went about twenty yards and ran face-first into a branch that was hanging across my trail. I had my head down the whole way watching where I was walking to stay as quiet as possible. When I looked up to push the branch aside, I noticed that it was not broken but twisted in a manner to block my path. The branch was close to the diameter of a baseball bat and twisted in the same manner as wringing out a washcloth. The only thing I thought that was odd at that time was it wasn't like that a couple of days prior. As soon as I pushed it aside and continued down the path to my stand is when shit started to get creepy.

That morning was dark; I mean really dark. You couldn't see your hand in front of your face dark. As I started walking the trail, I could hear something paralleling me beyond the brush to my right. When I would walk, it would walk. When I stopped, it stopped. I began to get very nervous thinking that it might be a cougar, as we have a large population in our area, even though the DNR won't admit it. Anyway, I picked up the pace and made it to my stand. I had a tarp on my seat that was frozen, and I thought that since I had around an hour till the sun started to come up, that I would drop it to the ground and try to scare away whatever was twenty yards or so to my right in the brush. Big mistake! It wasn't even twenty seconds or so after I dropped the tarp and hung up my bow that I heard the loudest tree knock ever, or whatever those idiots call it. It was the sound as if someone hit a home run in the middle of the woods. Not even two seconds later, something got up from my left and ran behind me back towards where the noise had come from.

I have been in the woods my whole life from around four or so, and could definitely tell that whatever was running was definitely on two legs. You could hear the pounding of the feet, and it was breaking and smashing everything in its way. It sounded like a freight train for about 10 seconds and then complete silence. I was frozen with fear. But I had to know what the hell was going on. I reached into my pack and grabbed my spotlight. I clicked it on and spun around to my right, and my whole life changed as I know it. I caught this absolutely massive creature in mid-stride. I would estimate it to be about 8 to 9 feet in height, long dark reddish-brown hair and extremely heavy. It spun and crouched behind a pine so fast, and it nearly disappeared. All I could see were these piercing reflecting huge eyeballs staring at me and an absolutely gigantic arm and hand were somewhat visible through the tree. I shut off the light and remember thinking that I was going to die in the woods that morning. I don't know if it was growling or just breathing, but I will never forget the deep guttural noise it was making, and then complete silence again. Now the only thing making noise was me. I had, at some point, grabbed onto my shooting rail, and it began to clatter as I was shaking so bad that I couldn't stop. I honestly don't know how I managed not to piss and shit myself. Once I gained control of my shaking, I immediately reached for my knife. I figured if it was going to come and get me, maybe I could try for an eye or something. I sat in the darkness with complete silence for the next 45 minutes or so until the sun started to come up. I didn't take my eyes off the place I had seen it all morning, but nothing was there. I was still extremely nervous and couldn't shake the feeling of being watched. About an hour or so passed, and I began to hear footfalls coming up behind me. I could tell it was multiple feet like a deer but still didn't want to look. So, I sat and waited for something to appear; I was still clenching my knife. It turned out to be a cow moose. She was calling, and I had no idea that a bull was bedded in a clearing about 200 yards in front of me until he started returning to call. I couldn't see him as the woods are very thick, but he made his presence known. My theory is that there were two Sasquatches, and they were probably going to get him. Any thoughts?

At around ten or so, I managed to pull myself together. I sprinted like a track star over to my brother. He immediately noticed I was nervous and asked me what all the noise was. I told him that I would tell him later and that I no longer wanted to hunt that day. He made me sit it out a couple more hours, and we left.

I told him what I had seen later that day, and he did not ridicule me. We still hunt the same area, and since then, I have found four prints and heard several things and smelt them a few times. I don't feel as if they are dangerous to a point.

I'm 43, and I have been walking those woods for years. I'm only 5'8 and weigh about 160. If they were aggressive, they could have snatched up my little ass at any time. But at the same time, they are wild and probably would react as any other wild animal if cornered or surprised.

Thank you for reading my story and for keeping up the good work. I joined one of those dumbass groups, and they were a complete scam. Weekend warriors in minivans. Complete idiots!

Once again, thank you for helping people, and your honesty is very much appreciated!!

Take care,
R Trettel

Surrounded In His Hunting Stand

Hi Steve,

I first discovered your YouTube channel while looking at hunting videos. I was mesmerized with your story about your wounded grizzly encounter. I have had two encounters in the Chattahoochee National Forest in north Georgia.

The first encounter affected my hunting partner more intensely than I.
We had camped out the night before our hunt and had set our climbers up on trees we had selected in some promising spots for whitetail that we scouted earlier that day. About 4:30, we made our way to our climbers, and I was set up about 1/4 mile from my buddy. I was about 30 yards from a very steep ridge overlooking a narrow ridge trail where I had several encounters in the past watching black bears and whitetail using the trail that crosses in front of my fairly concealed location.

My buddy was overlooking the same ridge 1/4 mile away on a knoll near some thick laurel that grew on the base of the ridge with several funneling deer trails below the ridge that he could watch down below.

Waiting for the first light is always exciting as the woods are very calming and quiet. Any noise by an animal definitely does not go unnoticed.

So, I'm enjoying the quiet serenity of the woods until about 15 minutes before first light when I began to hear what I thought were owls hooting, but they sounded louder than owls with more of a booming noise with much larger lung capacity than an owl. The noises then began to sound like whooping sounds, and I heard several whoops then a brief pause of about 2 minutes. I then heard three successive tree knocks. This was all coming from my buddy's area, and I was concerned. I thought my buddy might have been f*cking around. Then I realized that he could not duplicate these noises, nor would he be so irresponsible to screw up a hunt that we spent so much time and prep to set up for.

I then became extremely concerned once I rationalized this, so by now, I was on edge and listened intently. It began to get light enough where I could see it was very foggy out; actually, it was cloudy in our elevation, and I couldn't see but 30 yards away from me. Just then, I got a text from my buddy that said, "Get your ass over here." I figured he nailed a big ass buck with his crossbow and needed my help dragging it.
So, I immediately, I replied, "Okay, I'm coming." I get down, grab my gear and quietly head his way.

So just to let you know. We have been hunting together for 25 years, and we never talk loudly in the woods, and if we see each other, we always use hand signals or a quick whistle to alert our positions.

When I got close to his spot, I created the knoll and knew he was down the hill about 80 yards from the crest. As soon as he saw me, he yelled: "Get the f*ck over here....did you hear that shit?!"

I got a pissed off look on my face and put my finger over my lips like "Shhh."
He said, "No...f*ck that shit...those mother f*ckers surrounded my tree!"......"Did you hear that shit?"

By this time, I was about 20 yards away from him, and I could see he was white as a ghost and quite visibly shaken up. He was freaking out and shaking like a leaf. I've never seen this man scared of anything in the woods. But I knew he was serious and with the noises I heard, it began to sink in, as my mind raced.

Just then, he said, "They were making these whooping noises and hitting trees with sticks in a triangular pattern to communicate their position. They got closer and closer then started getting louder and were throwing large rocks near my tree, but it was too dark to see them; and LOOK, they left f*cking tracks!" He pointed to the ground about 20 yards from the base of his tree he was in and sure as sh*t, there was a set of prints in a semi-circular pattern pressed deeply into the matted leafy ground.

The ground was soft enough that the tracks sank about 3" deep in some spots.
To best describe these tracks is sort of, unlike most bigfoot tracks, were used to hearing about.

Instead of being unusually wide, these tracks were narrower like a human foot with a pronounced heel, a narrow arch that connected to a wide ball of the foot. The big toe looked to be the size of a serving spoon, and the small toes looked like they were one pad, possibly because heavily matted hair made them appear to be connected like one pad. This set of tracks was about 16" long. I couldn't believe what I was seeing.

Then it all just hit me as I took it all in, and suddenly I felt overwhelmingly euphoric. Almost like the air was charged with a calming agent. I calmed my buddy down when I said, "Holy sh*t....you lucky mother f*cker."

He said, "Lucky?... I almost sh*t my pants. Those f*ckers terrorized the sh*t out of me."

While I was mesmerized by studying the tracks, he was standing guard scanning our perimeter as one would during wartime while surrounded by the enemy. I told him, "I doubt they'll be back now that its light," and he calmed down a little bit but not much.

We began looking for tracks (together) because he did not want to leave my side. Crazy cause I've never seen him act so childlike. He was really shaken up, still wide-eyed and puffing on a cigarette with his handshaking.

We scanned the area, and I found three other sets of tracks. One at the edge of the knoll in a semi-circle pattern. Another one set about 70 yards from that, it looked like the tracks just appeared, then the last track was set really deep as if it rested its weight on its right foot while crouching to look at the trails below the ridge. It looked like it was trying to conceal itself behind a large white pine.

We found several spots where large rocks were just removed from the ground near the tracks. We saw some older tracks on the other side of the knoll where you could easily tell one straddled a log and lifted it to the side to forage for grubs in the soft soil underneath. There were scratch marks in the soil still. I did not find any hair, which is what I was hoping for.

At this point, my buddy was pretty stoked and seemed excited that our suspicions of these creatures had been solidified first hand. The tracks ranged from roughly 16"-18" long.

Both he and I have told our story to several hunters and DNR officers because we know what happened, and we don't give a sh*t if people believe us or not. We figure we will take a chance and maybe we will run into other outdoorsmen that have had similar experiences, which we have. Including a native American guy who shared a similar story and found tracks in a semi-circle pattern; also, which kind of freaked me out.

We have had confirmation that the creatures exist up there after talking to a couple of DNR officers that have seen and heard these creatures and have confirmed stories told to them by several hikers, hunters and campers. They told us that they believe they're migrating hunters, and we happened to be in their spot this season. They actually thanked us for being brave enough to tell them what happened so they can tell the other DNR guys to BOLO.

It was refreshing to talk to these guys that didn't treat us like crazy whack nuts because they have their own experiences, although we have shared our story with other hunters who think we've flipped our friggin lids and they laugh it off which we really don't care either way.

I've also had another experience in the same area, and I'd be willing to share that story as well if you're interested in hearing it.
Yes, you can use my name and call me if you'd like to chat.....like you have time for that...lol.

This all being said, I still don't fear going up there at night, and I won't let it spoil my fun....unless they try really hard.

-John Wintersgill

Not Once But Twice In Michigan

My background: I'm a "farm boy" who, in the early '80s, joined the Army and was assigned to 1/75th Ranger Battalion. I spent the next ten years as a Ranger and LRRP team leader. In those days, the woods were my home!

Encounter 1. Date: 11 July 1995, Time: 0400 Zulu (11:00 pm local), Location: North of Comins Mich. Latitude: 44.86700, Longitude: -84.0679 Weather: Clear; moon phase, full or near full.

We had a secluded Family cabin, deep in a cedar forest, on the banks of a river, miles from civilization. It was our base camp for family vacations, hunting, fishing and winter sports.

This particular night my family had gone to bed, and I went outside to gaze. Suddenly, off to my right, I heard a baby cry, twice, just across the river. I quickly made my way to the spot. There, in the moonlit forest, about 50 feet away, I could see what I thought maybe a small herd of deer (maybe 3 or 4). It did occur to me that bobcats and deer did not socialize, but I pressed on. All at once, a foul stench of wet dog, rotten duck eggs, cow farts and skunk's ass hit me! I had never smelled all things in such a strong combination.

Just then, "the deer," spooked and started heading north through the thick cedar. To their front, the ground rose a few hundred feet out from the cedar forest, giving way to open woodland. There was a foot trail, just east of me, paralleling the direction the deer were going, so I jumped on it and gave chase.

As I ran towards the hill, the sound of something big crashing through the forest was just to my left. I know once we hit the hill, the deer would head south (away from me) come to a small valley that cuts back west, ending up on the backside of this hill. So, I went over the top, expecting to cut them off.

As I crested the hill and started down the backside, the deer were gone? I could see small pine trees wiping back and forth violently at the north end of the valley. I couldn't believe the deer outran me, but I pressed on. Just then, I caught another whiff of that odd, foul smell (OFS).

If the deer kept going, they would run into another thick cedar forest. Hot on their heels, I believed they would head south, around a beaver pond and into a clear cut, logged a few months earlier. I moved southwest at a quick pace and soon emerged from the woods above the beaver pond. As I stood quietly, I heard then saw what looked like a very large moose coming from where I expected the deer to be. Had I been chasing a moose, making sounds like a bobcat and smelling like a city dump? The thought was still rolling around in my head when I realized, "this moose has no head, it had no backside either, and it's huge!!! Soon, this thing emerged from the tall brush and started uphill about 50 feet from me. I was paralyzed; my pants (real men don't wear underwear) sucked halfway up my a*s as the pucker factor went well passed 100%! There, before me, was a VERY large, hairy "man-like beast," built like an NBA basketball player with no neck! It strolled through the clear cut like it was walking through a parking lot. Unbelievable!

When it turned and headed directly away from me, I could see this beast had a back as wide as two men and shoulders the size of medicine balls. I could clearly see heavily muscled arms, chest, leg and back (all covered in hair). As it came to the edge of the clear cut, I made a mental note of a tree limb it narrowly passed undergoing back into the woods.

At daybreak, I took a big shot of whiskey and, armed only with a measuring tape. I headed back to the spot where I last saw the creature. When I arrived, I scanned the wood nervously as I fumbled with the tape. I hook the tape on the limb long enough to get the other end to touch the ground. I looked down at the tape and saw this thing measured over 10' tall! Then, I shit myself!

Encounter 2: Date: July 2016, Time: 0700 Zulu (0200 local), Location: Berrien Center Mich. Weather: Clear; moon phase, full or near full. I was in my motor coach, close to my in-law's house (where I would meet up with my wife). I had my window down as I came to the intersection of M140 and Pokagon Rd. Suddenly I was hit by a familiar stench, one I had smelled 21 years earlier! "I'll be darned," I thought, "there's a bigfoot around here!". Shortly after that, I arrived at the house, parked the R.V., crawled in the back and went to bed. I thought it was odd the dogs had not barked, but soon I was fast asleep.

The next morning early, the little honey came knocking HARD, on the door. "What that hell is wrong with you?" she said. Having been trained in the art of resist interrogations, I quickly turned the tables on her, "Awe, what's up?" I replied. "Why were you banging on the garage door last night?"; "You scared the crap out of the dogs and me! Slow down," I replied, "tell me what happened." Well, last night around 1 am, I heard something like a knob on an old-time radio being turned quickly. I could hear loud, rapid talking, but I couldn't make out any words. When I looked out with the flashlight, I saw the dogs cowering in their dog houses, scared."

My wife's parents live just east of Berrien Springs, Michigan. The house sat well back off the road and bordered hundreds of acres of farmland, orchards, vineyards and some marsh. The room we stayed in when visiting is above the garage; it looked out over the drive and the woods to the west. Just outside, three guard dogs barked their heads off over anything! This night, however, they refused even to come out. "What happened then?" I asked.

After the little honey scanned with the flashlight, she went back to bed to finish her book. A minute later, she heard something hitting the roof with a thud. Then, something (or someone) began rattling the garage door, followed by a loud series of bangs in quick succession. She did not know about Bigfoot, but I felt it was time she did. I told her the radio tuning sounds are forms of communications typical to Sasquatch. I also told her like most apes when Bigfoots, when scared or threatened, they throw things (rocks, trees, etc.). She was very skeptical but had never caught me lying, so, reluctantly, she believed me. I got the ladder and climbed onto the roof, where I found a large handful of rocks, enough to fill my hands, cupped together.

The garage door was clearly damaged as if something big had tried to push up on it! The banging noise was the spring braking in half. When the garage door repairman arrived, he was amazed. Besides having a sheared spring that would have taken thousands of pounds of force to break, some of the door panels were wrinkled. The repairman said it's as if a hydraulic jack had been used to lift the door. Apparently, Bigfoot (s) became agitated, threw rocks at the house then tried to open the garage door. They were scared off when the spring snapped.

I asked the little honey if she could remember anything else? "Yes," she exclaimed, "a skunk was wandering around too! I could smell it!" We spent the rest of the day watching Bigfoot videos on YouTube! She had never seen the Patterson-Gimlin film or any of the 100s of other clips.

I hope you add this report to your collection. With enough testimony, we may, one day, know exactly what these things are and how to properly deal with them. For now, my advice to anyone who asks is to avoid it at all costs! If confronted, do as you would if cornered by a giant grizzly bear, put your head between your legs and kiss your ass goodbye!

Thanks for your time, and be safe out there.
Best regards
J Cartier
Ironwood, Michigan

Newton County Texas

Steve,

Like you, I don't do anything with Bigfoot research unless it's to answer my own questions.

After having some strange things happen to me in and around the Big Thicket National Forest, I started to look into this subject. It led me to the BFRO and GCBR (they were a ridiculous kill group on T.V.) I kept to the fringes of the B.F. community as I quickly learned that these groups didn't mesh with what I was seeking. I wanted facts and info, not to be led around by the nose and told what was what. One good thing did come out of it. I met a solid dude, who like me, didn't want exposure but answers.

I met (I will call him Mike because he's a pilot for a major US shipping company and doesn't want to be mentioned by name because of his career path) in August of 2012. He lives up past Huntsville, TX, and I live in Orange, TX. Our first outing was what we now call "experiencing" because we aren't scientists, we aren't researchers was in the Angelina National Forest, and not much happened, other than Mike, 6'4" 250# got heat exhaustion. We did have an almost immediate friendship.

Fast forward two years. Although we were still very green, we had learned a few things, and one is don't go hiking around in the Texas heat with a 50-pound pack in August. What we really learned is, if you go into the woods looking, you most likely aren't going to see much. You need to listen and sit still. We still cruise the woods looking for different things that could be a place, but who knows. I've seen one footprint in 8 years.

Mike had a plan to buy land somewhere along a river in the deep woods, for his family and his love for the outdoors. I went with him to check out 90 acres along the Sabine River. The Sabine is not like many of the rivers in Southeast TX. First off, there's not a lot of public land on the Southern Texas side. So, it's hard to access, and there are not many towns it runs through. The property was paper company land that also leased out for deer hunting approximately 15000 acres in Newton County TX. This was March, so the thirty-minute drive into the land he wanted to see was desolate, there was absolutely nobody around. There were a few remnants of some makeshift deer hunting camps along the caliche road.
The terrain is small hills full of mostly Loblolly Pine and some Longleaf Pine. As you get closer to the bottoms, it turns to hardwoods, White Oak, Pecan, Hickory, Ironwood, some cedar and Yopon. As you get even closer to the river, it's almost solely Cypress. These 90 acres had all of it, including river access and massive Bald Cypress that ran right into the river's edge. We spent the better half of the day walking the land and looking around. It was cold that day (for March in Texas 45 degrees) and misting on and off. At about 530pm we made it back to his four-wheel-drive Dodge Dually and sat on the tailgate listening to a couple of Barred Owls making their calls.

At about 6 pm, it was getting dark and decided to head back to my land in Jasper County about an hour and fifteen minutes away. We hadn't experienced anything strange that day until I mockingly did a BFRO MoneyTaker/Bobo call. Which BTW neither of us does seriously. After about two minutes, as we were both climbing into the truck, there were two distinct knocks. I know you don't put much stock into knocks, but there's nothing in the Big Thicket that can pick up a stick and slam it into a tree. Other than the few people, twelve miles into private land and out of season. We sat another five minutes or so, and nothing else happened except the woods were now silent.

As we travelled up to the "T" in the road about a half-mile to make our Southernly turn to get us back out to the caliche road, it was now dusk. The last 300 yards of the dirt/grass road was up more of an incline that placed his headlights shining up off the road until we travelled over the final lip of the caliche road. The headlights lowered back parallel as we made our left. I caught movement immediately across the road. An abandoned trailer that had been burned up in the not so near past. It was approximately 25 yards away from moving left to right in the grass brush and small pine saplings scattered around the old camp. It or at the time I thought it was a he, was about 20 feet running towards the burned trailer. At the time, I thought it was teens who were going to ambush the truck with eggs or just trying to hide. I say teens plural because I thought nobody would be out here at night in the rain alone. As I got a better look, it looked like he was dressed in all black, wearing a hoodie and fast. I noticed how fluid he was also moving. I don't remember the arm swing or gate at all. I just thought it looked like he was floating for lack of a better word. I was not shocked or really anything other than confused. He disappeared behind the trailer, and a second later came out the other side, heading for a tree line about 30 yards away, which was at the bottom of a hill. The entire encounter lasted about 3 to 4 seconds. He seemed tall and lean like a pro basketball player. Shoulders were wider than the chest and waist. I remember absolutely no head movement.

We sat for a moment, and Mike sounded off irritatingly, " I ain't buying no land with a bunch of crackheads living around here." I was still trying to process what I had seen, and distractedly agreed. We drove back out and 10 mins later and halfway to the gate. It seemed like we woke up; neither of us had said much of anything. Mike turns and looks at me, "Dude, that wasn't a person."

I don't remember anything about the ten or so minutes between leaving and where we were. We agreed to go back and look at the abandoned campsite. I was reluctant as I hadn't brought my 45 that accompanied me in the woods. He said he had his 4570 behind the seat, which gave me courage after hearing that.

Upon returning to the deer camp, I walked to where I had seen him first. The grass that hit him at the lower thigh hit me in the chest. The distance he covered was over 50 yards to the tree line. We estimated it was less than 5 seconds for sure. At that point, I became very nervous, as if I was being watched. I didn't want to speak. I was afraid to talk above a whisper and felt compelled to leave right then. We both moved quickly to the vehicle, and Mike took off as fast as he could without seeming panicked. We both didn't speak much if at all until we hit the Farm to Market road. So, we both laughed at how not perceptive we were as researchers. I still, to this day, have to ask him every third call or so if he'd seen what I had seen. I had no reference for what I saw that evening. It must have been seven and a half or eight feet. I actually googled to see if any surrounding basketball players in our area were over seven feet tall.

The experience changed how I see the outdoors. I still go out alone fishing and hunting but never unarmed and not at night do I venture too far from the cabin when I am up at my place in the woods.

Steve Isdahl   The Day Sasquatch Became Real For Me   Copyright© 2020

Thanks Steve, for what you do. It's different from the others and appreciated.

Sincerely,
Tom Cobb

Government Worker In Chilliwack B.C

Hey, great channel, very informative. I am a retired government worker, and this is the reason why I will not go public with my experience. I have been hunting since the age of 15 years old. In the field of work I was in, military/law enforcement, I would have been sent for a psych eval and removed from active duty, if I ever spoke of this.
I still do not want to be recognized for this encounter, but I feel a need to tell the story. I was a scope sighted rifleman, so stalking a target is not new to me. I have received multiple training courses through my 34 years of service on how to cover and conceal myself. I'm multiple theatres of operations.

I was in British Columbia, Chilliwack, to be exact. I was told there were deer and black bears around Chilliwack lake. So, I decided to go scope the area out for signs of potential activity in that area. I passed the Chilliwack lake camp area for around 3 kilometers, parked my vehicle, with my wax tire marker to mark my way in, and my 12 gauge with sabot slugs. I walked for about 4 kilometers, found a good spot to sit, observe and just enjoy the beauty of the wilderness. There were absolutely no people around ATVs, motor cross, not even birds chirping, no squirrels running in the branches, just dead, not sounds, which I thought was weird. So after around 30 minutes, the environment was still dead, nothing. Very creepy.

I decided to change my location. This was when it started to get weird. I came upon a carcass; the weird thing is it was not mauled, bitten or even eaten. It was completely ripped apart, in totality. I knew it was not recent as the blood had turned blackish. So, knowing I was in a kill site, I decided to pull back a bit and observe the general area. I am now about 30 feet from the carcass, and the only way I can describe the smell that came over me was when a mop was left in a dirty bucket of water. I worked on farms my entire youth, and I have never smelled anything like it, I was almost dry heaving, just nasty.

I decided to retreat back to my vehicle, following my wax tire marker trail I made on the way in, I noticed that the marks were smudged, I am getting weirded out, and my hyper-vigilance is at max now.
I made it about a kilometer. There was something really heavy to my left. The ground had a slight vibration in it if I decided to put my back against a large rock and prepared for a fight, something was stalking me, it was smart and fast, and that smell just kept following me.

At this point, I charged my shotgun. After about 5 minutes hearing nothing, I continued my trail out. There were noises on my flanks, but not to close. When I was close to my vehicle, I made sure I was around 100 meters from my vehicle, after a shortstop of around 5 minutes, I proceeded to my vehicle. A large tree was leaning, hovering over it.

As you can expect, I drove out of there in a hurry. After about 15 kilometers, I stopped, and my legs would not move, as I sat and tried to make sense of what just happened, I realized I just got chased out, by something or things, there was definitely more than one. Well, I secured my shotgun and started to drive home, realizing I can never tell anybody about this; it would ruin my career.

One day something was in the woods, it was heavy, smart and aggressive, I knew it knew what a weapon was, and it knew I was ready to fight after I charged my shotgun it, they kept their distance.
I have been in the shit, life or death theatre of operations. I have never experienced anything like this, I have received training on how to understand your sixth senses and I have become very good and listening to my gut instinct. On that day, my instinct told me I was in a very dangerous situation, how I reacted probably saved me.

I am not a bigfoot believer, I have never seen one, but there is something in those woods, and it is not friendly. I have not been in the woods since, or have I hunted. I have moved out of British Columbia. I also lost a great passion of mine, hunting. Do I want to remain anonymous...hell yes! Nobody would respect me if I spoke of this. What the fuck could rip an animal apart like that, no sign of tracks in the kill area just animal parts???

Thighs As Thick As Telephone Pole

Hey Steve,

What you are doing is perfect. Thanks, and please keep it up.

My story is like dozens of others. I was bluff charged, screamed at, and followed by an angry Sasquatch. What I want to talk about are the parts that still disturb me.

Fifteen years ago, I was on a spring hike in the coastal mountains in central California. Three miles inside the Sespe Wilderness, I came on an old, empty campsite with a spring and shady oaks, so I stopped for a break. I cooled down, drank water and looked around, and noticed things were kind of strange. First, there was an old coffee-can that had been split open and laid flat, jammed a good six inches into the trunk of a tree. I couldn't imagine how someone could do that. It would be hard to get a sharp knife one inch into that oak.

The fire ring hadn't been used in weeks, full of leaves and rained on since the last fire. Nearby, dozens of twelve-pack boxes, crushed flat, were laid out to cover the ground like a mattress. It was out of place. In a wilderness area, people are expected to carry out trash and generally do. This trash looked like a year's worth of beer parties. At this point, I know things aren't right with this campsite, and I'm curious.

I checked out the spring. Cattails grew tall over my head, but there was a narrow path through.

The path led to where the grass was pressed to the ground, leaving walls of standing grass around, like a little room, about ten feet square. This was when the hairs on the back of my neck stood up. The grass under my feet was freshly pressed. Still wet and springy, but it hadn't sprung back up. Someone had been lying there very recently.

I felt a cold sweat. There was no one else on that trail; I was certain. No other cars at the trailhead, no other hikers, and no gear around. Yet some big living thing had made a bed in that grass, and it wasn't a bear because the little "room" was cut perfectly square, with sharp 90-degree angles.

I found what I did when I came back from the spring. I heard a rustle in a heavy brush, down a ravine fifty feet in front of me. I expected to see a deer until I heard branches snap. Big branches, and thundering footsteps. Bipedal footsteps, thump-thump-thump, as it ran up the other side of the ravine past me. I saw it, maybe twenty yards away, running flat-footed. Tree branches blocked my view of its head, and upper body. But I saw thighs as thick as telephone poles, calf muscles bulging, covered in short grey hair. It was broad daylight, and the sun gave the hair a sheen. The thigh and calf were at a 90-degree angle with the foot flat on the ground. Who runs like that? I could see the tendons behind the knee stretch as it launched away at an inhuman speed.

Stunned, I just grabbed my pack and left, quick. I didn't know what I'd seen. But part of me did know. There is a long history of sightings in the area. I hurried the three miles back to my truck, feeling eyes from the ridge above all the time, and immediately locked the doors. I drove a mile away before I stopped to piss.

So, this ate at me all the way home. It ate at me all week long. I'm an engineer—a critical thinker. I kept trying to fit what I'd seen into some kind of "real" scenario. It must have been a man. But why would a man be hiding in the bushes, and then come crashing out and run away? Could it be illegal pot growers? But what about the hair? The size? The incredible speed and stride? I had to go back and look.

I returned the following weekend. I couldn't go under the trees - too spooky - so I went around behind where the thing ran. There was a path, and I followed it up a long valley that turned to a steep gully topping out on a flat ridge. The other side of the ridge sloped into a bowl - a small, pristine canyon formed by a tributary to the Sespe River. The slope in front of me was an easy pitch down a Manzanita covered hillside. The chaparral grew just above my head, so when I started down, I couldn't see over the brush. I got fifty yards, or so, and a horrifying scream blasted from the trees in front of me. I can only compare it to the Velociraptor from "Jurassic Park." The sound was a screech and a growl, two-part harmony, so loud I felt a thump in my chest. My brain started looking for a reasonable explanation, and I concluded there had to be a backhoe and dump truck working down there because the screech almost sounded like metal on metal. Like a giant, rusty gate hinge.

I went to a little knoll ahead of me, where I could get a view over the brush. I could see there wasn't anything in that entire valley. No backhoe, no dump truck, no road. Of course not. It's a restricted Wilderness Area. This was when things got strange. This is the part I really want your listeners to hear.

It was finally dawning on me what screamed was some kind of animal. I also remembered what brought me there in the first place. I was putting two-and-two together. And then something came over me I can't explain. I started feeling hot. My skin prickled, and my knees buckled. And then someone entered my brain and said, "You don't belong here. Get out!"

I'm not sh*tting you. I didn't hear a voice. I just got this message, clear as if someone said it in my ear. It wasn't my thought. It was foreign - a thought projected to me in clear, concise English. And I immediately complied. I retraced my path for home, and every now and then, I could hear it pacing me.

I never felt so vulnerable. I don't blame people for being skeptical about "mind-speak." But it communicated with me, and its message conveyed pure danger. Not malevolent, but the kind of anger you might show a trespasser in your own home: "Get out, or I'll kill you."

In the years since, I've had one other sighting, and I've heard whoops and knocks and rocks clacked many times. I've seen footprints, tree structures and scat. I live in Arizona now, and most of my encounters have been here. They can be anywhere.

I believe they mean us no harm and want to be left alone. I've come to respect that and have quit hunting encounters. I carry a .44 Mag in the woods - not that it will do any good. They can disable us at a distance. Ultrasound is probably how. As an engineer, that makes sense to me. It's the intelligence they display that is spooky. And the sense of annoyance it directed at me. It had no fear of me, it meant business, and if I didn't leave, I might die.

I'm going to leave you with this picture. It's real - a skull and spinal column - stuck in a canyon cove in a place I won't name in the Four Corners area. An area with many sightings. I can't say what did this. Maybe an old First Nations burial? Or maybe a pissed-off wood ape? Stay safe out there.

You can use my name,
Andy Hall,
Tucson, Arizona

Maine Experiences From A Guide Family

Hey Steve,

I've been following you and your channel for quite some time now; I've watched every Sasquatch video you have made and have watched countless other hunting videos of yours.

I'm from Maine, and I grew up in a hunting family. My father is a master Maine Guide, and my grandfather is a professional Maine guide. I've been in the woods ever since I can remember, following my father around learning as much as I can. I've hunted and successfully harvested all of the large game animals in the state as well as numerous species of small game. So I know what is what when I am in the woods. I know enough to know how animals act towards humans.

In the fall of 2014, I was into my family's cabin on a pond about 20 miles outside of the town we live in. It's pretty remote. Being the road into the cabin is gated off, and it's a mile drive-in. There are four cabins on this pond that are all owned by my family. These cabins have been in my family since the 1920s. My great grandfather ran a hunting and fishing outfit out of these cabins. My mother, father, wife and I were at the cabin relaxing and just enjoying the peace and quiet. Me being me and being kind of intrigued about the whole Bigfoot subject decided to joke around and take two pieces of firewood and make two knocking sounds with them around 8:30. By maybe 9 pm, my father was already sleeping, so it was just my mom, my wife and me awake.
My wife and mom had to go outside to use the outhouse. But once they stepped outside of the cabin onto the porch, they instantly heard two knocks in the woods. Needles say they didn't walk all the way out to the outhouse and just decided to pee right beside the porch. They came into the cabin and told me what they had heard. I didn't believe them, so I went out and just stood on the porch. My mom joined me, and we heard walking right directly in the woods, not 20 yards from us. I had a very bright spotlight and shined it in the woods, and nothing. Turned the light off and instantly heard the walking again. Then we heard deep breathing—something with lung capacity, unlike any human. We rushed inside and told my wife what just happened.

None of us really knew what was out there, but we had an idea. We were not inside for long, then BAM! Something hit the side of the cabin. The cabin is set maybe 8ft from the wood line. I had enough, grabbed my shotgun loaded with a slug and went and stood on the porch. I was greeted with a high pitched, but deep scream 20 yards in the wood line and it was unlike anything I've ever heard. It did that four times then went back to making the breathing noises. I went inside, and my mom shut the curtains and we sat around the table. For a few hours. Nothing else happened to the cabin that night.

I still feel very uneasy going in there and my wife won't stay in there overnight unless we stay in the cabin. We've told a few people in the family, and none of them believe us as to what happened.

Thanks for listening, and keep on telling great stories. You can use my name if you want.
- Caleb Wade

Eastern Idaho Highway Sighting

Hello Steve,

Kudos to your efforts in creating a venue for people to express their Sasquatch experiences. My name is Joe Chace, and I live in a city in the Willamette Valley of Oregon.

In the late 90s, my then-wife and I and two little kids were driving home from a visit to the in-laws in Eastern Idaho. The trip makes for a long, all-day road trip, especially with two little kids that begin around four am.
I'll get right to the point.

We were travelling West on Hwy 26, East of Bend Oregon in the Ochoco mountains around early evening about an hour before sunset. There was plenty of light, but the sun was behind the hills and trees and not in my eyes. The wife and kids were napping, and I was in cruse mode, just wanting to get home and be done with this trip.

My story is very unremarkable and could be easily excused as a man crossing the road, but what rang loudly in my mind was the visual impression. As we crested a hill, the highway dipped slightly before ascending further into the mountains. The line of sight was open for over a half of a mile, and the lowest point of the highway was about a quarter-mile ahead (a few hundred yards).
As we crested the hill, I saw what I initially thought was a man walking out of the forest, crossing the highway from my left to right at an angle walking away. As I saw this, my first thought was this was someone that might need assistance because of the remoteness of the location then as it was crossing, it looked over its shoulder at us as we approached. As I saw it do this, my next thought was "Paddy." This "person" was one solid dark color with the same stride, swinging arms and the same head/shoulder turn as the Patterson-Gimlin film everyone has viewed.

The crossing lasted only less than ten seconds. We got to the point of crossing. I was looking for it, as well as anyone camping or a pull-off, creek or anything. There was nothing there but a solid forest on both sides of the road for several miles.

As I slowed to look around, my wife woke and asked what I was doing, and I said I saw something. She asked what I saw, and I said I think I just saw a Bigfoot. She was miffed with me saying that after waking her and closed her eyes to continue napping and nothing more was said.

It was, as I said, unremarkable, but the similarities between the P/G film and who/what I saw were pretty much identical.

Take it for what it is. Keep up the postings. I totally agree with what you're doing in this venue. I believe if I had an encounter with one of these. Like some of the close encounters, others have revealed to you it would be a soul-shaking, world view reset.

Keep up the good work,
J Chace

California Lady Huntress Encounters

Hi Steve,

My name is Dena Trumbly, aka Momma D. I live in Oroville, CA. I've been married to my best friend and hunting partner for almost 30 years. We have three children together. Our first encounter was approximately mid-October of 2005 in Forest Ranch, CA. During our C zone deer season.

We left our home around 10 pm to head up to an area then owned by a diamond match company. (A dear friend of ours worked for them and gave us the combo to the gate). My husband worked late that night, and that set us back a few hours to get into our spot for the next morning's hunt.
We finally got there, and because of the late hour and the fact that we had no moonlight, we decided to just sleep in the GMC Jimmy blazer. Our youngest daughter is with us. She was about ten at that time.

My husband and daughter laid down in the back, and I kicked the driver's side front seatback into the lounge position. After about an hour of falling into an uncomfortable sleep, I heard footsteps coming towards the truck. I immediately became awake and aware of my surroundings. As the steps got closer, I reached over and shook my husband, and I said, " Babe, someone is walking around our truck." He said, "no way." I said, "Shoosh, listen." The steps were definitely bipedal, and it walked completely around the front passenger side, stopped and then around to the back towards the driver's side. It stopped there for about ten or so seconds and then walked off, heading to the northeast of us.

About a minute later, there was an animal scream. It lasted at least 20+ seconds. My mind was racing. "What in the hell is that?" My husband uttered the words out loud. Little did we realize; our baby girl was also awake and listening. I've heard almost everything that lives in the woods call, yell, scream, tweet or chirp. You name it, and I can most likely ID it.

I'd never heard anything like this before, ever. It was approx. 150-175 yards away from us, and the sound was so piercing it was almost deafening.

We were so scared we didn't sleep for the rest of the night and left just as day broke. We never went back there, unfortunately, because our friend had seen a giant buck on multiple occasions in that spot, he sent us to.

The second time wasn't anywhere near as scary. Again, we were out deer hunting, but this time we were in Challenge, CA. This was about two maybe three years later.

The forest service /logging road gates were locked, so we parked and walked in about 2 miles on the forest service/logging road. I was in the lead. My husband was about 300 years back. I was coming up on a bend in the road. (Mind you, it's late summer) There was an embankment on my right (N/E) about 30 ft high with forest above it, then the road I was on and then a

downslope of about 30 ft to my left (S/Sw. That was a clear cut. It was at least 400+ yards before it became thick woods again.
I slowed my pace, knowing that deer tend to run ridges/fingers, so I needed to look for tracks or anything down in the clear cut, possibly feeding.

As I worked my way to my left, I noticed the road dust was hella deep, and I knew I'd see whatever was crossing that ridge would be easily identified and which way they were travelling, so on and so forth.
I saw several doe tracks and a couple of different good buck tracks.
I walked and scanned slow and easy. Then I saw a left, huge human barefoot print. It was heading west, downslope. It had to be at least 14+" x 4- 1/2 to 5" wide.

I knelt down and just waited for my husband to catch up to me. I scanned the wood lines waiting. When he got closer, he stopped and motioned, "what do you see" I motioned back, "come here." When he got to me, I pointed to the footprint. He said, " Who the hell would be out here, barefoot?" My reply, "I don't know, maybe a Bigfoot." We looked for more tracks, but the center of the road was so hard-packed that we couldn't find anything. I had that feeling that someone was watching us, and so did my hubby. We decided to head back to the truck and leave.

There have been more times than I can count of feeling like I needed to just get out of an area whilst hunting for no reason at all. I left anyway. I've told my encounters with many people. Nine out of ten times, I'm told I'm delusional or high or just have paranoid thoughts.

I know what I heard and saw. I didn't make it up in my mind. I don't use drugs, although I do enjoy a few glasses of wine now and then. I don't care if people think I'm nuts. Maybe I am, and I'm fine with that too.

Thanks for everything you are doing to make everyone aware. I appreciate you.
-Momma D

North Carolina And Wished It Never Happened

Steve,

I am sorry about the length of this story. It wouldn't achieve the real seriousness of what happened to me had I taken any detail from it. I understand you most likely won't use it due to time restrictions, and I'm fine with that. Still, at least you can grasp what happened to me and kind of get an idea of what I'm about and why I post on your pages and explain the things I do to some of your YouTube trolls that demand evidence or a body. My 30+ years of digging into this topic, the cover-ups, the lies, the TRUTHs that would blow the average person's mind away is just another day at the office to me. I've read 1000's of testimonials, stored 1000's of pictures and videos. I've also snagged about 80-100 people I've told about you that now follow you and will be behind you as you march forward with the real truth to the questions everyone has related to this topic.

If you choose to use my name, that is fine. I understand it might not be legal to use the name of the video I watched, which made me angry enough to come forward on a public platform finally... This is a true story and has kind of bottled it up until the last few months.

I posted this to a video on YouTube via Ray Nichols titled "Sasquatch Spotted by Campers," a video that really got me angry. I edited it at the time I wrote it because I wasn't nice. But here's my story. Feel free to see the video that created my reason for stepping forward.

People like Ray Nichols and these videos and hoaxes that make fun of the seriousness that it actually is, is why people won't step forward and tell the truth about what they have seen and what it did to them mentally. The reason people are afraid to come forward and say what I will.

It wasn't a joke when you got something like this looking you right in the eyes. Watching it watch you while you can tell it's calculating what it should do about you in its domain, you realize how massive it is and that you got it's 100% attention every bit of its focus is directly on you. At that moment, you have two reactions, and it's something everything on this planet has, fight or flight and then your brain's motor skills shut down. You're not doing anything because your stone is frozen. Totally and utterly helpless knowing damn well the gun you have for Protection will most likely piss it off even more. Even moving to reach for it isn't even an option at that exact moment in time; trust me when I say that. Don't get me wrong I wouldn't go down without trying to prevent my demise, but just the overall size and demeanor and the look it had was pure hostility. Just looking at its massive chest, the size of its head and hands. It's a very fit specimen that reminded me of one of those barrel-chested men you see on those tuff man challenges. The difference being this thing was three, maybe even four times bigger. It was wider than I was tall, and if it wasn't slightly bent over, its head would have been in the tree. It sounds farfetched, but it is what it is. Take it or leave it. Don't really care who does or doesn't believe me anymore at this point.

Its height reminded me of a giraffe exhibit at the zoo. I've watched hours and hours of "Bigfoot" footage trying to help me swallow that bitter taste it left in my mouth. I've come to the conclusion. The thing I saw must have been in its prime years, and if they have a hierarchy amongst Bigfoots, this one held one of the top seats. I noticed right off its black hair was clean, almost like it didn't belong in the middle of the woods. I don't know how to explain it. It had shiny hair and was actually well kept and maintained like it brushed its hair. I say this now, based on the majority of Bigfoot videos (hours and hours) I've seen and used the facts of what I saw and know was real to make a spot-on decision of what's real and fake of all the footage I've viewed. I can say without a doubt this was a bit larger 7-8ft, 100% 9ft or more, its head was in the trees and it was hunched over a bit.

It had intelligence, make no mistake, you could see it in the way its eyes looked at me, calculating. Was not even close to an ape or gorilla. This thing was a giant human with hair to put it simply. I was hoping to watch a video and just catch a glimpse of something similar to this.

I've seen the Sylvanian Bigfoot footage, and it wasn't that, and I've seen the Patterson video and wasn't that. It had a more human face, wide jawline. Mouth seemed lower than a human-like; there was a bigger gap from the bottom of its nose to its mouth. Its brow line was slightly protruding, but not like a Neanderthal. The face had no hair other than a beard that went all the way around the bottom of its chin. Its eyebrows were connected—a full line of hair across the underside of its brow-line.

I could understand someone not wanting to shoot because of the human characteristics, but that's not what stopped me that day. I can't put my finger on it to this day. But the look of it and how the odd feeling that came over me as I unknowingly got closer to it, felt like someone watching me. It knew I was there, and I believe it chose to let me see it.

When we both made that initial eye contact, it was a feeling of darkness, sinister, nothing in the realm of goodness. The surge of fear from what felt like it was part of a bigger plan, and I was smack dab in the middle of it. Kind of like when you walk into a room of people you don't get along with and you are the topic and nobody is saying nice things, and as you walk in, everyone stops talking and looks right at you. That's as close as I can get. I'll never ever be able to explain how demoralizing, humbled and at the same time worthless and feeble this thing made me feel. Your mental state who you might think you are curls right up in a ball and says, mommy. PURE FEAR. Instantly put my world into perspective and crushed my soul. At that second, you are a shell of a man, predator and prey.

It's changed everything inside me and how I feel about everything. That day will never go away; forever instilled in my mind's eye. I understand you wouldn't have any idea why something like this video for everyone to see could piss me off so badly. I am almost sorry to vent on you, but people like myself and others like me have had similar encounters and won't say a word to anybody, partly don't want to be laughed at because of videos like this that makes fun of the situation. Slightly still scared to death and even mentioning the ordeal brings you right back to that day. But mainly because they don't have the fuckin balls to stand up and say what happened and how bad it screwed them up mentally. Please don't insult my intelligence by saying this video is real. If you'd of seen what I saw, this upload would have never happened, not to mention this hairy guy here misses the mark by 3-4 ft, and I'd say 400-500 lbs and then some; hard to say.

Honestly, I rarely go public with this. I will tell anyone my story that asks me about that day. But for the most part, I keep that day bottled up. I will let you know, though.

It stared at me for 30ish seconds, and when I say 30, it felt like 30 hours. I still feel like I'm there when I recall that day or if I stumble across something that stirs a memory from that day. That 30 secs of my life can be remembered in such detail. Its eyes burned a hole in my soul. The way it was hunched over like it was going to jump towards me. It had the lowest, slowest growl I have ever heard in my life. Damn, I got chills writing that.

Steve Isdahl   The Day Sasquatch Became Real For Me   Copyright© 2020

There isn't anything I can't remember about that day. It's like it heightened my senses. Anyway, after it knew and made sure I knew it was my boss and I messed up by making the worst decision of my life that day by walking NW in the woods looking for morel mushrooms on Mother's Day trying to surprise my Grandma (she loves her mushrooms). It started to slowly turn its body as it took its first step away from me instead of towards me. It never took it's greenish-red odd colored eyes off me as the weight of the situation started to diminish. It was as much emotion as a person can take in 1 day believe me. It was like all the air was taken from me and then 30 secs later smacked in the face with a breeze. I should have played the lottery that day because I was extremely lucky to still be alive.

I got to see something like that up close and personal. It was unreal to me to see something that was so gigantic be so agile. It walked with flow; there was no jerk to its step. Its head did not bob up or down. If I hadn't felt its vibration and seen it walking away with my own eyes, I'd of swore it was floating with an attitude like "you're lucky to be alive. You punk ass human" for lack of better words. It walked away from me, staring back, stepping sure-footed away, like it knew the ground ahead of it and where it was headed. As it walked, I felt the ground vibrate from the weight of it walking away. It made me feel like I was supposed to feel it walking away instead of killing me on the spot, and that I was indeed lucky.

The growl it had continuously stayed low and didn't seem to stop till it turned it's back walking away. Must have lungs for days. That low sound it made kept me scared, and if I think about it, I can still hear it.

Lastly, my encounter was hands down without a doubt, the most horrifically scariest day of my life. I will admit the size and the all-around idea of it actually existing was breathtaking. I wasn't able to move or think until it was about 50 yards away or more. Even when my brain came out of backup mode, I still did not want to move. That's my story, and it's changed everything about me and took that 15-year-old boy right out of me. I grew up that day, not knowing up or down and rattled to my core.

Btw this happened in Brasstown, NC, IN 1986. I was 15, staying at my Gma and Gpas. Always played in the woods, and my Gpa taught me how to carry and use a gun when I was 10. He never let me leave the house without protection. I've always wondered if my Gpa knew about these beings and if that was the real reason, he taught me how to use and carry a gun at such an early age. That day the gun and I were both useless in every sense of the word. They literally lived in the sticks. A good mile from any neighbor and the woods circled my Grandparents trailer 5-10 miles in every direction.

It was really beautiful, but I'll say this now, looking back. Being that far into the woods, we (no-hair humans) are not in our element; we are in mother natures! To those who want to find a Bigfoot, Don't. To those that have, sorry. And I mean that.

-Thomas Harris

She Saw Two And Took A Picture

Hello Steve, my name is Patti Price. My father was a full-blooded Cherokee and believed in the old ways. He taught me all I know about hunting, fishing, and about the swamps, he told me always to keep my ear to the ground when in the woods; that was his way of saying know what's moving around you. To this day, I practice his teachings while hunting.

Now in 2019, I was hog hunting in south Louisiana with my son-in-law; he owns 30 acres behind his house. I had decided to walk back there to hunt one afternoon. I had killed a big bore a couple of days prior and dropped my phone in the creek. It was trashed, so I grabbed my iPad mini and stuck in my side leg pocket on my pants. That way, if I needed help, I could FaceTime someone, anyway I walked for a while and decided to sit with my back against a sapling. There was a group of pine saplings in-front of me. I could see where some hogs had been walking through.

I heard something big walking, and right away, I knew it was no damn hog! It was making a weird low humming sound and getting closer. I could hear the feet breaking suctions in the swamp. I had laid my 243 across my legs with one in the chamber. I went to get my iPad out, and that's when we locked eyes two female Bigfoots, one had a baby on her back.

Now, this is not my first run-in with these A*sholes, so I knew not to touch the gun! I slowly started pulling out my iPad, never losing eye contact. When I got it out, I pointed it in their direction. I glanced at the screen and took this picture. They never stopped walking. You can hardly see the other female because she's on the other side of the big one. I gave them some time to clear out, then headed back to the house.

That night, a male Bigfoot came up to the house and raised hell. He was hitting the house, trying to open the doors, and standing outside my bedroom window looking in. The picture of the footprint is at my bedroom window. These attacks were a nightly ordeal for weeks! Even throwing dead animals at the house, mostly birds. They have finally backed off, for now, anyway.

Hunters, y'all keep your ears to the ground when in their woods. If you read this, you can use my name. GOD BLESS YOU FOR ALL YOUR WORK.

-DIXIE MUD DIGGER

Florida Law Man Shares Story And Photos

Steve,

I've been watching your videos for a while now, and I like what you're doing. I also like and respect your D.I.L.L.I.G.A.F (do I look like I give a f*ck?) attitude. I'm a retired deputy sheriff, former Marine and also served in the Army Reserve. I have a very similar attitude. I also ran a small "mom and pop" outfitting business here in Florida for ten years. We provided hunts for wild hogs, turkeys, occasional deer hunts, gators, exotics and bow fishing. I've seen some pretty gnarly swamp and done my share of stupid shit over the years.

In late 2016 I was hog hunting in central Florida in a pretty crappy location. I've been in there before, and it was always creepy because everything down here will try to eat you, and most times in that area, you can only see five or ten feet in any direction. On several occasions, I had to use my bow to move water moccasins out of the way and find a path around a decent gator that wasn't interested in discussing who had the right of way.

I made my way to a marshy clearing about a half-mile into the swamp and found an excellent hog sign. I set my climber in a 25 to 30-foot pine tree. I was just high enough to see the clearing and have covered around me, about 12 feet off the ground. I was in the stand by early afternoon and intended to sit still dark when the hogs are most active in our area. About 5 PM I was watching several whitetail does that were about 70 yards north of me. They were feeding contentedly toward me, and my hog hunt was rapidly turning into deer hunt. Shortly before dark, the deer had closed to twenty yards, and I was trying to pick out which doe to shank. It was dead quiet, almost no wind, and I heard the most God-awful groan from behind me. It was SO freaking loud that I felt it in my chest! It was close, inside 70 yards. The deer broke camp as I've never seen deer run. No flagging, no bounding. Just OUT! Straight line, ears pinned back, tails tucked and about Mach 3. That pretty much told me that whatever I had just heard ate meat. Technically in my current location armed with only a longbow and three arrows, I felt like I was right in that meat group.

It took a few seconds to get my thoughts and my shit together, but I finally decided to take the deer's hint and un-ass the area. When I got to the ground, it was dark. I took my day pack and my bow, leaving my stand and hangers-on the tree. The groan was to my south, and my truck was somewhat northeast. I'd been walking for about three minutes and heard and felt the groaning sound behind me again. That's when shit got real for me. It was answered by an equally loud, higher-pitched whoop from in front of me. Whatever answered, the groan was between me and the truck.

At this point, I am really not liking this being surrounded. North and south were covered by those "things"; the east was super thick high ground and west was lots of water but more open. I went for a swim, circling northwest to the truck. I'd rather take my chances with the gators and snakes. I got to the truck pretty late, and the moon was up high. I found an enormous handprint on my truck's topper. It was super greasy. I didn't really know what to think of it, so I just got the hell out of there and went home.

I waited a couple of days and went back to get the rest of my gear. This time it was "full battle rattle," and I was going in prepared, short barrel 12gage and .40 cal Glock with extra mags. On the way into the swamp, I found big, deep tracks. They looked almost flat-footed. The tracks had almost no heel strike and pushed heavy off the ball. The stride was easily 45 to 50 inches and walking in line, like a heel to toe but full strides. When I got to my stand, I found two sets of tracks that met up about ten yards from my stand. All the tracks were either paralleling hog sign or in hog sign. I got my shit together and left.

I drove out a different way, looking along the swamp for more tracks and found them. I also found a mangled pig. The pig looked to have been forty pounds-ish. It wasn't shot, and its neck had been twisted around a couple of times. The legs were obviously pulled off, not cut or chewed. The hide appeared to be torn open and not cut. It had been pulled apart and eaten.

I've attached photos of the area, tracks, handprint and the hog kill. I didn't see "them" face to face. I don't care if I ever do. That's their swamp. It's almost 7000 acres without even a fire break in it—two and a half miles wide and over three miles long. I know what was going on out there and what I was in the swamp with. There is no way any human came two miles through that swamp to get behind me. No one came in behind me unless he or she was twice my 300-pound body weight and had 16 inches long, 6-inch-wide flat bare feet. I didn't leave anything in there. I need to go back and get it and haven't been back in there since.

I've told a few close friends, but this is the only "public" statement I've made. I know that tracks don't do much for you, but I have attached photos from my incident. You can use the story, photos and my name if they can be of help to you.

Keep up the good work,
Jack Dorton

Island Grow Op B.C. Sighting

The live show was excellent, looking forward to the podcast. The Trudeau comment was deadly, and I couldn't agree more.

I had a couple of encounters when I was younger and spent my entire life sharing these stories and getting ridiculed. A close friend of mine who once laughed at my story recently shared a story with me.

This story took place in September 2010 or 2011. A group that he was with was harvesting an outdoor grow-show operation on Hardwicke island just off the east coast of Vancouver Island near Sayward. The grow operation was a 30-minute hike from the beach.

He was cleaning up all the garbage from the recently harvested area, the group he was with took off down to the boat before him. He finished bagging up all the garbage and started making his way down the trail to the boat. He was probably 15-20 minutes from the boat when a large 9' male walked onto the trail in front of him, stopped and stared at him from about 40 ft. He told me the Sasquatch was more human than ape with dark eyes, dark brown hair and looked at him with an evil, angry stare. He felt the look was telling him to leave and leave now. The Sasquatch walked back into the bush opposite from where it came from, and my friend had no choice but to walk in the same direction and pass through that same area to make his way back to the boat. He blacked out from fear on the trip back to the boat.

Needless to say, this experience completely changed him, and he apologized for laughing me off when we were younger.

-L Fitzsimmons

Ohio Female Sasquatch Humming To Baby

Steve, my name is Jeff McComas. I am from the very southern tip of Ohio. I am an honorably discharged Navy veteran I served during the Persian Gulf conflict, and if you were to talk to anyone who knows me, they'd tell you that I do not lie about anything. In 1986 I had gone deer hunting in an old coal strip mine area that is now part of the Wayne national forest in Gallia County, Ohio. There have been many encounters with these things reported since the early 1800s in and around Gallia county.

Well, this is what happened to me; it was bow season 1986. I'm not for sure of the exact date. But I had scouted this area since early September. I built a few of the old-fashioned deer stands in a patch of woods that probably spanned two miles. In each direction, there were a few old strip mine roads and two old strip mine ponds. I tried to alternate between the tree stands going to a different one each day.

This day, I decided to go to the stand that was maybe 40-50 yards away from one of the old ponds. I got to the tree stand around 5:00 am it was still dark, cold, and foggy when the sun finally started to break. The fog started rolling back. I started hearing a buzzing sound, and I thought to myself there can't be any bees nest in this tree, especially as cold as it was. All of a sudden, I caught a glimpse of something out of the corner of my eye. I first thought it was a black bear, but as it broke through the fog, I made out what it really was. SHE was maybe 6'-7' tall and was carrying a baby one, and the whole time she was humming and looking at the baby.

I don't know if it was a newly born baby or if it was sick. But she walked to the edge of the pond, got a scoop of water in her hand and either gave it to the baby or wiped him off. But as quickly as she appeared, she turned and walked away through the thickest briar patch, and after that, I didn't hear the buzzing or humming anymore. I feel like that she was so into taking care of the baby one that she didn't notice me setting up in the tree stand.

This is probably one of the most uneventful encounters that has been sent to you. But it's absolutely true. They do exist, and I know it to be fact!

Again, my name is Jeff McComas, and I'm 53 years old, I have 12 grandchildren, been married to the same gal for 30 years, and a truly honest individual. Feel free to use my name and to tell my story, thanks!

Highway To Tofino, Again

Hi,

My story is directly related to a daylight sighting on Hwy 4 near the west coast of Vancouver Island.

One of my work associates was travelling to work (toward Tofino) at 9:30 am on April 12th, 2016. It was a typical dark west coast rainy day. He rounded a corner of Highway 4 near a bridge over a creek. As he was turning, he saw a large, dark figure running at high speed approximately 100 feet in front of him. He saw it jump from the center of the road and said he didn't think it touched down until it hit the right-side road bank (photo #1)

As he slowed his work van, he saw the subject standing at a tree line. Its shoulders were approximately four feet across. He said it was about eight feet tall, and he saw reddish hair mixed with black hair. It stood very still with its back to him. It was a dangerous corner with nowhere to pull his vehicle over. So, he slowed to a near stop. He called me that morning around 10:30 am when he got cell service back. (There's poor to no cell service after Port Alberni to near Ucluelet) He said he would investigate the area later that day after work.

He sent photo #1 of a muddy footprint later that evening. (iPhone photo)
I went to check the print about a week later. I measured the print with a tape (photo#2)
I set up two trail cameras. A week or so after that, there were three more prints by that time on the same westbound road bank. Nothing appeared on either of the trail cameras. I checked both cameras periodically.

April 28th, 2016, I had bought a high powered 50x optical 'Bridge' HD camera 1080i (60 FPS) 16 meg photos. On a hunch, I started recording the woods on the eastbound side only of the highway where my one trail cam was located. I zoomed way in to the woods and began panning back and forth, focusing on far away from trees and bushes. I recorded this area for about 3 or 4 minutes.

I then walked to the creek and recorded up the creek bed. There is a deep creek bed with many dark roots. I recorded this area for another three or four minutes in total. Moved away from the creek, then recorded a 2nd time up this same creek. Then I left the area.

When I got home, I checked the recordings and noticed something odd in the photo near this creek. I took a single photo from video-record mode and lightened the photo in a video editing program.
(Photo #3)

I believe that this is a Sasquatch. I have shown many researchers this photo. (Comparison photo) is important. The comparison photo (#4) is 40 seconds before photo #3.

Also, I should mention I have other subjects to show you but decided to start with this.

I do not like the negative opinion from the subject of Sasquatch nor the idiotic remarks of closed-minded individuals that you speak of on your channel. That was one big reason I did not share with the YouTube 'circus.'

You tell- it- like-it-is!! I appreciate this!!

Oh, and FYI I saw a younger, tall thin Sasquatch (with another person) in August of 2016 standing beside a tree in the same area ...I took a photo as fast as humanly possible (not well focused) ...But that is another story.
Thanks for the opportunity to share.

Cheers!
P Hetu
Nanaimo, BC

Short And To The Point, Washington

Hi Steve,

I live in SW Washington and do most of my hunting in the high cascades. Currently, 63 years old, and I have been fishing and hunting my whole life. Mostly archery, so tracking and reading signs is what I do.

I first found footprints back in '74 but wasn't until the late '90s in my hunting camp that things started to happen. I have been camping in the same spot since 1990, and to this day, I still spend the archery season there.

My first encounter up there was about three in the morning. The thing came in and peed on the front and back door of my army tent. Since then, every encounter aside from seeing the d*mn thing has happened.

Tree knocks so loud they wake you up. They push trees over, hoot, rocks placed on my kitchenette, rocks stacked behind camp, trees jammed into the ground upside down. Occasionally the hairs on the back of my neck stand up and alert me that something isn't right.

One night we packed an elk out and got back to camp a little after 3:00 am. Twenty minutes later, we heard the craziest language right outside the tent, which ended with a growl. So far, I have found tracks up there three times, one of which was about 20 inches.

From what I have witnessed, there is NO doubt of its existence. I think I will write a book, 'I Hate Sasquatch.'

Thanks for listening,
Colby

PS. So far, 3 in camp have seen it, and I don't care to! Keep up the good work!

Sandhills Region North Carolina

Hey Steve,

I live in Pinehurst, which is South-Central North Carolina, in what is called the Sandhills region. About 15 miles south is the Sandhills Game Lands. I like to duck hunt, but in this area, about the only ducks you can find around here are wood ducks.

So back in 2002, I was on my way to scout a creek bottom for beaver ponds when I saw one of these things. I had my Labrador retriever with me that morning, just letting him run around to burn off the excess energy he had before we got to the creek bottom. I was hiking near thick underbrush. To the left and the right of me were an open pine forest with broom straw and blackjacks scattered about the area.

My dog was running ahead of me; he would always stop and wait for me until I caught up with him. After he caught sight of me, he would continue on. As I got to the spot where I last saw my dog, he came back to me in a fast walk, not running. His hair was standing up along his back, ears pinned back with a worried look to him. As he came up to me, I called his name (Joe) what's up, boy? When he got to my feet, I looked up, looked to my left, then to my right towards the pines. I didn't see anything, but I noticed what looked like a burned-out pine tree stump that had been obscured a little bit by the broom straw.

Looking back down at my dog, I said, "what's up, buddy?" at that time, he jumped up on my right side. As I started to rub him, he was looking forward. Within a second of rubbing him, he lets out a low growl and jumps down and runs behind me. This makes me look up again. What I saw had just stood up from a crouching position. This thing was huge, standing on two legs about 8 feet tall, with broad shoulders and dark grey hair covering its body. I was stunned to see something this big, only about 30 yards away!

We stood there for about 2 seconds, looking at each other, and this thing took off running toward the thick underbrush. What was stunning is how fast this thing moved! Within two strides, this thing was moving at full speed and never slowed down as it hit the underbrush. The amount of noise from the underbrush was incredible. This thing was blowing right through it and never slowed down!

I listened until I couldn't hear any more noise, which was about ten seconds, maybe more. The only thing I could say was WHAT THE F*CK WAS THAT??? After about a couple of seconds, I began to shake with my hair standing on end. I turned around to get the hell out of there, and about 15 feet behind me was my dog, Joe. As he saw me turn around, he took off, never stopping to wait for me along the way, and was waiting back at the truck in the back corner of the dog box. So much for man's best friend! LOL! Anyway, on the fast walk back to the truck, at one point, I heard what a strange yell or yep was. I stopped, but never heard it again and couldn't pinpoint the direction. Since then, I have never been back to that area. I still hunt but not in that general area, and every time I go hunting or in the woods, no matter where it is, I always have that nagging thought about that day.

I have lived in this area for 50 years and never heard of anyone telling stories of seeing one of these things. Maybe in the smoky mountains, which is in the western part of the state. The only person that I ever told about this was my dad. And as guys do, they like to break your balls a little bit for fun. But afterward, he told me stories of the sighting in the Adirondacks of New York State near where he grew up.

Anyway Steve, thanks for taking the time to read my letter. Take care and be safe.

-Walt

Another Life Changed In Penn State

Dear Steve,

My name is Joe Lomeo, from Pennsylvania. I sent you this email earlier on, but it was short, and I didn't give you my name. I want you to share my name now because I know what I saw, and with so many people now giving their names, I feel ok with being in this group because these beings are real. I know you have our backs; we won't be laughed at.

My family leased 2200 acres back in the '70s through the '90s on a tract of land bordering Pennsylvania and New York. This event happened on the first Monday after Thanksgiving, 1993. We always went to our camp after Thanksgiving dinner. We would unload all our gear and sit our rifles in for the upcoming first week of the deer season.

My brother and I went out scouting and checking the deer stands to make sure they were in safe condition. We went into an area we never really hunted and found some really good signs. That night back at camp while sitting down to snack on more Turkey, we all let each other know what stand we would be going to. I told my brother, father, my two uncles, and cousin about the good sign my brother and I found and that I was going to head there in the morning.

This area was loaded with pine and fir trees along with a large pond and a dried-up old beaver dam. I headed out the next morning at 4:30 am and headed to the area, it's about a 30-minute walk from the logging road. When I got in, I sat in the area where I saw an excellent beaten down the runway between the pond and the side hill. I had a good hour and a half before first light, so I tucked into the pine tree I found the day before. The base of this tree was so rotted out, and I could tuck into the tree's perfect concealment.

The first 3 hours of light didn't produce any deer, and I decided to pour a coffee from my thermos. As I poured the cup, I heard something as if someone had stepped on a stick coming from my right. The ground was covered in light snow less than an inch. Steve, what I saw next made me feel paralyzed and frightened so much. What I saw was not a bear! No matter how hard I kept telling myself it was. This thing came from my right and turned going on a downslope towards the pond. It was then I picked up my rifle and put the scope on this thing. What I saw was a very human-looking ear, uncovered no hair hiding it. The head was very wide and had a slight point on top. The hair was dark brown, and the width of the shoulders was at least 4 feet across.

As it disappeared down the hill, it was then I started shaking so bad because I wanted to get out of there. I waited for over an hour before I got up and pretty much ran out to the logging road. When I told my family, they laughed and told me I saw a bear, I didn't push it, and I hunted the rest of the week close to camp.

I just want to tell you thanks for being a voice for all of us who will never be the same person while hunting again. It truly does change you when you see them.

Thanks, Steve.

Sticks And Stones In Ontario

Gday Steve,

I hope all is well. I would just like to say you live in one of the most mind-blowing places on the planet. My son and I took a road trip from here through the states up the coast through northern California, Washington state, to British Columbia. The back down through the province's home camping every night at state and provincial parks in 2017; 12,000 km in total. When we hit British Columbia, I wanted just to stay there.

I am now 54 years old and still-hunt whitetail down here in our back yard, so to speak—lots of eight and ten pointers on the wall.

When I was a young man, I spent every spring, trout opening in Northern Ontario. Near the Su. Our lakes were 3 hrs. back on old logging roads. No one but Natives and the odd fly-ins. Early May, we were the only ones there.

This spring was no different than any other. I was about 20 years old at the time. My buddy and I were trolling one afternoon close to shore as the lakes were feeding shallow just after the thaw, maybe 20 ft from shore. The old-growth timber was thick and very steep. We almost jumped out of the boat when a kerplunk 5ft behind the boat and soaked me! WTF, that was no fish jumping. I cut the motor, and then smelt something awful. "What the funk is that smell?" I said to my buddy. "Did you sh*t?"

We heard nothing. I thought right away it was a beaver flapping at us. My buddy said ponds or streams close, and that sounded like a 50-pound boulder hitting the water. We trolled up a mile or two then back as we were having luck. Again, roughly in the same spot, a 6-foot log 4 inches thick came out of the black forest at us. Again, that stench. We figured just a grumpy black bear was just waking up, and we pissed him off. We see lots up there.

After listening to your stories and others, I'm pretty sure it wasn't a bear. Bears can't throw sh*t; they tear shit up. We heard nothing. But we sure smelt something I can't describe. I've never really talked about it. But that encounter is etched into my memory as unexplainable.

Thanks, and good luck this year!!
Chris Rose

A Handful Of Experiences From Florida

I was born in Brevard Co., Fl, in 1950. I have lived here (except for 4 yrs. military) my whole life. From East to West is the Atlantic Ocean, the Intercoastal Waterway(brackish) then the St. Johns River. One of three rivers in the world that flows North from beginning to end until the '80s, because the river would grow in size from 200 feet to 2 miles wide. All that land was flood control. It could be fished, hunted (hogs), and frogs gigged all year.

West of the St. Johns was large ranches, farms and very large tracts of untouched land owned by corporations who left it open use. It was an outdoorsman's dream. My Dad, uncle and their friends were country people that gave nature every opportunity to give up what it wanted us to have. It was an all year-round event for them. They had milk cows, hogs, chickens, deer dogs, duck dogs, jeeps, airboats, outboards and all the stuff needed to have fun. My Dad started me young.

At 12 years old, I was trusted enough to go hunting with my Dad or my Uncle, with my bow or my 410.

At 13, I was turkey hunting when (what I was told later) must have been a panther screamed directly behind the tree I was sitting against. I froze and had never felt so small.

At about 14-15, I was with a friend in an 8 ft pram with a two hp outboard motor. We were trolling for speckled perch—every time we trolled by this one spot, we caught fish. We tried casting but got no hits. Troll by and catch fish. So, we just kept going back and forth. On one pass, I saw a big gator moving from the side of the river towards the middle. This gator was a lot longer than our boat, so I told my friend to slow and let him go across before we got there. He slowed, and the gator submerged. We were reeling in the jigs. Then all of a sudden, the gator tried to come over the front of the boat and slid off. It tried again and again as we were backing up.

Finally, on one of his tires, I picked up a 3 ft paddle and hit him as hard as I could on the nose. When he hit the water, he spun a 180 and knocked the front of the boat almost 90 degrees sideways. We both almost went out. As I was laying there half in half out with my face at water level and water pouring in over the side, I didn't feel as apex as I had a few minutes before.

Flash forward about ten years. The same friend that was in the boat with the gator and I decided to take my jeep out by Holopaw, Fl. to see if we could get to this hard to get to canal, to bass fish. We tried to get unstuck until almost dark, knowing we had a 5-6 mile walk to get back to the paved road. I knew if we angled East, we would hit the big flood control dike and have easy walking all the way. We had walked for about 45 min through the woods following cow trails toward the dike. Then we both heard a roar that, to me, sounded like a movie was starting. It sounded like a lion about 3/4 mile away. Hard to tell.

We walked about a mile, making good time up on the dike road. It roared again. This time it was half the distance and straight behind us not out in the woods. I had never heard a lion-like roar in the woods. Whatever it was, was trailing us at twice our speed. My friend said just to keep walking. We walked another 1/4 mile, and that thing roared very loud again about 50 yds back and on top of the dike. I immediately turned and shined my old flashlight behind us. No eyes. I shined both sides, slopes, no eyes.

I turned to ask or say something to my friend, and he was gone. He yelled, "Come on, hurry up." I did exactly that. When I caught up, he was about 1/2 way up a 10 ft high chain fence enclosure surrounding a spillway. When I got there, I turned to look to see if there were eyes. Then I put the light in my pocket and started climbing up the outside. All of a sudden, in the dark, I hear a total commotion going on inside the enclosure, and my friend is climbing back out.

Somehow, a 7 ft gator had gotten in there. I decided I'd rather be inside with the gator than hanging on the outside. When I climbed over, it was too much for the gator, and he bailed off into the spillway. We stayed there for about 20 mins listening and shining; and heard nothing. We climbed out the other side, walked the last mile and never heard that lion sounding roar again, to this day. But there was that less than apex feeling.

Flashback to 1963. My Dad comes home from work and tells me to get his headlight out of the boat. I went back into the house, and he had his shotgun and a box of shells on the table. This was not out of the ordinary for Dad and my uncle. My uncle walks in and asks me if my Dad had told me they were being deputies to be part of a posse. It seems there were some ape or gorilla running loose and scaring people out in Holopaw.

About 30 men hunted that thing for two days and nights; still nothing. They said it stunk so bad the dogs wouldn't trail it. Later, National Geographic did an actual investigation with hair samples and foot casts and determined it was what we call Skunk ape today.

Flashforward to 1980. My brother-in-law and I were squirrel hunting. We were about four miles West of the Lion Roar dyke and about five miles from Holopaw. We both had 22lr semi-autos. We were in an oak head when one squirrel decided to play, hide and seek. I told my in-law to walk around the other side of the tree, so one of us would get a shot. He had to walk around about a 6ft high 30ft diameter palmetto patch to get where he needed to be.

All of a sudden, he lets loose about ten shots as fast as he could. I hear grunts, the tusk sharpening chomping and palmetto crashing coming at me. The biggest wild hog I had seen in all my years in the woods came out 20 ft away, and he was mad. I did the same as my brother in law to turn him away from me. My in-law said it walked out of the palmettos about 5 feet in front of him, looked at him, and chomped his teeth. That is why my in-law opened up to him.
Now we had to deal with it. It was so big it never ran, just trotted. Probably 300-350 lbs. It went into a field that was open of trees and had patches of 3-4 ft tall palmettos all over. My in-law took off to get in front of it. I saw him stop and shoot another 8-10 times and start back towards me. I was standing on a grass path wide enough for a jeep. I figured by watching my in-law that it would cross that path about 50 ft away. I was going for a kill shot behind the ear. So, when he crossed the path, I only fired once.

He stumbled but kept going toward a little cypress head. I could see my in-law coming through the palmettos and ran to meet him. He reloaded again and started toward the cypress. I was putting more shells in my rifle when I focused past my magazine to see someone standing on the edge of the palmettos next to the path. It was about 50 yds away, just staring at me. There were still 2hrs of daylight left so I could see its eyes, nose, the mouth was closed, very short neck, couldn't see ears but maybe under thick hair. It had very wide shoulders, a thick chest and long arms. It had very little if any hair on its palms or bottom of feet. Its hair color was black with red tinges. I would guess about 7 ft tall based on the palmetto height he was standing in and probably double my weight of 200 lbs. Hard to tell with all the hair.

It stepped into the path. It looked at me, then just turned and walked away. I watched it walk 100 yards more down that path. Where it came from I, haven't a clue. I was looking at the field the whole time watching my in-law.

We killed the hog, but together couldn't drag it out of the cypress head. So we field dressed it right there and still struggled to drag it back up by the path. We could not pick the hog up. We even tried cutting down a tree to carry the hog between us, but it broke in half. We are both not weaklings.

We left the hog there and hurried back to camp to get our two friends and a buggy. We were gone 45 min at the most. When we all got back to the spot, it was gone. We took our friends to the cypress head to show them that it couldn't have come back to life and run away. The drag marks were there, but the intestines weren't. We walked back to where we had left the hog and started looking around. I noticed the pieces of the tree that broke in half, trying to carry the hog were gone. We found them down the path where it had walked out of the palmettos. They were put in a 'V' with the point facing the direction it took when it walked away from me. I knew nothing of bigfoot except I read they smelled bad, were hairy and big. I did know about making signage for travel. Who left the 'V,' and who was it left for?

That's when I told them what I had seen. They laughed at first, then went quiet. My brother-in-law never even smiled. He knew.

He now felt that less than apex awareness. I learnt at an early age; and was reminded of now it and then in my life. I think the awareness lessens the effect of inserting myself into ANY environment. BUT, also being cognizant that my arrival did not go unnoticed.

Glowing Eyes Out The Window

Steve,

I live in Monroe WI, 6 miles outside town on 70 acres on top of a hill, 1/4 mile from the road. I got a frantic call from my girlfriend yesterday at around 6:45 pm. She was home alone with our four dogs when they all of a sudden went nuts growling and barking at the front door. Hair up and all she said. She told them to be quiet, but they kept at it. When she went into the kitchen, something about 6 feet high saw her and began turning away as she snapped this picture.

I have a camera on the cabinet pointing at this window to watch the front-drive that has a ring of IR lights that are visible but do not reflect in the window. I stood where she took the pic with the lighting and did not see it. She said she also did not use the flash so she wouldn't reflect off the window.

There is a small tree there that could support a raccoon. She mentioned it sounded like somebody tapping on the house when this all started, and the same thing happened last week.

My beagle is currently in heat, so I thought maybe that had something to do with it.

Thanks for all you do,

Marko Bajic

Another One Never Flinched By Gun Fire

Hey Steve, I really appreciate the person you are and the attitude you have. I wanted to share my story with you. First off, I'm 25 I live in the central plains of America and have my entire life. So, I can fairly say I know what wildlife is here. I've heard of and seen the majority of it. I only state that to express later how blown away I was when my encounter happened. Now to my experience.

My brother (I don't want to name for his privacy) lives on a farm with his wife and daughter. I've had to help him take care of a few pests and mountain lions before, so when he asked for my help with what he thought was another mountain lion, I said, of course. So during the day, we looked around his land, trying to find tracks to see what we were dealing with; we found nothing. I told him I couldn't see anything and asked him if he was messing with me? He told me he was absolutely sure because of the sounds he heard the days before calling me.

I have to stop for a second to describe the area we were in. He has a built-in pond probably 30 yards away from a tree line, then on the opposite side of us is the house about 100+ yards away. We were about 15-20 yards away from the pond. Now, as I was explaining how I didn't understand that we didn't find any tracks, there was a loud splash in the water of the pond. He has no fish. I turned and pointed my Mossberg .30-30 at the tree line. My brother had his 870 Express Mag pointed in the same direction. We both exchanged the same look of 'What the hell was that?" Then he called out, "This is private property! Come out, and all is forgiven. No cops, no danger and no harm done." After shouting, he lowered his aim and put a hand in the air for good faith, and I lowered as well.

There was an odd silence for about 30 seconds. Then a scream I can only describe as something from Jurassic Park came from the tree line. I jumped and almost fell backwards, and I am not easily frightened. I aimed back at the line expecting a chorus of mountain lions to come out. My aim dropped when this human-shaped object came out of the tree line that had to have been well over 8 feet tall. My brother responded by calling out to the object that it has 15 seconds to clear off, or it will be fired on.

He started counting. By the time he hit six, it had begun walking towards us. We relaxed a little because we thought, "Oh, hey, whoever this guy is, is leaving." That thought left when it stopped and let out another yell. After feeling it in my chest, I knew this was going to end badly.

That thing charged us; the only thing we could do is hide behind our four-wheelers, run or attempt a fight. I have never fired all four of my rounds as fast as that day, and that thing stopped charging and just looked at us. Then just turned around and walked back into the tree line. We started the four-wheelers and drove back to his house, grabbed 2 of his AR-15s, a few mags and his dog Buckley then went back to the pond.

After searching the area with Buckley, we found zero blood. There were prints but no blood. My lever action holds four with an empty chamber. My brother's 870 Express Magnum holds four empty chambers. So four .30-30 and four slugs have no blood. How is that possible?

We both have no explanation, and yes, we are absolutely sure of what we saw. He took pictures of the prints, and he has yet to tell his wife of what we saw because he fears she'll mock him or leave him thinking he's crazy.

Feel free to share if you choose to and keep doing what you do for this topic. We need more people doing the work you do. As always, stay safe out there, buddy and happy travels.

-C

Mississippi

My name is Jason, I am 45 years old, and I'm from Southaven, Mississippi. I have been hunting and fishing my whole life.

One night myself and a friend of mine were driving to deer camp we had just turned on the gravel road that the camp house was on. As we came to a curve in the road, there was a sign posted about six feet up a tree. My headlights made the curve, and then I saw a dark outline of a man-like thing. It was at least two feet taller than the posted sign.

It slowly turned around the tree and disappeared in the darkness. I was totally freaked out and scared to say anything. I looked at my friend, and before I could say anything, he said, "what the hell was that?" I said, "I have no idea, but it was huge whatever it was."

We made it to the cabin freaked out and didn't want to tell any of the other guys. We just had to, though, and of course, they said that we were full of sh*t.

We both know what we saw, and to this day, still wonder what it was that happened. I've never seen tracks or got any pictures on trail cams, but I will tell you I know what I saw, and it wasn't an animal; it was not a man!

Road Trip Through BC Saw A 'Human-Like Baby'

Steve,

Hey, I just want to say thank you and thank god that i found you and your channel. i am so thankful for what you are doing. you are the only person on this planet that speaks the truth about this subject. you can use my name if you want i am, not afraid!

The bullshit out there on the subject is so deep, and the most recent on television expedition using algorithms to predict where a mythical creature might be... mythical? are you f*cking kidding me?

Most everyone on this planet is so preoccupied with iPhone, and computers, and have this self-righteous attitude. somehow, they have the perception that we, as a species are so smart. what will they say when they find out that there are people on this planet who are more advanced than us, on the evolutionary chain? maybe not in the realm of technology, but in relation to this earth.

We would no longer be able to use homo sapiens as the DNA baseline at the top of the scale. i can guarantee, if DNA were put against ours, it would tilt the scale in the opposite direction.

Like, for example... humans 100% (top of the scale) bonobo chimps 99.85% from human, regular chimpanzees 98%, great apes 97%, orangutans 94% etc.... if they included sasquatch DNA, it would say 115%... 15% in the other direction. my point being...why don't you place a human on a mountain at 10,000 feet elevation, in the middle of winter, with no clothes on and no tools? now tell me how long they would last. they wouldn't last more than 3 days. these people are far more advanced and in tune with the earth than we could ever be.

Now to my encounter. this is only the 5th time I've told this story to anyone outside of my family members. the four before you; I've almost been in fist fights with, and some i was talking to did not walk away cleanly.

It was May 1993. the end of my junior year in college at Arizona state university. my roommate and i had secured jobs on the Kenai peninsula, Alaska, through a good friend of ours, who had fished commercial salmon the year before.

My roommate secured his job with (jeff ransom) who owned the sites; he passed away the same winter in an avalanche. jeffs sites were on the mouth of the Kenai river.

I had a job fishing halibut for a 48-hour fish. the job was with Kevin Duffy, who was jeff ransoms brother-in-law. he referred me to Debbie naked, who owned set net sites just south of jeffs on the Kasilof riverside. I'm just giving you the background in case you wanted to verify, deb still lives there and in Hawaii in the winter.

We started our trek and arrived at the Canadian border in Vancouver. we headed on through whistler and the switchbacks, up 97 north, to Prince George, and then highway 16 west to hit the 37 Cassiar highway. on the map it was a single red line, which means a 2-lane paved road...not... it was 800 miles of 2 lane dirt and gravel.

So, headed north in my 2 wd 1986 Toyota pickup truck with 200,000 miles on it already. we stopped at Iskut BC to get gas and some food.

It was May 28, 1993, around 9 pm. i know this because i will never forget this day and what happened next. i go over it in my head daily. i can remember the scent of the forest in the air; a scent that i did not experience in Arizona. it was the smell of pure clean, freshly rained on forest, air.

When we pulled out of the gas station, i looked at my trucks clock, and it said 8:59 pm. the sun was on the horizon. i drove for about two miles and then pulled over to the side of the road because i thought i had left my wallet at the gas station.

After getting out of my truck i found it on the floor between my feet. i jumped back in and put it in drive. i was only going about 10 mph because i was turned halfway around putting my wallet in my bag behind me. my roommate in the passenger seat had his head down leaning forward, taking off his shoes.

As i turned and put both hands back on the wheel, i started to accelerate to maybe 25 mph. then about, i would say 75 yards ahead from the tree line on my right i saw what i thought was a grizzly bear at first glance, starting to cross the road. i was about to say "grizzly!" because at first glance that's what my brain said... another split second later as i took my foot off the gas, i saw something larger than a grizzly take its first 2 steps across the road, on 2 feet.

I basically froze as my truck rolled forward. the next thing i knew i slammed on the brakes, sliding a little in the gravel. my roommate who hadn't looked up yet, hit the dash and glove box with his chest and part of his face. i screamed, "bigggggg ffffoooootttttttt!!!!!!!!!" and came to halt.
My roommate looked up and went silent. he was staring straight ahead with eyes wider open than i had ever seen before. i looked back ahead and watched the 3rd and 4th steps. it never turned and looked at us, and we were at this time 40 feet from it. the funny thing is, it didn't look at us at all.

It was carrying a child in its right arm, which was high up on its chest. the child's upper torso was at her shoulder, and it was turned and looking right at us, peering back from behind the right side of her head. never took its eyes off of us the whole way across the road. her left arm looked very long as it dangled almost to her knees. when they entered the opposite tree line, i accelerated forward and slammed on the brakes where she went in and jumped out of my truck. My roommate said... "don't get out! what are you doing?"

But in saying that, he had already opened his door and was on his way out as well. i ran from my truck to the tree line and just stood there with my ears facing the trees. i heard not a sound; i stood there for five minutes in silence. i slowly backed away from the tree line, looked up and recognized the tree she went under; there was no way it was any less than 8-9 feet from the ground.

We got back in the truck and started driving. after sitting in silence for maybe two to three minutes, my roommate says, "did you see that?" i said, "yes, i did. did you see the child it was holding"? my roommate said, "that was a baby, a human baby." i said, "that was not a human!" he said, "no, i didn't mean it like that. i meant it looked like a human...what the f*ck!!!?????" when he said that tears started to come from my eyes. i had no idea why.

We drove in silence for the next hour until he said..."what are we gonna tell everybody?" i told him "i don't know I'm gonna tell everyone i saw a bigfoot and a baby." no one will believe us because people are idiots.

We started talking about the features of the child's face, the size of its eyes, and how it was looking at us. Then talked about the mother's height, hair color, and weight.
That whole summer in Alaska, every time i heard a noise in the trees, i would stop and just listen and eventually start shaking.

It changed my life forever. I've went over what happened in my head practically every day for the last 25 years. I'm ok with that because I've accepted it as a blessing and i embrace it. you've help make me now embrace it even more!
thank you for your channel!

Another Grow Op Encounter

I was in college, and every fall, I would drive to Warsaw, Indiana, on U.S. 30 to harvest marijuana that grew wild. Learning from past mistakes, I developed a system where I put a BMX bike in the car, then parked several miles away and biked in. I would strip the plants and haul trash bags to my extraction point, then drive back in daylight to a dip in the road and fill and go. I had this down to a science and only worried about alien abduction at that point in my life.

I had parked my car then biked in at dusk looking as local as possible. It was dark as I dipped into rows of corn to head back to the electric towers where I would topple and bag the marijuana. Going only a few rows in, I was walking comfortably when I smelled sure death directly in front of me. As it was dark, I kneeled down and flashed a small pen flashlight in front of me. There was a black and brown mass on the ground a few rows over. I clicked the light off. To my horror, I heard something come to its feet. I felt immeasurable fear and looked to my left to exit the corn when this thing snorted like a bull. I tore out to my left, knowing there were only a few rows of corn before an opening for the electric towers. I broke into the opening, but this thing was on my ass, and I knew it was going to overtake me. Just as I went to jump a small creek, it plowed me over.

I woke up, and it was daylight, meaning I had laid there for eight hours or more. I was literally pushed into the mud and had a hard time getting myself out. I wandered out to where my bike was and must have had a concussion as a school bus drove by, and children were looking out the windows at me. Knowing I was seen and the driver surely called me in, I got out of there.

I was so disappointed at not getting my weed. My fraternity brothers were sure I was run down by a buck and encouraged me to go back the next weekend before the first frost. I did return and parked far away and rode into my extraction point and hid the bike. Wary of walking in the corn, I went straight down the opening towards the electric tower. I had only gone a few yards past the spot I woke up in the week prior when I heard a radio squelch. I stopped and looked up at the tower. There was a man about forty feet up it, and I tore into the corn as he said, "he's running north." I realized I was surrounded by many men. I would drop and lie still, and I could hear them being guided to my location by the guy on the tower. They would get close, and I would tear off and drop again. I did this several times before they caught me. They had my bike, backpack and cutting tools etc. I was trying to act like a local and do anything not to admit why I was there or that I had a vehicle several miles away. After some pretty aggressive treatment, a State trooper pulled up, and a man got out and walked right up to me and said, "I found your car." I knew I was getting busted right there, but he pulled me up and walked me towards the tower the man was in.

It was dark, and I was getting alarmed, especially when I realized there were 12 or 15 men right where I had woken up the week before. This man pushed me right into the dried impression and said perfect fit. He then rolled me over and said, you either talk to us and quit the bullshit, or I'm going to throw the book at you with all my authority. Of course, I said I'm here to pick weeds, but he pulled me off the ground and walked me a few feet towards the corn and said, "I want to know what happened in there."

He was pointing into the rows exactly where I ran into the hairy smell on the ground. He looked right into my eyes and said I know you were here last week and something happened to you and I want to know everything. I told him about my system and how I had done this many times without ever being detected. He pulled me into the corn and at the spot I was standing before I ran, they had all the corn pushed down, and you could tell many men had been back in there. I told him my frat brothers' theory about being run down by a buck, and he kept going over and over it repeatedly asking about what I saw. After what seemed like hours, this man walked me back out to the road, and the State cop was still there. He walked me to the back-passenger door and opened it for me and motioned for me to get in.

As the State trooper was pulling away, he turned to me in the back seat and said I am a lucky young man to be walking away from this. I wasn't sure if that meant I wasn't going to be charged until he pulled up to the place my car was and stopped his car. I got out as instructed and saw my bike and backpack were next to my driver's door. He then said to me, "what happened to you out there"? I said I don't really know.

This happened just west of Warsaw, Indiana, in the US. 30 ....I would ditch my car at a place called the Pickin Patch and bike North to county road 600. The year was 1989.

Terrifying On Vancouver Island

Hello Steve,

I'm Terry Vibert. My background at the time was a former employee of Aeroguard Group in Pre-Board Screening Security as a Supervisor at YVR Airport for ten years. My story is quite vivid and freaking scary. It happened while I was on a mini-vacation in the year 2000 at Rathtrevor Provincial Park on Vancouver Island during the summer. Exact date I do not recall.

I was car camping. Yeah, I know about bears, so I didn't leave food in the car. The car was a white Chevrolet Cavalier sedan formerly owned by BC Tel. The back seat folded down and exposed the trunk, and there was just enough room with front seats pushed forward to sleep back there with a foam cushion and comforter and pillow.

The first night I went for a stroll through along the road to the beach. It was quiet there except for sounds of pebbles rolling around the beach as though something big was moving there. I didn't investigate but took in the milky way stars that were out that night and a small airplane circling around the sky. I began to return to the park where there were a lot of campers in the park that night and had lots of campfires and cookstoves burning as I saw the steam rising from the flames.

I then headed from the beach back to my car, which was parked near the caretaker's house with a white light atop a pole over the backyard. My car was in a stall next to a fifth-wheel trailer to the west of my car. The house was to my southeast, the showers were further east midway through the park & the beach was halfway across the park to the far east.

So, here's the frightening part. It was the wee hours of the next morning. I heard the unmistakable sound of footsteps booming through the forest. I woke up as the sounds were deafening and saw a man-like ape creature in all black walking on the gravel road from east to west right past my car! It was f*cking fifteen feet tall. It was just like the Patty film or the Paterson movie on Bigfoot, except it was a male as its chest was bare. It walked right past me to the west then stopped.

At that time, I ducked down under my comforter. Then when I heard no sounds, I picked up and saw it look into my stall area. Then it moved back in front and stopped and stood right behind my car. I was freaking out scared shitless. It then backed up to survey the area looking for me! There was no tent. Then I noticed its eyes; they were glowing red. Then it looked down and spotted me. My jaw dropped, and I was in awe, and I tried to scream but couldn't, and it mimicked my face. Its look of fear then turned to anger as it glared at me. It had buck teeth like a horse and a mouth as a human with a tongue. Its face was hairless, but it had a cone head and all black. It looked to be 15 feet tall. Its feet were sideways to me before when it was in my stall as it bumped the bumper with its legs below its knees. I estimate it had 24-inch feet, which were too bare up past its ankles. It had human-like feet. But its walk was dragging like as I estimated it was around 2,000 lbs.
It continued to glare at me, and I had a Pentax camera ready but didn't take a picture because it was angry. It never made a sound from its voice but walked past my car into the bushes between my car and the fifth-wheel trailer.

Next, I heard a man scream, "please help me; it's going to kill me!" As he ran into the trailer as it shook violently back and forth.

Then it was all over. PS Note its chest was at least two upright pianos wide, with thick shoulders and arms and hands as wide as a car door with palms bare and fingers four inches wide and 18 inches long. It was massive in stature.

(2nd email)

Hello Steve,
Please don't get offended or add WTF, but I wanted to add how this creature walked off away from me. I must add that I shook my shoulders and partially got up while still laying down on the bed, bracing myself with my elbows to take a look at this creature better.

Just as I shook my shoulders, it flexed and shook its shoulders back at me. Then in a few short steps, it proceeded to come really close to me. It was lowering itself down on all fours. Its head came right up to the back window glaring at me with buck teeth. It then moved to my left against the passenger side; its upright head filled up the entire window with its face!

I grabbed my crotch so as not to take a p*ss. The look on its face was one of bewilderment as I saw its eyebrows slant upward like an angled roofline. Then I hid next to the comforter, and it turned and walked away upright past my car.

I vowed never to camp again, and for the last 19 years, I have done just that. I never felt so alone and helpless as I felt that night. It's been a struggle, and I had nightmares for the longest time wondering if that creature would come back to haunt me by sticking its head against my bedroom window at night again. Just knowing I'm safe in the suburbs relaxes me now.

If you want to add this tidbit, so be it, Steve.

It Climbed Onto His Machine

Hi, how are you doing? First of all, I love your YouTube channel, and you may not know it, but you help people by getting them talking about our Sasquatch encounters. It helps us get this stuff off or chest. I am a 42-year-old Native Secwepmec from Chase BC, Canada, in the heart of the Shuswap. I have been hunting and fishing my whole life. I have been a logger for 22 years. I have had two encounters with these hairy men called Bigfoot.

Encounter Location: Spences Bridge BC
I was harvester for a logging contractor for a couple of weeks. During the night shift, I would usually show up at 3:00 pm and cut trees till 2:00 or 3:00 am. I was geared to go to work, and my boss called me and told me not to bother coming in to work. They were having problems with the alternator on the harvester and that they were trying to get one from Finning in

Kamloops.

The next day, my boss got a hold of me to let me know it was ok to come in and the machine had been fixed. Oh, I would like to say that when I worked in this area, I always had that uneasy feeling like being watched, especially when I serviced my machine.

My shift had ended at 2:00 am that day, and I headed to my truck. I was cutting in an area about 2 km from where my truck was parked. At about midnight, my machine started to lose power. The hydraulics were running sh*tty, and my lights were starting to dim. I was like ah f*ck the alternator is f*cking up. So, I tried to drive my machine back to my truck. Only made it a couple hundred yards until it died, no power at all.

Then I figured I would just walk until I realized I left my light in the truck. There was no way I was going to walk out of the bush with no light what so ever! You know how it is trying to walk over fallen trees on the ground, especially at night. You could get hurt. So, I decided just to put my seat back and sleep in the harvester instead. It seemed like I was sleeping forever when I heard a loud thud on the back of the machine. Right away, I just froze. My mind started racing, thinking about what that could be. I'm in the middle of a logging block with no trees around me. So, it could not be a branch or a stick falling from a tree.

Still frozen in fear for what seemed like forever, I hear a sound on the right side of the machine. It is the sound that I am very familiar with. The noise I heard sounded as if a person stepped on a car hood, and the hood pressed down. As I heard this, my face turned numb, and my blood got cold.

I am familiar with this noise because I've stepped up on the machine and walk on the hood to check the oils and antifreeze. I am like what the f*ck could be walking up on my machine in the dark? Could it be a bear or any other critters? I know it takes a certain amount of weight to push the hood down to make that thud noise.

I am still frozen; I can't move or start the machine. So, I think fast, and I turn the key to put the light switch on and look out the back window. I heard a loud 'thud' noise. The sound reminded me of how if you throw a bale of hay out of the barn and it hits the ground. Not even a second after, I could just see through the late-night mist, with my machines dim light. I can make out a ripped, black, harry, being running away. Holy f*ck, I almost sh*t my pants!

After I settled down and figured out what just happened, I looked at my watch and still had three or four hours until the day shift crew showed up. There was no way I was not getting out of the machine. It seemed like forever sitting there wondering if that the Sasquatch was watching me from a distance or if it left.

At about 3:30 am, I saw the light of the day shift crew coming over the mountain into our logging block. I was so relieved, and not long after that, my boss drove out to me in the skidder. He saw my truck parked on the landing and no machine and put two and two together and figured I was breaking down. I know what I saw that night, and it scared the sh*t out of me. I don't know what was worse, having that thing on my machine or waiting and wondering what was next after the encounter or waiting for the day shift crew to save me. I quit that job that morning and never worked night shift alone ever again.

My people have known these beings exist. Well, you know the story. Every time I go to work in the bush, I always do a tobacco or food offering, talking and praying to these beings, telling them that I need to work and feed my family and to leave me alone.

I also had another close encounter when I was 16, in Keremeos, BC, on the Chopaka Indian reserve, but I'll save that for another time.

You can use my name if you want, don't care what anybody thinks, or if they believe me or not.

Until next time,
Jay

Night Hog Hunting, It Tore Its Head Off

Steve,

My name is John Townley. Here's a little background on me. I am 38 years old and live in central Florida. I have been an avid outdoorsman and hunter since a very young age. Both my grandfather and my father started taking out hunting by age 8. At an early age, I fell in love with the outdoors and spent every available minute hunting, fishing, camping and anyway I could to be in the woods. My family has a very successful family-owned and operated business that my grandparents started in 1953.

About 20 years ago, we started leasing property just outside a small town called Morgan in southwestern Georgia. About ten years ago, the wild hog population went crazy there, and they were causing the farmers and landowners an immense problem. So, I found another way to spend time in the woods and this one gave me access 24/7/365, and that was hog hunting.

So that you know, I'm not one of these guys that goes anywhere and everywhere just to pull the trigger to kill shit. There are very few things that I will kill that I don't eat, and those are primarily coyotes or predators and pigs/hogs. Hogs are invasive and cause an amazingly ridiculous amount of crop damage every year. I have spent uncountable nights from dusk till dawn crawling around the woods, fields and swamps of Georgia. I use a handheld thermal unit to spot and find pigs and stalk up to them where I then switch to an AR-style rifle chambered in .308 with night vision to start shooting.

As a side note, this is more like pest control than hunting, but some people don't understand why we are trying to control the population of the pigs. I typically have someone with me just for safety as I also shoot suppressed, and the first round that hits the pig is louder than the report of the gun. One night in early February, a friend of mine and I was doing some night hunting, and we walked into a field where we saw approximately 20 pigs. Eight of these were very large, with two that stood out as the biggest, which were most likely the boars. We started off about 350 yards away as the hogs were about 50 yards out into a field. I know this area very well, and the woods behind them was a large swampy area. We stalked to the downwind side and got within 50 yards of the closest pig.

At this point, we got our rifles up on our shooting sticks, and each picked out one and did a countdown. One of the largest was on my right and the other closer to the rear of the bunch. We did a countdown, and the shooting started. I dropped one large pig and went for the other large boar that was close to the wood line. I shot him several times with a 150gr bullet but didn't stop him. My buddy had killed 4 of the other pigs, and as we gathered them up into one spot, we could hear this other one that I had shot squealing just inside the woods, so after gathering the others, we decided to go in and finish him and drag him out. At this point, I switched back over to thermal. My buddy kept his night vision on, and we slowly entered the wooded, swampy area. I could hear the boar growling and making noise but couldn't quite see him, so we kept moving slowly closer.

At one point, we stopped so I could scan, and to the left of where I could hear the hog, I saw something moving rather quickly, but I couldn't tell what it was. I thought it was probably just a white-tailed deer that we jumped. We went another 30 yards or so, and I spotted the large hog approximately 25 yards away from us when all of a sudden it spun looking to our right, which was 180 degrees from how it was laying. It started really growling and making some really vicious sounds that a hog can usually make when threatened. I quickly scanned with the thermal that direction, and what I saw next still makes the hair on my body stand on end. There was a creature or being that stood approximately 9 to 10 feet tall and very man-like just way larger and had longer arms. Still, you could tell it was built very muscular and hairy.

I whispered to my buddy, who was literally right next to me to raise his gun and look through the night vision as I started doing the same. When he got his rifle up, I could hear his breathing get faster and faster, and it was at that point I also was looking at this creature through the night vision. At this point, the creature was approximately 40yards away from us and was focused on the wounded hog. My buddy said, let's shoot it, and I said to wait it's looking at the hog, and as I said that, it looked directly at us.

I had an IR light on my gun which helps the night vision when there is little to no light, its eyes glowed as it looked at us, and then it let out a noise that almost made me crap myself and pass out, but I thought I have a semiauto 308 Aires at this thing. All of this happening in less than a couple minutes and what happened next was the most disturbing. As I switched my safety off, it looked back at the hog and moved towards it, and when I say moved in like two large jumping steps, it was over top of this pig and had a hold of it with both hands. The hog struggled for a second before this creature, with one hand, ripped its head from its body.
As it did this it let out another crazy noise like an aggravated brown bear growling, it dropped the body and tossed the head with the other hand and at this point headed for the field where

we came from, and yes it made noise going through the wet, swampy area but not like what a man would. My buddy and I stayed still for a minute till we could no longer hear anything moving. It was at this point we decided that if we saw it again, we would have no choice but to protect ourselves, but I think we were both in shock at this point.

We slowly moved back to the field, where we started scanning with the thermal the whole time seeing nothing until we got back to where the field was. The four hogs that we put in one place had been dispersed or thrown apart approximately 50 to 60 yards. Two of the smaller ones (150 pounds) were ripped literally in half, and the other two (200-250 pounds) were beheaded, and the largest one that I shot had been torn and ripped and thrown.

That same night over a half-mile away from that location, we spotted another group of hogs from the truck. We shut the engine off and stepped out to get on shooting sticks when from the woods in the distance came to that same hair-raising awful sound; we both jumped back into the truck and started it. The weird thing is that the group of pigs had run closer to us and bunched up into a group facing the woods. We didn't stay to see what happened. We just hauled ass outta there back to the house where we were staying.

Since this, I cannot get my friend to go with me anymore. I still go because this creature's intentions were not clear to me as if he was just there for the pigs or us. I will not go alone anymore, either. Thank you for sharing the stories on YouTube as I have only shared this twice only to be laughed at and ask if I was drunk.

Thank you so much for letting people like myself share their stories with others that have had similar encounters.

My Reply Email

John,

Thanks for the message. I am no stranger to cleaning up hogs as I have shot hundreds over the years at a close friend's place in Alabama. We use 308 with thermals as well as night vision. Did the thing give off a good heat signature?

You mentioned hunting another spot the same night. Was this after you saw it? And if so, how the F does someone do that?

Thanks again,
Steve

Johns Reply Email

Steve,

 Sorry, it has taken me a few days to get back with you, but to answer your question, the thermal signature I'll describe much like an animal with hair like a bear or coyote or wolf. Its face and head were very white as well as its hands and midsection, I guess, like the groin area. The rest of the body did put off heat. It was just a lighter color white, as I'm sure you understand since you're familiar with thermal. The little that I saw through the NV was definitely hairy, so that all makes sense to me as far as the thermal.

 And yes, I did continue to hunt that night. I just moved to an adjacent property, and we decided only to shoot if the hogs were in range, and we would clean them up the next day because neither of us wanted to go crawling back through the woods that night. That night did scare the shit out of me, but I'm not going to let it stop me from doing what I love. I have spent thousands of nights in the woods, many of them by myself and this is my first time seeing this thing. Also, it knew we were there, but after seeing how quickly it moved and not to mention the strength that's required to de head and or mutilate hogs of decent size if it wanted to get us or hurt or kill us, it could have with ease.

 I don't really know, but I think all the noise from the winded high is what drew it to the area. Also, the next morning when we went back to the area to remove the carcasses from the field, some of it was missing. I know this is just speculation, but I wonder if that thing returned and took the hogs as food?? It could have been coyotes as well though usually, they leave the carcass and just eat off it where it lays.

 I know you spend a lot of time in the mountains and areas where these things have been seen and yet you still go to these areas, and my situation is similar. I did look the next morning at the field's edge for tracks, but it had been really dry, and the clay was like concrete. I was able to make out what looked like a large toe and heel marks, but they were not very defined. If you have any more questions about this, please let me know also I'm curious if you have received any other stories from the southeast US, like Florida, Georgia, Alabama.

 On another note, I have always wanted to go to your area to hunt, specifically wolf, grizzly, Elk, and or whitetail/mule deer. If you offer and guide these types of hunts, please let me know as I would love to come up and do some backcountry hunting with you

 Thank you again for the content that you continue to put on YouTube as I really enjoy all your content and stories.

Be safe, and I hope to hear back from you soon.
John Townley

Tough Ex-Marine Says He's Not Going Back Ever

Just a share of something of my past. When I was in my early thirties, my uncle, and I were sitting by the lake fishing one night just talking like we always did about something and nothing.

That night I asked him when he was going back out west elk hunting that year; he said they weren't going back to that place ever again! I asked why?

Now my uncle was a very tough Ex-Marine who wasn't scared of anything in life. He spent too much time in dirt and mud in places and situations most people would never dream of—some of those stories he did share with me over the years. I had total respect for the man! But anyway, it took a while, but what I got from him was this. The fall before they were in the mountains packed in, himself and one of his hunting buddies were hiking into their spot. They came over a bluff, and first a smell so bad it almost made him sick. Then the feeling he used to get when he was in the Marines in a hot spot and something was about to go wrong. Then his hunting buddy said WTF is that? He spun around, and behind them on the trail about 50 yds, back was a figure very big and very tall.

They didn't freeze because of their service training. They held their ground and didn't make any moves that would be taken as aggressive. This whatever it was stood there and looked at them for under 30 seconds, but it felt like an hour and then it disappeared into the brush.
It spooked the hell out of him. He said I know what it was, the only one I've ever told this I'll never go back there again!

Then he said something that I think fits one of your videos. You said a fight between good and evil is going on in this world! He said boy remember these two things Fallen Angels and Giants one day that's the fight we will all see. It's not much of a story; it's just a share from one open-minded individual to another and thank you for the time you spent reading it and keep posting my interest will never stop!
-John

Something Is Living In Vietnam

Steve,

I was at Fire Support base Bastogne. West of Hue in 1970. They would have 3 of us go outside the perimeter over a hill that we could not see past and spend the night in a hole with a radio then come back when it got light out.

We would take turns staying awake and watching the tree line—a couple of hours before daylight. A dozen monkeys come by, then I realized two people are walking behind them. Thought it was game over—no time to react. I looked and did not see any weapons. Realized they were covered in fur. I calmed down and watched these two walk by. They were close, not over 15' away, walking left to right.

My impression was a couple, a male and female, with the male closest to me. They looked to be 5' and 4' 6" tall. Healthy looking. Real fluid walking, with a no BS look. I couldn't see much of her. They were looking forward to it. If he had turned his head, he would have seen me. She was beside him and was blocked by his body. I wanted to see her really bad; it was all I could do not to whistle and get them to stop. Not the time and place to be messing around. Never told anyone about it till years later when the Internet came out, and I read about rock apes.

Good, Great, Awesome story's you have on YouTube.

Thanks,
J Sloboden

It Spoke At Me And Was Angry

Hi Steve,

Something I do to deal with stress is to write a story about these issues or events. The majority of this story I composed a while ago. You probably have heard lots of similar stories to this, but for what it is worth, here it is. Sorry if this is a little long.

I would like to start by saying I am a person that loves hunting, fishing and the outdoors. I have spent the majority of my life as an amateur adventurer. I am now retired but worked at the same job for 40 years. My staff, coworkers and most of my superiors came to me to share stories and concerns or as a sounding board because I always try and see all sides of an argument and usually can work towards a win-win conclusion. I am a very rational person, so why do I have three memories while out in the bush that I cannot explain, and why do they haunt me to this day?

The first time I can remember being afraid in the bush, I was with my family, and we were staying in a little campground beside a stream located about halfway between Canmore and Banff. Sadly, the campground is no longer there. I was 12 or 13 and already very comfortable on my own in the bush. There was a well-worn trail that followed the stream back up the mountain, so I decided to take the hike to see what lay back there. I was probably about 20 minutes in and the bush was lush, green and very thick, but I also noted, very quiet. All of a sudden, it was like someone was talking to me. No sound, but an energy was coming from just up ahead, and I could clearly hear words in my mind, something telling me that I was not wanted there! I remember thinking, what or who are you? I received an immediate response; "LEAVE NOW"! The energy was dark, and it terrified me. I turned and ran back along the path. About halfway back, the energy was gone. It left me with a lifelong memory.

I was now in my early thirties and bow hunting elk in a mountain valley running east from Meadow Creek in BC. It was closer to the end of the day, and I was starting down the mountain heading back to camp, trying to be stealthy, walking along about halfway down the mountain when there was a wave of energy that hit me like a brick. The energy was very dark, and it scared me. At this point in my life, not much scares me. But that did so I forgot about the hunt and took off at double pace. After about a 1/4 mile farther down the mountain, the energy was gone. I remember telling myself, 'What in the hell was that?' Ironically about another 1/4 mile farther along, I did have a grizzly bear encounter with a mother and cub that I managed to talk my way out of (but that's another story).

Late that night, I replayed the events of that day over and over in my head, and it finally struck me that I remembered that same energy from the trail walk when I was young. It was like you would remember a nightmare!

Now I was in my late 40's and elk hunting along the North Saskatchewan River in the Fort a la Corne forest reserve in my home province of Saskatchewan. It was a very cloudy day with the threat of rain, and after hunting along for about 3 hours, I came upon a huge hillside of blueberries and decided to sit down for a while and have a snack. I must have been crawling around for the better part of a half-hour or so just enjoying the fruits of nature when boom, it hit me again! I know that dark energy. I jumped up and spun around. I saw nothing, but there was no mistaking the thoughts and feelings. This time I was determined to stick it out, thinking that this was all in my head? I could feel where the energy was coming from, so I surveyed the area closely. What I could see was a very bright spot of light on a bush. This was very unsettling as there was heavy cloud cover. After what seemed to be an hour but probably only minutes trying to face my fear, I heard a heavy thump to my right, I looked over towards the sound but could see nothing? I looked back again to where the energy was coming from. The spot of light had moved. I heard a second thump to my right again but much closer this time. Looking over, I saw a large bowling ball-sized rock rolling to a stop in the grass. Now that was tangible evidence that something was not OK! I could no longer see any bright spots of light but decided that there was something definitely wrong there and backed out with my rifle at the ready. Again, little ways down the trail, the energy was gone.

Thinking about these events have led to many sleepless nights. How do I come to terms with these memories? The only thing I have to go on are the thoughts and the feelings of the (so called) energy. But now to add to that the spots of light and a couple of rather large rocks (I think where) thrown! How do you rationalize all of this?

Now in my 60's I still hunt and love the outdoors. Always eager to learn something I may not know or hear stories from fellow outdoor enthusiasts, I started to follow your YouTube channel. Then the topic changed. I approached the Bigfoot stories with skepticism, but then elementals of the stories started to fit for me.

I want to thank you for your efforts.
Larry Brower

A Different Kind Of Experience From The U.P.

Hello Steve,

I have a couple of experiences to share. I'm from Marquette county in the upper peninsula of Michigan. I was 12 years old at the time of the first one. About 5 or 6 friends and I were in the neighborhood we grew up in. We were on a dead-end street that was up on a high ridge, and I was looking across a gully at another ridge that was about a 1/4 mile away. I noticed a dude jogging along the hillside, which was strange because there's a trail at the top, and where he or it was jogging, it was steep, rough terrain covered in leaves from the hardwood trees.

I pointed him out to my friends and said, "Hey, look at that dude in the white jogging suit over there." It was all white from head to feet, hands everything, white. We all just thought it was a dude jogging until we saw it leap up a ledge that looked impossible for a person to accomplish. At that point, we all started saying, "Holy sh*t, did you see that? It's a bigfoot!"

We all ran up the ridge we were on so we could keep sight of it for as long as possible. That thing covered some serious ground on some nasty terrain like nothing. After about 5 minutes of watching, it finally crested the hill, and we lost sight. The next day after school, we went to the ledge. It kept up to see how high it was, and Steve, if I'm lying, I'm dying, it was about 8 ft tall! That was confirmation enough that that wasn't some dude in a white jogging suit, but had to be a Bigfoot.

The second sighting happened about three years later. I was around 15 yrs. old. My two friends and I were sitting up on a power line ridge smoking cigarettes and shooting the sh*t, and about 400 yards away, I noticed a tree that looked like a dude squatting down looking at us. I pointed it out, and we all chuckled about it because it did look like someone. (A week or two prior to this, a dog from the neighborhood we lived in went missing.) Well, all of a sudden, that dog or one that looked just like it shows up by that tree and starts bouncing in circles around it and we all look at each other like wtf? And that solid brown tree stood up straight turned away from us and walked straight into the tree line. Again, we all at the same time, said, "it's a bigfoot!"

Its mannerisms were weird. It didn't even look at the dog. It just turned sideways and walked away, arms a swinging, with the dog following right behind. It never looked back. That dog never did return home to its owners, and we didn't mention seeing it either.

Thank you for doing what you do, and God bless da Yooper. Yooper is what they call us folks from the U.P. (Upper Peninsula of Michigan)

Strange Lights Scaring Hunters

Hello Steve,

I really appreciate and enjoy your hard work on this subject. I am 32, and I Grew up in north-central Oklahoma. I now live in southwest Kansas. I have hunted whitetail for several years but mainly spent my outdoor time fishing for big catfish and anything else that swims. I have not visually seen one of these beings, but I have had numerous unexplainable things happen.

My two trusted best friends, and I went on an evening hunt for whites, as we often did. We all had set up long distances from each other on probably a 700-acre property (I know small). We didn't succeed that evening, but that's neither here nor there.

We all walked out past dark to my truck. I was first to make it back and had already witnessed crazy green "orbs" moving through the woods....No way was it a human with a light or an animal's eyeballs reflecting. The first of my buddies to return reported the same thing. He and I were waiting for the 3rd of us to come in, and we both witnessed the lights 500 yards away. When our 3rd came walking up, he was shaking. He is a brave, tough dude, so I knew something was amiss. The first words he said were something like, "did you f*cking see that shit?!" We all concurred that yes, we had.

I have heard unexplainable screams while camping in the same patch of woods, seen broken trees etc. It is coincidentally ancient Indian ground.

If you would like I can do a better shorter rendition of my accounts but as you would say "there ya go" thanks Steve keep fighting the good fight

-Paul Hanger

New York And Red Eyes

Hello Steve. I'm sending this story without much apprehension because it is the truth. I lived in a small town 50 miles south of Buffalo, New York, where there's a lot of hills and extremely woodsy. The road that my folks lived on is seasonal and, at the time, one of three houses. At one point going down the road, it kind of bottlenecks, it winds sharply, and there is a real deep ravine on the west side for about a half-mile down the road.

Anyway, right before that part of the road, there was an old farmhouse that had collapsed, but the old wooden machine shed approximately 30 ft long, and 15ft wide was still standing. A couple of guys and I that lived on that same road were out on a bike ride that day because 35 years ago that what we did before the internet, we got out the house and did shit. I've forgotten to mention that I was 14, and the two brothers were 13 and 15.

We started looking around the old building and decided to see what was inside. It was pretty dark inside even though it was fall in the middle of the day. Being nosey kids, we just kept going all of a sudden in the back of the building we saw, and I do mean we, a large being with two red eyes, started to stand up. How do I know its eyes were red? Probably because there was enough light that could have made the eyeshine to the back of the building. I can't tell you how tall the thing was. It was wide and tall that much I can tell you. I was scared shitless and ran out of the building with them two right behind me. I was running so fast that the chain on my bike jumped off the sprocket. We didn't speak of this for a few weeks, and when I did and who was with me, I became a laughing stock. It wasn't until 30 years later that one of the brothers admitted to me what we saw that day happened. I really didn't give a shit because I did, and it wasn't until 2006 that I had another encounter. Not of the same magnitude, but an encounter. Thanks for giving me a form to share my story. You can use my name if you want. And thanks for being balls to the wall kind of guy.

Take care.

Attacked On An ATV

Steve,

Thank you for what you, David and Scott, have done. For bringing things to light in the world and bringing people together. I give credit where credit is due! Excellent job, and Thank you very much. I have been following you on YouTube since you started this project. A little about myself before I state my encounter(s)

I have been a firefighter for over 25 years, retiring at the rank of Captain. I have worked previously in law enforcement and at this time again in law enforcement division now. I trained and bred German Shepherds for many years. Been an outdoorsman all my life Hunting/Fishing/Hiking/Caving and just exploring the outdoors. You get the picture now. Lol

I have never told this before publicly! I have told a few others over the years and had the mindset I don't give a shit what people think or feel because I know I encountered something unnatural. It's changed my perspective on the outdoors. If anyone says I am a liar will bust your lip because I will never fear them as much as I encountered! That is a fact! Feel free to use my name if you decide to share my story. I did alter my friend's name with respect.

Here goes...
A Friend (I will call Tim) and I decided to ride the ATV. It was a cool, clear night in November 1997. This was a normal thing for Tim and I when we rode horses, camped, hiked, hunted together.

We doubled on my ATV because he wasn't at my house at the time. We live in N.W.Ga. At the foothills of Lookout Mountain. We were riding on a very old logging road on the side of Lookout Mountain, which had been our hunting grounds since childhood. We reached a point about ¾ up the mountain and stopped for a break. I had my HT radio to check-in at the house with the wife, which we do. Status check.

As we were looking down the mountain, we could see a direct line of sight to the house, which is about a mile. 1 1/2 as the crow flies, we made contact, but strangely the radio became static and broke Communication. No biggie, I thought. So, Tim and I decided to return back down the old logging road. Being a new ATV at the time, Tim wanted to drive it just a normal thing when us guys get a new toy. We reached the base of the mountain next to a field in which a mountain wash was in between us and the field where we entered the deep woods earlier. OK being on flat ground at very slow speed, the ATV flipped from rear to front violently we overturned we both were shaken up, scuffed a little, but not injured.

I stated what the F**k happened? I thought Tim hit a deep stump hole or something, but no the ground was flat on the logging road. Tim couldn't explain it either why we flipped from the rear to the front so quickly. We started laughing about the Oh WELL and CARRY on Mindset. We turned the ATV back over on all four tires, it being a 4X4 Yamaha Kodiak, which is very heavy ATV. Still giggling about what just happened.

Then SUDDENLY, a loud scream! The scream was so loud I could feel the vibration in me. It was like Surround Sound "LOUD" NOT A bobcat... Coyote ...Bear...Owl... or a Peacock!

We were both frozen in place. Never heard anything like this before. It was a Fear I cannot explain over overwhelming fear. Not like the fear of skydiving for the first time! IT WAS WORSE. The fear was like your soul was going to be dismembered. It almost felt like time stopped, like the moments before lightning strike; time froze paralyzed for how long? I cannot recall.

I said to Tim Let's get the F**K outta here. As we mounted back on the ATV, something caught my eye between the starlight and the reflective light from the ATVs headlight from the trees. I saw a figure at least 9 feet tall and broad on two legs with reddish eyes reflecting light from the ATV.
This was a NO D*MN BEAR! I knew this!

I yelled to Tim, GO! GO!GO! And which he did crossing the mountain wash and into the wide-open pasture, Tim changing gears as fast as possible. I was looking over to my right and behind to see if we were being preceded. Yes, we were, but this large dark figure was going from two legs to four. Its arms were assisting its running or pursuit at us.

At this point, we were in 5th gear and going 50 mph; and this Creature was gaining on us, which I could see from the starlight in this open pasture. In fear of our lives, reupholstered my 9mm pistol, which I knew I was completely under gunned.

Yes, it is hard to shoot from a moving ATV, but I felt I did not have a choice! I aimed center mass and began firing at this creature. Which was about 25 to 30 yards and gaining on us. I was going to empty the magazine until I was empty firing.

The creature began to veer off and then disappeared in the darkness. I could not tell the color of this creature, dark and massive Muscular moves at a speed and a stride unbelievable like watching something on a sci-fi flick, I guess like the movie "Predator."

Meanwhile, Tim was driving the hell out of the ATV we returned to my house. Shook up, trying to explain to our wives and my Brother. They couldn't comprehend what happened to us. Hell, we couldn't either. Then I didn't have a clue at the time over the years and my own investigation and research. I have more knowledge and know people are open and hearing other people's encounters. It's amazing the similarities!

Tim and I discussed this incident a few times and how the ATV flipped the way it did? If that creature came from behind, flipped it like a toy, with the weight of the ATV plus two grown men on it. Imagine the strength of this thing. Hell, it could have ripped us to shreds! We both agreed on that and how he had a Ruger44 magnum in a shoulder rig, and he was so frightened he said I didn't think of it. Heck, he was too busy driving the hell out of the ATV.

Tim doesn't have much to do with the outdoors after that. Honestly, I think the experience affected him more negatively than me. It took a while, but my love for the outdoors, I had to overcome it somewhat.

Steve, as you state and others, I am (always) observing everything when in the outdoors after that; because I know something could be there. After that night, I have had other encounters, but not like that night. Something I do with the younger folks or even kids I try to explain is always be aware of your surroundings and never go alone into the deeper forest at least take a dog or two dogs, preferably.

-David Espy

Record note:
Steve, I have spent years finding out what these beings are and which is so hard. I went from old microfilms in libraries before internet days, but to bring to mind these old stories are still locked away researching old newspaper articles is a key back then fake news wasn't quelled as bad.
I have talked with people that have encountered these creatures over the years. I build trust with them. I have learned a lot from these people. Some have passed on.

As far as Sasquatches or Dogmen, I don't know what or why this creature attacked us, maybe territorial? Were we a threat? Spiritual? WTF honestly, I feel lucky that I wasn't a victim of disappearing like so many others have.
I have had other encounters with these creatures since then. I have learned so much over the years that it just brings more questions. WHY THE COVER-UP? WHY THE INTIMIDATION? WHY THE THREATS?
1000s of people disappeared from young to old and all walks of life. These are people with families that have no closure! Really sad. If anything, we can do educating people like You, David and Scott, are doing.

We must find out why? These creatures aren't ape/monkey way too smart. Screw their missing LINK crap.

You mentioned about being in Ga. and Ala. Please let me know when or where I would love to meet you and share notes.
If anything, stories don't have to talk about the "Nephilim" all the time. Lol
Be safe out there in the woods, and especially around people, they are more dangerous!

Godspeed David Epsy

Knocked A Home Off Its Foundation

Hello Steve,

My name is Brian Gibbons, and I live in Northeast Tennessee. I live where Tennessee, Kentucky, and Virginia all meet. I'm 5 minutes from Virginia and about 5 minutes from Kentucky. Where I live is very mountainous and rugged, with several cliffs, deep hollows, and many miles of untouched forest.

I grew up hunting and fishing and competition coon hunting with hounds for years. I have hunted all over the U.S. and have never seen one of these creatures (Bigfoot); however, I have recently found footprints and have heard what I'm almost certain was one of these devils.

About a year ago, I was attending a little get-together at a friend of mine's house. While talking with several of my friends, a couple of ladies walked in that I didn't know. My friend introduced us, and we all started back talking again but now with a couple of real nice elderly ladies.

I'm kind of a talkative type person and can usually carry on a conversation with anyone. So out of the blue, I asked, "Has anybody ever seen a Bigfoot?"

And as quick as I did, one of the ladies said, "yes, I've seen one of those bastards, it scared the crap out of me." I said, "really? Tell me about it." She told me that she lives alone, way back in the mountains, and in a single wide mobile home and that one night, while watching television, there was a loud, hard, bang on the outside of her trailer. She had her curtains open, and although she lives miles from anyone, and on a dead-end gravel road. She thought it was some young teens just being assholes and trying to scare her. So, she hollered and said stop, I have a shotgun, and I'll use it if you don't knock it off.

In just another few minutes, bam!! It happened again, so she grabbed her shotgun and started toward the door, and that's when all hell broke loose—Bang, bang, thump, and extremely loud, guttural growls that she had never heard before. Needless to say, my friend was shaken up pretty badly, and the only thing she knew to do was to turn out the lights.

Strangely, this is when everything stopped. She knew that whatever had done this was not human because when all hell broke loose, and she went to turn off the lights, she could tell that her trailer had been knocked off of its foundation. The next day she called the company she bought the trailer from, and they sent three men out to put it back on its foundation. After they had finished, she asked them to try to knock it back off of the foundation or at least see if they could move it. They couldn't budge it.

After this happened, and we became more acquainted, she started telling me about other things that were happening. She said that she was hearing them scream at night. She began finding huge rocks, big twisted limbs, dead animals and a lot of other things that even you probably wouldn't believe.

I decided to try and find her some professional help. She wouldn't because she thought that if she told the authorities that they would put her in a nuthouse as she called it, so I took on the task of finding someone. I contacted a very popular, but very controversial person in the Bigfoot world, and he truly tried to help, but one of the things he wanted us to do was to offer them gifts. I sat down with her and discussed the plan, and in her sweet southern fashion, she said, give them gifts? For knocking my damn trailer off of its foundation? Hell no!

I just laughed and said, you know what, your right. I don't like the idea either. So, I contacted you, and you recommended Scott Carpenter. I eventually got a hold of Scott, and he gave me the best advice a person could get. Out of respect for Scott, I'll keep mine and his conversation between him and me. I will happily share it if someone is having a problem with one of these things, but I won't share it in a public forum for obvious reasons.

Thank you very much, Steve, for recommending Scott. He's a very good guy and very knowledgeable about these creatures. For those of you that think it's cool to offer them gifts, I can tell you first hand, that's a very dangerous hobby you have. These things are not to be trusted; they have hairpin tempers and will mess with you, just to be messing with you. I've never laid eyes on one of these devils, but I've heard them, seen their tracks, and have witnessed firsthand what they will do and can do when they are angry.

Steve, I can't say enough about how much you're helping people by letting them vent through you by talking about their encounters, you're actually helping more than you know.

God bless, and if you're ever in Tennessee, Kentucky or Virginia, look me up. I'll buy you some toilet paper and some hand sanitizer....lol

It Knew I Was There

My name is James Ferrell, and I'm from Michigan. I have hunted all my life. I have taken 100 deer or so with my bow; I've also got many coyotes and foxes. I know my animals.

I was hunting in Irish shields or Brooklyn; either way, I was hunting a big swamp. My brother told me not to hunt there by myself. Still, when you're young, you don't listen. I was chasing a nice buck for six days. My father-in-law shot at him from a stand. I'd put them in a wide massive 12-point 160 class; I wanted him badly!

I went in around 5:30 am and set up on a valley that had a creek that ran through it. I saw what I thought was a coyote peering the ridge. I watched as this thing came crawling on its belly over the ridge. As it slowly moved down, I noticed that it was not a coyote. The hair on my neck rose. It then dropped into the creek line; my mind said, what was that?

I watched and saw a head pop up 15 yards down the creek. I saw that it was looking right at me. It sent chills through my body as we made eye contact with each other. It sprang and leaped across the creek and pulled itself up with its arms and ran off on to feet. I just couldn't believe what I was seeing. I stayed in my tree till around 10:00 climbed down and got the hell out of there!

I don't know what I saw, but I can tell you it was not human. It had the ability to know I was there. It looked like a young black child with no clothes on.

I have a new perception of what's out there. Thanks for letting me tell my story.

-James

It Looked Like A Man In A Ghillie Suit

Dear Steve,

I have been listening to your channel for a while now. I enjoy hearing all of the hunting stories and bigfoot encounters. I am so glad that you take each one of the bigfoot stories seriously with no criticism or mocking. Thank you!

I have three short stories to tell. Two that involved both my daughter and I; and one that was my daughter's own encounter. All three occurred within a short period of time.

The first encounter happened at a popular trout fishing campground in Southern Missouri. It was September of 2012, and the campground was packed full of campers. This campground was located in a valley that was surrounded by the Ozark mountains. My husband, daughter, and I were camping in our large dome tent. We had enjoyed a full day of fishing and all of the joys that go with it.

After sitting around the fire, we decided it was time to retire for the evening. Just as I was about to doze off, I hear this loud, obnoxious noise. There was someone in the next tent, which was sawing logs with an industrial size saw if you know what I mean.

For me, a light sleeper, it meant "no sleep tonight! "It was very frustrating, to say the least. Sometime after midnight, the snoring finally stopped, but it was too late for me. I was wide awake. As I lay there in the silence, I hear this low wailing/howling sound. It went on for several seconds, moving up and down in pitch as it echoed off of the hills surrounding the campground. I live in rural Missouri and am very familiar with the local wildlife and the sounds they make. I have heard bobcats, coyotes, owls, and even bears. This was not a sound I had ever heard before. I also know what wolf and dog howls sound like, and this was not that either.

My mind immediately went to thoughts of Bigfoot. When we got home, I went online and searched for recordings of Bigfoot. When I finally found what I was looking for and played the recording, I was excited. It sounded identical to what I had heard. It was almost two years later before my daughter, Alyse, was brave enough to tell me she had also heard that same sound that night. Or should I say both strange sounds? The industrial saw and the Bigfoot.

In 2013, a Lakota friend of ours talked Alyse and I, into hiking up to Black Elk's Lookout in the Black Hills of South Dakota. This hike took place at the end of March. It was seventeen degrees with a foot of snow on the ground. Not the easiest hike to take when you have been sitting on your backside all winter.

We started out all amped up and excited about the adventure that was ahead. We were cutting up and joking around. Soon the conversation turned to that very subject. The Lakota are firm believers in Bigfoot. They say he walks between two worlds and has been seen regularly on the reservations. As our conversation continued, we soon began a Bigfoot calling contest. It was fun to hear our voices echoing out across the Black Hills. Before long, we were back to business with our hike and made our way towards an especially dense area of the forest. As we progressed into this area, we all started feeling very uncomfortable. So much so that we all became very quiet, except for the prayers that were being muttered just under our breath.

As we came out of that area, we began to talk about what we each were feeling. None of us visibly saw anything, but our Lakota friend was sure Bigfoot was watching us. We had called them, and they had come.

This next encounter is, by far, the most definite one. As I said earlier, we live in rural Missouri. We have a small farm with livestock that includes horses. In the summer of 2015, Alyse saddled up one of the mares and went for a late afternoon ride down our gravel road. About two miles down the road, there was a herd of goats. Alyse happened to ride that direction on this particular day.

It was very warm, around eighty-five degrees with high humidity. She was enjoying her ride, and the mare was doing great. They rode past the goat herd about a half mile then turned to come back towards the farm. As they were passing the herd a second time, the mare began to jig around and act spooky. Alyse then saw what was spooking the mare. There was a huge man-like figure standing on the hill just above the herd of goats watching them. He looked like he had full dark brown winter coveralls on or a ghillie suit of some sort. She reasoned that it couldn't be a man because who would wear coveralls like that in this weather and there was no reason for a ghillie suit. It was all Alyse could do to hold the mare back from bolting. She had to hold her back all the way back to the farm.

Thank you for taking the time to read these stories. They aren't as descriptive as most, but enough to make me a believer.

God bless,
Tina

P.S. I really do enjoy your channel, but the stories without the expletives are much more enjoyable, as I am an ordained minister.

Who Would Believe A 13-Year-Old

Hey Steve, do you believe these Sasquatch beings are Mortal or Immortal Beings? In all your world, travel and research and seeing one of these D*mn beings. What's your opinion? I, too, have had an experience seeing them. And am curious as well.

My story:
Who's going to believe a 13-year-old? My experience with these beings happened when I was 13; I'm now 37. I still remember that moment. I'm an avid hunter and have had that passion since I was born, luckily, I got the guts to share my story, and I'll believe it till the day I die.

I love your no-nonsense, no bs, honest, straight-up talk and attitude. And defend "good, honest, and hard-working people!"

Long story short, I was at a scout camp, camp out, it was after dark, and I walked to the cabin where my brother was. The cabin had a big glass pane window with the light on.

As I was walking toward the light of the window in the cabin, two massive beings stepped out of the trees walking side by side onto the two-track road with trees on both sides of the two tracks. I immediately crouched down so I could get a better look, let me remind you that they were 20 feet in front of me.

The light of the window between them and I really made their figures stand out! They were massive! One was I'd guess 9 feet tall and the other 7 feet tall. The smaller one was at the biggest one's shoulder height. As I was crouched, they kept walking towards me.

I called out my brother's name, thinking it may be him. The creatures stopped when I called out my brother's name, and both creatures immediately stopped and turned into the trees and disappeared "silently."

They walked next to a power line pole and into those trees. When they disappeared, I turned tail and ran back as fast as I would to the other cabin, which was about 75 yards away. I was silent for the rest of the camp trip. I just told everyone I was sick.

I still deal with what I saw. Nobody but my family believes what I saw. Seeing two is rare from what I've heard, maybe not. To deal with going back into the woods where these beings live, I took a stress management class in college, and our final exam was to "face a fear" and go face it. And write about it for the final exam.

Whether it's skydiving, asking a girl out etc. So, I went to the same spot and spent the night alone. I never said in the exam what I saw just that I was afraid of being in the dark alone. What I saw I saw. And facing that fear when I slept alone years later helped me deal with my passion for hunting and still going outdoors alone or with friends. Maybe telling that will help others feel they can go back and enjoy their passion outdoors.

Don't get me wrong I still have a hard time going hunting and camping alone, but I still do. The two beings I saw I know they were not human.

Without a doubt, I know they were Sasquatch/Bigfoot beings. Hopefully, my story can reach you and others who have experienced these massive intriguing beings. Stay safe. I thank you for saying, "you have my back" you have no idea. For what it's worth, I got your back too! Feel free to use my name.

Thanks, Steve.

-Justin

My Wife Screamed Uncontrollably

Good morning Steve,

It's been 25 years now since my girlfriend, now wife and I saw something. We never talked about it, but we were very shaken up that summer evening. I'll do my best to describe what happened.

Back in the early summer of 1995, I asked my wife if she wanted to take a drive up to Canyon Lake? Canyon lake is east of Phoenix, near the town Apache Junction, and the Superstition Mountains.

We spent the day fishing and just sitting by the water and having a nice picnic. It was a really nice day. It started getting late, so we decided It was time for us to head home. It's just over an hour to get back to where we lived at the time, so we started heading back toward Phoenix.

It got dark on us as we were driving home and anybody that's been to canyon lake knows it has switchbacks and it's a dirt road, or at least it used to be. So, as I was driving up the road, I was turning around a corner, and just in view of the headlights, something stood up from a crouched position and jumped down from a boulder and went behind some trees.

Mind you, there isn't much of any landscape or big forest trees in this area. I would call it the mid desert landscape—some Juniper trees, boulders, cactus, but nothing major. The area does back to a national forest but nothing that you would consider the forest, so my mind did not process it; my wife didn't say a word. I didn't say a word; we just sat in the car looking, and then whatever it was, it moved from the small trees to some large boulders.

It was big. I would have to say it was at least 8 feet tall, and it moved as a person would on two legs, and it moved quickly. Very quickly. That's when my wife started to scream as I've never heard her do again to this day. From it jumping down from the 1st boulder into the trees and moving 15 to 20 feet behind a larger boulder, I say I got at least 7 seconds of view of this thing.

It looked like it had dark black hair arms that came down to its knees. At the time we had a hatchback two-door car when my wife started to scream, I took off as fast as I could. The road was a bit rocky with some medium-sized rocks. I just wanted out of there. I broke the Muffler clean off, but no way in H*LL, I was going to stop!! It's been 25 years since this happened, and we have not been back since!

It Sometimes Doesn't Make Sense

I am not sure of the day or month; if I was a betting man, my guess would be May or June of 2015. The best I can narrow the time down is between 10:00 am-noon. (Because that's when I would take my 2nd smoke break if I was stuck in the warehouse)

Nothing out of the ordinary was happening that day that I can remember. I went out for my smoke break, sat down on my usual stack of skids (pallets), lit up my cig and started my watch for the normal wildlife.
I noticed the lack of bird noise, thought that was unusual, remember thinking, "little buggers are usually chirping' up a storm." Now I should tell you we had a 3oo foot radio tower and at the south edge of the property and a 250-300-foot cell tower.

The birds would be on those towers by the handful or whole flocks, depending on the time of year. That's the first area I visually scanned. Not a single bird on towers or electrical lines. Strange, I thought. I started scanning the trees for birds.

That is when my view on what's out in the woods changed forever. In a tree approximately 50-80 yards from where I sat.... halfway up the tree, its trunk splits into two, which creates a natural "V" shape. The space in the "V" was blurry to my vision, so naturally, I thought, "one of my eyes had gone wonky." I wiped my eyes, and it was still blurry, so wiping each eye carefully, one at a time while always keeping one eye on this thing this time. Still blurry in the "V" of the tree, which is 50- 75feet up the tree.

Now at this point, I'm like anyone that has seen the movie "Predator" I'm a little spooked and wondering if this is one of those things from the movie. It did not look like the visual effects in the movie. I could see colors through it, but it just looked like a massive blob of blurriness. Then I remember thinking, Nah... somebody's shrink wrap or bubble wrap flew up there and got stuck in the tree.

What happened next still to this day gives me chill bumps. I had no sooner thought this thing was bubble wrap stuck up in the tree, and the d*mn thing shifts and tries to hide behind one of the big branches.

I can still see it sticking out a little on each side of that branch. I CAN TELL YOU WITH 100 % CERTAINTY that was NO f*cking bubble wrap!!!

I threw down my cigarette and made a B-line back into the garage and sat at my warehouse desk, shaking uncontrollably for longer than I'd like to admit. Thinking back now, why I didn't say anything to anybody in the garage.

All I can say is that I was scared, embarrassed, and a little freaked out. (well a lot) Plus deep down inside, I KNEW that if I went right back outside with someone, that thing would NOT be there.

The next time I went outside, to do my afternoon runs, the thing was not there. Where I parked the company, truck put me 20 yards closer to that tree. I stared hard through the tree line and not a damn thing in sight, and the birds were back chirping & fluttering about.

Flash forward to 2019. I find the Missing 411 Hunted documentary. That was Sept. 21. Now I know the encounter that happened to me also happened to Mrs. Maccabee, near her house southwest of Lima, OH (2010). That encounter was approximately twenty-eight miles due north of my sighting down in Sidney, OH. When looking at the map, you will notice that the Maccabee property is within a mile or two of R.R. tracks to the east of them. The tracks (toward I-75) are the same R.R. tracks that run behind O.D.O.T., district 7 (Ohio Dept of Transportation), the place of my sighting—been rolling this info around my head the last couple weeks. A chilling conclusion that I have come to is if this blurry bubble wrap thing decided to hop a ride on a train. Who is going to think anything about seeing a blurry spot on a moving train??

Still, to this day, there are days when I really wonder if I haven't gone loopy. Then there are other days when reliving the feelings, I had that day, and I know that I saw something, and cannot explain what it was.

Was it an alien, military experiment, interdenominational being? I just can't say, but that thing moved in the tree and was trying to hide behind the bigger branch. Right when I was going to write it off, in my mind, as bubble wrap stuck up in a tree. You know, as a younger man, I always wished for an encounter with Bigfoot or a UFO. Maybe that is why I used to spend a lot of spare time in the woods of Ohio and the mountains of Colorado. (lived in the Denver area from '84 -'89) Now I would tell people. Be careful what you wish for.

Thanks, Steve. Keep up the good work and be safe out there.

It Threw Cinder Blocks

Steve,
First and foremost, thank you for giving "us" a voice, and my apologies for having to deal with some of my illiterate Patriots in the United States. Must be a bear reading through a lot of these emails. But I digress.

Summer 1990, late July to be exact. My brother and I decided to try our favorite smallmouth creek at night for flathead catfish—something we have done many times on our home river some 40 miles south. The night started off usual, dusk...semi-dark...total darkness. We always fished "bare-bones" at night—single, small handheld cheapo flashlights. My brother was half asleep, claiming to feel poorly. No matter, I'm fishing. He can do whatever. Across the creek, approx. 30 to 40 yards, something very fucking large came slamming through the thickest shit around like it was charging me as I was closest to the bank. My brother sat up a bit, and I asked if he heard that, and he agreed he did. Being me, I started chucking rocks in the area of the action. One after the other thinking, it was one of the landowners' cows that wandered off. It got quiet, like really fucking quiet. At that exact moment, a large rock came a landed close enough to me to get me pretty wet. WTF. So, being me again, I begin throwing bigger rocks in that direction. Yeah, I know, genius. That didn't last but two rocks when another large rock hit damn near at my feet as I was in the water at this point ready to go! Then a large, fast, powerful whoof like nothing I have ever heard came at me. My brother was in the car at this point, yelling at me, "Let's get the f*ck out of here NOW!"

It then began to fucking bark like a damned dog? But you could tell, it wasn't a damned dog at all. I was paralyzed at that point, not having a clue what this thing was. Better senses came over me after about 30 seconds or so, and I retreated like the flailing human I am.

The next day I was out there at 7:00 am to see WTF, yeah, that's just me. The "rocks" this a*shole threw weren't rocks. They were f*cking cinderblocks! One full, one was half of one. Cinder Blocks! 40 yards! I went across the creek. This area I knew well as it was a hotspot for large bass for me. The thicket it came through was 7 feet tall, and you couldn't see through it at all. The path was clear was Mr. or Mrs. A*shole plowed through. Not totally clear, but doable and behind this thicket were two dead Whitetails—one seemingly fresh, one well eaten.

I know why he was p*ssed off now, or she supposed. I never saw the f*cker, and I am thankful I didn't. I know full well what it was, nothing in Indiana can do shit like that. Worms, property owner, cows all accounted for an in pens for the night plus that's not his land.

Thanks for listening, never want to see one or be around one of these things again.

Regards,
J McDermott

I'll Never Go Back There

Hello, and nice to finally be able to tell you my story. I watch your YouTube videos all the time and also have a story to tell you.

I am 44 years old. I am currently bed-bound and disabled from a horrible accident at work in Florida, around 2005. I hit a 3000-pound bull with a semi. I did a few years of therapy and was able to go back to work.

About four years ago, I slipped and fell at my job three times in two days. Due to both accidents compounding, it's got me back to being bed-bound, and now I can't walk.

Back when I was around 21 or 22 years old, I was living in North Florida, Cotto, Florida, to be exact. A friend of mine asked me if I wanted to go hunting on a piece of land that his dad owned. His dad owned a huge piece of land like over 2000 acres in Compass Lake in the Hills Florida about 15 to 20 miles from my house.

So, I remember I had a 306 rifle, and my friend had a 308 rifle. We left to go hunting around 4 pm. That evening driving to the property was all unfamiliar to me. I have hunted in a track close to this property before. However, I didn't know the layout of this property and told my friend just before we parked that what if we got separated, I've never been there. I worried because I left my truck at my house, and we drove to the property where we were going to hunt in a two-man tree blind/stand.

My friend laughed at me and said nothing to worry about, he knew the land, and he said I was worried about nothing. Well, was he wrong?

We got to where we were parking the truck and had to walk for a solid hour to the hunting stand. As we were walking in, I noticed that there was literally no animal life around us at all. No birds, no squirrels, no deer tracks or any sign that life ever lived there. It was just a quiet, almost dead feeling walking into these woods.

We walked a fire trail the most of the way back to the hunting stand. At around 5:30 pm, we made it to the stand and climbed up and got settled in. I'm a great thinker and problem solver; I was sitting there thinking that it was already 5:30 pm and it gets dark at around 8:00 pm or so this time of the year. In my head, I did the math. I told my friend in a soft voice (so we didn't scare away any of the deer or hogs or anything) that we might want to head out in about an hour or so. I certainly didn't want to walk on a track that I wasn't familiar with to get back to the truck in the dark.

My friend again laughed at me and said no worries, brother; we had plenty of time before we had to leave. Over an hour went by, and I finally said to my friend, look, I'm headed back with or without you. I'm leaving now, so my friend said ok and called me a wuss.

We climbed down and headed back to the truck with maybe 30 to 45 mins of daylight left. We were about halfway back, and just like that, we had no light at all. It was dark, and we didn't bring a flashlight with us. I remember walking behind my friend when I started smelling a wet dog or animal smell; it was awful. Enough to gag a maggot, it smelled so bad.

Around 20 mins or so from the truck, we were walking on a small trail or fire trail, getting closer to a little island of trees that sits right in the middle of the trail just in front of us around 50 yards away.

As we got closer, the smell got stronger and stronger. We just put it off as a dead buzzard or a dead skunk. Then all of a sudden, there was a big bang on that island of trees in front of us. My friend and I stopped dead in our tracks. I said to him, "Hey, what was that?"

He was so scared he couldn't even answer me at all. I told him something big was on that island of trees just in front of us, and now how are we getting out of here and back to the truck?

Just as my friend was about to say something, there was a noise that I'll never forget. It was a roar that was so loud that the decibels shook the ground around us. I grabbed my friend and said we have to go and go now! We started walking away from the island of trees forward the right-hand side as to stay as far away as possible from the Bigfoot in those thickets of trees.

Around ten steps in, it started to roar again and hit the trees with a log or something. To be honest, I'm 250 pounds of muscle and was a football athlete all my life. I've never been scared of anything! This was different. I know that Bigfoot would rip my friend and I apart with no problems.

I dropped my gun and ran for my life back to the truck. My friend still had his gun; he was only 160 pounds wet. I made it back to his truck about 2 mins before he did. That's saying something because of our sizes that my friend should have beat me back first. Remember, I didn't know this property as well.

When we jumped in the truck, I looked at my friend and said I dropped my gun, let's go go go now!

I remember we drove home in less than half the time it should of and when my friend dropped me off at my house, he said to me "wtf was that?" and I told him that he knew what it was and that I'll never go anywhere near that property again.

My friend said, "Well, you dropped my dad's prize gun and that he had to go back and get it."

"Good luck!" I said.

I never told anyone what happened that night. The next day my friend showed up at my house and said that he found the gun but no signs of anything else.

I hope you tell my story on your YouTube channel, and please believe me and my story. I have nothing to gain by lying about it. It's been over 20 years now from the Bigfoot experience I had.

I am now 44 years old with serious health problems and felt I have to tell my story, and my friend and I are lucky to get out of there alive.

With An Alligator In Its Hand

Steve,

Thank you for providing a place for so many people like me to safely share stories of encounters that may never get shared without you. Everyone who's come in contact with one of these animals can spot a false story a mile away, and most are false, I believe. You have shared several that seem in line with the real feelings and emotions that come with an encounter. My story is short, just like the period of time I had eyes on the animal.

It's 13 years ago, early spring in the Everglades, a trip I had made for six previous years. There's no place in North America where you can replicate the experiences, you'll have in the areas along the Miccosukee River. My friend and I also fished the hardest places to get access to, for the obvious reasons. The areas we fish are mainly canals and are split up or separated by weirs (a super shallow area 30-40' wide) between canals where you can pull a boat threw but not drive across.

I was pulling my boat, 16' Jon boat, and my buddy Joe was standing up in the boat on gator watch. With that said, if Joe made any kind of sound, motion or gesture, I would be in the boat in less than a second. That's what happened, Joe was trying to get a word out but couldn't make his mouth, vocal cord or something work. Now I'm in the boat, and Joe points to the bank where an animal or creature stands with a small alligator in his right hand, maybe 40 yards away. In 2 steps, it was out of sight in the thick low brush. This wasn't a seven or eight-foot-tall thing, more like less than 6, muscular with balls of reddish hair hanging on it as if there had been more that had already fallen off, maybe shedding. Joe told me when he first spotted it, it had an alligator leg in its left hand and was eating it.

Now for the part that keeps us from telling others about the day that changed both our lives. We both could see a thick collar of some kind around its neck. It looked to be metal with leather, not 100% sure what it was made of as some of it was covered with neck hair. We both believe it was a tracking collar. I have searched the internet for years now and never came across an encounter like ours, have you?

My hope is if you share this, others may come forward that have seen the same thing. If there was a prayer of the animal being a bear or escaped monkey, whatever, I wouldn't be wasting your time. This was definitely the same animal others have spotted in south Florida that they call swamp ape.

That was our last trip to the Everglades, and within a year or so, we stopped fishing and hunting together and rarely talked. That all changed last week when Joe had a serious life-threatening infection that he shouldn't have survived. I had no idea until he called me and told me after 14 days in ICU, he's out of the woods and should be home in a week. Then he asked, completely at the wrong time, if I had ever told anyone about the Miccosukee wear?

I told him no but had been thinking about telling this Steve Isdahl guy that reads people's stories. Joe asked that I do just that. So, there you have it.

-Cur

Remote Northen B.C. Guiding

International War Games Interrupted

Hello Steve,

My name is Miles Jay (MJ) Akula. I haven't been into the Bigfoot phenomenon. I honestly used to laugh at it or think people just got a little too high in the woods or what a lot of people think is a case of misidentifying something like a bear. Needless to say, I feel like an absolute idiot after what I saw.

I joined the USMC back in 2016, right out of high school. I grew up in Nashville, Tennessee and had very little to basically no outdoors experience aside from what I've learned from the Marine Corps. I unfortunately haven't had the honor of being deployed to a combat zone (yet), but I've gotten to experience and see some awesome places and meet incredible people.

This past October, 12 guys from my platoon got tasked with doing a survival training course in California at the Mountain Warfare Training Center near Bridgeport, CA, in Mono County. We had to go due to the fact the marines brought over some guy from the UK, Poland and Mexico to go through the course, and I guess they needed guys to cross-train with them.

To be honest, I was pissed though almost the entire time because I already had to go through sere school (Survival, Evasion, Renitence and Escape) while a bunch of the other guys got to go to Little Creek, Virginia to train which basically meant go party with the Navy guys over there. So needless to say, all of us had our own shitty attitudes going. When we got there, we did about a 5-day course on some basic survival stuff, nothing too different from what we all learned at sere.

After those five days, we were simulating some war games with the "new" survival techniques we learned that were a part of this game the instructors designed, basically the last team to be found wins. We all got split up in our own teams, helicoptered out, and had to hide, and last as long as we could and not be found by the instructors and other guys that were a part of another course that were supposed to be using their techniques to find people.

We all thought we were pretty hardcore after a while, knowing that our little team was only one of two teams left. A helo flew overhead with a giant megaphone calling out our teams and another team's number, as well adding to our ego's knowing that the other team had some UK SBS guys in it. (Basically, the Brits Navy Seals) Everyone knew that team's number as we were all fangirling over those guys, haha. So, we were hot shit at that point, or so we thought.

We thought we were doing good. Until we thought we got caught by one of the instructors in a ghillie suit, as we got to the bottom of this mountain, we just got done climbing up and over. As we went down near a creek, toward the instructor in the ghillie suit one of my buddies shouted something like "well f*ck we thought we had a chance, should we head back sir?" after all, we all assumed we got caught and just wanted to shower after being in the cold mountain air and mud the past 14 or so hours.

It was then that this guy we thought was in a ghillie suit stood upturned and looked at us for a solid five or so seconds and started trotting up the mountain that had just taken us about 4 hours to get up and over, that thing went over it in about 5 minutes coming in and out of sight.

At that moment, I at least knew what we all just saw, and my buddy and some other guys in my team must have known as well from the looks we all had on our faces, as we were in absolute shock. One of the marines that was from Mexico said, "I didn't know you guys had monkeys here."

We all nervously laughed our ass's off at being as stunned and somewhat terrified as we were. Needless to say, I've been a believer ever since, and I used to think people were idiots who thought bigfoot was real. I felt we all basically wanted to be found at that point, at least at this point I didn't give a fuck about beating some SBS guys, I just wanted to get the hell out of the woods. After being found none of us said anything, still to this day, my buddy David and I are the only ones out of the other three guys in my platoon that were with us never bring it up. That night we discussed it a little, but really didn't carry on too much as we got interrupted by some "ambush fire" coming at our base. We all had to go survive that night out in the woods in order not to be found by the "Chinese." That night sucked. I didn't even think about sleeping.

I'll never be able to forget that day as everything I thought I knew that was real or fake completely turned upside down. I remember how nervous I felt, too, not cause we all had blanks, but because I still don't think we would've had a chance even if we were ready to smoke something, it was insanely massive. I don't want to estimate some bs size, but Steve, it was f*cking massive.
I've been on a Bigfoot binge ever since, and I've realized how much bullsh*t was out there. It

doesn't surprise me why I never bought into the phenomenon, let alone the rest of the world. When I came across your channel, I was at the point of pretty much giving up hope on finding legit people who had real answers. I remember seeing your video title, "my first experience" (or something to that extent) on my recommendations for about a week before I clicked on it and thought what the hell.

Let's just say I'm glad I found your page and I'm glad you cut out all the bullshit. You don't try and feed people bullshit you just tell people what you know and what people have told you. I've watched a bunch of your videos and love the hunting stories as well, "get down on one knee before firing at a bear you'll likely miss standing up due to underestimating the speed" quite possibly some of the greatest survival advice I've ever heard.

Thank you again and good luck with your adventures, I'm jealous of the lifestyle you're living, and it has given me some ideas on what I want to do when I'm out. Thank you again

-MJ Akula

Wilderness Guide Relieved To Share This

Hi Steve,

It's been such a dang relief to hear some type of "plan of action" on the reality of all these beings that share our planet.

I grew up on the Minnesota/Iowa/Wisconsin borders, along the Mississippi river valley, chasing whitetails, turks and trout at a young age. Summer vacation was walleye fishing deep into Southern Ontario with my family.

I'm now 33 years old, and am just at the beginning of the "Millennials." I was raised without cell phones and the internet. However, I remember my junior year of high school, and I was being taught about the internet. I feel that many people around my age (give or take 5-10 years) have experienced such a crazy frickin turnaround in this world and society. 9/11 was my freshman year of high school; war coverage was then covered on most tv channels in my house for the next couple of years. It seems so similar to the past; take some of the best young men and women in the country and go to war.

I was a stud of a young man, but ended up following my Grandpa and Uncles paths, and enlisted to active duty. Obviously, I was driven by the war coverage on the news, and all the heroes. Hell, I had girlfriends to impress like all the other 18-year-old boys in America. Thankfully after three years, an auto accident ended my time in the service.

I have had experiences with Sasquatch beings. Most recently was late August 2018 in remote Idaho mountains. I guide wilderness big game hunts via horse and mule.
It was about ten days before elk and deer season started, I was working with two other guides

packing in our camps, and many loads of hay. We were set up at a trailhead, with hitching rails for the animals and a creek nearby for watering the stock. The trailhead alone was at the end of an old forest service road hardly accessible by four-wheelers. We were on the northeast edge of the Frank Church-River of No Return Wilderness. Arguably the most remote area in the lower 48. Our camps were in the wilderness area, so no motorized anything, once we got on the trail.

One afternoon while wasting a little time, another guide and myself walked up the hill from the horses about 15 minutes to sit down in a spot with a small view. It was a very thick forest. After about 20 minutes we had finished our lunch and were ready to relax for another half hour or so. Not more than 25 yds down the hill and to my left was a small grove of like six big trees, with long grass around them. All around this grove of trees was tallish brown grass, in between me and these trees was a rockslide, so my view was not obstructed whatsoever. My eyes gazed down towards this spot when I saw a dark object slowly move behind the tree like the thing was peeking out with half its body, and then moved behind the tree to hide from me. I instantly began eliminating the animals that I knew weren't down in front of us right now. My first thought, of course, was a bear. But it would have to have been climbing the tree because it was high up the trunk where I saw the dark object slide behind the tree. As the seconds passed, I became quite interested, and I stood up. I expected to see something continue walking past that tree; animals don't hide.

I never took my eye off the spot, and I had already got the attention of my partner, who was sitting next to me, and he was also looking down the small shallow rock slide and into that small patch of big pine trees. I literally said out loud; I'm going to walk down there because I know I saw something, and it has to be there still.

Right behind us was a very short, steep rocky wall, maybe 15 feet up, almost like a creek bank, but we were high on a mountain. On top of the rock slide wall behind us, the dark pine timber started and didn't stop for literally dozens and dozens of miles. In front of us behind that small patch of trees, the dark timber started and didn't stop for dozens and dozens of miles.

I took one step down the hill toward that dark thing I saw. From behind us came a sound neither of us had ever heard. It was so freaking loud; it could not have been more than 20 or 30 yards away. It was completely unnatural. It wasn't a whoop, scream or whatever else noises people talk about, I've researched it all.

It feels dumb to try and explain what the sound was that we heard. It was like a wood instrument mixed with a different language, and it was within feet of us, but we couldn't see above the steep slope behind us. Neither of us had a weapon, not that it even matters. As curious as I am about the topic, that afternoon, I had no inclination to stick around and see what was in store for us. I feel they were trying to communicate. They wanted us to spot them behind the tree in front of us. Maybe. And the noise from behind us was not exactly a threatening noise. But we just wanted to go back to the horses, and so we did.

Here's the deal, I don't give a shit what new movie is coming out, or what Dr. Phil thinks is terrible, or what my president did 20 years ago THAT SHOULD BE ALL OF OUR ATTITUDES. Folks, where I'm from, don't even know that Sasquatch is even a topic of discussion.

You may be familiar with the new science that's been coming out about the power of our brains. And what we can accomplish through meditation. Dr. Joe Dispenza's newer book 'Becoming Supernatural' opened up my eyes quite a lot. And he has recently talked about the giant beings that himself and others see and his meditation workshops.

My biggest fear and concern is that we won't ever know what these things are. Of course, the Gov't knows something, but why would they decide to be completely honest all of a sudden. There is nothing more important than figuring out what the heck is going on in this world right now, yet so many people are brain dead to the idea that anything different is even happening right now IT'S CRAZY!

I live for the outdoors, horses and mules. I love my family, and being healthy is more important than anything because all we have to ourselves is our one frickin body.

Sorry for the rambling, I have so much to say and nobody to say it to. Thanks for the motivation, you're the freaking man.

Use my info if you want- Phil Flaskerud from Northeast Iowa

Numerous Incidents In Port Angeles

Hi Steve,

This is a photo I took. I could not see them but felt them. I was down at the creek by my home with my neighbor Linda. Linda wanted to meet the Sasquatch and see the area. We did have the Sasquatch cone down to the creek side where we were standing. It walked in the creek. It was huge; I would guess 800 lbs. I used to have horses and trail rode thousands of miles here on the Olympic Peninsula in Port Angeles, Washington.

I had the big Male look in my window one night. He was over 9 feet tall. My guess is 10 feet. He had beautiful brown eyes, wrinkled grey skin and facial hair. I was 15 feet away from him!

I've lived here for 20 years by McDonald Creek on Old Olympic highway.
I've been aware of the Sasquatch for the last six years. They have let me know they are down at the creek with screams, wood knocks, rock clacking, smell, growls, ran past me at mach speed while invisible!

Let me back up. I was standing by the creek talking to my new neighbor, Joey. He is a bowhunter, and he has been watching your Bucktail apps. So back to the creek, I could feel the Sasquatch, so I told Joey to introduce himself, and he looked at me like are you kidding! Yes, I was serious, but he wouldn't, so I told the Sasquatch who he was. I've been talking with

Sasquatch for the last two years. I know they understand English and who we are.

One day I took two of my German Shepherd dogs to the creek for a swim, and within minutes a Sasquatch on the other side of the creek yelled at us! I told the Sasquatch that I was going to leave and was sorry for my dogs barking! I didn't want it to kill my dogs either.

Last year I went out on my deck that faces the creek and told the Sasquatch to leave me alone. I did this because I was afraid. They did leave me alone. I know because the prints they left every night stopped. I spend a lot of time alone because my husband is building a cabin in Neah Bay, Wa. So, after a while, I went back to the deck and told the Sasquatch that I missed them.! They came back.

I walk my dogs down by the creek in a huge field. I've growled at twice. I believe they don't like dogs. They haven't hurt my dogs, chickens, myself, or my husband.

They have left me glyphs. Too bad I can't read them.

Oh, I know you are not a big fan of some of the so-called people in the Bigfoot world, but Ron Moorehead came to my property with his wife. Before they came here, I had tried talking to him about the Sasquatch living here and didn't get anywhere until I shared my photos. Bingo, that got them here.

You see, Ron and his wife live in Sequim, Washington. Ron said there are five other people in the area by me having encounters with the Sasquatch! I know Lessie across the creek from me is.

So Steve, what do you think they are? Why do you think they are so close to homes?

I am a dog groomer with a shop here at home. One of my clients is a retired federal agent for the National Park service. She has finally admitted that the Sasquatch are real and that they don't want people to know about them because they don't want people to shoot them.! I knew she knew about them!

I'm with you; we need to move on from the prints! Yes, most people are sheep. Just the way it is. I think they're scared of the unknown.

I felt the beings in the trees, so I took some photos. I got a photo of blue lights in the top area! I wonder what it is? I think it's the Sasquatch in energy form. Think of why they need the trees? Thank you for your time.

Port Angeles Washington

Breathed On My Neck As I Slept

I was in Jacksonville, Oregon, just north of Medford. With one of my cousins and one of my uncles. We were on my cousin's gold mining claim trying to strike it rich. I've been out in the woods my whole life; I live in Oregon. We were there for just shy of a month. My uncle and cousin had a tent. I slept on a cot under the stars next to the fire. It was an awesome trip. One night about three weeks in, I was going to sleep, fire going, dead silent, then I felt the breath of a very large animal sniffing my neck. I could tell this was huge. I could hear and feel its breath. I was so terrified I couldn't move, didn't even try to get the shotgun under my cot. I thought it was a black bear. But I was laying three feet from a full-on fire. Now I'm more confused than scared. I mustered the strength to look as it walked away.

I've seen bears walk; this was not that. It had a powerful gate, balanced, natural. Well, it walked down to the creek bed and up a steep mountainside. The creek was 6 feet below me, and I could see its shoulders and head above the creek bank. It took two steps up the mountain and was gone. I retreated to a two-man tent that had two men in it. The next day I realized if it wanted me dead, I would be. I slept under the stars for the rest of the trip. They, to this day, say I'm a bullshitter. But I know what happened and what I saw.

Coastal B. C. inlet

From A Navajo Reservation

My wife and I live in a very, very, remote area of the North-Western part of the Navajo Reservation in Northern Arizona. We have limited resources such as a consistent cell phone signal, and getting groceries is a two and a half-hour drive one way to Flagstaff, AZ.

I find you informative and let me clarify that too. It seems to me that when one (or a group) has an equal interest in a similar topic and connect, it becomes more than just informative, but yes, even entertaining. We look forward to seeing what has come next, and by that, I do not mean the Game of Thrones or those types of fiction. Some people will never grasp the idea that we don't need to be entertained with deceptive fiction and bullshit. Entertainment, according to Hollywood, does not necessarily mean having the truth involved.

My wife is full-blooded Navajo, and I am a 3rd generation Irish descendant. We've been married for 23 years now. We met at the Navajo National Monument as Park Rangers in 1995. She grew up nearby merely 6 miles away from that national monument. I was working as a Ranger that same summer we met.

My name is Patrick, and I want to relate an encounter I had back in 1986 in a state forest in Western Michigan. It was near Muskegon, Michigan, in the forest area of a smaller community named Revanna. It was late Fall, and I had just finished a seasonal position working for the Grand Hotel on Mackinac Island. I was in extremely good condition after running up and downstairs at this large Victorian Era Hotel. I was visiting a young love interest in Ravenna. Her cousins and Uncles needed my help to gather seasoned cut firewood left in the forest. I worked with medium effort, as I said I was in great shape, so the Uncles and cousins did not harm. I was to stay put in the designated area whilst the fellas went to get the tractor and trailer for us to load the wood.

As I enjoyed the autumn sunshine afternoon warmth, I suddenly heard a very loud tree knock close by me. I picked up a baseball bat sized branch nearby and proceeded to swing a Teddy Williams at a tree in front of me. It was a very loud clunk noise when I connected, and the end of the Branch snapped off four inches. It rattled my hands pretty good. Just then, without any sort of plan, I saw that there was a hollowed-out part of a large diameter tree where fire or lightning had made its mark. I was 6 ft tall and 170 pounds, and I was able to slip inside the tree and lean back with the sun on my face, warming me while the sun began to get lower now. I am not sure to this day why I did that, but a couple of minutes went by, and as I just leaned there, I smelled some sort of horrid smell of skunk and urine. Very strong indeed, eye-watering, really. Then I heard some rustling outside of the tree, and I listened intently, thinking I could scare one of the cousins or an Uncle.

As I sat in the sunshine with my eyes slightly closed just relaxing, I heard the rustling again and as I poked through the oval slit from the tree cave, I was in. I did not see anything right away, but I did hear a very low gruff, Heh heh heh heh... As though someone was amused at me and my tree cave. I then saw a flash of brown go past the tree cave entrance and then saw the second brown flash, and it was the largest set of feet and ankles I had ever seen.

Steve Isdahl   The Day Sasquatch Became Real For Me   Copyright© 2020

I froze, I somehow knew exactly what it was. I heard some brush being pushed against, and I jumped out of the tree, expecting to see the cousins or the Uncles to give them a startle. Not so, I was alone and again heard some rustling in the brush nearby. The cold gave me a shiver as it was nearly dark now, maybe five minutes of light left.

Jason, one of the cousins, was near me as I slowly made my way through the saplings. As we met up, Jason and I walked back to the truck, and I asked Jason if they heard three knocks often in this area? He said they were frequent in this part of the forest. Nearly dark now and I could see that Jason was unnerved, spooked somehow. He then said, did you see those guys that are over there? They have hoods upon their jackets. He pointed to a small clearing with many Maple saplings ringing it thickly. With the taller pines in the backdrop of night darkness looming, I saw the outline of the hooded guys walking away with the slightly lit horizon behind them; they moved into the thickest part of the forest. I could barely see with the light nearly gone from the setting sun.

We drove the truck back to the large farmhouse and met up with my love interest and her extended family whilst we unloaded the wood we had collected up. I was introduced to Jason's Auntie and Uncle that we had collected firewood for, they were very friendly. I asked about the tree knocks I heard. I had asked if they had encounters with tree knocks or more. This woman's eyes got really big, and she looked at The Uncle, just then he said that not many want to discuss that sort of thing as it often comes with ridicule to those that do.

The Auntie smiled at me as I told them about the tree knock and the tree cave I was in and the horrendous stench. The Uncle said, yep, you got them to come in and take a peek, that's for sure. I knew then and there that I was going to be on the lookout for anything like that for the rest of my days if I were ever in the forests.

The Sasquatch exists, and I knew it. I suspect these are differentiations of a Neanderthal-like species. Nope, it wasn't swamp gas, an eclipse, or a mass hallucination brought on by mushrooms in the water supply.

What a great platform to hear real people encounter these creatures. Thanks for the hard work, it is great to hear people stepping up to allow others to hear their experience.

I believe that the area where I was near: Muskegon, Ravenna, and Ludington, in a large forested area that leads along the western coastal area of Michigan all the way to the upper peninsula. It is not very populated in these areas for sure, or it wasn't back in 1986. I think it is a route used to migrate for them.

Another encounter I had was up by Flaming Gorge, Wyoming, in the early spring of 2014. My wife and I were travelling to Flaming Gorge Wyoming for a short vacation. We decided to stop at a pull-off area called Moose Pond. It had picnic tables and outhouses available, as well as a paved trail that led around the small lake. It was at the base of the mountains, and where the tree line of large Ponderosa Pines took over. While I walked near the lake, I saw a dead foot-long rainbow trout. It was belly up floating in the aqua-colored water; the color was from the Glacial flour runoff from the mountain.

The first thing that came to my mind was that the water might very well be unhealthy, and we should just go ahead and keep driving. My wife changed her clothes in the restroom. I continued to walk the path all the way around the lake. Then I heard the distinctive sound of children laughing, like at a playground. It came from the tree line, and I felt eyes watching my every move. I heard it briefly one more time before we left. As we drove away, I recalled someone had mentioned to me that they had heard the very same thing at an encounter with a Sasquatch family. I instantly knew what I had just heard. I told my wife, and she had heard it too. She was excited and said she believed it had been the big creatures.

As I said, we live in a very, very remote area, and my dogs often bark at Coyotes and wild Mustangs. However, there are times when they bark violently and then just cower and hide. These creatures are swift and know stealth tactics that Army Rangers only dream of. These guys are real pros in the bush, and they have had a very long time to dial in on their craft indeed.

I was in the Marine Corps and was trained in stealth tactics, but my skill level is not an inkling in comparison.

The Sasquatch Attacking Native Tribes in history and having battles are for real. They are still attacking us, grabbing our children, elderly, even our strongest and smartest that are naive enough to believe they are completely safe in the forests of North America.

Make no mistake people; some of these creatures don't give a hoot about your human rights. You may very well be the main course, and that could be wrong to some degree too. Maybe somewhere in between, like Humanity, not all of us are warm fuzzy creatures, from not so good experiences of life. Some are brutal in their outlook. Just saying.

Father And Son Terrorized On Hunting Trip

September 2015 N.W. Colorado. California park. Right on the other side of Sand Mountain. An 11,0000 ft peak from Steamboat Lake. Scouting Elk early September just before muzzle loading for my fall rifle hunt. My son (15) at the time and I (38 years old) I am an experienced big-game hunter with 12 years as a professional guide experience hunting Big game in NW Colorado. Elk, Bear, Mule deer, cougar antelope. We are camped at the entrance to California park coming from the Hayden Colorado entrance; This is my backyard. I lived there for 20+ years

At around 10 am, my son and I set up camp at the government corrals on top of California park. Anyone familiar with the country knows what I am talking about. At around 1 pm we struck out for some scouting to find recent game activity in the area. Being familiar with the area, we set out on a couple mile hike. We had lunch in the woods after a few miles and headed back to camp.

After returning to camp, I was tired and took a nap. My son was at the back of the truck in the cooler, making a sandwich. As I slept all of a sudden, a HUGE rock, literally the size of a bowling ball, landed 15 feet from the back of my tent. It startled me to the 10th power. I came out with my Glock drawn to see the aspen tree behind my tent still shaking from being hit with the rock. There is absolutely no explanation for it. We were alone on the mountain. Blew it off after looking around as just a freak thing.

Later that night, we had a campfire. We were in the same spot. Hit the rack around 10 pm. Around 2 am, it was completely calm, weather-wise, and I was sound asleep. All of a sudden, a very large tree came crashing down about 50 yards from the tent to the northeast of us. Absolutely scared the shit out of me: Pitch black, no moon, no wind. Freaking crazy.

After about 10 minutes, I finally got my heart rate back under control and laid down again. I was notching it up to some freak thing again. It wasn't 2 minutes later an incredibly loud howling kind of noise came roaring from the woods about 20 yards to our north. This is a thick alpine mountain environment. Wouldn't have been able to see what it was if it was daylight much less than 2 am. It proceeded to do this several more times. Then about 100yds to our south, there was a freaking reply to this thing that sounded almost identical. I was in the process of shitting my pants while I drug my half-asleep son to the truck in a total panic. We jumped in the truck, and I fired it up and honked the horn to try to scare them away. I drove the truck in circles, trying to get the headlights on whatever it was. Didn't ever see it.

After about 10 minutes, I turned the truck off. Literally, for the rest of the night, I sat in my truck with my Glock in my lap, and my window cracked, listening to tree knocks in the distance. My Glock is an S&W .40 cal. It's a badass weapon. I did NOT feel safe!!!!

Packed up at daylight and have not been to California park in Routt national forest in North West Colorado since. I now live near Yellowstone, and I am more comfortable dealing with grizzly bears than those freaking things.

They are real. That's not the only time I have been around them, but that's the scary one for sure>

Thanks for all you do, Steve!!

Peace,
Brian Crabb

Father And Daughter Terrified

Hello, I'm 53 years old. I live in the small town of New Trenton, Indiana, about 25 miles northwest of Cincinnati, Ohio, but it is still a pretty rural area. Where I spent the past 30 plus years deer hunting, and to say I love deer hunting would be an understatement. I hunt every day

I can. Some years even every day of all three deer seasons. Bow, firearm, and muzzleloader. Normally, I pick out one certain buck and hunt until I score or the season ends.

I'm sure you understand what I mean when I say I can identify all the animals in my area by just the sounds they make. Most animals have a distinct walk or call that is hard to miss after years of hearing them.

First, I want to say I believe in Bigfoot, and most people think I am a little crazy about it. Even my adult children think I've lost it, but I've never cared what most people think. I know what I've heard and what I've seen. That's all that matters to me.

It was an early spring night around 10:30 pm. The trees had just started to green out. My 15 yr. old daughter and I just watched a few of your videos; I have to say you have the best stories! I know to keep it short and quick!

I will start off with I'm an 18-year veteran, Military Police, I've become a local Police Officer here in east Texas. My Mothers dad was Choctaw First Nations American, and he always told me stories about the "big one"! I just thought of them as stories. When I was 10 in 1983, my Mother and my stepdad were driving me back up to my dad's in Paris, as we crossed the Sulphur River, I looked down into the river as I always had, to see how full it was, I saw a huge RED long hair Man. But he was covered with it!! It just stood there and looked at us and watched us pass! I looked at my Mom, her face was blank, mouth wide open and eyes just as big, I asked, "Did you see that?" she just shook her head yes.

Now while in the military, even stationed in Colorado, I haven't seen anything. Now I live in a small community in East Texas. I have 14 acres, and am an avid hunter; always have been. I live in a small one-bedroom cabin on a two-acre pond. I've been having my cabin slapped, it and rocks on my tin roof!

Hunting season comes close, and here in Texas, we can have feeders. I was going out to add corn to the feeders. I took a 22 for snakes, that's all.

As I was about to walk around a bush, then all of a sudden, this thing came alive!!! I mean, the bush was shaken, the big oak tree next to it was shaken, so I stopped, walked backwards a bit, watching this, thinking that maybe a black bear had come on my property. This thing keeps going on like crazy!!! So, I kept walking backwards, thinking, "Whatever this is, all I have is this 22, I have to aim for the eye!!!" I kept walking back. The further away I got, the more this would calm down.

Look, I'm 46 years old, and I have hunted all my life, and I have never run out of my own woods!! But this day I did! So, I reached out to a friend who knew a few guys with the BFRO, now don't get me wrong, I don't have a lot of faith in these guys, but I didn't know what I was facing, so they came out for a weekend.

We went into my woods and found a 17-inch bare foot in a creek bed! If I didn't see it myself, I

Steve Isdahl   The Day Sasquatch Became Real For Me   Copyright© 2020

wouldn't believe them! Then we started hearing chatter like I never heard before in the woods! After watching your videos and doing other self-investigations, I know that they are real! I think they come through during the fall and winter. But I don't hunt my woods anymore. Not knowing what I know now! My foot is 10", I'm 6' tall, this was 17", that would make it 9-10' tall!!

Please tell my story, but keep my name out of it! Being a cop and all!!

Thanks! And keep up the great work!!

Sea To Sky region B.C.

Another Concerned Father

My name is Carl Hall, Jr. I'm 53 years old. I live in the small town of New Trenton, Indiana, about 25 miles northwest of Cincinnati, Ohio, but it is still a pretty rural area. Where I spent the past 30 plus years deer hunting, and to say I love deer hunting would be an understatement. I hunt every day I can. Some years even every day of all three deer seasons. Bow, firearm, and muzzleloader. Normally, I pick out one certain buck and hunt until I score or the season ends.

I'm sure you understand what I mean when I say I can identify all the animals in my area by just the sounds they make. Most animals have a distinct walk or call that is hard to miss after years of hearing them.

First, I want to say I believe in Bigfoot, and most people think I am a little crazy for it. Even my adult children think I've lost it, but I've never cared what most people think. I know what I've heard and what I've seen. That's all that matters to me.

It was an early spring night around 10:30 pm. The trees had just started to green out. My 15-year-old daughter and I were working on the chicken coops op in the backyard. There are about 50 yards of flat yard. Then the wooden hillside. These woods are part of a 500-acre farm with only a few houses on it.

When I first heard the first three knocks, I told my daughter it was the neighbor boy hitting something with a bat. I knew better. The knocks were too high on the hill to be him; the force of the impact was hard that a major leaguer could produce. They were at least 150 yards out on the hillside. Well, past his house. We just went back to work when the second set of knocks rang out. The power of the knocks was undeniable. Man, this thing was strong, and to make it worse, these were right above us on the first flat on the hillside.

Even though it was dark and with only a small flashlight, I could see my daughter was scared, but before I could think of what to say. Whatever made the first knocks, came running towards the second noisemaker. His strips were long and heavy—Thud, thud, thud. No doubt, it was on two legs.

Whatever was running had no flashlight. I would be able to see it if there was one, but the area is too thick to run through in the dark without a light. The ground it covered in 6 or 7 seconds was impossible. It was only about 50 yards from the second set of knocks when it happened. A loud heavy huff is the best way to describe it, which brought our runner to a halt.

My daughter was losing it by now. She was trying to hide behind me, but she still wanted to make sure nothing was coming out of the woods towards us. I was trying to tell her it was just boys playing in the woods, but she knew better.

Neither one of them made any more noises for the next few moments. Then came a softer thud than before, almost like a heavy smack on a tree by a boxing glove. Then a loud crash of a good size tree hitting the ground. That was enough for both of us, so I pinned my daughter to my back and walked backwards to the house.

The next day, I walked out into the yard. I just stood there looking into the woods. My daughter came out and said, "you want to go look?" Without a word, I started up the hill. It didn't take long for me to find the downed tree. It was a semi-dried oak with a 10-inch diameter. The one thing I know for sure is, this tree didn't fall on its own.

These next parts I'll keep short and sweet. Two weeks later, my two daughters and I were driving past a clear cut through the woods. The clear cut is for a pipeline. It's a good spot to see deer cross. Sure enough, there were three does standing close to the road looking back up the hill. I glanced to see what was up the hill just before we lost sight of the gap. There it stood behind a cedar tree looking down the hill. The tree is a six-footer with its head and shoulders above the tree. I turned around as soon as I could, which only took a few seconds, but all the animals were gone.

My daughter that doesn't want to believe also saw it but refuses to talk about it.

Thank You,
Carl Hall, Jr.

Another One From British Columbia

Hi Steve,

First off, I want to say that I really enjoy your YouTube channel, direct, honest and none of the fluff.

My name is Randy B; I'm a 52-year-old guy who has been fishing, hunting and guiding for most of my life. My story began in 1996 when a good friend of mine and I were deer hunting in a place called Botanie Valley, North of Lytton, near a lake called Pasulko lake.

It was late November, and there was quite a bit of snow on the ground. We set up camp below a high ridge, made a fire, and it was late, dark and cold. Sitting around the fire having a beer, my friend said he felt like something was watching us, I too got a bit of an eerie feeling but didn't want to mention it, we turned in for the night and woke up early to hike to our spot. Walking up the tree line to the ridge above our camp we found some huge human-like footprints in the snow directly above our camp, we both stopped and looked at each other, we couldn't believe this, I remember thinking we should have gotten out of there, it really shook me, but my buddy wanted to follow them.

We followed the tracks for quite a distance into the thick forest where there wasn't any snow. I think one of us even took some photos, wish I knew where they were now. I was on edge the rest of that hunt and couldn't wait to get out of there. A few months later, I contacted a Bigfoot researcher, his name was Rene and explained everything that we saw, and I think he recorded it somewhere.

My hunting buddy and his wife were down for a visit from Barriere a couple of weeks ago, and I mentioned that Botanie Valley hunting trip. He said I know exactly what you're going to say, lol. He has never told anyone about those tracks we saw, and I didn't want to talk about it in front of his wife.

I have never told anyone besides that researcher and now you about this because I don't want people to think I'm nuts. Anyway, I consider myself lucky to have never run into one of these things face to face, the footprints scared the hell out of me enough.
Cheers,
Randy

It Killed A Huge Elk

This was the summer of 1983. I was 13 years old and went on vacation with my family to my grandmother's home located in Superior Montana, a small town just before Missoula Montana.

The drive there is long for a kid, but we finally made it. The plan was a week and a few days to hang out. One of the days, my Dad Uncle, an older cousin with my older brother and myself were going to go trout fishing.

One of my Uncle's brothers was a forest ranger. He told my Dad and my Uncle about a really nice fishing spot and not a spot for die-hard fishermen, but told it was a great spot. This place was called Little Joe or Joe's Creek.

This was the morning of the day of fishing we got up before sun up how my Dad and Uncle did things, so we got the gear load and off we went my Uncle's brothers showed my Dad on a map where the best place to go, so that is where we were heading.

Sun is coming up and we are on an old logging road heading up thick forest and both sides as I can see. My Uncle says we are at the spot, so my Dad parks the van. We get out, grab our gear, and polls, and head off to the creek. We all got our polls in. It was great, good hits, and clear water. Everything was perfect. We spent the morning mostly in one spot, but then it began to die off. It was warming up and going to be a hot one that day.

We all walked down the creek a bit to find other spots. For most of the day, we had been up and down the creek a mile or two. The creek we been up and down at one section had a large curve to it with a high embankment on the inner side. I would say it was close to 30-40 ft high. I passed through that part of that creek a dozen are, so times walking back and forth.

We were all at this time fishing a bit lower than the curved part of the creek. My Cousin, Dad, Brother, and Uncle all decided to go back up where we started that morning. As we got to the curve, we see in the creek a big bull Elk dead in the creek. It was not there until now, and its neck was broken like spun around.

My Dad, Uncle and Cousin looked at it closely and said it was still warm. This just happened. I ask how it happened? Dad and Uncle didn't know my Cousin said it must have fallen from up there, pointing at the top of the embankment. He said it must have slipped off and broke its neck on the way down.

I was 13, so I was ok, but I was in awe of such a massive bull elk it was the size of a horse. At this point, my Dad, Uncle and Cousin decided to go to the first spot and my older brother, and I decided to go down from where the elk was and a bit further than we had been.

As we went down the creek it split around the tree in the middle of the creek my brother and I thought it was a good place to fish. As we got to the tree and the piece of damp sand, we stood there, and my brother looked down and said, "what is that?"

I also looked down at what he was pointing at. In the damp sand, there were his footprints, as well as mine, but there also was a large bare footprint in the sand. My older brother looked at me and took off running up the creek leaving me standing there. He was at a dead run and he was fast so I thought why is he running like a fool and thought to myself why is my cousin fishing in his bare feet?

My Cousin was tall 6 "4 or so. The creek itself was more than twelve feet across, and I'm looking at the footprint comparing to mine; it seems huge. It was wider than both my feet together, and as long as my fingertips to my elbow. At this point, I still think my Cousin has huge feet.

I look to my left. As I look up the creek and the direction where the footprint was coming from, I see on the bank another footprint; toe dug in more, and it was of the left foot. I turned back to look at the footprint I just seen, and it was the right foot too. I went back to it and was going to look the way it was going, and I heard something large ahead of me and seen the bushes or whatever they were, pushed to the side like someone went through them. Then I smelled something bad, like an old musky skunk.

I froze. The hair on my head felt like it stuck out straight on my head, arms, and legs. I saw something so massive back passed the thick vegetation, by the trees, standing and watching me, rocking side to side. It was dark, but it was way bigger than my Cousin. I didn't know what to do. I wanted to cry or scream, but I froze in fear.

Then I heard a crack of a branch, it set me into a panicked run up the creek. I didn't look back; I just ran and ran right to the van. I got in and locked all the doors, laid on the floor and cried. I was so scared. Then I heard noises outside the van like someone was walking around it. I laid motionless on the floor. It felt like an hour that I laid there.

I heard my Uncle and my Dad calling me. I got up off the floor, looked out the windows and seen nothing. I was scared to say a word. Still, I had to. So, I yelled out the cracked window, "here in the van Dad."

My Dad saw I was scared out of my wits and asked what was wrong? I said, "I think I saw a Bigfoot." He looked at me like I was crazy.

My brother was not saying much about it. He was like, "We saw a footprint, it looked like." and I was like, "It was!"

I asked my Dad can we please go now? I don't want to be here and began to cry because I was so scared. He asked where my poll was? I told him I left it down at the creek. He wanted me to go get with my brother, and I said, "NO, I won't. I'm not getting out of this van."
My Dad was a bit mad at me, so my Uncle said he would go and get it. We all waited for my Uncle Bud to come back. He did without my poll and said to my Dad it's time to go now. The look on his face said enough that he was scared as well. My Uncle never spoke about why he got scared that day to anyone or me.

To this day I don't fish in creeks in the mountains alone or at all. I was 13, and now I'm going on 50. I don't hike alone in the mountains where I'm from Mt Hood region. There are always two or more people if I go. I've seen bears and wolves in the wild. They didn't scare me as much as that did in my whole life.

I've told this to a few people, but they think I'm lying or telling a spook story; it's not! If my brother was still alive, he would tell you we saw that footprint together.

Police Officer Can't Hunt His Property Anymore

Hello, I just watched a few of your videos, and I have to say you have the best stories! I know to keep it short and quick! So, I will start off with I'm an 18-year veteran, Military Police, I've become a local Police Officer here in east Texas.

My Mother's Dad was Choctaw First Nations American. He always told me stories about, "the big one!" I just thought of them as stories.

When I was 10 in 1983, my Mother and stepdad were driving me back up to my Dad's in Paris. As we crossed the Sulphur River, I looked down into the river as I always had, to see how full it was. I saw a huge RED long-haired Man. But he was covered with it!! It just stood there and looked at us and watched us pass!

I looked at my Mom; her face was blank, mouth wide open and eyes just as big. I asked, "Did you see that?" she just shook her head yes.

While in the military, even stationed in Colorado, I haven't seen anything. Now I live in a small community in East Texas, and I have 14 acres. I'm an avid hunter, always have been. I live in a small one-bedroom cabin on a two-acre pond. I've been having my cabin slapped, it and rocks on my tin roof!

So anyway, hunting season comes close, and here in Texas, we can have feeders. I was going out to add corn to them. I took a 22 for snakes, that's all.

Black bear feeding on protein near Vancouver Island beach

As I was about to walk around a bush, all of a sudden, this thing came alive!!! I mean, the bush was shaking, the big oak tree next to it was shaking. So, I stopped, walked backwards a bit, watching this, thinking that maybe a black bear had come on my property. This thing kept going on like crazy!!!

I kept walking backwards, thinking, "Whatever this is, all I have is this 22; I have to aim for the eye!!!" I kept walking backwards. The further away I got, the more this would calm down.

Look, I'm 46 years old, and I have hunted all my life, and I have never run out of my own woods!! But, this day, I did!

I reached out to a friend who knew a few guys with the BFRO. Now don't get me wrong, I don't have a lot of faith in these guys, but I didn't know what I was facing. They came out for a weekend. We went into my woods and found a 17-inch bare foot in a creek bed! If I didn't see it myself, I wouldn't believe them! Then we started hearing chatter like I never heard before in the woods!

Steve Isdahl   The Day Sasquatch Became Real For Me   Copyright© 2020

After watching your videos and doing other self-investigations, I know that they are real! I think they come through during the fall and winter.

I don't hunt my woods anymore. Not knowing what I know now! My foot is 10", I'm 6' tall, this was 17", that would make it 9-10' tall!!

Please tell my story, but keep my name out of it! Being a cop and all!!
Thanks! And keep up the great work!!

You Can't Not See Once You See

Hi Steve,

Thank you for creating this forum to educate and, in my case, help me heal from the experience I had. I had a face to face encounter with a male Bigfoot in the 1st week of October 2016, in the upper peninsula of Michigan.

He was massive, well developed and very healthy looking—jet black hair with an oil-like sheen in the sunlight. Long arms, powerfully built like beyond steroids. Hair was very thick, and I only knew it was hair by the way it was stringy looking on the forearms. Chest breastplate was like slate gray color leather, which was not hair covered and did not have a weathered or cracked, dry appearance. The face was flat; straight lips did not show teeth. The nose was flat. Eyes were black with no white or pupil showing. The face was the same color as the breastplate and did not have a weathered appearance. The hair on the abdomen had some white/gray streaks starting at the xiphoid process wrapping around the diaphragm and streaked down into the groin on each side. I did not see male genitals. Upper legs were massively built like true tree trunks. I did not see from the knees down.

Time was about 1:30 in the afternoon. The temp was around 60. Mostly sunny day, but we were on the north slope of an east/west running ridge of mix timber, pine, hemlock, cedar and poplar/aspen trees. Sun was at my back and in his face through the canopy, which showed the oil-like sheen on the hair.

The wind was from SW @ maybe 5mph. I did not smell it as it was a crosswind. The entire ridge was covered with tree snaps, x's on the ground, and maple tree bends. There were also two pine trees that had branches knocked off, and they were woven into a shield or blind like structure. This being wanted me to see it.

I was looking at a tree bend, and it made a noise to make me look at it. Not a grunt or growl, maybe just a smack or thud on a tree. I looked and told myself that it looked like a deltoid and bicep muscle. Then my brain put the whole package together, and we were eye to eye. I started to back up in pure fear of what I was looking at. Maybe 30 feet for 30 seconds, I'm not sure. Scared shitless and can't really remember getting back to my truck at maybe 200 yards away. It did not follow me, and I thanked the Lord for that. I have had other unexplained events in the woods from age 14-54.

I currently live in NC and really am not worth a crap in the woods anymore. Other than opening day of rifle deer season, I never travelled in the woods with a weapon or even a knife. Your recent story of the torn cedar bark hit home. I found four cedar trees striped the same way, and they all showed five nail marks in the shape of a huge handprint. I believe they use these markers for night navigation as the ones I found ran in a straight line for a half-mile. Use this as you will, please caution people not to go looking for them. You cannot unsee what you will find.

Respectfully,
Larry Hintsala

Myself and friend high above Goldbridge B.C.

Just Standing In The River

Hi Steve. I live in Colorado and was always skeptical about the existence of these things until about ten years ago. One of my brother's came out to visit from the east coast and wanted to do some rock hounding. I live in Duenna Vista and we have a bunch of savage wildernesses all around. I took him to a place well known for gathering garnets and cool rocks. Now I must add that I have worked in two different state prisons and am very keen on details and horrible situations. Facts and accurate report writing are a must. Both my brother and myself have 20\20 vision and have been in the woods our whole life. Hunting camping fishing you name it we have done it. We were up on a cliff side approximately 300 feet above the Arkansas river in Brown's canyon when I looked down at the river. What looked like Backache from Star Wars was standing near the river about a hundred yards downstream.

I say Backache because the colour of the hair was the same only in comparison Backache would have been much skinnier. I tapped my brother and said look right there it looks like a freaking Bigfoot! Are you seeing what I'm seeing? He affirmed that I was not hallucinating and we just stared at it for about 5 more seconds. The creature was looking in our direction and I know it was watching us also. It took two slow steps back without moving its arms as if trying for minimal noticeable movement and disappeared in the trees. We stood there for a few more moments trying to make excuses for what we clearly saw. It was the strangest experience I had ever had. Again, I must say it was summer and no hunting season was on.

I own a ghillie suit and it was not that because at that distance I could see hair. I could not make out the details of the face at that distance but it appeared fairly flat with no prominent features. As far as my feelings were concerned, I was more in amazement than fear. We had the high ground and some reasonable distance from it and my jeep was just over the other side. I cannot deny the evidence of my own eyes and have gone over the scenario in my head for years. I would not have wanted to be any closer to it because it was very big and powerful looking.

I always carry in the wilderness but looking at that thing my 45 would probably have felt like bee stings to it. The experience has not kept me from the wild because I figure the law of averages. One experience in my life at 47 years old. I'll probably never see another one. If the subject comes up, I tell my story to people and like you don't care what they think so feel free to use my name. Your channel is one of my favourites for both hunt stories and this subject. Thanks

Shawn L Ague

A Scout Sniper Shares With Us

Hi Steve,
I recently discovered your Channel on YouTube as we just got Netflix on our Smart TV otherwise, I'm not socially connected at all so this is a whole new thing for me. I'm hooked on your channel and I appreciate your straightforward honest approach to dealing with issues and people. Little background on me I'm 57 and have had a lifelong passion for deer hunting, trapping and fishing. I've spent hundreds of hours camping, scouting and hunting the western states pursuing my passion. I spent 11 years in the USMC Recon most of which as a scout

sniper. I was involved in many missions all over the Middle East and Africa and Serbia and saw a lot of combat and horrible things. I can handle myself in the woods or anywhere else.

My son he is also a very passionate Outdoors man, hunter found you on YouTube and convince me that I needed to write you and tell you my story he's one of only a few people I've ever told but he knows my word is the only thing that matters to me so if I said it it happened. I watched some of the TV shows and heard some of the broadcasters and personalities and all seem to think that this is some sort of a joke I wonder how much time they spent in the woods? Or how much time they spent with mortars going off around them and .762 AK-47 rounds flying by their face I wonder why they're word would be more honest than mine.... douche bags.

All the vent you'll get out of me... it was 2006 I was hunting in Central Oregon on the east side of the Cascade Range trying to kill a big black tail I had my base camp set up at about for 4000 feet I think in a small clearing about four miles from any road. I had spent the first two days scouting and found a buck that I wanted to try for so on the third morning I set off an hour before sunrise and started heading up the slope to a good spot where I could easily glass a couple Meadows at first light. I got set up, leaned my rifle against the tree and started wiping the dew off my binoculars and opened up a power bar. It was still a little too dark to see so I started tuning my eyes into the meadow while I ate my breakfast. I had made at least 20 DIY hunts in Western States in my life but never to this particular area as I have never killed a big black tail and this was supposed to be a good area.

Not having the funding for an outfitter/guide I always went by myself on public land and had a good time. So first light comes and I start glassing the meadow I heard some noise off to my left the West it sounded like something was coming up the ridge it was going to come out in a small neck down that fed into the meadow...so I turn and got my rifle up assuming it was a deer. I can see movement in the brush about a hundred yards to my West but the brush was thick enough I couldn't make it out but could tell it was not a deer...Eventually I could make out that it was upright so I assumed it was another Hunter.

He got to the edge of the meadow and stood there kind of crouching behind some bushes... so I'm getting a little pissed off as someone ease's got in the same exact area I was in and I hadn't seen a soul in the two days I scouted or even any human tracks so I rose up slowly and whistled at the guy waving my right arm over my head to let him know "hey there's a hunter here go somewhere else... " he immediately wheeled to his right to face me directly when he did that I could see he was immense across the shoulders I thought holy Christ I'm 6 '2" 220 he made me look like a child. As soon as he saw me even though it was dimly lit, I could tell we were looking at each other and he ducked down in the bushes I thought what the hell?

So, I set my rifle back against the tree and stepped out into the meadow so he could get a clear look at me. I started walking towards him. I want to hunt this area. I want him to go somewhere else. There was plenty of time for him to leave and do that.... I took about 5 steps and he stood up again and this time I could tell it was not a man it was just too damn big and covered in hair he started grunting at me and shaking the bushes in front of it my rifle was still leaning against the tree where I had originally sat but I raised my Weiss up and looked at his face.

Steve Isdahl   The Day Sasquatch Became Real For Me   Copyright© 2020

I can't tell you a ton of details as I was totally startled but he had dark hair certainly all over what I could see except for the face there was a lot of Flesh on the face broad forehead broad nose big lips and a huge set of shoulders and chest I could never see his legs very well because of the brush.

But I have sent spent countless hours looking through binoculars and a rifle scope and I know exactly what I'm looking at when I'm looking at it and this was no man and it was no ape and it was no joke and it was a no dumb ass in a ghillie suit.... the whole instant only took a matter of minutes but it never stopped grunting and growling at me and shaking the bushes though it never came out in the clearing or towards me any further it certainly made me feel like it did not want me there and I was in danger.

He was downhill from me so it was hard for me to get a judge his height but the bushes were clearly four to five feet tall and it was well above those I'm going to guess it a good seven or eight feet tall with shoulders a good 4ft across with massive arms and head were also massive in proportion to a human.

I was within 95 yards of this thing with a clean line of sight looking through quality Optics. I've never seen anything like it before or since and I do not ever want to see another one. It was a truly a spooky deal I instinctively backed up I picked up my rifle shouldered it and centred the cross hairs on his face it stared at me intently and very menacing it would have been an easy shot but something told me inside not to shoot something told me it was absolutely the wrong thing to do so I held my rifle up with my right hand and raise my left hand over my head and looked at him in a submission. I didn't know what else to do...I slung my rifle, picked up my backpack and headed back down the trail to Camp never looking back...

I never heard him or saw him again. I got back to my tent and packed up everything headed down to the truck went to town. I stayed the night in town and then I drove to a new hunting area 35 miles to the north to finish out my trip the next morning, I didn't want to waste my tag and waste my Bible vacation time so I tried my best play ended up unsuccessful in filling my tag That season and yes I was rattled the whole fucking time.. I've only told my family and a few close friends my story. My son believes me I don't know if anyone else does or doesn't I don't really give a shit I've got nothing to prove to anybody. I know what I saw and like I said a man's word should be enough.

Thanks for hearing me out I really appreciate what you were doing it's nice to have a sounding board to get this off my chest it's been almost 14 years and I relive it every single day I cannot get it out of my mind everything that goes bump in the night what makes a sound in the woods gets my immediate attention isn't that crazy question mark especially after what I've been through? LOL what a fucking world we live in huh Steve? Be careful my friend and God bless feel free to contact me anytime you can share my story with others if you want

Temper F

Steve Isdahl   The Day Sasquatch Became Real For Me   Copyright© 2020

Kurt Johnson

A Disabled Veteran Shares

Hi Steve, my name is Sid Daugherty (pronounced: Arty). I am a disabled veteran and served 6 years in the U.S military.

I am from North East Tennessee and I was raised in Southwest Virginia (not West Virginia). Around 1999 or 2000 my wife and son and I owned a place in southwestern Virginia outside of Bristol VA and TN. We lived there for around 10 years before we moved to TN. We had a dog that was part Husky and I don't know what and he was huge. His back came above my knees and just below my waist and he weighed around 125 pounds or more. He liked to kill groundhogs and would bring them to the door and sit until I acknowledge him. I loved that dog. I can say that I never knew of that dog backing down or being afraid of anything except one time.

Where we lived was out in the country and was remote enough that we would have to drive 20 minutes to town. There is a place called Gum hill that isn't far from where we lived and the old folks will tell you of something there they call " The wood booger". There is a video of a Bigfoot crossing a creek in front of a four-wheeler that has been on TV and Moneymaker and his crew came in to do whatever they do. That place was just a mile or more from my house.

One night my dog had gotten agitated and was throwing a fit. I went outside to calm him and see if I could see what was making him so agitated. He was on the front porch and as I opened the door, he ran to me. I had my gun and walked down the steps out into the yard with my dog beside me. As we came up to the creek and just out of the range of the house lights, he reacted fierce. There was a smell that hit me that I have never smelled since it before. I can't describe it but the closest I can get is that it smelled dead, and skunk y and like a wet dog all at the same time. And it was so strong that it pushed me away from it. But my dog was barking and showing his teeth like he was going to fight something. As I backed up a little, because I didn't want to get sprayed by a skunk, my dog took off. He hit the creek wide open and was across it in a blink. He was throwing a fit and then he yelped and came running back. That dog was terrified! He was trying to get between my legs and was shaking

.

I backed up and had my weapon up ready to fire if something came out and walked backwards to the house and safety of the light. My dog ran to the front door and was clawing at the door to get in. Even though he never came inside. I stayed outside waiting to hear something or see something but never did. All that was there was that awful smell. Then it just went away. It never came back and I never found the source of it. My dog ran into the house and went under a table beside my bed and wouldn't come out until the next day. And I had to drag him out then.

I've never experienced anything like that before or since. I asked around from neighbours to see if they had noticed or seen anything and that's when I learned of the " Wood Booger". What ever scared my dog did something that nothing else ever did. And I sure never wanted to find out. I have a pretty good idea what happened that night. You can use my name if you like. I have told this story and have been ridiculed and made fun of but I'm the type of person that could careless what people think. I know what happened.

Vancouver Island B.C.

Coastal British Columbia

Hey Steve,

I hope you and the missus are doing well, staying safe, and healthy.
I've been watching your videos, as well as Scott Carpenter's, and of course Dave Paul ides'.
I know that I asked you not to use my name when reading my previous emails, but I've changed my mind, not that you need or want to now anyway.

I feel that because so many people have had the courage to come forward and be okay with you using their name with their stories, that it's time I did the same.
So, feel free to use my name, my buddy. Even with my previous stories. We're all in this together.

Here's another story for ya, sorry for the length.

The last year that I went to Chelsea was 2007. We didn't camp at the site where I had my sighting, but we went back because I wanted to see the place again.
Looking at google maps now it looks like the area has become an industrial park of sorts.
When I was there in '07 with Robert, the access road for the pump station was blocked of with a 6' pile of dirt and rocks right at the entrance. I had a Land Rover back the and had no problem trailblazing through the thick brush around it, and we carried on down the road.

When we were approaching the clearing we had camped in, about 75 metres away, a turkey vulture, that was in that clearing, rushed onto the road and took off flying directly towards us while looking behind itself. It flew right towards us and wasn't any more than 30cm directly above the roof of the rover. I could see the feathers on its belly through the sunroof. It was that closed.

Robert looks at me and says, "I've never seen a turkey vulture fly towards people. It looked like it was being chased."

We drove on, and when we came to the clearing on the left side of the road there was garbage strewn around and a stand-up freezer lying on its side with the door open, flat on the ground. Inside the freezer, were two large plastic ice cream tubs, like the ones you get the no name ice cream at Dominion in, and they were chalk full of something red, with the lids on.

We were suddenly hit with a powerful stink of rotting flesh, mixed with shit and who knows what else. It was enough to make us gag. Because of the stink we decided to drive on to the pump station. When we reached it the road across the right of way was blocked with boulders that I couldn't drive around so we decided to park the truck and carry on by foot.

When we got to the other side of the right of way where boulders were again blocking the road, we heard a commotion of branches breaking and trees shaking back by the truck and pump house, but when we looked we couldn't see what was going on, but the noise was still there. We shrugged our shoulders and carried on. I was just hoping that my truck wouldn't have broken windows when we came back.

We hiked for a couple kilometres down the road. On the left side was a sheer drop off to a ravine below. We decided to stop for a snack and a drink, we sat down with our legs dangling over the edge, and spoke quietly.

It was only minutes when we started to hear movement on the ridge above us. Someone was walking up there. We couldn't see them but we could hear their footsteps, and we could hear talking. A loud mumbling, and it was a familiar sound but we couldn't make heads or tales of what was being said in a very deep voice.
We stayed quiet, and listened. We stared at each other; eyes wide open. We knew what we

Steve Isdahl   The Day Sasquatch Became Real For Me

were listening to. The footsteps and mumbling receded in the direction we'd come from. Each of us took deep breaths and started talking about what we just heard.

The ravine was about 30' deep, and there was a lot of Sasquatch sign in it. We stood up, brushed ourselves off and carried on down the road. Another kilometre or so on, we took a game trail off the road and followed it to a steep trail that went down towards the sound of a river rushing below.

There were trees pulled down over this descending trail. I climbed down under the first one, about a four-foot drop. Down in this it was dark, with a ledge that was about a metre and a half square. Trees had been pulled in arches over this trail. It was really dark, so dark that I couldn't see to the bottom end of the trail, and it was still the middle of the afternoon.

That was enough for me so I climbed out. I wasn't about to try this descent; it would have been pretty hard to get back up without ropes but I could believe someone with four-foot-long legs would have no trouble with it. We headed back, but the game trail seemed to have disappeared. We couldn't tell where it was. My video camera batteries had all gone dead too. We had a video camera; each Robert had my digital still camera and I had my 35mm. I was out of film.

We bush whacked our way back to the road. This is where things got scary for a bit. We lost each other. One minute we were only 3m apart laterally, the next, Robert was gone. I couldn't hear him. I called out repeatedly, and never heard a reply.

It felt like I was being watched, and I thought Robert was ranking me. It seemed like it took me forever to reach the road again. When I did, I was maybe 500m further from where we had taken the game trail. No Robert on site.

I walked back towards the pump station. Calling for Robert when he finally answered and came out of the bush on my right. "What happened to you?" He asks, why wouldn't you answer me."
"I didn't hear you. I've been calling your name almost since we last saw each other."
Neither one of us had heard the other calling.

We decided to head back. We talked about how weird the experience there had been. First, the batteries going dead, then losing the game trail that had been so obvious before, and then losing each other. The weirdest part was not being able to hear each other calling.

When we got back to the right of way, I was relieved to see my truck in the same condition I left it. We climbed in and drove back up the access road towards the clearing. When we got there the two ice cream tubs were opened and empty, sitting on the ground a few feet from the freezer.

"Holy shit!" I yelled. "Those F ING tubs are empty!"

I stopped the truck and we both got out. We each examined the tubs. No damage whatsoever. No scratch marks. No tooth marks, no punctures. Someone, or something with thumbs, had pulled the lids off and consumed the entire four or five litres of what turned out to be raspberry preserves by the smell of it.

We were dumbfounded. Nobody in their right mind would have eaten something like that out of a discarded freezer. Inside the tubes were clear giant finger smears, where the preserves had been scraped from the inside. There was only a spot of it left in one of the tubs.

Suddenly there was a loud racket of leaves shaking behind us that scared the shit out of the two of us. At the same time, myself and Robert jumped in the air and spun 180 degrees around. He with my little digital Canon, and me with my empty 35mm. Ready to take pictures.

There was nothing there but a birch tree swaying back and forth furiously. Easily making a five-foot-wide arch at the top. Two ravens suddenly fell out of the top of the tree as it was swaying. One looked like it was falling on its back and the other was just falling.

At the same time, they spread their wings. The one falling backwards righted itself as it spread its wings and the two of them flew away without a peep, or a squawk. The only sound they made was the wings of their feathers brushing together as they flew off. "It was just ravens," I said to Robert. "Yeah," he agreed. Neither one of us wondering at the time how two ravens would have gotten a thirty-foot-tall tree to sway violently back and forth, in five-foot arch at the top. Never occurred to us until we were halfway back to his house.
How F's up is that?
Anyway, that's already too much for now. I still have a couple more to share, but that will wait for another time.

Make sure you watch your back, my buddy.
Cheers,
Ricardo A

Near An Albertan City

Hey, how's it going?

So, I saw something recently on TV that made me decide to tell you of my encounter with something a couple of times now.

First of all, I live in a small city in central Alberta Canada where I would say things like this aren't supposed to happen. Things like this, you hear of happening in the mountains and various other places, but not here. Which is why I'm dumbfounded by what I'm sure I saw.

One day last summer, I stumbled upon a parking lot at the edge of town. Kind of just out there at the edge of town where it's not really close to anything. There was one of those red garbage cans that wildlife can't get into because of how it's shaped and the fact that there's a handle on it that requires a hand with a disposable thumb to operate. There's also a brick out house that's supposed to clean itself after any time someone uses it. Right beside that is a trail head for a multi-use pathway that goes through the trees and around the small lake that's part of the town. While I was having a smoke, I thought that I should bring my bike here and go for a ride down there. So, the next day I brought my bike and rode around the lake. It's about a ten-mile ride to go all the way around and get back to the start where this trail head is.

Anyway, as I was riding through trees, I could hear something big moving through the trees. I stopped and tried to see what it was but couldn't see a thing in there because the bush there is actually pretty thick. Not being able to see anything in there I got back on my bike and rode on.

A couple of days later, I stopped at the same parking lot for a cigarette on my way home. It's a nice quiet place with very few people around. It's a nice peaceful place. It's between eleven thirty and quarter to twelve at night when I pull in there and the sun hasn't long been set. A full moon is rising in the east behind the trees at the far end of the parking lot. I get out of my car and light my smoke. I take a drag off it and I hear the lid of the red garbage can dropping shut. It's loud enough that I turn my head to look. I can't really see much because that part of the parking lot doesn't have much light from the rising moon because of the thick trees. I think that I can see something moving, but can't see clearly enough so I shrug it off.

The breeze then changes direction and that causes the smoke from my cigarette to drift straight into my face, so I turn around. I'm now facing north and away from the brick out house I mentioned earlier which is on the south side of the parking lot. I'm still parked right by it near the west end of the parking lot. The parking lot stretches to the east of where I'm parked, maybe 60 to 70 yd, and there's a sign at the end and some posts with reflectors on them and another garbage can. There are trees on three sides of this parking lot and a field on the north side of it. So, I'm smoking away, and out of the corner of my eye, way to my right, I think that I can see something moving. So, I turned and looked, but whatever was moving stopped, and therefore I can only see a large shadow like thing there. I'm about to shrug it off when I notice that whatever that shadow is, it's casting a shadow now on the parking lot pavement.

The light of the moon is behind it and some of it is getting through the trees, which is causing the shadow on the pavement. I'm not sure what I'm seeing so I look intently at this dark thing standing there. I notice that the top of it is pretty much even with the top of the sign on the sign post. All of a sudden, I see that the reflector on one of the smaller posts at the tree line is coming into view and then going dark, over and over as if something is moving side to side and intermittently blocking out the light that's being reflected. I'm beginning to get afraid because I now realize that there's actually something standing there.

Something that I can't really see clearly, and it's also something rather big. I then start to hear, what sounds like a rumbling sound coming from that general direction. There shouldn't be any sound coming from that direction because there are no businesses or even any houses in that direction. It's just wilderness over there. Suddenly I can feel a huge amount of fear. It started at my feet and quickly went up the back of my legs and then my back until I could feel the hair on

Steve Isdahl   The Day Sasquatch Became Real For Me   Copyright© 2020

the back of my neck standing on end. I put out my smoke, jumped back in my car and got the hell outta there.

Anyway, I'd pretty much completely forgotten about that when I found myself pulling into the same parking lot last Sunday night for another smoke on my way home. As I was pulling in, I remembered the incident and turned on my bright lights to survey the parking lot in a big circle before stopping for my smoke. I saw nothing so I stopped and got out of the car. I'm looking towards the east end of the parking lot where I saw something the summer before as I smoke my cigarette, when I hear the strangest sound coming from behind me and to the right side of the brick out house. I turn around and am actually able to zero in on pretty much exactly where to sound is coming from but I can't see what's making the sound.

The sound that I'm hearing doesn't sound like anything I've ever heard from any wildlife that's in this area. It sounds like two sticks being clacked together really fast. Like in sets of maybe five or six clacks, and then a pause, then five or six more clacks and then a pause and so on. And it kept repeating. It was really intense because the sound got louder and louder and then faded off quickly and then got rather quiet. It seemed as though the sound was coming from the short grass to the right of the out house. So, I think that maybe someone is playing a prank on me so I move to my right to see if there's someone standing there around the corner of the out house. Instead of seeing anyone standing there, I see two dim red lights to the right of the outhouse and up in the air pretty close to the height of the roof line of this brick outhouse.

That's between nine and ten feet up. I think to myself, that's odd. So, I take another look to see if maybe those are some distant street lights or something peeking through the trees. I look to the right and up a bit and sure enough, I can see street lights from a nearby residential neighbourhood, but they are way brighter and not red. So, I look back at the dim red lights, and notice that they are moving slightly from side to side. I'm now starting to feel a lot of fear again and wondering to myself WTF is that? Just then, I hear what maybe sounds like a breath or maybe an exhale. So, I put out my smoke and get in my car and get the F out of there.

Now what convinced me that I should tell you about this was a TV show that aired on Tuesday. The show is called "Expedition Bigfoot". It was at the end of the episode (#4), when two of the scientists had put out some apples to draw a Bigfoot in, and they heard something nearby.
When they turned to look, the female scientist exclaimed that she could see "red eye shine"! When the camera man managed to focus in on it, I couldn't believe my eyes. The red eye shine looked just like the two dim red lights that I saw just a few nights earlier. The hair on my arms and the back of my neck stood up and my arms were covered in goosebumps! My heart was racing! I couldn't believe what I was seeing.

It was then that I decided that I needed to tell someone about what I saw, and you were the first one I thought of because every time you post a video, you post peoples stories without judgment, and I appreciate that. I've been listening to the stories you tell from other people who have had various encounters on your channel for a while now and never once thought that I would ever have any kind of encounter of my own, like ever in my life. I'm not going to tell you that I actually saw a Sasquatch, because to be honest, it was really dark there on Sunday night and I couldn't actually see anything except for those two dim red lights that seemed to be moving slightly from side to side. But I saw and heard something!

Anyway, I'd be honoured if you posted this story some time. BTW, I gotta tell ya that its okay if you don't believe me. Most people wouldn't anyway. That's kinda why I'm not really revealing a lot about myself or where specifically I live, but I do know that this really happened. My name is Peter, and this is a true story.
Thanks
Kindest regards
Peter

PS. I also believe, from all of the stories I've heard, that Sasquatch are sentient beings that we should just leave alone, and never harm! I hope you feel the same way. Thanks again.

Frozen ocean Kodiak Alaska

Another One From Oregon

Hello Steve,

My name is Mark Marcus. You can use my first name when sharing if you decide to share my story. I have more than one story about Sasquatch but let's start with the first one. I am willing to take a polygraph and can assure you what I tell you actually happened.

I am 60 years old and born 1960. I have two brothers, one 14 months older and one 26 months younger. This story happened between 1969 and 1971. We were living in Lincoln City Oregon. My dad had three river lots along the Silent River on the south side upstream about a mile from the Hwy. bridge where the natural gas pipeline crosses the river. My dad bought a Honda 70 trail bike that was gold colour. Three speed automatics. My brothers and I would take turns with it at the river lots while our dad was fishing.

As we got more confident with riding the Honda 70 the area, we rode expanded. The road to the property was built through wet lands like a dike road. We started riding clear to the main road which was a gravel road back then and paved now.

A spur road off the dike road to the East was an access to the pipeline that went over the hills. Later this road was the access to the cabin that was built for the movie "Sometimes a great notion" also called " never give an inch". One day I decided on my turn with the Honda 70 I was going to go on that spur road. As I was going on the road it started going up hill. I had only been on level roads and was not happy with my choice of the spur road I wanted to turn around but needed to find a wide area to do so. I'm still a little kid and turning around on an incline was out of the question so I kept going. Ahead of me I could see it was levelling out at the next corner. That was going to be the spot to turn around.

As I approached about 100 feet away, I saw something cross the road. It was about 3 to 4 feet tall, black and on two feet. It went into the wide area on the left so now I don't want to stop there and was a bit scared. As I approached the spot where it crossed, I looked to the left and there it was, standing in front of a bigger one that was like 7 or eight feet tall and had an arm holding across the chest area of the small one. The third one was like 10 or 11 feet tall. Yes, there were three of them together. I was really scared at this point and hit the throttle of the Honda and kept going. I went clear to the river and the road stopped there. I was trying to figure out how to get back to the river lot as I could see it downstream fry where I was at.

I spent some time trying to figure out how to get back but the only way was to go back the way I came from. A few hours had passed and the sun was going down so I headed back down the way I came from. As I approached the wide spot where the three were at, I was glad they were gone. Before I got all the way back, I had to turn on the lights on the bike. About a quarter mile from the river lots I see something in the road. It was my dad looking for me. I stopped the bike and tried to talk to my dad. He was pissed and was scolding me for being gone so long.

He finally stopped yelling at me and wanted to see what happened. I told him the story and called the three bears with a flat face. My dad got mad again and said bears are not around here and they don't walk on two feet. Now I am grounded.

About a month or two later my dad says I am sorry for not believing you about the bears. He said he was at the river lots and saw a bear and took a picture of him. It was a cub bear in a tree. The camera he used was a Polaroid instant photo he used at work. He showed me the picture and I said that's not what I saw and I told him the ones I saw looked nothing like that.

Steve Isdahl   The Day Sasquatch Became Real For Me   Copyright© 2020

They had no snout and a flattened nose and on two feet long arms and a lot bigger. He got upset and said he doesn't want to hear it anymore. I never called them Bigfoot as I never heard of Bigfoot or Sasquatch but I know they were. This was my first encounter and it was a close encounter as when I was as close as 40 to 50 feet away and could clearly see all three of them. They looked very close to one of your photos. I will send it with this letter. I love what you do and appreciate your work. Mark

Hi Steve, had a sighting dragging a buck out of state game area in Commons county Michigan 4th day gun season 2013.I've been hunting for 45 yrs. spend a lot of time in the woods,3 to 4 weeks a season camping hunt a flooding area roughly 6000 acres, lot of swamp with islands with some nice oaks on them. The DNA plants a few rye fields back there also, where I shot a nice 8 point that evening.2 days previous to this we had a bad storms blow thru the area with a lot of rain on the 17th.raised water levels in the flooding a lot, we have to cross an area that has a big culvert for draining mud lake to a swampy reason the way out that afternoon the 19th we noticed a lot of dead fish washed up on shore. Well anyway shot a buck that evening in the farthest rye field a way from camp maybe a mile. Forgot the deer cart back at camp, so we took the slings off our rifles to drag it out, whatever takes. Took a shortcut a little piece of high ground next to the swamp. Come out to the trail that leads back to camp. Standing there taking a rest, no wind temp about 24 degrees. You can see your breath going straight up in your head lamps. It was dead quiet.

Roughly 150 yards in front of us sounded like a bowling pin hit a dead cedar, then there was another tree knock in between us and the rye field where I shot and gutted the buck, the third tree knock was between us and camp. Still had roughly 1/4 mile down the trail back to Gotham to the edge mud lake and I told my son wait here and I'll go get the deer cart for the last 300 yards instead dragging Itasca I got across the little dam, water is roaring from the rain 2 days earlier.

I heard splashing next to shore just past the dam. I thought what in hell is that splashing and I can hear over the roaring of dam., got closer to the sound and turned my headlamp up looking down in the tags I was on a slight elevation.

This thing slowly looked up at me at about 15 yards away its eye was as big as around as a bottom of a pop can, brilliant blue. Its head was very wide, we locked eyes for a few seconds was standing in 2 feet of muck and the tags were about 5 feet tall. Its head was about 1 foot above the Tangshan it took off thru that shit it was as fast as a bolt a lightning. It was dark but could see its silhouette, looked to be maybe 4-foot-wide at the shoulders. I yelled at it as it was hitting the other bank, get you son of a bitchily the scope on it out of instinct 2 rounds left in the 06. almost let 1 go over that things head to send it on its way.

I either carry a 350-rem mag or a 450 marlin now. Sincerely Tony Montague, you can use my name. to my friends that don't believe me, you don't spend enough time doing what you love! Steve love your channel.   Keep up the good fight, and hunt hard. PCs. that thing was eating those dead fish that washed up on shore and forgot to mention that.

Steve Isdahl   The Day Sasquatch Became Real For Me   Copyright© 2020

A Correctional Officer Wrote In

Steve, my name is Rick and I am 48 years old and have worked in corrections for 24 years and have always been a straight shooter. Every story I've told has never been twisted or exaggerated at all. I can't stand people who exaggerate and twist the truth. I've been watching your channel for about a year now and I appreciate what you're doing, it takes guts. I grew up in a military family and at the time of my incident we lived in military housing just off the base. I now live-in south-western Oregon but at the time in 1979 I lived in Massachusetts. Behind the military housing where I lived was a whole lot of woods.

I've never seen anyone go back there except me and some of the other kids I played with. I was 8 at the time and I told my neighbour friend who was about the same age, to get his bike so we could go to our spot in the woods which was a trail head that led into the woods just a 5 min bike ride down a dirt road. I took off a minute or two before him. I arrived at the trail head and set my bike down and began walking up the trail which went up a small hill then down into the dark forest. I liked to practice being stealthy when I walked in the woods so I don't scare animals because I like to see them.

Well as I walked quietly up the beginning of the trail a Bigfoot was walking the same trail in the opposite direction coming towards me from the forest. We damn near ran into each other I shit you not. We were both walking up towards the top of the small hill so we didn't see each other until we both crested the hill then we were visible to each other. I never heard it coming; it was silent. As soon as we saw each other we both stopped walking and froze facing each other.
We were about 10 to 15 feet apart. This thing was walking just as smooth as a man except it was huge, I mean massive. It was the classic Bigfoot build, 8 to 10 feet tall covered in dark fur and a huge shoulder width and an extremely powerful build. No human is built like that. Bigfoot was the only damn thing it COULD have been. It never made a noise and I sensed that it was just as surprised as I was and it felt like, oh shit! I've seen what I do! I sensed intelligence as well.

After seeing this which was about 1 second, I immediately took off back towards my bike and saw my friend pulling up on his bike. I was soot scared I screamed go go go now! I took off back home faster than I have ever ridden a bike, I could have beat Lance Armstrong no prob. I didn't make out facial features on the creature because I was coming off a sunny road into the dark forest looking at a dark hair covered creature and my eyes hadn't quite adjusted yet but there is absolutely no doubt it was a Bigfoot. I was literally 10-12 feet from it. Also, in about 2012 here in Oregon I drove deep into the woods to visit Colin lake by myself one day. It was the off season so nobody was around. That's where I experienced wood knocking for the first time so one must have been eyeing me. Thanks for all you do Steve these things are real and very interesting to say the least. I'd rather keep my full name out at least until I retire in just over a year.

1st Of Two From Ohio

Greetings Steve,

I must say that your straight talk about Big Foot has been refreshing. I am 63 years old and have been a believer, since I was very young. I would like to share a couple of stories and some happenings with you from my childhood.

My name is Linda Bowers and I grew up near Lima, Ohio, which is farm country and extremely flat in the Midwest of the U.S.A. The little village, Spencerian, I lived in was an old canal town, on the Miami Erie Canal. The canal was constructed to get supplies up to Fort Toledo through the Black Swamp area, when the state was young.

My granny and I spent a lot of time together. She'd been born in the little village in 1902, and when married, had moved into a house right across the road from the canal. My home was just across a very large pasture field from there. There were many wooded areas, amidst the farmed fields. In fact, one of the largest stands of virgin woods in the state, was just outside of the village and had been in the same family for generations.

I asked my granny one day what a Boogie Man was. I don't even recall where I'd heard the term. She said that they only came out at night; which was why we needed to be in at dusk. They'd been known to take children. She went on to say that they were huge, with long, black hair all over their bodies, they were dirty and stunk. Right then, my mother had asked granny to stop telling me about that. She'd said she didn't want me to be scared. I begged to know if they were ghosts, animals or people. Granny said she didn't know. She had never acted as if my question was odd and she would never have informed me of what they looked like, had she not believed it to be a living being.

My first story took place when I was about 10. I had gone to a girlfriend's house whose dad farmed and they lived about 5 miles outside of our village. We had decided to hike out to a wood quite some distance away with a pond that they owned.

We walked past her horse who was in a paddock beside the barn. Then down a tractor path between the farm fields that led to an old cow pasture with huge, old trees. The pasture had not been used in decades and the grass had grown up a couple feet high under the foliage of the big, old trees. We needed to traverse the length of the pasture, go through another field lying fallow and then we would reach the woods with the lake.

Approximately half way through the abandoned pasture, stones began to come flying by us and landing all around us. At first, I thought they were acorns but then I saw several and one hit me. They weren't falling down; they were being thrown across and coming at a high rate of speed.
I became frightened and told my friend that someone or something was hiding and throwing stones at us. She realized that stones were flying by also, but couldn't understand where the perpetrators were hiding. I pointed out that the trees were so large that a person could easily hide behind them or could squat down in the tall grass.

We yelled at whomever was hiding and told them that we knew they were out there and they'd better stop it. We were going back to the house and get the men. They would be back.

On our way back, we noticed that the horse who had been standing near the fence relaxing when we'd headed out; was now trotting nervously back and forth, shaking her head and snorting loudly as if in fear. When she would stop briefly, she would paw and dig at the ground. We could tell she was scared or preparing for a confrontation. We both thought she sensed whatever had been in the old pasture.

Once we were in the house, my girlfriend told her mom that someone had been hiding in the field, throwing stones at us. She told her mom she should send my friend's dad and brother out to see. Her mother thought we were letting our imaginations run away with us. My friend told her how frightened the horse seemed to be but her mom was certain she had probably seen or smelled a coyote.

Let me interject that when night came at my home, it was very quiet. I would be unable to get to sleep for quite a while and would listen to the night life. Many evenings I would hear an owl hoot and then in the distance another hoot back. We had no trees except a dead one in the direction the hoots were coming from. I can recall asking my dad how I could hear owls hooting if none were around. I had a horrible feeling that birds were not making those hoots.

Several times the dairy farmer, a couple of fields over from my parent's home, had some of his calves taken. He usually had a herd of 60-75 head of cattle. My dad was a councilman and eventually the mayor, so he would end up hearing about thefts in the area. It was concluded that the theft would entail at least 2 to 3 people pulling it off, to be able to hoist the calf over the fence with no evidence left behind. Now, I see those things in a much different light.

My second story took place when I was about 12 yrs. old. I had a girlfriend spending the night at my home. We'd decided to sleep out in my tent, in my yard.

Mom and dad's property consisted of 3 acres in lawn with over 100, mature trees that were hundreds of years old. We had a barn close to the house and beside one outside wall of the barn was where we kept big metal garbage cans with lids that fit quite snugly. There was a lot of food and scraps that would be thrown into them. We burned everything else. Along the adjacent wall was our dog pen with our two dogs. They had a house and a good-sized area to run around in. The only time they were inside the pen was at night.

My girlfriend and I were sleeping in my old, canvas tent, not too far away from the house and barn but in an area that contained a lot of large trees. We were lying in our sleeping bags talking. It had been dark for over an hour.

Suddenly, I heard the sound of a lid being taken off one of the garbage cans and dropped onto the ground. I said, "be quiet, there's something in the garbage." My girlfriend asked what I thought it was, and I replied that it was probably a raccoon. They had the ability to take lids off. Then we both began to smell the door of a skunk. My girlfriend said she wanted to make a run for the house and didn't want to be outside anymore. I said no. I didn't want to be sprayed. We'd never get the stench off.

All of a sudden she said, " they're talking- do you hear that? That's not a skunk! They are talking. I can't understand it though." I listened and sure enough something was being said. It sounded like the kind of gibberish that you'd hear when watching a Japanese movie about the Samurai warriors. There were definitely two talking.

She began to panic and wanted to make a run for the house again, but I felt sure we'd be caught and told her so. These were obviously people, since they were talking to each other. She kept repeating that she couldn't understand why people would be in the garbage. I said maybe hungry migrant workers, but none of the farms nearby had any and I knew it. She immediately said, "they aren't speaking Spanish."
I certainly thought these people were the worst smelling people I'd ever smelled. I had been to some of the migrant camps though and they smelled nothing like this did. The people were clean and nice. This was a skunk smell.

I told her we had to pretend we were asleep. She asked what we should do if they tried to open the flaps on the tent. I told her to scream as loud and long as we could. Strangely the dogs weren't barking at all. That was totally uncharacteristic of them and puzzled me. Suddenly the foraging through the cans was over and we both froze. The sound of the lids going onto the cans signalling us to be quiet. We heard walking but it went by us. As I pondered that as an adult, I think they were heading to our large garden, further out into the yard and by the pasture. We planted all kinds of vegetables and had many, many currents, gooseberries and a highly productive pear tree. Across the pasture was my granny and grandpa's home with another big garden, cattle and the canal. The old mule trail still ran down the length of the bank and would have made a great place to walk on. They could have fished anywhere along the banks.

The next morning, we hurried to the garbage cans and saw the lids on them. When we went into the house, I told my mom that something had been in the garbage. She commented that it was probably raccoon. She asked if we'd put the lids on. I told her they were on. Her comment was that we must have been hearing things because animals would not have replaced the lids. My girlfriend was furious with me for not telling my mother that it was someone talking, but I knew it would have been pointless.

I thought a few years later that my encounters were The Ohio Grass Man or Sasquatch or the Boogie Man. My dad had relayed the information he'd heard about ape type men messing with road workers out west and their equipment. It didn't occur to me that they would be confined just to the West. Then Patterson's film had come out also.

My dad felt that an unidentified primate was a distinct possibility. I don't know that he ever dreamed it could inhabit Ohio. My granny obviously felt the Boogie man was real, but I never discussed with her what she might have known.

I am a firm believer that what happened to me was because of a Big Foot. I have kept abreast of reported sightings by people over the years, within a 20-mile radius of my parent's home. I believe they are among us, always have been and always will be. I hope that the public will not continue to be kept in the dark, which is why I am so grateful to you for what you are doing.

2nd Of Two From Ohio

Hi Steve,

First of all, I would like to apologize for having sent this to the incorrect email address, along with the previous email that I sent to you as well. I see now, it was for questions. Very sorry, but hope you see it.

This is Linda, from Ohio, again. I wanted to let you know about the activity that continued at my parent's home, long after I was grown and had moved away. I am not certain of the year this particular conversation I had with my dad took place; but it was around 1994. I judge that by the fact that the dog I had gotten when I was 18 years old, and still at home, had died at the age of 18. This would have been after the dog's death.

Bamfield B.C.

He was a mixed breed German Shepherd and Golden Retriever. He was never put away, as our other dogs had been at night, and he roamed the pastures, woods and farm country. If anyone or anything showed up at our home though, he would show up. He was a large dog and could be formidable if need be. You'll understand why I mention him later.

My parents had continued to have a garden, but as the years had passed and they'd aged, they'd planted less. Eventually, it was just some tomato plants and green beans that they would put out. There were still long rows of those delicious currants and gooseberry bushes that had been so plentiful and had been producing since I was young. Of course, the old pear tree was still there too.

We, meaning my husband, sons, and myself, had come back to Spencerian to visit. It was a time in the summer when the bushes would have been covered in berries and the pear tree laden with fruit.

I had asked my older son if he'd help his little brother to find a pear to eat. I asked my older son to be sure, if his little brother wanted to eat a pear from the ground, that it didn't have bugs in it and wasn't rotting. Once my younger son came back inside, I asked how his pear was. He said they couldn't find any. I told him I would find one for him. I figured his brother had just lost patience dealing with him.

To my astonishment, there wasn't a single pear on the tree and not one on the ground. My biggest shock was that the long rows of gooseberries and currants were gone. I stood there and pondered why my dad would have removed the bushes. The berries were delicious! My mom and I had spent an entire afternoon the summer before, picking gooseberries and had not even begun to make a dent in the bounty. I could not imagine why there were no pears. Mom and dad weren't fans of them but I had always loved them.

I came back into the house and asked mom if they'd allowed someone to pick the fruit and gather up what normally fell to the ground. I also stated my shock at all the berry bushes being gone. She said someone had stolen the pears. I asked what she meant by that. Had they seen someone and caught them; how did they know that? She said to ask dad, but she knew he'd found footprints. She said he'd ripped the bushes out because he wasn't growing them for others to steal.

Once dad came home, I had asked him what had happened with the pear tree and why had he ripped out the berry bushes. He said that he had only gotten a pint and a half of berries from the bushes and the pear tree had been stripped overnight somehow. I told him mom had mentioned that he thought they were stolen and he had found the footprints of whomever had done it.

He said yes, he had found many prints. He also seemed rather nervous at that point. I asked what kind of shoes the perpetrator had worn, could there have been more than one person and were the prints really good ones that could be cast. Also, I asked if he had called the police; having been the mayor, he knew them all. He gave a little laugh, his nervous one, and said they were bare feet. I said what!!! Why would someone be out in a garden plot in their bare feet stealing fruit? That didn't make sense. How could anyone take all the fruit in one night? They would have needed lights, to pick the berries I thought.

He explained that yes, they were bare foot prints. He said they were the biggest feet he'd seen. He said that his foot was a size 10, which wasn't big, but these were so large that he could put his foot in it and they didn't begin to fill the print. He said he thought maybe it was one of those Big Foot. He said he knew it sounded crazy and he would never have believed it, if he hadn't seen it himself.

He went on to say the tree had been stripped and ground cleaned up in one night and nearly all the berries too. His thought was that the dog, who had passed away the Fall before, had deterred them somehow. Now that the dog was gone, there was no longer an alarm system or reason for them to stay away.

He said he didn't like the idea of having fruit that would draw them to the property. Finally, he surmised that he and mom would not have the benefit of harvesting the fruit any longer, since the Big Foot knew it was there. He said in fact, he was going to cut down the pear tree also.
I possibly should have told dad that I knew they had come for decades, but I had seen the fear in his eyes. I knew that sharing my experience would only exacerbate that. It frightened me to know that as my beloved, aging parents slept; these beings were pillaging their property. Dad was a man in his late sixties then and he just wanted a safe, quiet existence and to golf daily. The Big Foot or Grass Man, just wanted to eat and our home was a part of their all you can eat buffet.

Steve, I hope that you and your efforts, will enable others to learn what our ancestors have always known. They are among us, and they are like us; in so much as they want to protect their families, thrive and survive. Whether we call them The Boogie Man, Ohio Grass man, Big Foot or Sasquatch; they are real.

I applaud you for what you are doing. You are presenting what people have experienced. I have never told people, except for my sons, these accounts. I appreciate you providing a safe platform in which to do this.

I wish you safety in your adventures and good health in these troubling times.
Warm Regards,
Linda

Stalked In A Parked Car

Hey Steve, you are a Pisser and great work. I'm a Vermonter who lives in the mid state, and right on the borderline. I was the owner of a mining business, with deep pits and very large waste piles of large rock, some 100's of feet deep, and high on top, surrounded with endless acres of deep woods. The nearest town was a mile away from this one. This was 1976 or 77, close enough. One night about 11 PM, we drove up there, a lady friend in tow, to talk and maybe get acquainted a little better for I had guests at home and this was spur of the moment. I bad. We parked near one of the pits on a cement hard roadway, enjoying the isolation for many reasons. We were in a Volkswagen Beetle, and being a warm evening, the windows were rolled down. It was safe, secure, and on the small chance anyone was to drive in, chances zero, we would hear them, for it was a location where you could here a caterpillar sneeze from 20 miles. About 15 minutes into our chat and a shared beer, I heard a big tree break about 1/3 of a mile to the south, just past the end of one of these huge quarry's. I thought it a little odd, but trees do fall in the spring, and outside of deer, there was little to give concern. Plus, in my youth, I had bigger fish to fry. Maybe 5 minutes later, but still 1/4 mile away, it sounded like some brush breaking with maybe some light hoot or noise, but I was still not concerned. The radio was on, but very low so it bothered little. I parked, I had spun around so that all I had to do was start the car and go straight and I'd be back on pavement. The back of the Beetle was towards the Woods and the Noise. So maybe 10 or 15 minutes from then, quietly at first, then gradually louder, so from behind, it heard this very stealth 2 footed walk, trying to sneak up behind my car. My companion didn't hear a thing but saw that I was on Red alert, and had the Hair on my back up like porcupine quills, and Goose Bumps the size of Baseballs, and this odd feeling of fear, I don't think I froze up but outside of Pointing towards the back window, I went for the Ignition and I don't think it ever took that Bug longer to start.

When it came to fife, I only had my Mirrors to look behind for my frigging fight or flight was heading for the Moon, and whatever was behind me was just being illuminated by the Tail Lights, and could have grabbed my bumper if so inclined, just maybe the starting car startled it for a second. All I remember seeing was a waist, and whatever there was for a head angled out of sight too high. As I made my escape, my guest manages to turn and look out the back window of the beetle to which gave her a Look of fear like one cares not to see.

Other than a dozen Holy Shits from me, a Dear God, Huge and Monster or something from Her, she then remained silent and just reverted to hand signals until I dropped her off at her Home in Total Shock. I was not much better. I asked Her what She saw, but just said She never wanted to know. Our paths never crossed again. Whereabouts unknown, just like my Boxers from that Evening. Steve It was Huge. 9 Feet easy I would say. And very dark Hair I believed, but the red from the Car tail lights could throw what I thought was Black Colo off. That was a quarry I was running and had to do it during the day, but with Company or one of my Men.

I could never go over there alone again. Day or Night. I had to go in there again the next AM with an Employee, and found a few very odd scuffs for tracks and some Other Tracks that were like two concentric circles 6 inches in diameter. I know the Woods but never thought Squash was around here

When till of late. And that quarry and old structures are a perfect habitat for them. I'm quiet, humble and love people and life but am disabled now for never having a man or woman work with me that I didn't do their job too, but it was tough on the body. My company is well known, me, purposely, not as much but one could figure it out quick. Thank you for helping people open up. Now I wish I could get my body to do the same.

Call me Fred, but it's _____to you. Stay safe.

Innocent Day Trout Fishing

Please forgive me for my typos and grammar. Steve one reason people are afraid is because of ridicule. To some people ridicule is one of the worst things that can be done to a person. I feel that people need validation of these creatures to put those who ridicule and make fun of back in their place. They need an underdog so to speak. No one wants to be different, singled out or have fingers pointed at them. I have a short story of an experience I had as an 18-year-old teenager in the mountains of Colorado. I was in a remote area by steamboat springs. I think the year was 1987 and it was spring.

I was camping by a river in an old broken-down cabin that belonged to a friend's family. one morning I decided to go trout fishing and enjoy the morning air and what nature has to offer. I was not at all prepared as to what I was about to see. I started to trout fish when a pebble or something hit the water in front of me. thinking about this is giving me goosebumps as I speak and I am 53 now.

Anyhow I kind of dismissed the idea of it being a pebble but maybe some fish had started to hit the top of the water. Again, another pebble was thrown into the water and this time I figured it was coming from a tree across the river by a squirrel or something. Still, I figured it was nothing to worry about. It was then about that time I noticed there were no birds chirping or doing what birds do. I noticed it was dead silent other than the breeze and the water making noise.

I knew there were bears in the area but all I had with me was my little .410 shotgun. I knew this was not enough to kill a bear but maybe deter it long enough for me to get back to the cabin. It was about this time I noticed movement up on the rocky slope with pine trees. I saw something with reddish brown hair and it got up and started to move across the hill. When I say got up, I mean it stood up. At first, I thought it was a couple of bears that were together and both were standing up to get something out of a tree. I could just feel something was off so I started to walk back towards the cabin with my little cap gun in tow and it was then I realized it was not 2 bears standing up together it was one big creature and it was looking at me.

You know I hunt and have hunted all my life and when I think about it now I know what I saw was not fake, when you hunt and you have been around enough animals you look at their eyes and their demeanour, this creature was most definitely real, he, she or it had my attention and we both knew it. The funny thing is it wasn't really showing aggression but just letting me know hey I'm here you're in my spot, or maybe it just was curious about me and what I was doing. I never turned my back on the creature and even though it was across the river I decided I had enough and started walking backwards never taking my eyes off the things.

I stumbled over rocks and stumps to get back to the cabin because I was basically walking backwards. It never left and just watched me walk away. I got back to the cabin and my friend who was still sleeping asked me where I went. I told him and told him what I saw and I thought we should go. At first, I was reluctant to tell him because of the ridicule but as I told him he did not look surprised and he said they have always been here and they have never bothered anyone before. don't use my name, you can use my story if you want.

Sorry for the typos, I did this on my phone and as a healthcare worker it's hard to find time to do things these days. Take care and please please understand sometimes the people who need the proof are the ones who have experienced something and they are the ones who are asking for proof for themselves to know they are not crazy. One thing is certain, I live in rural Missouri now and I love to hunt, but when I do, I lock and load as soon as I start walking. If I ever see one here, I will quit hunting and sell my small farm. thank you for your time.   B@#*&#

Trailing out after 90 days in remote B.C. Mr. Macarcani and I.

Alabama And Warned

Hello Steve, I'll try to keep this story as short as I can. I grew up in Alabama on my family's 64 acres of land. It's been in our family for three generations. We are outdoors men that's always hunted our land for food on the table. It's how we live. My grandfather always told us to stay out of the hollow passed the rock quarry. Don't hunt there or you will die. The hairy man won't come out of there unless you fuck up and go there. My grandpa never bullshit anyone at any time. I'm 59 and I spend most days in the woods. It's part of me. I have seen these beings throw my scope and even up close one evening. I was on top of the mountain one evening before it started to get dark. I saw the hairy man walking into their cave with a large buck on his shoulder. Two grown men would have trouble carrying this huge Lama buck. This giant had no problem with it at all.

Steve Isdahl   The Day Sasquatch Became Real For Me   Copyright© 2020

The Daddy of this family is over seven feet tall and weighs over four hundred pounds. It seems like a shit story but in my kid's life it's true. My Daddy told me not to go there and I've told my sons not to go there. It's the only way for us to stay alive on our land. They've got about ten acres and we've got the rest. My grandpa told me they were there long before he was born. These fuckers are not Apes. They are people that have been in hiding for hundreds of years. Only one of us has gone in there. It was my grandpa's brother. He was ripped to pieces and left in a tree for them to find. My Grandma told me about it when I was a kid. It's not Just a bullshit story to scare the kids. It's a true story that we take very seriously. I've got grand kids that watch your channel. They ask that you don't use my full name. Their friends wouldn't believe it and kids are so cruel to each other. So, thank you for listening to my story my friend. I will send you another one soon that happened to my two brothers. Keep up the good work and tell our stories. More people need to know what is going on. Thanks again
Michael Rogers

Another Police Officer Admits It

Steve, I want to thank you for speaking out for so many people that's lives have been turned upside down because of these creatures. Your enthusiasm has become contagious!!
I know from your past posts that you really like encounters that are being told by police officers, those who are or have been in the military and Government employees such as park rangers. Etc.

I spoke with my best friend a few days ago who just happens to be a police officer. He has retired from his first job and now is serving as a deputy in the county that I live in to make some extra money now that he's retired. In the course of our conversation, I asked him if he had ever had any calls about these creatures, and he said yes, however, he was in a hurry and told me that he would call me and tell me about them later.

I myself have never seen a Sasquatch, however, I'm positive that I've heard them. I have found prints and have a cousin by the name of Steve that works for the United States Postal Service. He is one of a handful of people that I would trust to watch my children, and his word is solid. He's one of the best people I've ever met, and he has endured unimaginable ridicule over the encounter he had back in the mid 70s, even by his own children.

Steve's story goes like this, he was squirrel hunting and was sitting in an old grown up logging road against a tree facing north, to his east side was a small hill, to his west side was a hollow and his back was facing south against a dead Elm tree.

Steve told me that he heard the leaves rustling, boom, dead squirrel. This happened a couple times, they were coming from the western hillside travelling east to where Steve was sitting, and then he heard the leaves rustling again, anticipating another squirrel, he steadied his 20 gauge shotgun and got ready, but to his surprise, it wasn't a squirrel, it was a 7 foot tall solid white bipedal creature. The creature was about 10-15 yards from Steve and it stopped dead in its tracks and looked at him. Steve said that it was only for a few seconds but it seemed like an eternity and that everything went into slow motion. The creature then went east toward the hollow, stopped, and hit a tree with the palms of its hands several times. He then said it let out a huge scream that he could feel in his bones.

Steve was only 15 or 16 when this happened and when I asked him what it looked like he said that he was too afraid to look it in the face but that it was tall, solid white with 4-6 inch hair covering most of its body and that its arms went down past its knees.

Steve's story will be on Sasquatch Chronicles in the near future. I know that this story isn't long, but I want to thank Scott Carpenter for helping me help an elderly lady that I know with her Sasquatch problem.

Her name is Cathy but she doesn't want it used. She had her mobile home knocked off of it's foundation by a Sasquatch, and she also had sticks, rocks, big limbs and several other things thrown at her mobile home. We contacted one of the biggest names in the Sasquatch world for help. He said to leave gifts to make peace with the creature(s). When I told her that, she said, "gives the slobs gifts for knocking my trailer off of its foundation and driving me crazy, "hell no". I had to agree with her, so I contacted you and you said to contact Scott Carpenter, and you were right, Scott knew exactly what to do, my friends Sasquatch activity has ceased. In closing, thank you, and a big thanks to Scott Carpenter.

What people don't understand is that these creatures are dangerous. I'm sure they're a lot like humans, you've got good ones and you've got bad ones, but the facts are that we don't know very much about them. Just read the Missing 411 books and I think that most will agree that 85% of the cases are Sasquatch related. Thanks again Steve for your Stories, both hunting and the Sasquatch stories.

I have had both hips replaced and had my left foot sewed back on and had been sitting at home, being lazy and feeling sorry for myself, but you have inspired me to get off my butt and to get back in the woods, and that's what I've been doing. So be careful out there and thanks for helping so many of us in one way or the other. I'll send you some more stories after I talk to my Sheriff's deputy friend. Have a good day Steve, and again, thank you for your honesty, and you do not give a shit attitude. Signed by Brian Gibbons, and yes, you can use my name.

Steve Dahlia,

Father Of 5 In Washington

Hi Steve, my name is Andrew Strengthen. I am 32 yrs. old, engaged and father of 5. First time mailer, long time follower of How to Hunt and your Blackmail tactics. I live in SW Washington state, not far from Mount Saint Helena.

First of all, I'd like to tell you how much I enjoy your blackmail videos and information. My number one passion is hunting big, old, smart black tails. I also archery hunt elk, as well as rifle hunt predators. Unfortunately, we can no longer run dogs however I have experience with dogs.

I was for a few short years a big game hunting guide in Northern Idaho. Hound hunting predators as well as guiding archery and rifle deer and elk hunts.

It was fall of 2019 after close to 25 years in the woods I saw something that has left me stressing every time I have to hike in the dark going in or coming out of the mountains. It was rifle deer season and I was hunting a massive 4x4 that I had seen the year previous. I judged him around 20" wide and 15-16" tall. Around here that's a very big buck. Let's just say he was my very own "Zeus the Moose". Although he definitely was not the calibre of your "Zeus the moose"! The only downside is that buck lives in the middle of nowhere. From my house to the beginning of the logging road is a 30-minute trip. Then It's an hour drive up the logging road to the very end of a certain drainage main line. Then it is an 8-mile bike/hike to where I want to hunt this buck. In order to get all the way up to where I want to be by daylight, I have to start my bike/hike a couple hours before daylight.

It was on this bike/hike trip up the trail that I saw something I have never seen before. The weather was rainy and drizzly as well as thick coastal fog rolling in and out. I had reached a point in the trail where I wanted to walk as it was a very large patch of big timber with a long flat stretch of trail that has a major game trail intersecting. I have seen animals cross at that point many times. There was enough light that I could see approximately two hundred yards.

I was slowly pushing my mountain bike with my left hand and holding my .270 with my right. As I turned my head from looking off to my right I looked straight down the trail at the point where the game trail intersects and saw a 7-8 feet tall massive statures being, black in colour, walking in steady stride across the trail, looking at me the entire time. The one detail that stands out the most, more than its size, colour, or even threat level was how long its arms were, well below the knees with a significant constant sway in motion with each step. I froze in awe and shock at what the hell I had just seen. I didn't move for several minutes.

I was by myself however I wasn't scared of leaving. To be honest it was like my brain couldn't really comprehend what I just saw so I started telling myself anything to explain it away. "Oh, it was just a bear", "maybe it was a real wet deer or elk" "it could have been a hunter in dark clothing without orange on" (orange is required during rifle season in WA.) I finally felt assured it was something else other than what I had just seen and continued on. I walked up to the point where the being crossed the trail thinking I would see a deer or bear track to explain it away however there were no tracks or anything. The ground was a hard orange brown clay however it was raining and surely if anything on hoof or anything with claws walked there it would have left a track. I looked and looked and found nothing as far as tracks.

The sighting lasted literally seconds. However, it was long enough for me to tell that there was no way in hell it was a bear, elk, human, cat, or deer. I have successfully killed every forementioned species with many of each species. I have hunted, fished, camped, and worked in the woods for close to 25 years, I have seen some things in nature that most people Simply would not believe it could happen involving known species, bear, elk, deer, bobcat to be exact. But I have never seen anything like what I saw that day. The more I replay in my mind what happened I am convinced I saw "Bigfoot". I feel very awkward even typing this. I have only told three people what I saw that day. Two are my friends and hunting partners and one is an uncle who I have looked up to and inspired me to hunt since I was a kid. All three of them literally laughed and gawked at me and told me how there is no proof. No game trail videos. No bones. No bodies. So, I have never brought it up with anyone since. Not even my wife or children.

It is very assuring to see someone speaking truth to power on this subject. I seek zero publicity. In fact, I would appreciate it if you don't share my name online. I don't need anyone thinking I'm crazy and harassing my family or I. If I didn't have a wife and 5 kids, I would care less about putting my name out there. Hopefully you understand this point and don't let that take away from the truth of my encounter. Feel free to share on a video however please just leave my name out. I live a very normal life. I'm not on drugs. I'm not psychotic. I am a very healthy, stable, honest hardworking man. I have a family and do my best in raising, teaching, and providing for them.

I have accepted what I see and I am at ease with accepting it. What I saw is what many would call "Bigfoot". I know what I see. Nobody can tell me differently. I don't even try to convince people at all, I know and that's the bottom line. It's very frustrating that there is not more information on these beings released to the general public. It's very frustrating there's not more open, honest research being done to reveal the truth. You my friend just might be the one to reveal all that is being kept or silenced from the general public. Keep doing what you are doing. I (we) are behind you.

Thank you kindly:
Andrew Strengthen

P.S.
Please keep up on Blackmail Videos as much as you possibly can. There is nobody else who can match the information you put out as well as incredible video regarding hunting, patterning, and targeting trophy blackmails. I truly enjoy your Blackmail videos.

Remote outfitting cabin in B.C.

I Felt Awe And Joy Seeing It

Hi Steve, love your channel, watch daily. My encounter was on a summer morning while I had taken my truck and little chainsaw on a firewood run for my camp. Not the usual endeavour for a woman at 50yrs old. I had a camp about 20 miles east of Oak ridge out a forest access road all the way to the end. Where the road ended was a grove of old growth trees more than 250 feet tall. Here two large creeks merged and the trout fishing was incredible. Peaceful, quiet and serene. I never felt uncomfortable there. I felt watched over. One morning while out on a wood run, I stopped at a spring pond on top of a mountain at the end of that road. My favourite place to have lunch. The birds there would land on my hand to take food. They never saw humans in that area. They had no fear.

As I was eating my sandwich- looking out over the forest just below me I saw someone walking towards my position in the distance it looked be a person, but as it drew closer- maybe 300 yards away - I realized by the height ,the length of its strides and that it was ducking under the lowest branches of the Ponderous Pines that are the only trees growing in that locale and altitude. You know how high up the lowest branches of that tree species are. I stood there watching it come closer- no fear in me - just an incredible feeling of awe and joy. It stopped and just stood looking at me from maybe 50 feet. After a few moments I raised an arm in greeting a few seconds later it raised its arm, turned and strode off through the forest until I could no longer see it.

The Day Sasquatch Became Real For Me

To this day I feel that it had caught my scent on the wind that was blowing past me into the direction he came from. Curiosity drew it to seek me. A human female high in the forests alone. He had no harm in mind for me or I would not be here. I watched your video tonight where you spoke of First Nations people in Alaska and their experiences and then spoke of a man who had become a Buddhist and their feeling that the Hairy people are not all evil, just like humans. There are just too many stories coming in about positive experiences with the Forest Kings. I left that mountain top that morning with the knowledge that they exist, and a feeling of wonder that he came to visit me out there.

I have not been to that mountain top since that day. Not because of fear- but respect. It is THEIR HOME out there. I never told this story not just to avoid ridicule because I can care less if people believe me or not. I am a great deal Cherokee, a civilized person. I never spoke of that day because I feared for the safety of the Bigfoot family that lived there. I did not want some 'yahoos going hunting to kill them a sasquatch.' Your show may have started off ' how to hunt' but what it has turned into is a forum where people who have had strange experiences out in the forest can tell their story with no fear of being singled out for ridicule. Thanks, brother. I can tell you my name. I am Kathleen Durham, and I am proud that a Forest King showed himself to me.

Keep up the good work, Steve, we need men like you who tell the dickheads to just f#$%k off. You are spreading truth as related to you by people who have no hidden agenda. Just stories to tell about strange goings on in our National Forests. I am 68 years old now. I was 50 when I saw my friend out there. Long enough for them to be safe from hunters. Yeah, I rambled a bit but I wanted it to be easy to visualize.

A Navy Veteran Writes In

I am a retired Navy veteran living in southern Idaho. I grew up here in Idaho and returned here a few years after I retired from 20 years of service, after seeing the world, spending half my career on aircraft carriers. I also am a recent college graduate now thanks to the GI Bill. I got married a few years after I got back to Idaho. I also remarried, my wife and I met at our 30th high school reunion and got married a few years after that.

My wife and I occasionally drive the Korean/Jordan Valley loop through the Towhee mountains in southern Idaho and Oregon for a day trip. One day, as we were passing a meadow, with cows and a stream, I glanced over to my left to see a Bigfoot walking away. I slowed down and said "Oh my god!" My wife asked what?! I looked again, and instead of Bigfoot; I saw a... cow?! Walking away from us. Seriously? Seriously.

I saw the back end of a cow, walking away from me at a bit of an angle. I figured something in the background, coupled with that cow made my mind think "Bigfoot!" The illusion didn't last long, but it did leave a lasting impression.

I can still "see" that Bigfoot, walking away, in my mind's eye. It was very tall, with black hair all over. They say the mind can play strange tricks on you. I'll have to agree. I'm wondering now though if that was really what I saw. One day last year I was at an area gun show, wearing a Bigfoot shirt. One gentleman looked at it, and asked me if I was a believer; when I said of course, he told me his story.

He grew up in Northern California. I don't recall exactly where, but the area was mountainous and heavily forested. He mentioned there was a creek he and his brother liked to fish. This creek was hard to access from the road, and the only real way up or down it was by walking along the creek. One day he and his brother fished up that creek to a waterfall, about 15-20 feet tall, and while his brother was fishing below it, he decided he was going to climb the waterfall to see what was up the creek from there.

He climbed up the waterfall, and as his head peeked over the top, he was surprised to see a huge hairy figure nearby, about 15 yards away, squatted down on the shore of the creek bed, taking a drink. As he looked at it, it looked up and saw him, and he clearly heard in his head the creature wonder "How did YOU sneak up on ME?" Then it stood up, about 8 feet or so of reddish-brown hairy manlike creature, turned around and started walking away. The man blinked, and a deer was walking away; he blinked again, and it was the creature again. Which led me to wonder, was it really the cow I saw walking away from me that day in the Towhees? Thinking back on it, the Bigfoot I saw was black. The cow I saw was brown. How's that for weird? I guess I'll never know for sure what I saw that day.

I've been a believer for a long time, since I was a kid, but other than seeing the upper part of something tall, dark and human shaped duck behind a tree in the northern Idaho mountains when I was a kid, I've never seen one. Which is OK with me, seeing how some people get pretty freaked out and scared by their encounters. I don't know if that was a sighting either, but I can remember that pretty clearly too, about 40 or so years later.

Take care Steve and thanks for standing up for us regular people, and for the truth. I really appreciate you, and the stories you share. You are welcome to use my name.
Sincerely yours,

Lauren Ne her

I Smelled Rotting Flesh And Dog

Hello Steve,
My name is James and I really enjoy your channel I respect the hell out of you, not only as an extremely experienced hunter and bushman but for what you are doing about this subject and what you are doing for those who are just looking for answers for what they have experienced and not have to worry about the repercussions of ridicule and disbelief. I do have my own theories on what these beings are but I generally yield to folks like you who have had so many experiences and who have rubbed shoulders with others who have actually gone out with boots on the ground and have done their own research. However, I would say the biggest reason I

respect your point of view is because you put the first nations people's histories and knowledge at the top of the list of people to listen to about this. I think those people who scoff at the natives' beliefs, oral history and their experiences are ignorant, small minded and so full of themselves that they wouldn't know whether to scratch their watch or wined their ass when it comes to these things.

I truly believe that all Native tribes had a better handle on their surroundings then we could even fathom. Let's see... should I listen to some jackass who goes out running around whooping and banging sticks on trees and claim they caught a glimpse of one so there for they know more or the guy who's people thrived in some of the most inhospitable territories known to man with sticks and rocks for thousands of years? Places that still claim the lives of people who have gone out with modern equipment to this day.

Anyway, I digress for now and I will finally share my story. I am the Program manager at a group home for at-risk teenage boys here in Utah. I know when someone is lying to me and I am very good at sifting through the bull shit and recognizing the truth when or if it arrives. Teenagers are like wild animals, just don't turn your back to them because they will eat you.

I was born and raised in Jackson Wyoming and spent my youth running around the woods and mountains from the southern end of Yellowstone through Grand Tetons National Park and the surrounding mountains of Jackson itself. My ancestors settled Jackson and the surrounding areas and they fought for every bit of what they had and I was raised the same way. You take care of you and yours and help those in need and if it's broken then fix it and when you give your word, then you honour it. Back home we call that cowboy logic. It's the only way I know how to do things so when I told this story to someone, I thought I trusted and who I thought would help me out. Instead he said what I saw was impossible and would never happen... WHAT IN THE FUCK! So, I just kept my mouth shut about it for a long time until I found How to Hunt and I slowly started to trust my memories again.

When I was around 10 years old, back in 1990 I had a friend who lived down the street from me who got a horse for his birthday. So, I saddled up my horse and we hit the trail. Back then kids like us could take off for a few days before anyone started worrying. I think I remember that we rode those poor horses all over that country for 3 days. The second and third day we went way up this canyon called Cache Creek Canyon to see how far we could make it. We got to this place where they had put a covert in way back when they were still logging the area. The covert was sticking out of the rode and had holes in it and it looked pretty gnarly and we found that our horses would jump over it so we must have ran them back and forth over that dam thing for an hour until the horses were all lathered up so we decided to unsaddle and let them cool off. I remember clearly that my horse had his ears pinned forward and would give a little sort now and again clearly concerned about something off in the timber but I couldn't see anything.

Then I smelled something awful, a rotting flesh mixed with a wet dog smell. The first thing that came to my mind was it must be a dead elk because that canyon is a migration route for elk in the fall and spring so I told my buddy that I was going to go check it out to see if I could acquire some ivory. So, I went up to the base of this cliff that was about 60-foot-tall and trees blocked the area between where my friend and the horses were and myself. As I was scanning the area I looked over to my right and there was this giant black man standing right at the base of the cliff. The evening sun was behind me and the way the shadow played off the base of the cliff I could only see the top half of this man.

Now, normally that would be cause for concern I suppose but, in my mind, it was another mountain man who decided to quit civilization and live off the land like in the old days. I had been with my dad and grandpa when we had met other men who would come down to stock up on supplies and then head right back up into the mountains so I really just thought he was one of them. Yes, he was huge! But again I was an ignorant little country boy who up to that point never met a black person before and the only thing I did know was what I saw on TV when we would watch the Packers play and all I knew is that those black folks were bigger than white folks and usually better at sports then us too. LOL so in my mind I that's what I was seeing. The man was enormous, with long dreaded black hair and fairly long beard that was silver up the middle of it. This is where it gets weird. He was bald on the very top of his head and I remember that it looked raw and possibly cut up or something and I was thinking man that looks like it hurts.

Another thing I noticed was his head was fairly pointed as well. He was wearing what I thought was a black bear skin coat because it was pitch black hair covering his upper body but I could see his massive shoulder muscles and biceps moving under the hair. I'll nearly forget the look he gave me; it was a look of annoyance. I knew the look well because I was a really annoying kid back then. But he was more concerned about something else up the ridge because he would look up the ridge and study it for a bit then back at me like I was in the way or something. I don't remember how long the encounter lasted but it seemed to be a couple minutes maybe a little more. He then lifted his arm and grabbed a ledge on the cliff wall and kind of leaned against it.

Then my buddy called out to me and he snapped his head over and so did I and when I looked back at him he just pulled himself up the cliff and grabbed another ledge with his other hand and repeated it like 2 more times until he was at the top and disappeared from view. I yelled to my friend "did you see him?!" and as he walked up to me, he asked "who was that?" Later on, several years later I tried talking about it with him and he claimed he didn't actually see anything or anyone. I was sure he saw him though.

Anyway, a couple years later we were taking a pack trip up to a place called Turquoise Lake and I remember I was 12 because that spring my cousin and I were taught how to train our first colts and we rode them on that pack trip. We got up to that same covert which was even gnarlier then before and our colts wouldn't cross over it so as the rest of the group went on ahead, we stayed behind trying everything to get them fillies to go over that covert. After a while we had to take a rest so we just sat and talked for a bit. I was on my horse when I realized that I was standing right next to that cliff and I was eye level with the ledge where that man had put his hand on. Let me repeat that, I was on my horse and I was eye level with where his hand was. That was about 9 foot from the ground. I then proceeded to tell my cousin the story and what I saw but he immediately blew me off saying there was no way I saw a man that tall climb that cliff basically only using his arms. Even then I hadn't thought much about it. It wasn't until 2007 is when I started getting into Bigfoot and I saw a drawing of one that some guy had drawn after he had an encounter. I thought my mind was going to quit me. I scrambled to find a paper and pencil and I went to town frantically drawing and my hands were shaking so bad but when I was done, I stepped back and just stared at it.

There he was the man I had seen so long ago and all I did was make the creature the other guy drew bald and with a beard and it was exactly what I remembered. Now, say what you will but I swear I believe I may have seen a Bigfoot that day. The only thing that doesn't make sense is the fear people and you have described. I didn't experience that, maybe I was to dumb or innocent or both to have even thought to be scared, I don't know but in my mind these beings are a lot like us. They will get mean and aggressive if they feel like they or their family are being threatened and I can only imagine how scary that would be but, in most cases, they just slip away further into the woods. I don't want to down play what you and others have experienced but I really believe they normally wouldn't want to harm us as long as we're far enough away but then of course there's probably some dick heads out there too just like we have in our species so caution must be taken at any rate.

I don't give a rip if you use my name or if you want to share this. I'm too old and tired to give a shit what some pricks think of me and I can tell that you are telling the truth about what you saw and I know you are an Honorable man who wants to help people and anymore I've learned that you're the kind of person to float the river with. So, keep it up man you are doing a good thing
All the best - James
PS if you would like to see that picture, I drew of what I saw then I will be happy to send it to you.

Roans Creek North Carolina

Good day, I hope you are doing well. Feel free to use my story...or part of it, as it runs a little long...

Late Fall, early Winter of 1980 in the rural mountains of NC, near the Va./Tn border in an area called Roans Creek. I was 14. I had spent the majority of those years hunting and fishing. In my 14 years, I was never over a 2-minute walk from the woods. Living in a rural setting without siblings left me 2 options, 1) set on my ass or 2) get out in the woods! I loved the outdoors and spent every hour I could hunting or fishing. I had NO FEAR of the woods. I would walk 45 minutes in total darkness to my deer stand, hunt all day and return home after I could no longer see 10 feet in front of me... I never gave it a second thought. The woods were my private Heaven...little did I know, they would soon become my worst nightmare.

I came home from school with time to grab the Beagle, Hunting vest and my trusty .410 single shot. I ran across the road, down my Great Uncles driveway, turned left up to the old Sawmill landing. I released Katie. She started her "Z" pattern, nose to the ground with an occasional "loophole" to assure me where she was. Katie was trained to circle the rabbit and push it back to the hunter, unlike many dogs that you have to follow. I climbed up on a pile of old slabs to secure a better view. Probably 4-5 foot high. She was cutting back and forth through Mature White Pines, between 30-40 foot high. They had been planted in nice straight rows after the depression ended...roughly 1933?? The reason I mention the straight rows, is so you can picture how the setting sun's light would light up the open areas. I could see Katie crossing back and forth...and occasional "loophole"...so very relaxing. Then out of nowhere, Katie yelped as if she was being hurt. We've all heard dogs in pain and scared, a long continuous crying yelp. I focused my sight in her area, about 80 yards out. NOTHING...then her cries became further away....as she ran away...cries that went out of earshot...crying out the entire time, until I could no longer hear her.

My eyes never left the tall pines. I then saw something moving through the rows. The sun was at an angle to my right...I could only see its "shadow" as it came closer. Bear? Horse? Uncle Rex??? 70 yards...60...50. The landing of the old sawmill was about 30 yards long, circled with 4-5-foot-high slab piles. I last saw "IT" to my right at about 40 yards. I climbed off the slabs to my left, this allowed me to see up the rows, as the slabs blocked the sun to my right. I eased along the slabs, moving closer to where I had seen IT... I swung out wider, so I could see around the slabs at the end........then my world changed forever.

The next 20 seconds takes 10 minutes to explain. Time moved in slow motion, as I can recall every step I took and each eye blink. A horrid smell engulfed the area. Almost like a "musk"??

warm, yet piercing. I'm sure you know what I mean by "musk"...if that makes sense. Every hair on my neck stood up, my senses were in overdrive, I wanted to throw up, I knew I was being watched...and I knew IT was close. I turned to my right, and just on the other side of the slabs was Bigfoot. 15 yards away. I could see him from his waist up. His head was semi pointed...no hair on forehead, cheeks or nose. Wide nose, thin lips, square teeth, with deep dark eyes. His shoulders were freaking 'huge, the size of basketballs...chest was defined as well as any body builder...arms went past his knees and they were 27-29" thick...he had some "guns". Hair colour was dark, kind of grey/brown.

I froze, I told myself, "there's no such thing as Bigfoot"!! I looked down, rubbed my eyes, when I looked back up... he was still there. I rubbed my eyes again and dipped my head down and to an angle...STILL THERE...at this moment I turned and ran maybe 10 yards...again I said, "NO SUCH THING!!!" I stopped, turned around...He had stepped up on the slab pile.... My God! It was 10-foot-tall...shoulders 4-foot-wide, thighs 38-40" thick...I'd say it weighed 700-800 Lbs?? That's it...it is real, I threw my gun to my shoulder...then thought, I will only make this thing MAD...I lowered the .410 to my waist,,, keep in mind, I was looking this creature in his eyes...when I lowered my gun, time stood still, I could hear him breathing.

This may sound crazy, but I never felt threatened...the eyes were firm, but I didn't see "EVIL". I leaned hard to my right...so the setting Sun would be hidden behind a large Pine Tree behind him...He leaned his head to the other side and gave a light exhale... GAME OVER ! when he moved, I turned and ran through the thorn bushes, down the hill, jumped halfway over the creek, landing in the middle, I tripped coming out the other side, falling on my rear...just in time to see HIM following me down the bank. I could see my house, 100 yards to go...I began screaming....MOM >>>MOM !! I jumped over the barbed wire fence, catching my boot...just on the tip, just enough to trip me up, just enough to turn my head and see HIM stopped at the creek.

My mother had heard my screams and was on the porch at the top of the stairs. I came flying up the steps. My jacket torn to shreds by the bushes...my face covered in scratches. Mom said, "you are white as a ghost, what happened"? About the time she asked...this creature began a blood curdling scream as it paced back and forth along the creek, just in the shadows of the Pine trees. 10-15 minutes of pacing and screaming...it stayed there until well past dark. Mom kept asking, "what did you do"?? what did you make mad?? Needless to say, I didn't sleep that night.

Next day...I come home. My mother says, "get your gun and get up there and find Katie, she never or why it came back that week. If it had wanted to "get" me...it had me at the sawmill...and it never ran after me...it just followed me. END OF STORY---

What's your thoughts?? Your personal story stands the hair up on my neck...but I think there are some of us who "believe"...we are attached to Nature...we have our 6th sense working, where most people have had it bred out of them. I know when I'm being watched. I know what I smell. I have no doubt that these Beings know "who" can see them...or sense them. I have had numerous "tree knocks"...too many to remember. I've had 6-7 rocks thrown near me (different times) ...and even had a rock tossed at me in my tree stand! I think rock throwing is just a warning...not to hit us...and even sometimes, just playing. I feel these Beings around me. I feel no threat from 99%...but every now and then, I get the feeling of "GET THE HELL OUTTA HERE"... as if some of these creatures might not be as "forgiving" if we walk up on them. I could go on for hours. My wife and I live in Rural NC Mons about a mile from Tn. on a hundred acres, mostly wooded. We respect all wildlife. We only kill what we are going to eat and try to see that the animals have food during the winter...I think "THEY" know our hearts...they know we're never going to shoot at them, or bring in News Crews to try and film them...etc. I'm sure you have 100's of stories also...not all encounters last 3 minutes...most are just simple Tree Knocks...Rocks...Smells and the KNOWING they are watching...that uneasy feeling. I don't expect you to read this novel...maybe you'll like the "MAIN" story. I have some PICS also, just got to find where I put em. I send you another email with the pics. Sorry so long winded, I ease up on next report. came home"...and you need to "get back on the horse"...it was probably a wild Boar and if you don't go back in the woods today, you will let fear win and never go back. I grabbed my .410 and out the door I went. I didn't make it 4 steps down...BLOOD CURLING DEATH SCREAM!!!! Mom even said "STOP, Get back in here!" You could see the shadow of this creature strutting back and forth...about 20 feet back under the Pine trees...after about 5 minutes my Great Uncle called the house, mom answered, he asked what the hell was wrong with me and what was I yelling and screaming about?? She informed him of what was occurring and he left it at that. That creature paced back and forth until dark...he would only "YELL" when I came out.

This went on for the next 2 days, but only when I was there. Finally, Saturday came. I was looking forward to catching up on lost sleep.... NOPE! A little after sunrise, a knock on the door, in walked my Uncle, my grandfather along with his 2 brothers, one of which owned the old sawmill...and the same great Uncle that had called earlier in the week. "We need you to come with us...why in the HELL did you tear up the sawmill !!??" Uncle Rex is good to you...and you repay him by throwing shit everywhere. We went together to see the sawmill. There were slabs everywhere!! The entire landing area was covered. I got one more ass chewing...until I pointed out the 20" bare footprints...and pointed out 300 Lb chunks of stumps thrown around and the 22 foot Steel I Beam guide for the mill tossed on it's side...they looked at each other, walked around with hands on hips...then across their chests...then they came back. " Dick, we think it's best if you stay outta the woods for a while." No argument from me!

Over the next couple of weeks My Great Uncles would drive to the old sawmill about 30 minutes before dark and I noticed their truck lights would come on from time to time throughout the night. I never heard the "scream" again, well, not from the sawmill and not for 38 years. I'll never know why it screamed...why it paced

Chief Engineer From San Francisco

Steve,
My name is also Steve, am 58 years old, and have had a passion for being an outdoors man

and horseman since I was a child. I have never spoken about what I am writing to anyone but your no BS videos and personality have prompted me to write. I am mentioned in a report by another person and will explain how I am connected. I live in Northern California, about and hour north of San Francisco, with trips to Kodiak Island, Montana, and BC being just a few of the destinations that I have considered privileged enough to include in my outdoor resume.

My grandparents lived near Seattle Washington on Hood Canal where exploration of the forests and back country were the activities of annual visits. When I was 12 my grandfather gave me two local publications on Sasquatch that included the Peterson Gremlin stills that still captivate me and the public to this today. I somehow knew deep down in a place I do not discuss the sightings and reports were true, but have never had a direct sighting or felt compelled to have to prove it to myself. I can't speak for you, but I have never seen a Narwhal in person, but believe the photos, videos, zoology, and reports that they exist. There is no deep pressing desire for me to gear up, travel above the arctic circle, and see one saying, "yep, they exist".

My current job is Chief Engineer of a low rise building in San Francisco. Prior to this position I was a firefighter, musician, and general contractor for 28 years. I consider myself to have been cut from a similar stone as you in that I do what I set my mind to no matter how small with integrity and passion keeping a Texas Toilet Paper mentality (that you don't take shit from anyone) as my core attitude. I would love to meet you someday as people of our nature seem to be becoming few and far between these days.

That said, and without further character validation, I will tell of why I am writing. My folks lived and raised me in a rural Nova to neighbourhood located in Marin County, California. We lived on a remote private golf course with nothing but open space watershed between us and the ocean some 30 miles away. Coastal black oak, lowland forests, and chaparral dense undergrowth comprises 80% of the landscape with redwood coniferous pockets on hill top regions mixed in. Tue Elk, mountain lions, bobcats, fox, coyotes, and coastal black tail were the species that made up our local protected species. Hunting was not allowed. Not exactly what most would consider " Squats" terrain.

When I was 19, I was practising piano in our backyard rehearsal/Au pair unit. Without warning, the hair on the back of my neck and arms stood on end. It didn't concern me really as I had experienced this many many times but usually when alone hiking or hunting, but never indoors. I stopped playing the piano for a moment in response to this " feeling" when a very loud and staccato impact came from the top of the sloped shed roof above my head. It was the type of impact that can only be described as blunt force and shook the whole building which measured 16'X40'. Not a small space.

I initially thought someone had jumped and slammed both feet hard down on our roof and thought someone was messing with me. Then reality set in as the fenced in backyard roof line was 12' off the ground and was not accessible from our street unless you came through the main house or side gate. No were trees or items to climb up and access the roof. The berm on the back of the property was better than twenty feet so accessing the roof from the golf course was just not possible. A fear came over me which I can only describe as deep and primal. Confused, I killed the lights, hastily went into the main house, and put it behind me as something I could not explain. I have never told anyone of the experience.

My musical band mates would cross the golf course from an adjacent street sometimes and come over through the main house side yard to the practice space. Freeman Young was one such band mate who, to this day, tells of his experience of walking to my house one evening along a tall roadway retaining wall when a 6' tall hair covered being jumped from the top of the 14'-16' wall and landed in front of him in the street to access the golf course. He said and I quote, " I thought
it was a large baboon". It looked back at him and hissed. He did an FBFB interview with Jeff Anderson in 2013 in which he describes the incident you can google and hear. How does this relate to me? I am the friend I mentioned in that interview who lived on the golf course. I now know that the " something" I heard jump on my roof that night could have only been one of those beings as the roof line and yard fencing was in the physical capabilities as described by my friend and there is no other practical explanation. This is the first time I have ever spoken about my experience.

Steve Isdahl   The Day Sasquatch Became Real For Me   Copyright© 2020

Anyway, please keep up the videos and share. In my opinion it is very important. If not for you and the others that have decided to come forward, I would have never written this letter. My name is Steve Mani (you may use my name) and appreciate your time. Have a great day, stay in the saddle, and keep the frog side down. Steve-

A Fellow Hunter Trapper Angler

Steve,

I am 53 years old and an avid hunter, trapper and fisherman. I was even on the outdoor channel for a time as I was a pro staffer for a game call company and we had a TV show. I saw my first Sasquatch when I was 12 on a family visit to Muir Woods in California. I was obsessed with steel head and there was a stream full of them right next to the walking path. I left my family to get closer to the fish. I guess I was about 100 yards from my family when I rounded a bend in the stream. I climbed over a big rock and I was about 30 yards when a guy squatted on the edge of the river. We locked eyes and it seemed like he was trying to kill me with his stare. As he stood up, I could not believe how fast he moved. His hair was dark brown. His face only had hair around the edges and he kept his eyes on me as he literally stepped across the creek. I saw greyish hair on his back and muscles like a bodybuilder. The creek was like 20 feet across and he cleared it with one hop. I could not get out of there fast enough. No one believed my story, not my parents, my brother or anyone for that matter. Jump forward to the year 2000, now I am married and living in northern New Jersey.

I shot a huge buck one morning early and the arrow seemed a bit far back. I decided to give it some time as it was November and I was coaching football at the High school nearby. I went to the game with the intention of tracking the deer after the game. We followed the blood trail about 150 yards to where the deer died. Steve you know what the ground looks like when a bow-killed deer expires. There was a 10-foot circle covered with blood and hair. Blood like someone spilled a five gallon pail.....but no deer. The bears are huge here, but a bear would have chowed on the deer first then dragged it a distance and either hid it or left it to come back to. There were no drag Mark's, no blood trail, nothing but a carbon arrow broken into little 4- or 5-inch pieces. Turkey season the following year I was hunting behind my house every morning of the season, about a square mile of private land. I kept jumping what I thought was a bear on the edge of a swamp at the base of a steep ridge. It happened 4 or 5 times in the dark and the " bear" would move off about 50 yards and stop.

It was always at first light as I was hoping to hear the turkeys gobble on the roost. One morning I was late getting out so I was creeping slower than usual and an owl hooting as I walked. When I got near the area where I was jumping the bear, I stopped to owl hoot. As I did, I heard someone running toward the ridge. It was the thump thump of a two legged being, their feet hitting the ground not the leaf shuffling a bear makes on the run. Then I saw it as it neared the top of the ridge, taking these huge strides he RAN up what I would have to literally have to use all fours to get up. As he topped the ridge all I could see was the face staring at me from when I was 12. I knew what it was. I haven slept right since 2001. At our camp 20 miles from my home we had a deer taken from the inside of a pickup with a cap on it.

The T handles of the cap were closed but not locked. Whatever took the deer had put its hands-on top of the cap and left Mark's where the hair on its arms had disturbed the dust and dirt. The guys I was hunting with just said a bear took it. How many bears can open T handles and walk away with a 100-pound doe, leaving no drag Mark's or evidence. They mimic the owl calls from a distance when I am turkey hunting sometimes, and shadow me on my way out of the woods after deer hunting. People have laughed at me forever for what I have told them is out there. I am so thankful that you are doing what you are doing. I am a big dude,6-4, 300 pounds. These things could twist my head off like I opened a beer bottle.

I coyote hunt at night a few times a week all w hell out of there. I am never going to stop doing what I love to do, hunting and fishing, but it is not the same once you know you are not out here alone. There is something about knowing you are not the top dog in the woods. I know you know what I mean. They walk around my house at night in the summer, they shadow me sometimes when I am out hunting, they are here and no one wants to admit it. The BFRO idiots were more concerned with having me pay 400 dollars to go on their freaking expedition, than coming up to see the area where I live. As soon as I said they were human like and not apes, they dismissed me like I never existed.

Keep pumping out the videos brother, I know how time consuming it is, but just getting this off my chest to someone that also knows these Damn things, as you describe them, exist is helping like you can't imagine. Many thanks brother. Jimmy Ginter, usually alone. Not any more. I had scouted a spot-on state land one Saturday after deer season ended, to coyote hunt later after dark. Driving in around 10 pm I came along a 6-inch tree across the road that was just wide enough for one truck. I had just been there a few hours before in the daylight. I got out to move it but the tree had been twisted around five feet off the ground and bent over the road. As I looked at it, I felt like I was being watched. That feeling of impending doom swept over me. They did not want me in there, so I jumped in and got the

Another Ex Combat Veteran's Story

Hello Steve,

I am 51 years old. I'm an ex-police officer, combat veteran and an avid hunter, fisherman and outdoors man. I was raised in south central Ohio, where I've been hunting nearly my entire life. I've seen or experienced every type of animal in the forests of Ohio, including black, and bobcat.
My experience with one of these creatures happened 18 years ago, on private property, near a correctional facility in Hocking county, just south of Lancaster, Ohio. This private property's boundaries end at the correctional facility and the Hocking National Forest. It was October, and the rut was in full swing. It was a cold, overcast, late evening hunt for white tail, and I was heading to my favourite spot, where I had harvested a few nice bucks. From the house, where I parked my vehicle, you only have to walk a quarter mile into the forest to be in whitetail heaven.

The walk is up a steep hillside, and my favourite spot is at the base of a small 30-foot rock that goes straight up.   There's no way to climb this, without climbing gear.   The only way to go up there is to walk around it, which is about 200 yards in either direction.   What you find is a plateau, and the edge of the prison's property line.

As usual, I sat down with my back against this sheer rock wall, and I was facing the house down below me.   There's a major deer trail that goes from my right to left, and is ranged at 30 yards.   A fantastic spot, due to wind direction, which blew directly towards my face, concealment of the rock wall, and the elevated position. With the added conveniences of being so close to my vehicle, and a bright security light, mounted on a telephone pole, there was never a concern to bring a flashlight.

This area is full of the annoying population of squirrels. Although they are small, they make so much noise.   And, every hunter knows the squeal noises these things make when they see you. As I was waiting for my trophy whitetail, I was occasionally being hit by acorns.   I honestly didn't think much about it.   I attributed this to the pesky squirrels that were all around me.   But I soon found out that this activity was not from the squirrels.

It eventually became so dark that I was unable to see. So, I stood up and began my journey towards the security light, as I have always done before. After I had walked approximately about 30 yards, I literally jumped from the top of the rock wall, and landed, with such weight behind it, my original thought was that a tree had just fallen. I stood there perplexed, as I did not hear it roll, or crashing branches.   It landed with only a huge thud. And, as I was frozen in place, intently listening, what I heard next chilled me to my very core.   It was breathing. Each breath was very long and deep.   I stared into the direction of the noise long and hard.   I was trying my best to see through the forest, in pitch darkness. I could barely see my hands in front of my face.   Then, it made a powerful "blow noise" towards me, like a deer, when it is alert to your presence.   But this thing was no deer. The noise was way too long and powerful. Thoughts of what else it could be in Ohio, came rushing through my mind.   When I came to the conclusion that nothing that I know of in this state would, or could accomplish the 30-foot jump, or the long drawn out breathing, or that powerful of a warning signal, panic began to set in.

It took two steps towards me, and I began to run with everything I had towards the security light. If anyone has ever experienced true darkness in the woods, you know that you can't see a thing.   As I ran, logs, fallen branches and vines were constantly tripping me.   I would fall on my face, and slide to a stop.   This must've at least 5 times.   Each time, I could hear it walking behind me, and stop each time it fell. I heard it taking very heavy steps behind me, and then stop each time I stopped. I kept thinking that whatever this thing is, it could have me any time it desired. I had never felt this vulnerable, or helpless my entire life.

As I finally reached the bottom of the hillside, I put my back against the light pole, and faced towards it.   I brought my gun to my shoulder, and began scanning with it, and I had every intention of shooting it at the edge of the light. But, in a surprise move, it did not exit the woods on the same path. Instead, I caught a glimpse of its nocturnal eyes about yards to my left.   The security light made its eyes light up like a nocturnal animal. The only problem was what I was seeing were the eye were 6 feet or so off the ground. His eyes are all I could make out. Then, it turned and walked back up the hill side. I was left shocked at my experience, and I've never gone back. It began to haunt my nightmares, and It still does to this day.

Thank you for allowing me to share my unnerving experience,

David

Myself and client, remote B.C.
HowtoHunt.com

Sent in From Alaska

Hello Steve,

I'm a truck driver in Alaska, I haul double trailers of produce nightly from Anchorage to Fairbanks and on occasion to the Aiken Peninsula with Homer Alaska being the furthest point.

This last winter my company hired a kid just out of trucking school and he needed training so I volunteered to help him.

In the training he needed chaining experience and mountain experience with an 18spd while pulling doubles, it can get squirrel if you don't know what you're doing.

We were driving through Donaldson Alaska on the Aiken Peninsula around 2am and just before the big hill I decided to pull over and chain up plus we both were jumping at the bit to release ourselves; the kid was riding shotgun.

We both step from the tractor, as soon as my feet hit the icy pavement, I hear a gut curdling scream from the other side of the rig, I instantly thought bear but then thought no! It's winter... I ran over and the kid was in shock, he pointed to a wall by a boat sales yard and I looked over. I couldn't believe my eyes! It looked like something you would see in a movie. King Kong is real. This giant ape like creature was at least 10' tall and 4' wide shoulder to shoulder. It looked more frightened than us.

What I remember the most was the long black hair like a bear, humanoid face and it had hooves like a goat, not hands! I knew this "Bigfoot" may not be of this world. I grabbed the kid and we quickly left. My life is changed forever.

I did some research after the sighting and someone told me of a disabled guy that travels around Alaska and WA getting good footage of these things. He has a Facebook group called: Tracking Sasquatch I guess Bigfoot doesn't hurt him because he's disabled, id if there's truth to that or not.

This encounter changed my life completely, I don't drive a truck anymore and I actually have a hard time sleeping or doing anything at night. I now fear the woods. I never imagined something like this could change lives so drastically.

There's a video I just saw with the prime minister of Canada reporting his knowledge of 20 or more aliens on this planet some of which are giant bugs and not all of them are nice. I have a copy of the video if you can't find it.

Thank you, Steve, you may not know this but you are definitely helping me and I am sure many more people.

Central Arkansas

Hey Steve, I ask that you only use my first name which is also Steve. I've got an encounter to share with you and your listeners. It's probably not as interesting as most encounters you read but it was real and very intense for me even if no one believes me. It happened in September of 2012 in central Arkansas. It was a month before archery deer season (whitetail) and I was out scouting and checking game cameras. Things started out normally. I made my way from camera to camera and looking for deer signs. The land I hunt is private and barely under 200 acres. Only myself and two of my grown sons hunt on this land but more times than not, it's just me. I would say the biggest part of the land is lob lolly pine. Open timber in places and super think underbrush in others. There are four pastures and there's a section of huge open hardwoods. Mostly giant white oaks that fruit some of the largest acorns I've ever seen.

The hardwoods are where I started. There are cattle on the land so tons of cow trails that I walk looking for deer tracks as they walk these trails sometimes too. I made my way out of the hardwoods and walked one edge of a pasture till I hit the section of open pines. Most of these pines are good straight, telephone pole quality trees. Great for climbing stands.

Eventually, the underbrush starts getting thicker and thicker and if you aren't on a cow/game trail, it can be quite difficult to make much headway. As you go even farther into the thickets, the bigger pines are more spread out and there are tons of different sized saplings of a large variety of trees. Mostly sweet gum (or golden amber) trees. I would say the average thickness of these sweet gums at head level would be the diameter of a Louisville Slugger.

As I started getting close to this area. I felt what many who have sent in their encounters have said. I felt a sense of dread. Like I was being hunted or stalked. My mind immediately thought black bear. Through the years we've seen a few then I thought about coyotes but they would most likely be rabid to consider attacking an adult. Those thoughts came and went literally in a second or two. I immediately knew it was something else. I didn't want to give in and accept what I was thinking it could be. I was frozen in fear. I felt I should head to truck and leave but I still have a few more cameras to check. I know I stood there for no less than five minutes. I finally told myself to get a grip before I had a heart attack as my heart was beating of my chest. It was then I started noticing several of these baseball bat diameter trees that were broken over. I would estimate the breaks were around ten feet up the trees.

I also noticed that the tops that were broken over all pointed at me and they made a half circle in front of me. Okay so now I'm legitimately freaked out. I'm seriously waiting for the heart attack. The sense of dread is now completely overwhelming and even though I grew up hunting these woods, I found myself completely disoriented.

I soon realized that I was on a cow/game trail. I also realized that either way I go on this trail that I will come out in one of the pastures. And I had the clarity to know where I was, if I could just make it to any of the pastures and would know what direction to go. As I contemplated whether to go forward or turn and go the other way, I heard something that jarred my whole system. Immediately after hearing this sound I had clarity. The dread completely disappeared and curiosity took over. What I heard was a child crying. Not a baby necessarily but a toddler maybe. Any feeling of fear was gone. Now it's just curiosity and concern about this kid that must be lost in the woods. I'm guessing the cries are maybe 50 yards ahead and I take a few steps. The woods in front of me exploded with snapping limbs and timber shaking and holy crap something is coming my way. Suddenly there he was. The cause of dread and fear was standing right in front of me. I say "he" because trust me, there was no doubt. There was no doubt about his manhood. I have to say that for the most part, most descriptions fit perfectly with this dude. Had to be a four-foot shoulder span. Legs at least as big around as my torso (I'm 5'8", 220lbs). Definitely a body rippling with noticeable muscles but no six-pack abs. In fact, I'd say he had a bit of a belly. Jet black, shiny hair all over except for what skin you would see on a bearded mans face. The hair seemed to be less dense on his feet and the top of his hands. His skin colour reminded me of the colour from a charcoal Gray pencil. Not the skin colour of a black man or any other race I've ever seen. Dark Charcoal Gray is the best I can describe it. My house has 8-foot ceilings and he was easily that tall if not a little more than that.

Okay, so this is my take on what I saw and what I didn't see. What I saw was a massive man. This was no ape. Not half ape/half man. There is absolutely no doubt. I'll even say this. He was actually a fairly good-looking man. And yeah, not really a noticeable neck. I never noticed any Oder. . Enough with the description and back to the story.

So, he has just ran up and stopped right in front of me. Ten yards max. So, we eye one another for maybe 5 seconds and then he slowly turns and looks behind him. Holy crap! There's another one. I'm Guessing 6'6". Noticeably smaller than he was. This one was about 20 yards farther behind him and although I'm not positive, I'm guessing it was female. I say this because although I never saw a juvenile with it, the crying I had heard hadn't completely stopped and I'm pretty sure this was mom walking away with a toddler. As soon as she started to take off, big boy looked back at me. He then raised his arm and pointed. Not at me. But as if to say I needed to leave. I know thatch what he was telling me. As I walked away, my surroundings started becoming familiar again. At this point I wasn't scared as much as I was just uneasy. I made it to my truck and headed home. I didn't sleep at all that night. This is the first I've spoken about it. I know this sounds stupid but I always felt if I said anything, he'd know. And somehow, I'd have to answer for saying something. Even as I tell this, the hair on my neck is standing up. I really think he knows.

I still hunt there but not nearly as much as I used to. I definitely avoid that section of woods. I've been within 100 yards or so but I feel I shouldn't go any closer. Although I'm sure They aren't always in that one little section, I feel like it's off limits to me. I've never seen a Bigfoot track out there. I have found broken trees since then but I haven't felt they were in the area at those times.

Oh. The one I'm sure was a female was more of a dark, rich brown colour than black. I couldn't make out too many details or features on that one except for the height and colour differences. Again, I never could make out the on that was crying.

I completely believe they are another race of people. The whole sixth sense thing you talk about, I fully believe you're right. After experiencing those feelings even before I saw him. They can tap into something we can't and bring feelings of fear and dread and disorientation. It has to be their first line of defence. I can say that I wouldn't mind seeing one again but, from like 100 yards away and it not be pissed off. I sure didn't get that warm and fuzzy vibe from him.

Please use my first name only.
Thanks,

Steve (Harmon)

Raised To Know Of Them

Hello,

Growing up my Dad told me Sasquatch is a real thing. His is a good and true story, maybe I'll send it to you another time. I want to tell you my experience.

Back in 2012 I was living near the city of Baltimore. I had my own successful business, a house and a workshop in a great town. I was a strong young man. Unfortunately, or fortunately now that I look back was diagnosed with a serious illness and given little chances of survival. This changed my life forever. I put up a good fight, survived the surgeries even awful chemo & radiation that I did against my intuition for my family's wishes. And even my long stay in the hospital. But then realized I had to change my environment to be well. I sold the house, workshop and shutdown my business in order to move to the mountains of Appalachia. I purchased a foreclosed cabin close to a very large wilderness area. I live there alone. My family and friends are still in the city.

The first strange thing I noticed here are the glowing orbs. I though maybe it was just my imagination until one rainy night I was driving home from seeing a movie with my close friend who was visiting. We were about to turn on the road I live off of and there it was. We saw a bright orange orb above the tree line near a pond. I asked my friend, what do you see? She saw the same thing I did. I asked her what to you think that could be. She said she didn't know. It was raining hard and foggy. Yet this thing was bright, about the size of a beach ball I'd guess. As we approach in the Jeep the thing just disappeared. I've seen the orbs on three occasions as of now.

Now for the scary part. And I have this on video so I know the exact date and time. I can try to send you the video if you want. That evening I was in the back-yard cooking steak camp style outside in an old wood stove beside my workshop. It was dusk, I was talking to my Mother on the phone as I was just finishing cooking and about to go inside. I had her on speaker phone. I mentioned that I was about to go in and that I heard something in the woods. My Mom said "aren't you afraid up there all alone?" I said no Mom, you know after all I've had to go through, I don't feel afraid of anything anymore. I went inside the cabin had the steak and settled in for the night. At 12:45 I woke up to my cat going crazy. He is a big Norway forest cat we rescued from Baltimore. He has never acted so strange. He can sense where wildlife is around the cabin and I can usually tell when and where there is a bear or bobcat based on his behaviour. There is a screen room on the back side of the cabin, my cat has a pet door to use the litter box. As I opened the door from the great room to enter the screen room my cat went nuts and jumped against me repeatedly as if he was trying to say don't go out there. That's when I heard it walking and it was big, really big. I have had experiences with bear this was different. The screen room is up against the woods, tall trees with a creek running below. There's no flood light on that side just a light inside the screen but with that on I can't see out so all the lights where out. The noise it made was loud, I don't know how it was made but sounded like a bang. I got my iPod and hit record and captured the sound. I felt my body having chills all over and I knew something was off. I closed the door and tried to look out the windows but I couldn't see anything. My cat stayed in also and this was strange because when there is an animal, he always wants to observe from the screen room.

I had a hard time sleeping and got up early. I went out the workshop and found this huge pile of scat on the board that I use as a ramp to put my motorcycle inside. I've never seen poop like this and I wish I had taken a photo. The scat was centred perfectly on the board and there was one large impression on each side as if something squatted there. Now it frustrates me that I did not document this part. I left the poop alone and after a few days of rain it was gone. But not from my mind. It was bigger than a dinner plate, I could see it was wild because there were undigested seeds, big seeds about the size of my thumb. As well as buds and plant fibre. So, what I suspect is, that these creatures' poop on raised structure, I heard it mentioned only once I can't recall where on someone's video maybe one of yours not sure. While exploring the wildlife area on Jeep we have seen odd structures and even a large tree inverted. I though that was significant but my friend though maybe a storm caused it. To me it seemed intentional like a warning sign.

I hope this helps you, I think hunting is great but I don't hunt. And I don't think this being should be hunted. I never actually caught sight of it but I don't have to or necessarily want to now. I have a firearms restriction sadly but I am armed best I can. I still go into the woods, but now I take precautions and try not to go out alone.

Thank you for your good work. I'd like to remain anonymous. So, until next time when I send in my Dads story. Be well,
-A Friend

The Teeth Were Extremely Over Sized

First, please refer to me as "Ted" if you do decide to share my encounters. Thank you for that. I have been an avid fourth generation outdoors man my entire life and I have always wanted to share my story with someone like you (an avid outdoors man). At the time of this encounter I was 10 years old. I was squirrel hunting in August with my 410 shotgun that was my great-grandfathers on a piece of Wildlife Management Area property (WMA). I had hiked and hunted in those woods on my own and with my grandfather for years before and I still use those woods after my experiences but I have NEVER been in those woods without reminiscing that memory from so long ago.

It was around noon and I was on my second trip to the woods of the day. I had just shot a grey squirrel with my single shot 410 and went to pick it up and... upon picking up the dead squirrel I turned around and noticed something walking towards me. Not a word was exchanged and all I did was raise up my squirrel to show "this thing" my HARVEST. The reaction "this thing" did was to open its mouth and showcase its teeth. The teeth were extremely wide and OVER SIZED! I never said a word and then "this thing" walked off through the timber. The entire encounter lasted about two minutes. "This thing" was about five feet tall, very thick, had matted hair covering itself, the head was pointed with a gradual slope, no smell at all, dark facial skin with sunken eyes, and lastly "this thing" was calm and I never felt threatened at all. I told my grandpa and dad about my experience and they deducted it was an older African American with odd camouflage.

Fast forward 25 years or so... I was bow hunting 250 yards from the squirrel ridge I had my encounter and the second strangest thing happened to me. It was about 15 minutes to sundown and I could hear something walking through the dried corn rows and then a gust of wind blew from me to the cornfield where the noise was coming from. Immediately at 40 yards whatever it was stopped in its tracks. At that moment I felt like something was looking right at me and MY NERVES SPIKED!!!! There was no movement or sounds for almost 10 seconds (which seemed like an eternity) and then all of a sudden SOMETHING ran off with such force, violence, and speed I was immediately concerned. I stayed in the tree stand until dark and then walked back to my grandparent's house which is about a mile total. The entire time walking back in the dark I had a feeling that I was being followed / stalked. I have been in those woods 100's of times since and not one thing happened I could not explain. These two moments in my life are very curious to say the least. I continue my journey for answers and in my quest, I have found similar stories and descriptions to my experiences which makes me feel better. I do believe what I saw was something I have never seen since but with all my heart and honour I believe I was supposed to have had that experience. Lastly, thank you for taking your time to allow people like me to share my story with
Matt aka "Ted".

The Tracks Alone Scared Her

Hello Steve,

I have become a big fan of your channel over the past few weeks after viewing your video talking about Bobby Short and the events that took place at Bluff Creek. Up until I found your channel, I used to think that Sasquatch were a joke (likely due to the bullshit "finding Bigfoot" television shows with the people running around in the woods saying they "heard something" when a camera man steps on a branch off camera). Being an outdoors man myself, I love to go hunting and fishing. I live in the Pittsburgh area and have seen your typical black bears, deer, and other critters roaming around western PA. My family also used to have a house in Deep Creek, Maryland where we would go ever since I was a child. Although I have personally never seen a Sasquatch, I am very fascinated by them and the experiences people share with you on your videos. The story I have to share with you is not of my own, but it is my grandmothers.
She just recently turned 78 today but is still as sharp as anyone I know. She not only had 4 kids, one being my mother, but she had also beat cancer, passed hundreds of kidney stones, and now suffers with vision and auto immune disease due to medical malpractice during a retina surgery. She is tough as nails and has some of the greatest morals of anyone I know. She has suffered much of her life but because of this is very wise and has an extremely positive outlook on life. She is my role model and I even have her birthday tattooed on my chest as a reminder of how important she is to me. She is the kind of person who is genuine and would not lie about anything to anyone. I remember a story she told me when I was a kid about these footprints that

she had seen but I didn't remember all the details. Just recently, I brought up the subject of Sasquatch since I had been watching your videos a lot just to see what she would say. I acted like I had known nothing of what she was talking about so she would retell me the entire story from her perspective.

She said that in the early 80's, she was at her sisters' cabin in Somerset County, Pa when they woke up early in the morning to let the dogs outside. Somerset is not only home to the Flight 93 Memorial but a ski lodge called Seven Springs that I have gone to at least once a year since I was born and my grandmother loved the place, hence why she was at the cabin. I had never been to this property, but she said that the cabin was up in the mountains and had several acres between lots. There was a backyard that was fenced in with a pool, but other than that, the house was surrounded by dense woods. When they stepped out the back door, it was just starting to become light outside and there was a fresh snowfall on the ground. In the snow, just outside the house, my grandmother, her sister, and sister's family could see that something had walked through the yard, stepped over the fence, and continued walking past the property. The area where the tracks came from, and where they continued towards, now has power lines built near it, but she said that back then there was nothing there.

She said that it was an area where a human would have had a hard time navigating through and would have had no reason to go towards since there was nothing but dense forest of the Appalachian Valley for miles in that direction. She said that the tracks were huge, and that you could see the toe prints defined in the snow. I asked her if it was that of a size 14 shoe, and she said "Way bigger". Aside from the tracks themselves being huge, what she said sold her was the way the thing climbed the fence. She said that the fence was every bit of 7 feet tall, and they could tell by the way the snow on top of the fence was disturbed that whatever it was must have picked it's leg up (like a wrestler going over the top rope) and stepped over the fence. She said that after seeing the tracks and the way the snow was moved on the fence, she could not rationally make up what it was that walked through the yard. It made no sense to her, and she had seen many bear and other animal tracks in person and in photos throughout her lifetime. Lastly, she said that after investigating the tracks and seeing them up close, she said she almost wanted to leave the area it scared her so much.

I do not know if Sasquatch live in that specific area, and this was 30 some years ago, but I would like to hear your opinion on this story. I know that there have been many sightings in the Allegheny National forest but I or anyone that I know, to my knowledge, have never seen one. In watching her body language, my grandmother was even visibly shaken when telling the story. It definitely bothers her still to this day because she knows that it wasn't an animal the way it stepped over the fence. I know this is lengthy, but thank you for taking the time to read my email, and I will look forward to your response.

Sincerely,

Dan

Another Career Military Man Wrote In

Hi Steve hope all is well been following your show for sometime now, and it's time I told my story. Bit of back ground served my country England for 12 years all over the globe 5 tours from Ireland, Bosnia and Afghanistan so seen my fair share of shit, face to face with some of the evillest bastards on this earth, terrorist have personally threatened me and my family and countless engagements. But nothing comes close to this here goes. I was sent over to Canada Alberta to do some training bk in 1993 1st day me and a friend decided to go to for a walk about, get to know the area bumped in to few Canadian soldiers a few words exchanged and one shouted back font let the monkeys keep you awake they laughed, we just looked at each other then carried on. Now bare with me because this is a bit of a puzzle to start with as it's over a few years between incidents.

While out on exercise, a few of the guys said they were woken up in their sleeping bags been pulled along the ground I heard this a few times over the weeks also there kit, rations and other bits going missing, nothing came of it also an incident of one soldier missing found the next day miles away from his platoon this is live firing so can get very dangerous at times, he said he couldn't remember why he got separated but felt that he was followed during the night by some animal? Nothing more was said. 1995 I returned to Canada to do another job spent around 19 months out there, just as before I was going out to check the lay of the land a group of Canadian soldiers were just coming in looked like they had been out a few day's looking at the state of them, you going out one asked your you staying out don't know I replied Fucking monkey's watch your bk he said, I replied OK thinking heard this before, I noticed the guys had there heads down they looked pretty worn out.

A few months on, one of the guys said you seen Scott, no why I replied his crying going on about seeing 3 bears WALKING TOWARDS HIM ON 2 FEET ON A TRAIL while out walking, I immediately thought Walking 2 FEET. I went to find him this was just a few hrs after his encounter I couldn't find him anywhere, the following day I asked around where he was, his gone a guy said, what do you mean gone, gone bk to his regiment, I knew straight away why. I found the guy who told me about this, he just didn't want to talk about it so I left it there. Was September now I remember this well cause I lost 2 of my best friends, and I was feeling very down and lost was a bad time in my career for me, I decided to go for a drive weekend break had an old pickup truck and just drove not really going anywhere in particular, I stopped for a break in a beautiful Area not far from Great falls been on the road 2 days now sleeping in the bk of the pick up, I decided to go for a walk there was a trail and a tree line about a mile walk away so of I went about 100 yards away from the tree line I see a coyote just stop on the trail never seen one so close up ours eyes met just staring at each other, I suddenly feel uncomfortable the dog keeps glancing bk and forth from the tree line, now am really feeling anxious not cause of the dog but what's in that tree line the dog moves backwards and forwards then just disappeared in the grass am left staring at the trees centre and left and right in that tree line something or things are telling me to come closer I cant explain this but my heads telling me no.

I don't know how long I was there but now I'm so scared, I've never felt so much fear to the point I felt sick I slowly got my legs to walk backwards keeping my eyes on the tree line, I then turned and ran, like a bad dream I got in my pick up and never looked bk, I must add I wasn't drinking alcohol never had a drop those few days, I still think about it to this day what was in those trees. The months go by and then my Battalion comes over for an exercise, one night while out I was with another mate we were parked on a hill overlooking a large bowl down below where a platoon of men were all sleeping, it was around 2.30 in the morning clear sky's you could see a good distance with out using any aids, my friend was asleep I noticed a group of coyotes down below looks like they were looking for a free meal, now I was thinking is this what happens when someone feels there been dragged in their sleeping bags, could a dog have that much strength?, I watched them for a while getting bolder by the minute, then suddenly there body language changed.

4 of them ran of one direction 2 the other then one was just standing there looking up the hill, I looked through my night vision now this peace of kit I was using was incredibly powerful top of the range, then all of a sudden 3 human type figures just stood up one after the other all different sizes that's the 1st thing that stood out to me on adjusting my sights I could clearly see what the largest one was a BIG FOOT no doubt about it. It was standing at 9ft the 2nd around 7.5 and the other 6ft I knew this by using the kit I had, to measure how far away they were plus the ground they were in, I had been there the previous day, I looked at my mate still snoring away and just left him to it.

The details on the tallest was easy to see, now the shoulders wow so big could see his eyes no colour couldn't make that out, they were all looking in my direction then just turned and walked down in to another valley, could see the hair swaying of his arms even the calf muscles,, am just smiling to my self, to me this was the last peace of the puzzle. I recently told my daughter about this she believes me, you know there's so many people that know about these creatures especially where I was it's common knowledge if your in the right crowd, well that's my story I think about them every day am glad I saw them and I've always believed they existed, there was a spate of orbs and even a couple of visits from the FBI will tell your about that next time round.

PS STOP USING YOUR OXYGEN ON THOSE PERFETIC LOOSERS WHO RIDICULE OTHERS KEEP UP THE GOOD WORK, MEANS A LOT TO ME TAKE CARE.

IAN

My Encounter

Hello Steve, my name is David Hayes and I am a 54-year-old husband, father and grandfather who also served in the navy, straight out of high school. After which, for several years, I had many carpentry types jobs until finally getting a job working for a major factory, as a production supervisor, for over 20 years. I had 2 strokes in the last 2 years and my working days were finished. I have nothing to lose now and while not as "in your face" as a lot of encounters, mine was one I'll never forget.

Enough of me, I want to thank you for what you are doing for those out there who have no place to go, to tell their story. This is very important; people need to tell someone to help start the process of getting over the experience. To keep it to yourself will not aid in recovering. While I haven't had the unfortunate experience of actually seeing one of these freaking things, I have had multiple experiences, in the woods, that have no explanation. The worse of which I am going to relay to you and your viewers now. I am hoping it helps someone, with a similar situation, to understand and hopefully get over they're own experiences.

This all took place on one of the longest mountain ridges here in Central PA. There is a mountain ridge, called the Bald Eagle ridge, that runs South West to North East and runs for about 60 miles. It's the last mountain ridge before hitting the Appalachian plateau to the West. It's a very beautiful part of the country and the state. In these mountains there are very few homes. Most of the population of this state lives in the valleys and not in the mountain tops, so they are pretty secluded.

About 10 years ago my wife and I, along with my 25ish year old son and our 2 grandchildren and one of their friends (all the children were between 8 and 10 years old) all went for a walk at the reservoir, that supplies all the drinking water for this area. (Central Pa. USA) This reservoir is set back about a mile from the main road (rt 150) and now is an area for walking and hiking. But back then it wasn't used by many people at all. It was formed from damming the creek that runs down through this valley. The small lake that was formed is beautiful and is abundant with fish and surrounded with the usual wildlife. But most of all it's secluded.

Let me first say that until having 2 strokes, in the last 2 years, I was an avid Hunter and fisherman. And taught my children and grandchildren to get out and enjoy what nature we have.

Steve Isdahl   The Day Sasquatch Became Real For Me   Copyright© 2020

So, with that being said, I and my son was armed, as we always are, to protect us from any animals that may not have the best intentions. We started out a little later than planned but things were going great and so far, uneventful. We walked about a mile or 2 up into the mountain and was on our way back, about 3/4 of a mile from the truck, and by this time it was about 9pm and dark. Everyone had a flashlight. We always take them for reasons like this and we were here before, at the same time, with nothing to be concerned about.

So, it was business as usual and we were all carrying on and enjoying the outdoors and the walk. I want to make clear now, that I got a very uneasy like feeling, for no reason. I wish I could explain it but can't. I know that doesn't make sense but I just had a very weird feeling. Then I heard what sounded like heavy foot steps, faintly, but I could hear them over the sounds my family were making, in front of me, on the trail. It sounded like something big, walking above us, straddling the side hill, to our left. It's a very steep side hill, and the trail we were on was cut into it for humans to walk on. My son was in the lead, followed by the 3 children, my wife and then myself bringing up the rear. My son stopped, which stopped the rest of us, and he said "listen". "Dad, do you hear that?" I was already listening hard, and again, I could hear what sounded like someone walking to our left, on the steep mountain side of the trail.

I'm not going to lie, it startled me. But after gathering my senses I shrugged it off as a deer or some other animal and told my son to keep moving. But him, myself, and the rest of the group were now focused on what was following us in the upper side of the trail. We were all moving forward and were not panicked, but focused.

Just then I heard what sounded like a very large branch being broken from a tree. My son and the rest of the family also heard it. Then it sounded like a tree or a large bolder was thrown. It was loud. Very loud. I've heard trees falling over from wind, in the woods, while hunting and that's not what this noise was.

There was no wind that night, it was very still and the woods were silent, up until this point. We then heard what sounded like a very heavy person running. This was all happening about 20 or so yards up the steep side hill to our left. At this point I calmly said to my son, who was now shining his light on the mountain side, trying to find what had made that noise, "start moving...!" We all started to walk, fast, to get back to the truck. All the flashlights were focused on that side hill but we could see nothing but trees. And the rest of the walk was uneventful. The whole way back to the vehicle everyone was on end and our senses were all on high alert. I don't know what made that noise that night but I know what it wasn't. I've been in the woods long enough to know what the sounds are and what we all heard that night was a deliberate made noise. If I had to make a guess, I would say something ripped a tree from the ground and threw it. That's what it sounded like to me. The rest of the way back to the truck was uneventful. We saw no eye shine and heard nothing else the rest of the way back to the place that we parked the truck.

We no longer walk there after dark and even in the daytime we are on high alert. There are many people who walk there now, since they turned it into a public walk and mountain bike area and we have had no other incidents while walking there. You can give my name, I don't care

Steve Isdahl   The Day Sasquatch Became Real For Me   Copyright© 2020

what people think of me, I'm at that age now where I don't care. I know what I heard and felt that night and my whole family still talks about it. I am in the minority in that I was not alone when this happened and my family still brings it up and talks about it to this day.

Thank you, Steve, for give people an outlet to share their encounters. I'm sure this will help a lot of people. It doesn't really bother me, I'm always on my guard when ever in these areas.

Bully Hater From Montana

Steve,

I have been watching your YouTube videos. First, I watched them because I am and have been a life long hunter, then I saw one on the subject of Sasquatch where you discussed bullying on a hunting forum. I really liked and appreciated your take on the subject...especially where you talked about hating bullies.

I hate bullies too. I was a cop for 27 years, which kind of brings me to what I experienced last year in Barrett's Montana.

As I said, I was a cop for 27 years. I approach things with "open minded cynicism" in other words, I like evidence. I want to be able to see it, touch it, feel it, test it, and then make my decision. Anyway, I retired from the department three years ago. I am from northern Arizona. I have been around black bear, mountain lion, coyote, wildcat, and even a wolf. I have hunted most things in North America that can hunt you. I also worked Gangs-Narcotics for 20 years and worked around and against human predators that can and WILL hunt you.

I am not given to flights of fancy or unreasonable fear. I am not saying I was never afraid...you'd have to be an idiot to not be afraid when you're getting ready to breech a door knowing there are armed men on the other side who would rather kill you than go back to prison. But I never let that fear stop me from doing what I had to do.

So, I retired from my department just over three years ago and after a while, decided I needed a second career. I taught school for a semester and really didn't like it, and o a fluke my best friend and competitive shooting buddy said "Let's go to truck driving school", so we did.

My buddy and I drove as a team and spent all of last winter in the mountain states, seemingly running from Phoenix Arizona (near where I live) to Shelby, Montana. We used to overnight in Barrett's Montana at a Sinclair station that had a cafe, a small store, and parking for about 20 semis. It was a regular stop for us, so I am and was familiar with the area. We stopped this night and I was in the driver's seat and my buddy was sitting on the lower bunk in the sleeper. We had a movie on the DVD player and I was paying half attention to that and half attention to my laptop when I caught some movement past the driver's window.

Bear in mind, this is a small facility, and it is 100 yards from the freeway, but generally surrounded by a large field with 3 to 4-foot-tall grass and thicket that goes right into foothills and mountains. I looked to the mirror and saw the BIGGEST (presumed) man I had ever seen step behind my trailer which was 70 feet behind me. I said "Jesus, that was the biggest mother_____ I have ever seen! Damn! "My buddy popped up and looked out the passenger mirror and said "No shit" and told me he saw a "big guy" walk between the space between the rear of our trailer and a truck that was parked next to us.

I didn't think anything more of it for a while, but then I realized that when I caught the movement next to me the head of "the guy" was nearly at my shoulder level which was ten feet off the ground. I was in my 2019 Freight liner Cascadia tractor. The bottom of the window line on my door is 9 1/2" feet from ground level.
My cop brain went into "assessment" mode and I thought..."No, he couldn't have been that tall. There must have been a shadow casting on my window". I wasn't even considering Sasquatch. I was in "What do I know, and what does the evidence tell me?" mode. But I was tired, and put it out of my mind. I finished up and my partner and I went to our bunks and killed the TV and lights. The only noise was my APU running to keep the heater running.

I fell into a very light sleep which was unusual because I usually sleep like a baby. I am totally comfortable in my truck, but not this night. It's like I felt like I was hovering between sleep and wakefulness. Around midnight, I really had to pee. Since the store/cafe was already closed by 9pm, I climbed out the passenger side of my tractor to "check the chains" (pee between the tractor and trailer near the snow chain hooks). The truck that had been parked next to us was already gone, so the space was open from my truck to the grass field.

For some reason, I felt like I was being.... hunted? Watched? Maybe not "actively hunted" like prey, but definitely I was aware of something predatory being aware of me. I have been hunted by criminals. I have been around predatory animals, and I have never felt like this before.

I finished quickly, and looked around and scanned the grass field in the quarter moon light and had a feeling, a deep-down feeling that I should NOT move toward the field. It was like a pheromone instinct that signalled that danger existed if I did. Like all the hard-wired primal instincts of survival just told me not to move in that direction.

Then I heard "oomph". Not like someone hot someone in the gut, but just a low verbalization of "oomph". I got back into the truck and locked the door. felt like there was "something" out there that was dangerous...but only if I did something to trigger an aggressive response.

I got back into my bunk and made sure that my Glock 10mm pistol was in the cubby by my head (being a retired police officer, I can legally carry in all 50 states), but I also made sure two spare magazines were close to hand as well.

In the time I had been trucking, I never felt as though I had to do that...not even when parked in downtown Detroit! Something was telling every fibre of my being, that there was something out there that was, while not aggressive, it WAS dangerous.

I tried to put it out of my mind and listened to a podcast while trying to go back to sleep. I slept a little bit, but I had a sense of foreboding. At 3am, I sat bolt upright reaching for my Glock. I saw "it" whatever "it" was go by the front of the truck this time in the space between the building and my truck. I moved out of my bunk to the passenger side window and only caught a faint and fading shadow moving into the darkness out of the faint glow of the low sodium lighting on the building 75 yards away.

I was up now, and there was no way I was going back to sleep. I got out my coffee maker and started a pot of coffee and got dressed. I still had 90 minutes on my electronic log before I could go back on duty and drive us out of there, but all I wanted to do was leave ASAP.I drank my coffee and kept looking out of the windows of the truck but didn't see anything else. The sun started coming up and with the light, the sense of foreboding retreated. I could see all around the truck and the few other trucks parked in the lot and out into the grass field and up to the building.

My buddy asked from the top bunk why I was up so early. We literally had an extra day and a half more than we needed to drop the load we were hauling so we had planned to do a 34-hour reset at Barrett's. I told him what I had felt all night and he quietly said "Me too".

When the sun was fully up, I walked all around the places where I had seen "it". I was using my cop brain again, and realized that the hard-packed gravel would hold no tracks, especially as cold as it was. I walked to the edge of the grass field and while there was a trail...it was a game trail where I am sure deer moved through, so there were no large footprints visible.

When the cafe opened for breakfast, my buddy and I went in to eat a meal we didn't cook in the truck microwave and tried to figure out what we had experienced and seen.

I am firmly convinced that I saw Sasquatch. I took the known and the unknown and the puzzle pieces put it into the one logical assumption that could be made.

At any rate, we decided to put a day of driving between us and Barrett's and get to a larger more populated truck stop or terminal to do our 34-hour reset.

Sean Francisco
Florence, Arizona

The Appalachians

Hey Steve, thought I would pass on kudos to you for the great work you are doing, as I have been one of the many that have been ridiculed and looked at as an idiot whenever I pass along my story.

I'm not the greatest writer so bear with me. My name is Wayne, I live in the Appalachian Mountains of North East Tennessee, along the North Carolina and Virginia border.

My encounter occurred in late summer of 1984, three of my friends, myself and 2 dogs a collie and Alaskan husky were camping in the woods as we normally did while school was out, so we thought we would get in one last hoorah before school started. We constructed a heavy lean-to from 6-inch green poplar logs and covered it with laurel and hemlock branches, it was something to be proud of, outside the structure we built a nice fire pit from large rocks, and collected a good bit of wood to burn, mostly dead fall.

A few days after completing our build we decided to camp, we ate, and began the usual talk and kidding that normal teenage boys go on about, you know GIRLS and the such. Around 1A.M. or so as 2 of us were inside our lean-to, myself and another friend were on the other side of the fire pit in front of the lean-to, the youngest of the group told us to be quiet , that he had heard something behind the lean-to, so we began teasing him, not more than 2 or 3 minutes passed the same friend and our other friend that was outside with me heard a low growling from the same direction, and said I don't like this I think we need to leave, when all the sudden our dogs began throwing their noses in the air, pacing back forth ,whining, when all the sudden a loud roar and scream along with an ungodly chatter erupted and absolutely shot us into a panic we broke loose into the woods with no light ,or way to find our way out, we were running for our lives, running through briers , bouncing off trees and falling on rocks we were a bloody dirty mess when we finally came to the nearest house and began beating on the door for someone to let us in.

But we soon realized that our friend and his dog were not with us, so we went a little way back toward the edge of the woods and began calling for him, then the lady that lived at the house came to the door and asked what was going on, we tried to explain it to her and, she told us to just get in the house, but we couldn't leave our friend, after what seemed like 10 minutes our friend finally came out of the woods ,and as he was walking out he was carrying his collie in his arms, he told us that whatever it was , was behind him. Our friend was in tears and white as a sheet, the husky was barking uncontrollably ,but would not go toward whatever it was, the lady that lived in the house called us again to come inside, so we did, she calmed us down, and had a bit of a chuckle at our expense, she made us a bed in her basement and told us we could stay there for the night.

All was well or so we thought, when we heard one of the lady's daughters scream and the dogs began pitching a fit looking toward the door to the basement. The lady came down the stairs along with her two daughters, a double barrel shotgun and a cordless phone calling her husband, and after the sheriff's department, her daughter began to tell us that she had heard a noise on the back porch. She looked out the back door and noticed a large hairy naked man running from the porch toward the driveway that connected to the basement.

We stayed together in the basement till her husband and the sheriff arrived, but were very disappointed to be told by them that a bear probably chased us out of the woods, but I know it wasn't a bear and there couldn't have been just one of these things with all the chatter and screaming going on.

Later on in the early 90s I bought my first PC and always had a fascination with the Bigfoot thing, so I began going online and doing some research, one day I was on the Oregon Bigfoot page and listened to the Ron Morehead recordings and bam, there was the same loud ungodly chatter screams and moan we heard 10 years before. It sent chills down my spine, I told my wife the story and it even scared her.

I have told my story to a few people mostly family, I'm kind of reserved in telling it to others after being scoffed at a few times screwed I was there they weren't.

Anyway, thought this would be a good one to share with everyone.

Thanks Steve.
Wayne Proffitt.

Rocks Hurdling

Hello Steve, first off thank you for what you do, I feel like I can finally get this off my chest after all these years. I live and grew up in central Wisconsin. About 30 years ago when I was about 12 years old, I spent a few weeks during the summer at my grandparent's cottage which was on a small lake in central Wisconsin. I spent most of my days exploring the wilderness which surrounds the lake. One afternoon I stopped to take a rest in the shade on the banks of a feeder creek that drained into the lake. As I was relaxing, I was startled by a loud splash in the water upstream from where I was sitting. I couldn't tell what made the noise right away but soon after a large rock came hurdling out of the thick brush about 25 yards to my right. Another big splash this time closer to me. At first, I figured it was one of my younger cousins messing around but quickly decided that there was no way in hell that one of them could possibly throw that big of a rock that far and high. Every hair stood up on my body and as bad as I wanted to run, I was frozen with fear.

After a few minutes I finally mustered up the nerve to leave. As I started to head back down the trail to the cottage, I had the overwhelming feeling that someone or something was following me. I heard a stick snap behind me and I quickly spun around. About 15 yards behind me a hair covered figure stood in the trail. It was only about 5 1/2 to 6 feet tall and had reddish brown hair but none on its face. It did not seem threatening for some reason but actually looked curious. We stared at each other for what seemed like forever but was probably only seconds. I raised my hands above my head to look larger. My grandfather told me that if I came across a bear to do this and yell. This sure as hell was no bear but it felt like the right thing to do. I yelled and waved my arms, hoping that it would be startled and leave but instead it copied my motions. I put my arms up, it put its arms up etc. this went on for a few minutes and it finally must have grown tired of this game because it suddenly turned and disappeared back down the trail. I took off as fast as I could running while trying to wrap my young mind around what the hell just happened.

As I approached the road that lead to the cottage, that damn thing was somehow now in front of me, it stood in the ditch blocking my way to the road. I froze in my tracks. It raised its arms above its head and waved them up and down, almost like it wanted to play the "game" again. I couldn't move, I was fascinated and scared shitless at the same time. But then something changed, the air felt heavy and I was overcome by an overwhelming sense of dread. The creature suddenly took off like something scared the hell out of it. Everything was suddenly silent. I heard a rustle in the brush to my left. I assumed it was the same one again but when I looked there stood the most massive, terrifying thing I had ever seen. It stood at least 8 feet tall and was probably 4 feet wide at the chest. It had the same face as the smaller one that I had seen but its eyes were different. Not curious like the other one, this one's eyes were absolutely menacing. Huge dark black eyes that seemed to pierce my soul. To this day I have never felt that type of evil presence and hope to never again. I thought for sure that it was going to rip me to shreds and leave me for dead. Instead it just screamed/roared at me, then as quickly as it appeared, it spun and vanished into the woods.

Needless to say, I ran like my ass was on fire all the way to the cottage never looking back. I told my grandfather what happened and strangely he didn't say anything, he just nodded and patted me on the shoulder. Had he seen it before too? We never spoke of it the rest of my visit and I have never told anyone but my wife this story until now out of fear of ridicule. Sorry for the long email but it feels good to get this off my chest finally. I always laugh inside when I see the "Finding Bigfoot" type of shows/websites because who in their right mind would want to look for these fucking things on purpose, what a joke! I hunt and fish regularly and to this day I always feel uneasy in the woods. Thanks again, feel free to share my story, keep spreading the truth.

Vancouver Island

Hello Steve my name is Ken Salmond and I live in Parksville B.C. I will try to keep this short but have several experiences I will pass on. I'm a Hunter by nature started as a kid in Victoria and at 73 yrs. old I have a fair bit of experience I mention that to clarify I know the Bush and I know Tracks.

1st. Exp. In 1976 I met a Man a few yrs. older than me his name was Norm.

One Day Norm invited me and my X to Dinner at which time he pulled out a Polaroid photo that astounded me, it was a picture taken on a Sunny Day from no more than 40 yrs. I still clearly remember it and did view it twice; it was a tall creature walking through some Aspen trees and it was clear as a Bell. My guess about 7 ft. tall not big and heavy like Patterson photo but lean and extremely strong looking, I could clearly see face from the side view and its whole Body except feet as grass was about a foot tall, photo was from the Interior as I recall. Aspen Trees.

I want to go on with details but will take a lot more writing so short version not an ape, thick lips wide flat nose moderate brow ridges sloped forehead and almost no neck, It would have to turn body to look back I also remember it looked happy and that's because the corner of its mouth curled up a bit. Hair was short like a Deer and similar in color, no fat long arms that looked extremely strong and dark patch under arm I think was sweat. I could see muscle definition and tendon in arm and legs. My thought was it looked like a young prime adult was confusing as remember thinking it's not Ape it's not Neanderthal it was confusing.

This Haunted me for yrs. finally in 2012 I contacted Dr. John Bendernagle and met with him at his House in Courtney. Told John about this and it was great to be able to talk to someone who didn't brush me off. I had not talked to Norm sense the late 70s as I had Moved up Island so I grabbed phone Book and dialed only guy in Victoria with his name and Norm answered. I Drove to Victoria and we met, he was now in his 80s and in a wheel chair, he still had picture but in one of many Boxes in his Basement, I Offered him $500 for picture and I would Pay for someone to search it out. I also set up a meeting with him and John but by then John was Sick but on his last trip to Victoria for Chemo he did stop to meet Norm. Unfortunately, John Passed a few Weeks later and Norm about 3 Weeks after John so I lost all contact.

John did give me several Photos and two Plaster Casts of tracks that I am thankful for but best part was finally meeting a Man that I could talk to as like you said in one of your Videos It never leaves your Head.

In 2014 I had another experience I also met John to talk about, in short, my Wife and I took a Trip up past Great Central Lake in late March and into Strathcona Park trying to reach Oshinow Lake. Got stopped by Snow next to Ash River. I walked up the hill looking for Deer or whatever Tracks I could find. There was nothing until I came across 8 huge 17-inch tracks in the Snow that stunned me. So, clear I could make out small details and Dermal ridges I could describe in detail as some interesting details but your probably asleep by now lol. If you want details let me know. Thanks for listening and thanks for the Work your doing as it's so frustrating not being able to talk about what I know is real.

Do not care if you use any of this and as for Polaroid Pics fading over the years not so much, I have Pics of Norm and two other friends Dragging a Moose we shot up at Aiken Lake North of Manson Creek back in 76 that is still pretty clear. I'm done, you have my e-mail and my cell is 250-954-7295 I have nothing to hide from. Cheers Ken

Germany

Hi Steve,

As a passionate angler and outdoors man I stumbled across your channel some time ago and I just can't put into words how glad I am that after all the years there finally is someone, who would rather listen than ridicule- only not to have to question ones' own outdated belief system.
I am agnostic (so please leave me alone with all that Nephilim BS) 52 years old now, served in the German Military during Cold war times, spent almost a decade of my life undercover for a foreign agency in a counter terror unit to fend off the scumbags in my Homeland after 9-11 and spent a year as a Risk Management advisory for the German Governmental Development Organizations in Afghanistan, where I witnessed stuff you wouldn't want to dream of. This lifestyle doesn't really go well with Family life as you might imagine, but nevertheless I am

married and we have three wonderful kids. Except for coffee, good Irish Scotch and loads of Cuban cigars I don't do any drugs. I am based in the Frankfurt, Germany area, where the really creepy stuff started a while ago.

Frankfurt Airport is a mayor hub over here so it's not unusual to see quite a lot of Lights and blinking stuff in the skies at night, but in September 2014 I was totally perplexed, when I stepped out to get some fresh air after I've had an argument with my beloved. I lit one up and noticed three huge flaming orbs hovering over the vast valley the City of Frankfurt is located in.

At first, I didn't pay much Attention as there was a storm coming up, so it could be some strange weather phenomena. I thought. I expected to see some flashing Lights at the sides of the "orbs" as the moved across the sky, identifying these "fireballs" as airplanes as they came nearer, towards the part of the northern part of the City where I was, but the more I was baffled when these orbs hovered over my neighbourhood without any flashing Lights at the sides, there was no Sound emanating from them. About 300 meters above. These things- instead they came together and shaped a triangular formation and then accelerated at Incredible Speed and vanished up into the sky with speed I hadn't thought would be possible.
I tried to Forget about this Event as good as somehow possible, because I couldn't find a sober explanation. The next few years I was assigned out of town and only recently made it back home to my family again. When I was back, I was really astonished to see on my favourite crime show that is broadcaster on our state sponsored official TV channel one of these strange missing 411 cases. Obviously fellow citizens are also vanishing in a split second in our country.

You can crosscheck this and for the rest of my report I am willing to take a Polygraph. Over here, we have been ordered to walk alone or in pairs unless it's Family members due to the plague. Our schools are closed, so I have to teach the kids at home a lot now and to forbid them to munch too many Chips and other unhealthy stuff. Two days ago, I needed just to get away from all the crap for a while, so at around 22:40 hrs I took a short walk outside and enjoyed being on my own at the end of the busy day. My usual walking exercise takes me through a park, which is not well lit at night, but you can adapt to darkness pretty quickly, as you know as a fellow outdoors guy.

Once I entered the park, which is right between my quarter and the nearby Autobahn I felt that there was some presence to my left, but I couldn't get my eyes on it, as there was a line of thick blackberry bushes along that side of my path. Usually at that time of day everybody has already walked the dog and very rarely there are People around, so I stopped Walking and listened carefully. Just that second, I heard something behind the bushes Walking and making a noise that came close to a mating call of a fox. So, I felt relieved again, and wanted to start walking.

Then all hell broke loose; Whatever that Thing was, it was scampering back and forth behind the bushes while yelling louder and louder nonstop. I usually Keep strong minded, calm and focused in stressful situations, but this was so fucking intense that I was somehow brought down on my knees and although I kept a clear mind, I started spring like a Little Boy.

I couldn't move at all and kept hearing the being roaring in my direction. I cannot Forget these screams Never will and I burst in tears writing this down.

They are truly Bone shaking and I am in Tears just thinking of that encounter. I tried to stand up as I wanted to get away but I found myself totally immobilized and everything went pitch black. I focused hard on my breathing and was able to lift my head slightly just to see a jogger approaching. Now it gets really weird as when that guy with his headlamp was approaching, he didn't seem to notice at all and just ran by only a meter away from me still on the Ground. I thought this is it and I was going to die there, but a few seconds later the Growls stopped and I was free to go.

I didn't tell anybody including wife and Kids. They would not understand. Especially my Kids won't see me in this condition as we used to watch your Sasquatch Videos together and made jokes about it. Feel free to tell my real Name at your discretion. I am sick and tired of all that bigotry and all the cover ups. I have no clue what These Things are and I just want to live a normal life again. Started drinking heavily since my Encounter but will get over it as I did a few times in my Lifetime. Wish you Godspeed. Stay safe and thanks for all that you do. Thomas (don't even try to pronounce my Family Name)

Called One In?

My wife and I live north of Tulsa, OK on what was then 240 acres of open field, creek and woods. On the other side of us is a very large tract of heavily covered woods. Our son was on the creek one weekend night hanging out with some friends and had a bonfire going. My wife and I decided we were going to sneak down and scare them. We slipped up to where they were in the creek bed and I broke a very large stick and they got silent. I had a predator call and I blew in this thing as loud as and long as I could. They were scrambling to get in his truck and get the heck out of there. My wife and I ran back to the house before they got there and they come busting in telling us their ordeal. They got some nerve up and wanted to go back down there and see what it was.

My wife and I were sneaking back down there to scare them again and was walking along a huge treeline that ran along some railroad tracks that splits our property. We didn't have a flashlight and it was very dark. As we got about half way there, we heard what was the most evil, low guttural growl that I have ever heard. It literally felt like it was within arms length and head high with me. It almost felt like I could feel the vibration from what ever it was. I told my wife, holy crap what is that. I had sense that this thing was pissed and didn't want us there. We went back home and still don't know what it was. Have you ever heard of anyone calling up one of these crypt-ids with a predator call?

Memory From Childhood

Steve,

I'm one of those not subscribed lurkers that has had multiple encounters with these things.

I was 7 years old living on a dead-end road next to a gravel pit. I was out in front of my house alone when something caught my attention. I started walking across the street, I got about to the middle of the road and looked to my left. Standing there motionless in the tree line sky lined with his back to the gravel pit was one of these things. It stood about 8' tall with shoulders about 4' wide all black with no noticeable neck. I was frozen staring at it for at least a minute. I was about 40' from it and it there's no doubt in my mind what I seem. I turned and ran to my house went inside and told my father there was a Bigfoot outside. He mustn't have believed me because I remember him days later running out of the brush trying to scare me. I remember thinking to myself "he didn't believe me". We lived about a mile from the Mohawk river in upstate NY and spent our childhood every day in the gravel pit and down by the river with never having another encounter.

Years later I would go hiking up in the Adirondack mountains with groups of my friends into Keene valley. We would go off trail and camp at a pretty isolated spot in an open area with a beaver dam and a nice trout stream running through if. We woke up the following day and had planned on hiking Dixx mountain. I didn't feel good so I decided to stay at camp instead of doing the half day hike. After everyone left, I started feeling better so decided to do some trout fishing. It's a smallish shallow stream. I was fishing the bends in the stream. I would take a few casts and walk a little way to the next bend and cast again. I remember I was standing there and decided to move again when I took one step and all hell broke loose to my left. This was a violent bluff charge. No vocals, just limbs breaking. I didn't put two and two together until years later. It was a scary situation and thought I was done for when I realized it wasn't coming, it was going. And it kept breaking branches until I couldn't hear it no more. nothing else happened that trip.

The other encounter was again hiking in the Adirondack mountains. I was with a group of 4 guys. It was a total calm day. We were hiking along when out of the blue we hear the unforgettable crack of a tree being pushed over right near up. We didn't see the tree fall or what pushed the tree over but it stopped us in our tracks. Again, I didn't put this together until years later when hearing other stories of these things pushing trees over to scare people out of there area.

My older brother was solo hunting at Indian lake in the Adirondack mountains at a hunting cabin. He got into the hunting camp before nightfall planning on getting up at day break to hunt. As soon as it got dark out, he heard something outside the cabin making a ruckus. He said the noises kept getting closed. Until this dam thing was right outside of the cabin screaming. He said it sounded like a big person screaming but what alarmed him was the duration of the scream and the fact that the windows were vibrating. He said he crouched down in the corner of the cabin with his gun loaded until day break. He decided to just leave and not go hunting. He also told me about a story our dad told him about being at the same cabin with his hunting buddies that were part of the hunting came. They decided to hike a near by mountain and plant an American flag on top of the mountain. The strange part of the story was the "bear" that was yelling at them when they got to the top of the mountain.

You might be wondering why I never put two and two together with my other encounters. As a young child seeing one of these things. It was such a scary encounter that I all but forgot about my encounter with this think. Until my older brother told me about his encounter. That's when I started to look into this subject online. And that's when I seen a picture of the thing I seen as a child and it brought the memory back to me. I have spoke to my father about going into the house telling him there's a Bigfoot outside. He confirmed everything that I remembered was correct and that he remembered me coming into the house telling him there's a Bigfoot outside. I didn't press him anymore about the incident because he's gotten pretty old and didn't want to make him feel bad about blowing me off. I was born in 73 and remember watching some old movies about Bigfoot with the guy from Star trek that showed the Paterson Gimlin film.

I have watched every video you have done about this subject and have the utmost respect about your reasons for doing what your doing. You can't imagine how it makes me feel knowing I'm not crazy. Use my story if you wish I'll understand if you don't. I'd rather you don't use my name as I'm sure you understand.

Never Seen My Dad That Scared

Hello Steve

I can't remember if I already shared this with you or not.

When I was a young child. 6 or 7 we lived in Oklahoma. It was a very rural area houses could be 1/4 of a mile at the closest to miles apart. Well our family would hang out in the living room at times to watch TV together. It was one of these nights 8 to 10pm in the evening after dark. We heard something rumbling through our trash can in the back yard. Our couch in the living room was up against the back window which you could look out to see the back yard. Me my father and mother were on this couch when we heard the noise. The trash can was maybe 30 feet from this window in the centre of the yard. My dad went to look out the window when whatever it was decided to scream. It was deep it was loud and it was long. I have never seen my father frightened before this or since. But whatever it was it scared all of us badly. My father went to the other room and got the rifle. It was only a 22 but it was all we had. After the scream none of us could work up the courage to look outside. Whatever it was it was big. I have never heard anything like it since.

I am now 55 years old a veteran and hunted plenty when I was younger before I got hurt. I've been following your channel for a couple of years now and this story has never left our family. I only told my younger brother and sister about it a couple of months ago and basically got laughed at. Unfortunately, Dad was sitting at the table at the time and confirmed the event.

Thank you everything you are doing. I feel like I've gotten to know you through your channel and am grateful to you and all those people who are sharing their experiences.

Thank you

Randall

Seven Feet Tall Just Looking At Me

Hopefully I found the right guy, Steve. My name is Ron, I was born, raised, educated all within 10 miles of my parent's house, which I now own.

Always looking for a reason to ride my dirt bike, I got a under the table gig afternoon/evening, working at an auto repair shop, approximately 2.5 miles from home (by road travel). After dinner, around 5:30pm, I hopped on my bike, and left for the garage, the first 1 mile is via a small, paved road and the remaining mile or so was a dirt road/trail a few hundred yards, then up a steep, torn up rocky hill. Once a broke over the crest, I went 100 -200 feet, here the trail was smooth, wide, with a fairly open view of a local creek below (Oriskany creek) and the small paved road I just came on. Just for reference, I was less than 1/4 mile from a long ago, defunct park, and about 1/2 a mile from the county dump. I stopped, shut down the bike, got off to look back at the view and have a cigarette.

Almost all the leaves had changed colour and fallen down. I'm guesstimating a 200 -250 foot, very steep drop to the creek below (Oriskany creek), about 50-60 feet below where I was standing is a dirt bike path going down the hill, at a fairly shallow angle. After about 1/2 a cigarette, I walked back over to the edge, to look around some more, I noticed a guy on the lower trail watching me. After what seems like 3 or 4 minutes (probably 25 - 30 seconds), I realized it wasn't a guy. It was at least 7 feet tall, very broad shoulders, and wasn't wearing clothes. It was a med/dark grey hair, with what looked like streaks of black. I hit the bike, booted the kicker and flew out of there. I've never been back to the area by myself, actually never even with others. I've had 2 other weird happenings within a 1/4-mile radius of this spot, both with the same guy, at night, with many months in between. Have a great life, stay safe and keep on telling everyone.

Ron Chamberlin.

Hells Canyon Oregon Screams

Hello Steve;

Thank you for taking interest in those of us who have had encounters with the Watchers in the woods or Big foot.

My story is from a deer hunting trip from the mid 1990's that took place in Hells canyon on the Oregon side, our family has been hunting this area since the early 1960's. We hunt at an area near Dug Bar, the end of a two-track bump and grind road that takes hours to travel from the end of pavement. There is designated wilderness that begins at Dug Bar an area of steep canyons and rim rock with forest back in the wilderness area. Back in the day the mule deer hunting was good, but with the introduction of wolves the hunting is now poor.

This hunt began like many before, consisting of two of my cousins and me, they pitched a tent and I slept in the back of my old ford pick up as it had a steel canopy with Plexiglas windows all around. My cousins' tent was about 25 yards away and we were a stone throw from the river.

The weather was mild with clear skies and a full moon. We turn in early just as it's getting dark. I could hear my cousins snoring loudly as I lay in my sleeping bag in the back of the truck. When the moon came over the canyon rim it was so bright that no other light would have been needed to walk around camp. I'm a light sleeper, at about 10 pm this loud screaming starts, close to camp, this was not a growl or the scream of a cougar I was amazed at the volume and pitch of the sound! the screaming continued for about 15 minuets. No animal or human could make this sound, what ever this was had amazing lung capacity. I was closed up in the back of the truck canopy with my rifle and a flashlight, I tried in vain to see what was making the scream but it was a bit forward and seemed to be to just outside of camp. I did not want to give away my location so I did not turn on the flashlight. After the screaming stopped, I kept watch for most of the night but saw nothing. In the morning I asked my cousins if they heard the screaming (I knew they had not as they could sleep through in coming artillery), I got a shrug and " nope ".

I'm soon to turn 70 and have had many experiences in my life that are " Taken with a grain of salt " by those who were not there. And this is one of them. I have had another encounter but have not seen the Watcher. Not so sure I want to.

You encouraged me to share my story, after listening to other accounts of screaming I knew there are others that might benefit from my story.
Best regards and keep extra ammo in your pocket. My name is Gene Greiner ok to use my name.

Less Than 30 Feet Drinking Water

About ten years ago, I was working at a small college in south Louisiana. I lived in the same area but not in town.   I lived about three quarters of a mile from the bayou Mallet watershed tract of woods about 100 miles long following the Bayou Mallet.

On another road out here lived a family who I was friends with and knew very well.   Their son had this experience and was very shy about it.   Now, this family is 100% trustworthy to the point of having the demeanour of Jack Webb on dragnet TV show, only the facts man. I know this event to be true.

During the hunting season, their 19-year-old son went duck hunting in a flooded field along Bayou Mallet. It was devoid of any cover except a large tree that had fallen over.   The young man got into the leaves and branches of the tree and made a blind.   After sitting about 30 minutes, he heard a noise behind him. He thought he was the only hunter out there but figured it might his father or cousin who he hunted with coming to meet him.   But as the sounds got closer, he caught sight of something black and reddish coloured move toward him. He froze in fear. It was a big foot.   The creature came to the water's edge squats down and began drinking some water.   This animal was less than thirty feet from him but the favourable wind and his concealment did not give away the boy's presence. He was afraid to move or breath as this huge animal was that close to him. After a minute or so, this creature stood up and walked along the edge of the water until he

Entered the woods about 150 yards away. Soon as the Animal was out of sight, he ran to his 4-wheeler and got back to his home ASAP. Upon reaching home, he told his dad of what had just transpired. Like most folks but to a higher degree his Father was skeptical. So, he urged his son to take him to where the encounter had happened. Boy he did not want to go back. But his father persisted.

When they got there the foot prints were undeniably big foot tracks. After the father confirmed the story as true. They rapidly went back to their home to gather their feelings.

I know this is a second hand story, but I believe it because of the father's and son's reaction while telling the story and Their inability to lie or fabricate such a tale because of their honesty.

I have hunted the swamps of south Louisiana for 53 years. I have had experiences myself. So, I believe these guys.

Thanks for bringing these stories out to the doubting public.

A Fellow Hunting Guides Experience

Hello Steve,

My name is B.W., first of all I appreciate and respect what you're doing for the many people who have seen these things. Thanks brother!

Let me tell you about my self. I grew up in the piney woods of East Texas and came from a family that has a long history of hunters, as in that's all we did, hunt and fish. My great great grandfather was one of the last hunters to harvest a Black bear in East Texas, back when they still had bears to hunt here. I served in the US Marines, was a deputy Sheriff afterwards for a short time and after 2yrs decided that wasn't for me!!

Then after a life spent in the woods, decided that the guiding life was for me and have been a full-time hunting guide for the last 33 yrs. Started in Montana guiding for everything from deer to Big Horns back when you could still buy a tag over the counter. And have had a long career back home in Texas.

The first time I had seen one of these guys, I was 5 years old. We hunted deer back then the old south way, with hounds and shotguns loaded with buckshot. It was a very cool and bright morning and the hunters were lined up a power line right of way that cut through the property. The property was located in the Sabine River bottom in Panola County Texas. Anyway, the Hunters were spaced about 200 yards apart down the right of way waiting on the dogs to run a

Steve Isdahl   The Day Sasquatch Became Real For Me   Copyright© 2020

buck their way. My father picked the end of the line down by a high-water slough that crossed the right of way. He put me into the bed of the pickup and told me to stay put and he walked about 50yards up the line to wait on the dogs to run a deer. We hear the dogs strike and he moves about 25 yards further down. And I noticed movement in the tree line down by the slough and at first thought it was a deer but it was to dark in colour and it ran out on 2 legs, it must have been a young one because it was only about 5 to 6 foot tall. In my juvenile mind my thought was why is a man running around in a full-length fur coat. Two things that I remember vividly is he was holding his leg while running like you see in the old western when the cowboy had been shot skipping and limping and the second thing, he was fast, to fast for a man to be running with a hurt leg. I yelled at my dad to see and when I turned around it was gone.

Later that morning I told what I saw and was chided and told I would be seeing pink elephants next.

From the time I was old enough to hunt by my self, I have been whistled at, pine cones thrown at me tree knocking, found saplings woven together or snapped, heard calls, so much that I thought it was part of the way the woods were!! It wasn't until I saw the second one, that made the world change!!!! I was sitting in a tree stand about a mile and a half from my first encounter, 17 years old and an old hand at being in the woods, or so I thought at the time. Getting to be magic time on an overcast day , woods were dead quiet nothing moving when all of a sudden in the cane thicket in front of me a sweet gum tree started to shake violently, the tree was about 8 inches across at the part I could see over the cane and was whipping like you would a small young sapling . Then it roared a deep guttural sound that vibrated in my body. Steve, I have been charged by wounded buffalo, had an elephant kick dirt on me, but have never been as afraid in my life as I was that day, I was in shock couldn't move frozen. He shook the tree again. I was so afraid I jumped out of the stand and shot into the air because all I could think about was, I don't want to piss it off more and I don't have enough gun!

I could hear it running though the thicket away from me so I jumped on my 3-wheeler and floored it. Haven't been back to that place since.

You talk of being aware of your surroundings,6th sense, you are right on the money! Have been in a lot of places, throughout the years it's went off, I don't stay in those places. My brother had an encounter when he was 13 that he won't talk about and won't go to the woods alone anymore. I have directed him to your site. Anyway thanks for letting me vent and thanks again for what you are doing , as of right now if you read this please don't say my name because I'm still guiding for a bey well known outfitter and known in SCI and Dallas safari club circles and still have a few more years left God willing !

Hunter From Arizona

Hi Steve, a few weeks ago you had a story from BP agent in Arizona. This is what I seen in App. 1992 I was camping in the Upchuck mys. I was having coffee when all I heard was this loud screaming sound. So, I was looking in direction of noise and what appeared was a tall dark-haired thing about 100 yards away standing behind a juniper tree. I made eye contact and chills ran down my spine. I could see it was big and covered in hair. At first, I was thinking an old mountain man with bear skin coat. It just looked at me then was gone. Now years later I am sure what I seen was one of these things. Even today when camping sometimes at night I hear what sounds like something hitting a tree with something.

I am 64 been outdoors all my life so positive it was not a bear. Enjoy what your doing and yes, we need the truth.

Thanks
Mike K

Eating Deer And Throwing Cinder Blocks

Steve,

First and foremost, thank you for giving "us" a voice. And my apologies for having to deal with some of my illiterate Patriots in the United States. Must be a bear reading through a lot of these emails. But I digress.

Summer 1990, late July to be exact. My brother and I decided to try our favourite small mouth creek at night for Flathead catfish. Something we have done many times on our home river some 40 miles south. Night started off usual, dusk...semi dark...total darkness. We always fished "bare bones" at night. Single, small hand held cheapo flashlights. My brother was half asleep, calming to feel poorly. No matter, in fishing he can do whatever. Across the creek, approx. 30 to 40 yards, something very fucking large came slamming through the thickest shit around like it was charging me as I was closest to the bank. My brother sat up a bit, I asked if he heard that and he agreed he did. Being me, I started chucking rocks in the area of the action. One after the other thinking it was one of the land owners cows that wandered off. It got quiet, like really fucking quiet. At that exact moment a large rock came and landed close enough to me to get me pretty wet. WTF. So, being me again I begin throwing bigger rocks in that direction. Yeah, I know, genius. That didn't last but two rocks when another large rock hit damn near at my feet as I was in the water at this point ready to go! Then a large, fast, powerful woof like nothing I have ever heard came at me. My brother was in the car at this point yelling at me "lets get the fuck out of here NOW!". It then began to fucking bark like a damned dog? But you could tell, it wasn't a damned dog at all. I was paralyzed at that point, not having a clue what this thing was. Better senses came over me after about 30 seconds or so, and I retreated like the flailing human I am.

Next day I was out there at 7 am to see WTF, yeah that's just me. The "rocks" this ass hole threw weren't rocks. They were fucking cinder blocks! 1 full, 1 was half of one. Cinder blocks! 40 yards! I went across the creek, this area I knew well as it was a hot spot for large bass for me. The thicket it came through was 7 feet tall and you couldn't see through it at all. Path was clear where Mr. or Mrs. Ass hole plowed through. Not totally clear, but doable and behind this thicket were two dead White Tails. One seemingly fresh, one well eaten. I know why he was pissed off now, or she I suppose. Never saw the fucker and I am thankful I didn't. I know full well what it was, nothing in Indiana can do shit like that. Worms, property owner, cows all accounted for an in pens for the night plus that's not his land.

Thanks for listening, never want to see one or be around one of these things again.

Regards,

J McDermott

PS.
Didn't catch a damned catfish either, something that really pissed me off!!!!!

The Roar Shook The Ground

Hello and nice to finally be able to tell you my story. I watch your YouTube vids all the time and also have a story to tell you. OK I'm currently bed bound and disabled from a horrible accident at work ..I am 44 years old and around 2005 I hit a 3000 pound bull with a semi in Florida and after I went to a few years of therapy I was able to go back to work and then around 4 years ago I slipped and fell at my job 3 times in 2 days and due to both accidents compounding it's got me bed bound and cant walk.. so that's my current situation, but back when I was around 21 or 22 years old I was living in north Florida, in Cottondale Florida to be exact and a friend of mine asked me if I wanted to go hunting on a piece of land that his dad owned and my friends dad owned a huge piece of land like over 2000 acres in compass lake in the hills Florida about 15 to 20 miles from my house.

So I remember I had a 306 rifle and my friend had a 308 rifle and we left to go hunting around 4pm this evening and I remember the drive in to the property was all unfamiliar to me., now I have hunted in a track close to this property before but I still didn't know the layout of this property and told my friend just before we parked that what if we got separated and that I've never been here before and I was also worried cause I left my truck at my house and we drove to the property where we was going to hunt in a 2 man tree blind/stand. My friend laughed at me and said nothing to worry about and he knew the land and he said I was worried about nothing. Well was he wrong. We got to where we were parking the truck and had to walk around a little over a solid hour from the truck to the hunting stand and so as where walking in, I noticed that there was literally no animal life around us at all.

No birds, no squirrels, no deer tracks or any sign that life ever lived there, it was just a quiet almost dead feeling walking into these woods. We walked a fire trail the most of the way back to the hunting stand. So, at idk around 5:30 pm we made it to the stand and so we climbed up and got settled in. Well I'm a great thinker and problem solver so I was sitting there thinking that it was 5:30 pm and so it gets dark at around 8pm or so this time of the year that we was hunting so in my head I did the math and told my friend in a soft voice so we didn't scare away any of the deer or hogs or anything, I told my friend that hey bud we might want to head out in about an hour or a lil over cause I certainly didn't want to walk on a track that I wasn't familiar with back to the truck in the dark. So again, my friend laughed at me and said no worries brother and that we had plenty of time before we had to leave. So an hour went by, then more time and so I finally said to my friend look I'm headed back with or without you but I'm leaving now, so my friend said OK and called me a wuss., so we climbed down and headed back to the truck with maybe 30 to 45 min left of day light left. So where about half way back or a lil closer and just like that we had no light at all.

It was dark and we didn't bring a flashlight with us and I remember walking behind my friend when I started smelling a dead and wet dog or animal smell, and it was awful it would gag a maggot it smelled so bad. And now around 20 min or so from the truck we was walking on a small trail or fire trail and we was getting closer to a little island of trees that sits right in the middle of the trail just in front of us around 50 yards away from us and as we got closer the smell got stronger and stronger but we just put it off as a dead buzzard or a dead skunk. So about 20 yards from the thick island of trees in front of us and all of a sudden there was a big bang in that island of trees in front of us and my friend and myself stopped dead in our tracks. I told my friend hey what was that? And he was so scared he couldn't even answer me at all, so I told my friend look something big is in that island of trees just in front of us and now how are we getting out of here and back to the truck?
And just as my friend was about to say something there was a noise that I'll never forget, It was a roar that was so load that the decibels shook the ground around us., so I grabbed my friend and said we have to go and go now so we started walking away from the island of trees forward the right hand side as to stay as far away as possible from the big foot in those thickets of trees and around 10 steps into it ,it started to roar again and hit the trees with a log or something so to be honest I'm 250 pounds of muscle and been a football athlete all my life and never been scared of anything, but this was different I know that the bf would rip me and my friend apart with no problems. So, I to be honest I dropped my gun and ran for my life back to the truck. As of my friend still had his gun and he was only 160 pounds wet and I still made it back to his truck about 2 min before he did and that's saying something because of our sizes that my friend should have beat me back first and remember I didn't know this property as well.

So when we jumped in the truck I looked at my friend and said I dropped my gun and to let's go go go now...so I remember we drove home in less than half the time it should of and when my friend dropped me off at my house he said to me wtf was that and I told him that he knew what it was and that I told him I'll never go anywhere near that property again. And my friend said well you dropped my dad's prize gun and that he had to go back and get if. I told him good luck and to not go at dark ever. So, I never told anyone what happened that night but the next day my friend showed up at my house and said that he found the gun but no signs of anything else. I hope you tell my story on your YouTube channel and please believe me and my story, I have nothing to gain by lying about telling you my story. It's been over 20 years now from the Bigfoot experience I had and now I'm 44 years old with serious health problems and felt I have to tell my story and myself and my friend are lucky to get out of there alive. Please tell my story and please believe me.

Steve Isdahl   The Day Sasquatch Became Real For Me   Copyright© 2020

Get The Hell Outta Here

Good day, I hope you are doing well. Feel free to use my story...or part of it, as it runs a little long...

Late Fall, early Winter of 1980 in the rural mountains of NC, near the Va./Tn border in an area called Roans Creek. I was 14. I had spent the majority of those years hunting and fishing. In my 14 years, I was never over a 2-minute walk from the woods. Living in a rural setting without siblings left me 2 options, 1) set on my ass or 2) get out in the woods! I loved the outdoors and spent every hour I could hunting or fishing. I had NO FEAR of the woods. I would walk 45 minutes in total darkness to my deer stand, hunt all day and return home after I could no longer see 10 feet in front of me... I never gave it a second thought. The woods were my private Heaven...little did I know, they would soon become my worst nightmare.

I came home from school with time to grab the Beagle, Hunting vest and my trusty .410 single shot. I ran across the road, down my Great Uncles driveway, turned left up to the old Sawmill landing. I released Katie. She started her "Z" pattern, nose to the ground with an occasional "oohhllpp" to assure me where she was. Katie was trained to circle the rabbit and push it back to the hunter, unlike many dogs that you have to follow. I climbed up on a pile of old slabs to secure a better view. Probably 4-5 foot high. She was cutting back and forth through Mature White Pines, between 30-40 foot high. They had been planted in nice straight rows after the depression ended...roughly 1933?? The reason I mention the straight rows, is so you can picture how the setting sun's light would light up the open areas. I could see Katie crossing back and forth...and occasional "oohhllpp"...so very relaxing. Then out of nowhere, Katie yelped as if she was being hurt. We've all heard dogs in pain and scared, a long continuous crying yelp. I focused my sight in her area, about 80 yards out. NOTHING...then her cries became further away....as she ran away...cries that went outta earshot...crying out the entire time, until I could no longer hear her.

My eyes never left the tall pines. I then saw something moving through the rows. The sun was at an angle to my right...I could only see its "shadow" as it came closer. Bear? Horse? Uncle Rex??? 70 yards...60...50. The landing of the old sawmill was about 30 yards long, circled with 4-5-foot-high slab piles. I last saw "IT" to my right at about 40 yards. I climbed off the slabs to my left, this allowed me to see up the rows, as the slabs blocked the sun to my right. I eased along the slabs, moving closer to where I had seen IT...I swung out wider, so I could see around the slabs at the end........then my world changed forever.

The next 20 seconds takes 10 minutes to explain. Time moved in slow motion, as I can recall every step I took and each eye blink. A horrid smell engulfed the area. Almost like a "musk"?? warm, yet piercing. I'm sure you know what I mean by "musk"...if that makes sense. Every hair on my neck stood up, my senses were in overdrive, I wanted to throw up, I knew I was being watched...and I knew IT was close. I turned to my right, and just on the other side of the slabs was Bigfoot. 15 yards away. I could see him from his waist up. His head was semi pointed...no hair on forehead, cheeks or nose. Wide nose, thin lips, square teeth, with deep dark eyes. His shoulders were freaking huge, the size of basketballs...chest was defined as well as any body

Steve Isdahl   The Day Sasquatch Became Real For Me   Copyright© 2020

builder...arms went past his knees and they were 27-29" thick...he had some "guns". Hair colour was dark, kind of grey/brown.

I froze, I told myself, "there's no such thing as Bigfoot"!! I looked down, rubbed my eyes, when I looked back up... he was still there. I rubbed my eyes again and dipped my head down and to an angle...STILL THERE...at this moment I turned and ran maybe 10 yards...again I said, "NO SUCH THING!!!" I stopped, turned around...He had stepped up on the slab pile.... My God! It was 10-foot-tall...shoulders 4-foot-wide, thighs 38-40" thick...I'd say it weighed 700-800 Lbs?? That's it...it is real, I threw my gun to my shoulder...then thought, I will only make this thing MAD...I lowered the .410 to my waist,,, keep in mind, I was looking this creature in his eyes...when I lowered my gun, time stood still, I could hear him breathing.. This may sound crazy, but I never felt threatened...the eyes were firm, but I didn't see "EVIL". I leaned hard to my right...so the setting Sun would be hidden behind a large Pine Tree behind him...He leaned his head to the other side and gave a light exhale... GAME OVER ! when he moved, I turned and ran through the thorn bushes, down the hill, jumped halfway over the creek, landing in the middle, I tripped coming out the other side, falling on my rear...just in time to see HIM following me down the bank. I could see my house, 100 yards to go...I began screaming.... MOM >>>MOM!! I jumped over the barbed wire fence, catching my boot...just on the tip, just enough to trip me up, just enough to turn my head and see HIM stopped at the creek.

My mother had heard my screams and was on the porch at the top of the stairs. I came flying up the steps. My jacket torn to shreds by the bushes...my face covered in scratches. Mom said, "you are white as a ghost, what happened"? About the time she asked...this creature began a blood curling scream as it paced back and forth along the creek, just in the shadows of the Pine trees. 10-15 minutes of pacing and screaming...it stayed there until well past dark. Mom kept asking, "what did you do"?? what did you make mad?? Needless to say, I didn't sleep that night.

Next day...I come home. My mother says, "get your gun and get up there and find Katie, she never came home"...and you need to "get back on the horse"...it was probably a wild Bore and if you don't go back in the woods today, you will let fear win and never go back. I grabbed my .410 and out the door I went. I didn't make it 4 steps down...BLOOD CURLING DEATH SCREAM!!!! Mom even said "STOP, Get back in here!" You could see the shadow of this creature strutting back and forth...about 20 feet back under the Pine trees...after about 5 minutes my Great Uncle called the house, mom answered, he asked what the hell was wrong with me and what was I yelling and screaming about?? She informed him of what was occurring and he left it at that. That creature paced back and forth until dark...he would only "YELL" when I came out.

This went on for the next 2 days, but only when I was there. Finally, Saturday came. I was looking forward to catching up on lost sleep.... NOPE! A little after sunrise, a knock on the door, in walked my Uncle, my grandfather along with his 2 brothers, one of which owned the old sawmill...and the same great Uncle that had called earlier in the week. "We need you to come with us...why in the HELL did you tare up the sawmill !!??" Uncle Rex is good to you...and you repay him by throwing shit everywhere. We went together to see the sawmill. There were slabs everywhere!! The entire landing area was covered. I got one more ass chewing...until I pointed out the 20" bare foot prints...and pointed out 300 Lb chunks of stumps thrown around and the 22 foot Steel I Beam guide for the mill tossed on it's side...they looked at each other, walked around with hands on hips...then across their chests...then they came back. " Dick, we think it's best if you stay outta the woods for a while." No argument from me!

Over the next couple of weeks My Great Uncles would drive to the old sawmill bout 30 minutes before dark and I noticed their truck lights would come on from time to time throughout the night. I never heard the "scream" again, well, not from the sawmill and not for 38 years. I'll never know why it screamed...why it paced or why it came back that week. If it had wanted to "get" me...it had me at the sawmill...and it never ran after me...it just followed me. END OF STORY---
What's your thoughts?? Your personal story stands the hair up on my neck...but I think there are some of us who "believe"...we are attached to Nature...we have our 6th sense working, where most people have had it bred out of them. I know when I'm being watched. I know what I smell. I have no doubt that these Beings know "who" can see them...or sense them. I have had numerous "tree knocks"...too many to remember. I've had 6-7 rocks thrown near me (different times) ...and even had a rock tossed at me in my tree stand! I think rock throwing is just a warning...not to hit us...and even sometimes, just playing. I feel these Beings around me. I feel no threat from 99%...but every now and then, I get the feeling of "GET THE HELL OUTTA HERE"... as if some of these creatures' mite not be as "forgiving" if we walk up on them.

I could go on for hours. My wife and I live in Rural NC Mtns about a mile from Tn. on a hundred acres, mostly wooded. We respect all wildlife. We only kill what we are going to eat and try to see that the animals have food during the winter...I think "THEY" know our hearts...they know we're never going to shoot at them, or bring in News Crews to try and film them...etc. I'm sure you have 100's of stories also...not all encounters last 3 minutes...most are just simple Tree Knocks...Rocks...Smells and the KNOWING they are watching...that uneasy feeling. I don't expect you to read this novel...maybe you'll like the "MAIN" story. I have some PICS also, just got to find where I put em. I send ya another email with the pics. Sorry so long winded, I ease up on next report.

PS. can't believe you didn't leave that Meth Head under some stump for Grizzly bait...what a scumbag!

It Was Paralleling Us In The Cypress Trees

OK I'll make this quick as I can I have two stories to tell.
First one happened about three years after getting out of the Navy. About 1973. I was hunting in the Atchafalaya Basin, south central Louisiana. My father, myself and my friend and hunting mentor, Frank. Frank was the best hunter and woodsman I have ever, even till today, known. He was part Native American and had a sixth sense about nature unlike anyone else I have known. We were hunting about 1.5 miles from any road. The Basin was flooded and we were hunting in water from six inches to four feet deep.

Frank killed a nice little four-point buck. My daddy and I went meet him just about 300 yards away. It was decided that daddy would take the guns and go on out the woods to the truck and wait for Frank and Me to "float" the buck out which is easier than dragging or poling a deer out.

but to do so we would have to travel through the woods on a different route than daddy and would take us a little longer.

As we were floating the deer out, I realized that some "thing" was paralleling is on the left of us about 30 yards away in the thick Cypress trees.   We were alone except for daddy who was by now at least five or six hundred yards ahead of us. We had a pole cut about six feet long with a rope tied in the middle and each of us having the pole across our waist. We were walking side by side.   I stopped when I heard the foot steps and looked behind us off to the left saw nothing. When I turned around Frank was looking at me with an amused look. I asked him do you hear that he smiled said yes and started walking again, the walking off to the left started again.   I stopped again.   But when I turned around, I caught a glimpse of black go behind a tree. Problem was the black was up in the tree not at the water level. I saw water rippling in the swamp but the black movement was too high to be in the water I thought. Frank told me let's go don't worry with him.   This confused me.   Frank knew "him?"   This time instead of walking facing the direction we were walking I turned and walked looking back at which time I saw a tall black figure passing between the trees.   At this time, I started really putting an effort into pulling the buck out. Frank just chuckled and told me that I did not have to worry, "let's just get to the truck."   The splashing sound of walking followed on the side of us another 15 to 20 minutes until we arrived at the truck.

We loaded the deer and I turned to tell my dad what had happened Frank put his hand on my shoulder looked me in the eyes and just barely shook his head no.

I did not speak of it that day or any day for years then telling the story only once to some younger hunters who just laughed and gave me the you full of shit look. I have not spoken of it again until this email. You are right about one thing for sure. Once you have an experience such as this, the woods are never the same.

Years later maybe 20 or so, I had stayed on my deer stand, until dark thirty, in the same general area. That night I heard three distinctive loud knocks. I said to myself at that time damn I wish I had not heard that, but I had.   I left carefully and alertly and went back to my little camp, about two miles away. I had a bourbon and said this is for you Frank as it reminded me of Frank and our time together. But I was not as afraid as the first time but very aware.

Hunting Camp

Hi Steve, I live in SW Washington and do most of my hunting in the high cascades. Currently 63 years old and I have been fishing and hunting my whole life.   Mostly archery so tracking and reading sign is what I do.

I first found footprints back in '74 but wasn't until the late 90's in my hunting camp that things started to happen. I have been camping in the same spot since 1990 and to this day I still spend the archery season there. The first encounter up there the thing came in and peed on the front and back door of my army tent at 3 in the morning. Since then every encounter aside from seeing the damn thing, has happened.

Tree knocks so loud they wake you up, pushing trees over, hoots, rocks placed on my kitchenette, rocks stacked behind camp, trees jammed into the ground upside down, and occasionally the hairs on the back of the neck area alert me, something isn't right. One night we packed an elk out and got back to camp a little after 3 in the morning. 20 minutes later we heard the craziest language right outside the tent which ended with a growl. So far, I have found tracks up there 3 times, one of which was about 20".

From what I have witnessed there is NO doubt of its existence. I think I will write a book, 'I Hate Sasquatch'.

Thanks for listening,

(aka-Colby) you can use Colby if you want to tell this.

PS So far 3 in camp have seen it, I don't care to, keep up the good work!

Eyes The Size Of Soda Cans

Hey Steve,
I'm glad I discovered your videos on you tube as I am an avid outdoors man for over 40 years. I enjoying listening to your hunting stories and the way you present them in a down-to-earth no bullshit kind of way. I especially enjoy listening to all of the Sasquatch stories and it's good to know there are thousands of people willing to share their own encounters. I have my own encounter to share with you today but first I'll give you a brief description of my background which may help lend credibility to my story.

I was born and raised in Iowa which is in the heart of the Midwest and is well known for big whitetails. After high school I went on to college and graduated with a doctorate degree in a health care field. I'm probably more educated then most people but I've always considered common sense and woodsman ship skills more important then book smarts. I still live in Iowa in a city of several hundred thousand people. Once you get outside of town the area is predominantly agricultural with the exception of timbered areas that border the creeks and river systems, not exactly ideal Sasquatch habitat!

As mentioned earlier I've been an avid outdoors man my whole life having harvested well over 30 Pope and Young whitetails by bow. My biggest obsession is trapping however, and I've run long trap lines all over Iowa for mink and raccoon. I've also done taxidermy as a hobby so you could say when it comes to wild animals in my home state there isn't anything, I haven't seen up close, or so I thought.

So here is where my Sasquatch story begins. It was November 10 or 11th of 2017 and I had been bow hunting on a property 2hrs from home. After an unsuccessful hunt I drove the long route back which usually put me home around 10pm. As I got off the interstate and started heading through town my route takes me adjacent to a major river with scattered wood lots and housing developments. I was approaching a wooded area to my right and the river was about 300 yards to my left. Keep in mind Steve this is smack dab in the middle of town. I always keep an eye out for deer especially during the rut as I've had many close calls with bucks running in front of my vehicle. As I was approaching a curve in the road my bright lights illuminated a set of large amber coloured eyes off in the distance. As I closed the distance to maybe 50 yards I was in shock because the eyes appeared at least 8ft off the ground and were absolutely huge. These eyes appeared to be the diameter of a soda can and about 5" apart. By this time, I had slowed to maybe 10mph with my high beams pointing directly towards whatever it was that was standing just inside the woods along the edge of the road. What I saw next shocked me. I was able to make out a very large creature covered in brownish-black hair standing on two legs looking directly at my vehicle. It was huge! It all happened so quickly that I didn't even think to stop the vehicle for a better look. As I drove past the creature, I knew without a doubt what I had just seen. A Sasquatch!!

Since then Steve I've had a couple other experiences but I'll leave those stories for another day. I personally find these creatures fascinating and would love to have another sighting despite so many people having negative experiences with them. I find it even more amazing that these creatures are willing to travel in very close proximity to people and yet remain undetected the vast majority of the time. Anyhow, keep up with the good work Steve and feel free to use my story and name.

Best Regards,

Steve Olson

3 Steps To Cross A 32 Foot Roadway

Hello, Steve how you doing. Watched a few of your videos. Welcome to the club, just kidding. So, you have seen a Sasquatch, so have I and it been out in the great north. I seen and felt the presents of one in 1976/77 was about 14 years old. It has changed me quite some bit. When I look at it, it woke me up. Lived a bit out in the woods before seeing it on Vancouver Island. Me and my brother used to take a short cut on a path along the tree line. It was weird that we would be walking then we came to this point that I called the invisible line in the forest. Then all of a sudden, the hair on the back of the neck would stand on end and fear took us over. My brother was a faster runner then I and he would always say last one through is going to get caught by the town drunkard, the troll, every time we would go through, he would call it something different. It was winter then so it got dark early, we got out of school at five so by the time we got to that area it was dark so we would always take the long way home. It wasn't till spring break that me and my brother took my go cart up to the three hills, where houses were being built. We were having a great time, it was starting to get dark when my brother asked if I wanted to go down the hills before it got dark, I said yea. We were close to the top of the second hill and we both looked up and half way up the third hill this gigantic creature took 3 steps to cross the 32'

Steve Isdahl   The Day Sasquatch Became Real For Me

roadway.

The hair went up just like in the pathway and terror sank in. Don't ever remember that go cart going so fast as my brother was pushing it. Two or three years passed before I seen the Patterson footage and realized what it was. A year or so after seeing that footage I started asking natives and hunters about the subject. Some of the natives told me stories about their grand fathers seeing one, but, some of them believed in them. They were told not talk about them as they would be told they were crazy.

The majority of the hunters would laugh at me and they would go on about being in the woods most of their lives and never seen any thing as crazy as that. They would also accuse me of drinking or doing drugs. Since I have moved down island to Nanaimo I am still talking and asking mainly local natives and have collected many sittings. I wouldn't call my self a researcher; but I have found some structures and a few other interesting happenings regarding areas I have left apples and walnuts etc. So just to let you know they are living well on Vancouver Island. I also believe they are very intelligent and the ones I have had happenings with are not evil like those that want to shot one. I also believe they aren't all evil and have heard many interesting happenings regarding these grand beings. I know you are a busy man, a reply that you received my email would be nice even if it takes a while to receive. A believer and a knower. Dave

9 To 10 Feet Tall And Broad

Subject: Bigfoot

I subscribe to your YouTube channel and I am glad there is someone like you being the voice to this topic. At your discretion you can use my name. My name is Brian Anderson. I am 55 come the 14 of March. I am ex militarily. I served with various units in the United States Army. I was infantry, 11B. And an outdoors man and love to hunt.

I have heard yells, seen sign before. Back in 1985 while hunting mule deer in the Rockland mountains in Idaho. I have hunted this area a lot and new the area.

I had set up under a group of pine trees that provided excellent cover and coverage of a small meadow about the size football field. I was set up and have never failed to get my buck in this area. As the sun lit up the meadow, I noticed that the normal sounds were not present and it smelled god awful and that's when I heard movement at the farthest left corner. I didn't need to scope to see this thing, my god it had to be 9 to 10 feet tall, black hair, and very broad. It covered the distance fairly quickly and when it stepped out of view I quickly turned and went back to my truck and left.

I haven't hunted that area since. Instead when I get the chance to go home and hunt, I hunt the Minadoka desert. I won't hunt the mountain without someone with me.
I thought I would let you know or at least share my 1st experience with you. I know your not

going to laugh about it.

Thank you for what you do! Keep it going.

Sincerely,
B Anderson

Terrifying In New York

First of all, Thank You for taking the time to share the encounters of real witnesses to this phenomena. I live in upstate New York I am 62 yrs. old I've been hunting and fishing since I was a kid with my dad. I had my encounter when I was 14 years old, I went with my parents to my grandparents house on a mid summer Sunday afternoon , my dad and I would always take the time to walk back to a reservoir behind their house about a 20min walk thru the woods to go fishing.

The reservoir is a freshwater supply for the local area and is patrolled by local encon officers. That day my father decided he wasn't going to go back with me, I have gone a few times by myself before and he told me like usual to stay on the trail and if I wasn't back in an hour or so he was going to come find me.

I walked back to the reservoir started fishing and immediately felt weird like I was being watched
in fact after about 20 min all I wanted to do was leave,   so I did and headed back on the trail only to hear leaves crunching and snapping of twigs above me on the hillside, I'd stop, the noise stopped I'd go I would hear it again, I thought I was going to meet up with the encon officer following me out of the woods to arrest me or write me a ticket but I was wrong... I then heard a loud crunch above me and I stopped and thought OK I'm going to stand here and wait for him to come down to me, maybe he will just warn me and not get my dad involved but then a tree above me started shaking violently, back and forth, I bent down to see the base of the tree , I could clearly see the base of that tree but there was nothing there shaking it.

Then there was a loud thump in front of me on the trail I could feel it in my feet but saw nothing, then a super loud yell in my face that I felt rumble my chest and vibrate my whole body it was at that point I took off running as fast as I could out of there, I didn't look back until I got to my dads car. I stood there catching my breath waiting for something to come out of those woods but nothing did, I didn't see anything there confronting me that day on the trail and I never told anyone about this especially my dad for fear of him doubting me, I still don't know what that was, but maybe with more people coming forward with encounters we will be able to get the truth out.

Thanks again Mike from NY

Battle Creek Michigan

I have told my encounter to numerous people but I get laughed at called crazy and more. Maybe most people didn't believe me because they felt that I was a little girl when I seen Bigfoot. I was 13 years old and that was in 1978 So, this has been quite some time ago. But I will never forget what I saw. My sighting was in Battle Creek Michigan in Calhoun County. My uncle had a small farm and I lived next door. My uncle had horses and I was allowed to ride them. So, whenever I could I would saddle up my horse mostly riding in the paddock which my uncle had about 7 acres of land. At the back of the paddock was pine trees and off to one side of those trees was a swamp. You have to bear with me I feel like I have to tell the whole story and it's a little long. So, I'm riding my pony named Rocky near the Pines going over this little jump I had set up. This Pony had a habit of shying away from everything. If there was paper on the ground or anything shiny, he would freak out.

So, I'm taking him over this jump when he stopped dead in his tracks and was acting scared. I thought at first there was something on the ground that spooked him. But this time it wasn't the same my pony was literally shaking from head to toe every muscle in his body was shaking. His ears were perked up and he was snorting over and over again. So, I got down off him and checked him out. To see if he was hurt. He wasn't hurt. So, I followed where his head and ears were pointed and was looking along the ground for paper or a pop can or anything shiny. I'm walking toward the Pines slowly looking at the ground. And I walk right up to hairy hands and feet. At first, I didn't even know what I was looking at. All that kept running through my mind was there was a hairy man squatting in front of me.

This hairy man had his head down and wouldn't look at me. So, I decided to reach out and try and touch his arm. Thinking for some reason he needed help. And just at that moment he decides to stand up. I know that I must have had a look of horror on my face. I wanted to scream but there was nothing, no sound I am standing there shaking like my pony. I'm looking at this hairy man in amazement or horror or both. I'm now standing face-to-face with this Bigfoot. standing so close that I still can't believe it. I can still describe what he looks like even though it's been many years. When he was squatting in front of me. His hands were over his knees almost touching the ground. His hands weren't as hairy as his upper arms. His feet were the same way. I could see the skin under the hair on his hands and feet. The skin was grey not pink or black. When he stood up. I could see that he had short blackish brown hair on his legs and chest and he was about six and a half to seven feet tall.

I could see his face clearly, he looked like a man but also look like an ape. His nose was flat and wide and his teeth were large and square like if you put Chiclets in your mouth like teeth. He was looking straight down on me. His eyes were brown but you couldn't really see the whites of his eyes he had chimp eyes. And he had a pointed head. He had facial hair a beard with no moustache no hair around the eyes or forehead he had curly shoulder length hair. We were so close to one another that we could have reached out and took each other's hands. If he wanted to hurt me, he could have done it easily. He could have ripped my head off my shoulders. After looking at each other for what seemed like forever. He breaks his gaze looks up at the horse. Spins around on one foot, starts walking. looks back over his shoulder at me.

Steve Isdahl   The Day Sasquatch Became Real For Me   Copyright© 2020

Looking at his back I see that the hair on his back was matted and was red. He kept walking stepped right over the fence and walk straight into the swamp. And that's when I ran, I tried to get the pony to follow me but he was still scared and wouldn't move I tried telling my dad and my uncle my sister and brother you name it. but they laughed and laughed. they told me I'd seen a man in a fur coat but this was in the middle of July. So, I hope that you believe me because every word is the truth. And like I said until the day I die. I will never forget this experience even though it scared the hell out of me. I hope someday I will see another Bigfoot.

Thank you.

A Copy Of A Letter Between Friends

Jim,

Thanks for the find.

For years our Boy Scout Troop would go to Pagosa Springs area Colorado and run its own summer camp. I usually ran or helped to run the rifle range. Behind the camp was a mountain that showed me that it had a very strong high energy field. So, one day I told my two older sons that I was going up that mountain and track down the epicentre of that high energy field (HEF).

As I approached the epicentre, I knew something was watching me. I never saw or heard anything. I did have a 1911 pistol at my side. I am very skilled at arms. But now I know that would have been pretty much useless in defending my person from one of these critters. I backed down before getting to the epicentre due to loud warning lights of caution going off in my spirit.

My first wife had a high percentage of Comanche Indian blood. Over the years her sensitivity of these type of things transferred to me. So, I can sense things to this day that most have no ideal are there. Our children do have Comanche blood running through their veins and they are even more sensitive.

A few days later another adult and I went to the HEF epicentre near the top of the mountain behind the Scout camp. The other adult also sensed we were being watched. You don't ever know for sure what is watching you when you are being watched. But I knew. I don't think it was a bear or cougar. Most likely one of the much more deadly critters. I was relieved as we came down off that mountain, especially as we got closer to the Boy Scout camp. We were watched and followed until we were almost to the Scout camp.

Several years later, the road leading to where we set up the Boy Scout Camp each summer got washed out. The authorities never opened that road again. I think protecting the secret of what was up there came into play in their decision to not open the road. This affected several ranches in that area as well as a public camping area. Still it was not reopened.

The High energy fields are associated with gold. But they also attract these really bad critters. This is why many a prospector went missing. The Indians were always blamed. And in some cases, this was the case. But the main cause was because they were snatched by one of these critters.

They are very quick and very strong. They use the HEFs to help flow a lot of energy into their bodies. This gives them incredible longevity and strength. It also reduces the amount they have to eat to maintain health. They can initiate rain fall from these HEF and often will do so before they go hunting to dampen their smell from scaring off their prey.

When they get out of their territory, the authorities will try to give them more space. If it interferes too much with what humans have established, they will send in special force troops to thin them out and push them back to their old boundary areas.

Every year dozens are snatched by these and other unknown critters. Humans send out search parties to no avail. What they need to do is to immediately track down the high energy fields in the area when someone is snatched. This would work a lot better than the typical search parties which have proven to be pretty useless.
I have some evidences of their existence including testimony of a friend and two sons. I am 100% convinced that they exist. And I have high regard for their speed and strength. They are not to be trifled with.

You are welcome to forward this email to your subscriber or anywhere else you think there may be interest.

A Sasquatch Swimming To Get A Deer?

Steve.
Love the YouTube channel. Had a big scare a few months ago that got me into your channel. I don't really want to talk about that particular story just yet. I was about to but in waiting for you to come out with more videos, I discovered the missing 411 deal and instantly put enough together that I would like to talk to David so the evidence can be properly put together before being discussed. Don't worry I won't leaving you without an interesting story to share.
I'm 27 now but when I was in 1st or 2nd grade (Idk I was home school ed) my 2 older brothers and I had taken the hunter safety course in mason county so we could carry our own rifle while hunting with dad. It was there I learned I was left eye dominate but right-handed. Makes shooting awkward. The instructor saw this quick and told me to shoot left-handed. Reluctantly I did hit the centre every time. Still disappointed in how I had to now shoot, the instructor thought me how to blink in a way to retrain my eyes so both were good shooting eyes. Big thanks to that guy however my parents then put me in public schools where they thought I had Tourette syndrome because I would train my eyes in class. Anyway, towards the end they played several videos about gun safety and survival and shit. But as a little kid I was wondering about one video in particular as it was of a Sasquatch swimming after and dragging out a deer. I was upset and wanted to know why he was killing the baby deer and he smiled and looked down and said"

its not a baby deer, Sasquatch is really big".

Hadn't quite understood until seeing one in person and I don't think people's stories are quite grasping the concept of how freaking big they are. Anyway, they overall decided I had passed the coarse but would be too young to have my orange card. Heart broken that I hadn't achieved my goal and would have to go through the course again without my brothers with me, at least I would get to see that Bigfoot video. Although the following year they decided not to play that video and when I asked about it, it caused a shuttle panic. I remember he put his has on my shoulder to turn me away from the crowd when I answered his questions on how I new about that. I could tell he didn't know what to do but the class was over and my dad waiting so I left. Just thinking it would be neat if someone else that took that class validated that story.

I don't know how you do this shit on a cell phone Steve. I'm trying to keep it short but still give you my story and yet I feel like this is super long. Maybe reading/telling the stories and not typing them is how you maintain the channel ha-ha. I bet you'd get a lot more stories if people could phone them in. Any keep it up, its super important people like you tell the truth. I can send you charts on how they test calmness in the lives of society through people's heartbeats based on structured data. Meaning it proofs the people react better to knowing the truth over bullshit. People can sense shit on a level that's not yet been explained. And Bigfoot being the missing link has a tremendous impact on religion. Its not that the government is hiding us from the truth, they are protecting us from it because as a society, we freak out to big news. Remember Y2K. That's when these charts start by the way. Thanks Steve I hope this gets out and don't use my name please.

Retired Air Force Fire Fighter

Steve,
Been watching your videos for about 3 months now, and have gotten my wife interested in them too. Unlike some viewers, so far, I have enjoyed all I have watched. (Hunting and Bigfoot) My wife loves your backgrounds.

I thought I would write and tell you about our experiences at Salt Fork State Park in Ohio. They have not been jaw dropping compared to others you've read, in my opinion, but it may help others. That is all we can ask for in life, that we have done something in our lives that has benefited others. As a retired firefighter/ paramedic and former U.S. Air force firefighter I hope I have made a difference.

Anyway, here I go. This may be too long for you to use, but feel free to break it up into smaller segments.

I have believed these Beings are out there ever since I saw the Patterson Gimlin film before it was known as the Patterson Gimlin Film. My parents took me to see a movie around 1968-1970 and the P/G film was shown before the movie. I was 10-12, and we lived in the country. My brothers and sisters ran the woods and creeks all the time. We never heard or saw anything unusual. Over the years I forgot about Bigfoot, after all they were in the Pacific Northwest. Probably 10 or so years ago I got interested in the subject again from The Finding Bigfoot Show. From the first show or two I was thinking these idiots could not find their ass if somebody showed it too them. In about 2011 we went to Salt Fork Lake to check it out and do a little hiking. It was early March still very cool mornings and afternoons. As soon as we entered the woods from the Primitive Camping Area (A.K.A. Bigfoot Ridge) We heard a howl far in the distance that sounded like a combination dog howl and owl hoot.

About 45 minutes later we came to one of the horse trails they have and it was next to a ravine that was at least 60 degree downhill and about 50 feet to the bottom. We stopped and just looked around enjoying the view. I just happened to look down and right there between my feet was a bare human looking foot print. But when I put my size 11 hiking booted foot in the print it was at least 3 inches longer and 2 inches wider and 3/4 to 1 inch deep. This part of the trail was clear, no rocks or leaves and the print looked fairly fresh, like that morning. The ground was not so soft that I would leave a print that deep, and I do not think anybody in their right mind would be walking barefoot in the woods this time of year or any time, they would be a bloody mess. This print appeared to have come from the same direction we did except it crossed the trail and went down the ravine.

We were not looking for Bigfoot just out enjoying ourselves. We continued on working our way down to the lakes edge. After a small lunch and a rest, we moved north along the waters edge. The water level was still down from the winter draw down so we were walking on the dry lake bed along the woods. We found a cemetery that we did not know was there so we stopped to check it out. There were very old and one or two new grave sites. We noticed it got very quiet, no birds songs, nothing but silence. We stayed there for 30 minutes and took the driveway out to the paved road. If you go straight out the drive and down the road you go to the Water Treatment Plant for the park, and if you go left it takes you over 1/4 mile uphill to the parking lot of the Primitive Camping Area. My wife was getting tired so she sat down on a rock and I went to get our vehicle.

I started walking and after a couple of minutes I heard something walking through the leaves up on the 6-8-foot bank off to my left. I could not see anything but, if I stopped it stopped, I don't know why I didn't climb the bank to look but I did not even think of it. When I got back to my wife, she was walking up the hill toward me. She told me that woods were strangely quiet and she was hearing twigs snapping and what sounded like something walking through the leaves towards her. We left without any event.

Move ahead to 2013 after I retired and we bought a 22-foot pontoon boat with 1/2 camper enclosure that we can zip on and camp on it. At Salt Fork you are allowed to boat camp. We started going there fishing and motoring around the lake and around 4 or 5 in the afternoon we drop anchor, put the enclosure up and fix supper. This first time camping on the boat we stopped at a narrow spot on the opposite shore from the Stone House. We were only about 15 feet from shore this time with a small ridge beside us. I started setting up the grill when a large rock hit the water close to the boat. I did not see it hit nor did I see what threw it. But I have thrown enough rocks in to water to know what it sounds like. I looked up and around the ridge and said "Hello" but I never saw anything or heard another sound the rest of the night.

The next time we went we anchored about 200 yards south of the first spot we'd camped on the lake. This spot was where a horse trail came down to the lake. Before dropping anchor, we beached the boat and did just a little hiking. This time I was looking for footprints. I found some just a short distance from the boat. Bare human prints again 3-4 inches longer and wider than my boot and they turned off the trail and went uphill thru the brush. I could see where the toes dug into the soft earth as they moved up. My wife was right there and saw them also. That night we had an uneventful evening watching the stars and planes flying over. About 2 AM I woke up to the "who cooks for you" from Bard owls. I woke my wife so she could hear them and started noticing that we were hearing them from the surrounding hills. They were all around us. Is this normal? I unzipped the back door stuck my head out, and total silence as soon as I did that. We have never heard a Bard owl there since. I think it was this same time camping later in the night that I felt like I woke up to something on two legs running through the water along the shore. The thing is I am hearing this but I could not move. I wanted to get up and look out but couldn't. I was not afraid I just could not move. Was I dreaming? I am not sure.

I am not sure what year this next time was, but we had our 5-year-old granddaughter with us. She fished all day never complained, and never caught a fish. We anchored for the night at the same place from my last story, put the sides up and our granddaughter wanted to fish some more. My wife went into the camper section and about that time our little one hooked my shirt at my shoulder. I can't get the hook out one handed so I am calling for my wife to help and she won't answer. I call 2 or 3 more times and finally she comes out and gets the hook out. Later she whispers to me that she saw a Bigfoot watching us from the bank behind some brush. She said it was about 3-foot-wide at the shoulders and she saw from the upper chest up. Had no hair on its face, not human but human looking face with medium length shiny dark brown hair on its head and shoulders. She said it sort swayed side to side while it watched. She was afraid to take her eyes off it or come out to help me because she did not want to scare it off. We were about 40 feet from shore and it was probably 8 feet back from the edge. Where it was, I think it may have been 6 feet tall. When my wife told the local BFRO about it she was Poo Pooed and Poo Pooed again by Cliff Barack man at a Bigfoot Conference we attended later. Never again will I attend one here.

Another time there we camped back close to the first camp site but a few yards farther south. At this spot the rise up to the same ridge is gentle and 40 yards to the top with very little brush from the lake to the top of the ridge. From the water to the top of the bank is about 4-5 feet then the gentle slope to the ridge. That night we were watching stars and planes like we always do. We spotted a light in the sky brighter than any stars right over top of us moving north to south. We watched for 5 minutes maybe and it just went out like someone turned off a switch. We are sitting there like what the hell? There were no other lights on it that would make me think it was an airplane, just the white light. We have seen this same type of light twice and both times it goes out the same way. Later that night we were sitting with our backs to the ridge and we start hearing something walking down the hill through the leaves, swish swish coming down the hill. I am trying to gauge about when what ever it is gets to the bottom before I turn my Boxlite flashlight on. When I turn it on it lights up the whole hillside and there is nothing there! What the hell? I don't know.

We have not been getting over there as much the last few years due to busy around the house and health issues. Maybe this year we can get back to it.

If you can use these great if not, I will not be pissed. Not my style. Keep the videos coming if you can. Be safe up there in those beautiful mountains.

Feel free to use my name.

David Baughman (Pronounced Boffman)
2/24/2020

5 Or 6 Dogs Chasing It

Hi Steve,

I enjoy your no BS you tube channel. I have had a couple of encounters with these beasts I would like to share with you.

First, let me explain, I grew up in the woods hunting and fishing and hiking, etc. And I know what the animals are out there. In other words, I know what a bear is and what it's not. I was born and raised in Bellingham, WA which is where these two stories took place. And I've spent a lot of time fishing in BC, in the Caribou. So, I am quite familiar with your area, just as a side note.

Anyway, the first "encounter" took place in a small neighbourhood near where I grew up. Granted it was a long time ago, I was 9 years old at the time and I'm 57 now, but I remember it like it was last night. My brother and I were staying at a friend's house and sitting on his front porch. We could hear some dogs barking in the distance which were getting closer and closer to us. Before long there was this hairy manlike thing running across the lawns of the houses across the street from us with about 5 or 6 dogs chasing it. It appeared to be about 7 or 8 feet tall and was covered in hair from top to bottom. It was running very fast on two legs with its arms kind of stiff down to its sides. It didn't fit the "normal" description of a Bigfoot as it was kind of slender looking. Maybe a juvenile? That was on the outskirts of Belling ham, where there was a lot of woods around at the time.

The second occurrence was 4 years later when my brother and I were together on a deer hunting trip up the north fork of the Nook sack river. This area, incidentally, is known for some sightings. My brother and I met up in some green timber. It was snowing pretty heavily at the time with big, heavy, wet flakes which were accumulating at a fairly rapid pace on the ground. We came up on some tracks that looked like human barefoot tracks, but they were about 15 to

17 inches long. Like I said, it was snowing pretty good at the time and there was no snow in the tracks, so this thing was there just ahead of us. The snow was heavy and wet so the tracks were as perfect as they could be. We could clearly make out each toe, ball of the foot, heel, etc. Unfortunately, it was way before everyone carried cell phones, so no pics. We followed the tracks for a couple hundred yards into some heavier brush and decided that we should turn around and head back to the pickup, as it was getting to be dusk.

Feel free to share. Maybe through you, somebody will believe me. Not that I really care that much. I know what I saw. Hey, maybe instead of "Honesty" you could call your new podcast "I know what I saw". Or not...

Regards,

Jim Suggs

Two Massive Beings At 20 Feet

Hey Steve, do you believe these Sasquatch beings are Mortal or Immortal Beings? In all your world travel and research and seeing one of these D@mn beings. What's your opinion? I too have had an experience seeing them. And am curious as well.

My story: Well...

Who's going to believe a 13-year-old? My experience with these beings happened when I was 13 and I'm now 37 and still remember that moment. I'm an avid hunter and have had that passion since I was born, luckily got the guts to share my story and I'll believe it till the day I die. I love your no nonsense, no BS, honest straight up talk and attitude.

Long story short, I was at a scout camp, camp out and it was after dark and I walked to the cabin where my brother was. The cabin had a big glass pane window with the light on.

As I was walking toward the light of the window in the cabin, two massive beings stepped out of the trees onto the two-track road with trees on both sides of the two tracks. I immediately crouched down so I could get a better look, let me remind you that they were 20 feet in front of me.

The light of the window between them and me really made their figures stand out! They were massive! One was I'd guess 9 feet tall and the other 7 feet tall. The smaller one was at the biggest one's shoulder height. As I was crouched, they kept walking towards me.

I called out my brother's name thinking it may be him. They stopped when I said his name and turned into the trees and disappeared. They walked next to a power line pole and into those trees. When they disappeared, I turned tail and ran back as fast as I would to the other cabin. And was silent the rest of the camp trip. I just told everyone I was sick.

I still deal with what I saw. Nobody but my family believes what I saw. Seeing two is rare from what I've heard, maybe not. To deal with going back into the woods where these beings live, I took a stress management class in college and our final exam was to "face a fear" and go face it. And write about it for the final exam. Weather it's sky diving, asking a girl out etc. So, I went to the same spot and spent the night alone. I never said in the exam what I saw just that I was afraid of being in the dark alone. What I saw I saw. And facing that fear when I slept alone years later helped me deal with my passion of hunting and still going outdoors alone or with friends. Maybe telling that will help others feel they can go back and enjoy their passion outdoors.

Don't get me wrong I still have a hard time going hunting and camping alone but I still do. The two beings I saw I know they were not human. Without a doubt I know they were Sasquatch/Bigfoot. Hopefully my story can reach you and others who have experienced these massive intriguing beings. Stay safe. I thank you for saying "you have my back" you have no idea. For what it's worth I got your back too! Feel free to use my name.

Thanks Steve.

~Justin

Every Email Counts

Steve, you're a true Patriot. I will try to be quick I'm a former DJ my wife a pizza girl manager of pizza places. We met in 98. She was born in Missouri but as a baby moved to Alaska. As a teenager when her father who had a brain aneurysm working up north on the oil fields in Dead horse was relocated to Arkansas. As a teenager she and her bother and sister and friends would cruise the off roads and party. She is the most truthful person I've ever meet she knows of my crazy military background and has taken me to this location on our honeymoon and other occasions.

She was in the car with friends and family and had to pee. Got out of the car and walked into the wood she heard some noises but thought just a possum. Then looking up saw eyes glowing looking at her she thought is was an owl from the noise she heard but then it stood up not flying but then saw an outline of something much bigger than an owl, then snort and run away. She doesn't like to tell her story to anyone. When she did back then people said she wasn't abducted because she was bearing couldn't have babies. We've never had children and she had to have a hysterectomy before she turned 40. I've seen things in my life that I wish I hadn't, she still likes to go camping and chooses to stay in a tent rather then a cabin. We sit around the fire and ask if there's any other medical condition we might have.

They are smarter than we know, I'm part Cherokee and more often when we are in the woods, I feel a calmness as if someone is watching over us rather then danger. We have been back to Seward and the Kenai numerous times, close to your neck of the woods, but only heard of stories. We will stick it out in the Midwest and hope good people like you continue to bring the light that may some day shine on the truth that helps those that have had encounters need to come forward without ridicule.

Thank again E&C

Terrifying To See It Hide From Me

I live in Pennsylvania and hike alone often; I've had this sixth sense feeling before on hikes and usually turn back. A couple days ago I was hiking up the mountain taking pictures and was pretty close to the top when I got this weird feeling like something was watching me, so I stopped and just listened for a couple minutes and snapped off a few shots. This spot gave me a bad vibe and I decided to not go any further up the trail. After 2 or 3 minutes of just being quiet and listening I could hear something moving towards me from uphill but it didn't sound that close, the sound stopping now and then.

There were boulders all around me and I was nearly at the top of the mountain. I kept listening but hadn't heard it for some time. I had just taken a photo of the valley to my right when I instinctively turned to check behind me, I looked to my left which I kind of had my back to and something quickly moved behind one of the boulders. It moved so fast I barely saw anything; it was really freaking weird. Whatever it was had been watching me and it quickly hid when I turned but not fast enough, all I saw was black fur slide behind the rock. It was terrifying to have that feeling and then to just barely see something hide from me. I know black bears could be in the area but they're hibernating right now and they aren't that stealthy. They don't hide from people and I've lived here my entire life and never saw one.

The weird thing is there isn't a lot of ground cover where I was, mainly just groups of boulders buried into the mountain, some small den-like spots in the boulders, and trees. I stood there for maybe 30 seconds and stared at the group of boulders and the spot where it had been, silence. My heart was racing as I replayed what I had just seen and my mind was on fire knowing I absolutely just caught this thing creeping on me. I turned and hopped on a few boulders and ran back to the trail. The sun was setting as I was on top of the mountain and I had an entire hike back down to do. I kept looking back the whole time and snapping off shots with my camera, the entire time feeling like I was being watched. This was one of the first times in years that I've hiked without headphones, and the first time I've stood my ground when I had this feeling that something wasn't right. I carry a firearm but something tells me it wouldn't do much good. This thing crept up on me and was watching me take photos from 15 to 20 feet away, it was way too close when I spotted it. Follow your intuition, if something doesn't feel right you need to take action and get out of there. This isn't the first time I've felt hunted in these woods.

A Quick But Lengthy Guide List

It has been a while now that I frequent your juicy rants on you tube. It has taken me this long to gather my stones to speak to you, although informally. The scenes capes are what draws me in. Many places you portray I have also traversed during 25+ yrs. Of mountaineering. From the Yukon to the Baja. I want to stress... I am not petting myself nicely. It's just what I did. Much like yourself. Without crazy details that make me shake typing this, I can say that there are a few areas that left me paralyzed in B.C. that are worth mention.

When you spoke of cedar bark tearing my ears perked. I found the exact same description in small patches 25 ft. High in a grove in the adjacent valley of the Tantalus range heading north from the towers across from Squamish, where I lived for a time around 2000-01. Strange I said!!!! Less than 6 months old? It couldn't have grown up to there?

Oh well. It was September... it was a week long solo trek so I set up camp in my bivy. My motivation. To try out some climbing gear I had just bought. My second night I heard trees being whacked. I thought windfall...or something. Day 3. My climbing gear by the base of my sad attempt the day earlier.... gone. My top rope anchor.... shredded. Yup... I booked er. I kept thinking, look at all that untouched terrain to the north. I have the pics. somewhere. I try not to think about it.

I will just tell you locations as I would rather sit around a fire and share beers with you than sound like some attention-grabbing loony.

Gold River... Dead salmon missing no one around for miles?
Elk river trail...Strange sightings + trail markers gone?
Della Falls... Uncanny calls and timber shaking?
Big interior mtn. Off topic a bit, but strange unconventional lights above moving at mach 4. All directions.
Rainbow glacier north side 5km. in. Deadly silence...not a chirp! Wt. No predators to see for miles?

The Lion Ears. 5day solo. Being followed. It triggered an avalanche. spooky shit man.
Needless to say, that I still trudge on into the wild as it calms me. It is my hope that one day we can shoot the shit like normal humans and share a bit and maybe find time to laugh about some things. I got some guide doozies for ya too. Nootka sound in particular.

Shoot me an email n maybe one day we'll meet. Good work brother. I am a stand up for the small guy kind of fella too. Proud of you! Fuck those douche bags...all of em, truth is truth!

Swamps Of Louisiana

About ten years ago, I was working at a small college in south Louisiana. I lived in the same area but not in town. I lived about three-quarters of a mile from the bayou Mallet watershed tract of woods about 100 miles long following the Bayou Mallet.

On another road out, here lived a family who I was friends with and knew very well. Their son had this experience and was very shy about it. Now, this family is 100% trustworthy to the point of having the demeanor of Jack Webb on the dragnet tv show, only the facts man. I know this event to be true.

During the hunting season, their 19-year-old son went duck hunting in a flooded field along Bayou Mallet. It was devoid of any cover except a large tree that had fallen over. The young man got into the leaves and branches of the tree and made a blind. After sitting for about 30 minutes, he heard a noise behind him. He thought he was the only hunter out there but figured it might be his Father or Cousin who he hunted with coming to meet him. But as the sounds got closer, he caught sight of something black and reddish colored move toward him. He froze in fear. It was a bigfoot.

The creature came to the water's edge, squats down and began drinking some water. This animal was less than thirty feet from him but the favorable wind and his concealment did not give away the boy's presence. He was afraid to move or breath as this huge animal was that close to him. After a minute or so, this creature stood up and walked along the edge of the water until he entered the woods about 150 yards away. Soon as the animal was out of sight, he ran to his 4-wheeler and got back to his home ASAP.

Upon reaching home, he told his Dad of what had just transpired. Like most folks but to a higher degree his Father was skeptical. So, he urged his son to take him to where the encounter had happened. Boy he did not want to go back. But his Father persisted.

When they got there the footprints were undeniably bigfoot tracks. After the Father confirmed the story as true, they rapidly went back to their home to gather their feelings.

I know this is a second-hand story, but I believe it because of the Father and son's reaction while telling the story and Their inability to lie or fabricate such a tale because of their honesty.

I have hunted the swamps of south Louisiana for 53 years. I have had experiences myself. So, I believe these guys. Thanks for bringing these stories out to the doubting public.

Another Game Guide Shares

Hello Steve,

I appreciate and respect what you're doing for the many people who have seen these things. Thanks, brother!

Let me tell you about myself. I grew up in the piney woods of East Texas and came from a family that has a long history of hunters, as in that's all we did, hunt and fish. My great great grandfather was one of the last hunters to harvest a Black bear in East Texas, back when they still had bears to hunt here. I served in the US Marines, was a deputy Sheriff afterwards for a short time and after 2yrs decided that wasn't for me!!

Then after a life spent in the woods, I decided that the guiding life was for me and have been a full-time hunting guide for the last 33 yrs. Started in Montana guiding for everything from deer to

Big Horns back when you could still buy a tag over the counter. And have had a long career back home in Texas.

The first time I had seen one of these guys, I was five years old. We hunted deer back then the old south way, with hounds and shotguns loaded with buckshot. It was a very cool and bright morning, and the hunters were lined up a power line right of way that cuts through the property. The property was located in the Sabine River bottom in Panola County, Texas.

Anyway, the Hunters were spaced about 200 yards apart down the right of way, waiting on the dogs to run a buck their way. My Father picked the end of the line down by a high-water slough that crossed the right of way. He put me into the bed of the pickup and told me to stay put, and he walked about 50yards up the line to wait on the dogs to run a deer. We hear the dogs strike, and he moves about 25 yards further down. I noticed movement in the tree line down by the slough, and at first thought, it was a deer, but it was too dark in color, and it ran out on two legs, it must have been a young one because it was only about 5 to 6 foot tall. In my juvenile mind, my thought was, why is a man running around in a full-length fur coat.

Two things that I remember vividly is he was holding his leg while running as you see in the old western when the cowboy had been shot skipping and limping and the second thing, he was fast, too fast for a man to be running with a hurt leg. I yelled at my Dad to see, and when I turned around it was gone.

Later that morning, I told what I saw and was chided and told I would be seeing pink elephants next.

From the time I was old enough to hunt by myself, I have been whistled at; pine cones were thrown at me, tree knocking, found saplings woven together or snapped, heard calls, so much that I thought it was part of the way the woods were!! It wasn't until I saw the second one that made the world change!!!!

I was sitting in a tree stand about a mile and a half from my first encounter, 17 years old and an old hand at being in the woods, or so I thought at the time. Getting to be magic time on an overcast day , woods were dead quiet nothing moving when all of a sudden in the cane thicket in front of me a sweet gum tree started to shake violently, the tree was about 8 inches across at the part I could see over the cane and was whipping like you would a small young sapling . Then it roared a deep guttural sound that vibrates in my body. Steve, I have been charged by a wounded buffalo, had an elephant kick dirt on me, but have never been as afraid in my life as I was that day. I was in shock and couldn't move frozen. He shook the tree again. I was so afraid I jumped out of the stand and shot into the air because all I could think about was, I don't want to piss it off more, and I don't have enough guns!

I could hear it running through the thicket away from me, so I jumped on my three-wheeler and floored it. I haven't been back to that place since.

Steve Isdahl   The Day Sasquatch Became Real For Me   Copyright© 2020

You talk of being aware of your surroundings, 6th sense, you are right on the money! I have been in a lot of places throughout the years where it's gone off, I don't stay there.

My brother had an encounter when he was 13 that he wouldn't talk about and won't go to the woods alone anymore. I have directed him to your site. Anyway, thanks for letting me vent and thanks again for what you are doing. As of right now, if you read this, please don't say my name because I'm still guiding for a very well-known outfitter and known in SCI and Dallas safari club circles and still have a few more years left God willing! Keep plugging.

Chapter 7 – Closing And The Proof

"Where's the proof?"

The real question should be, "what the hell happened to our communities, WHY is everyone a liar?"

In my world, The People are the proof. When a respected member of your community or family comes forward with concerning news, you listen, you take measures to protect you and yours as well your community. WHY does the modern human mind operate so flawed today? Why and who has placed the cap on our ability to learn, see what really is going on with this world of today? Why are we being mislead and lied to? Those are the questions which come to mind non stop after seeing one of these beings.

Once you start to dig, you soon realise there is much more to this than a simple large hairy un acknowledge being, much more. This is why my lack of respect for those "big names" in the "sasquatch community". Every single "big name" knows very well these things are not monkeys or gorillas, I know this, I would bet my life on that fact in a millisecond. I have mutual contacts who know and communicate with everyone of these, "big names in the Bigfoot communities"

Think about it, a "PHD" in anything stays focussed on foot prints? "metatarsal breaks"? for exactly how many years? And NEVER advances yet happily stays stagnant selling foot casts? Sasquatch trinkets? Booking appearances? Charging reality shows large $ to appear in Netflix specials? Um, NO, not an intelligent one who wishes to find out and share the facts.

Who in their right mind would boast of, "researching Sasquatch for over 25 years", and never come up with anything new or solid answers? WHO? I'll tell you who. Those who have either chosen to stay silent due to being paid to OR those who find it much more lucrative to remain on the narrative, that's who.

Let's look at David Paulides as an example. He was hired to investigate this "bigfoot thing" years back. Being very thorough, professional and intelligent. Well versed in finding out facts, him and his team including the likes of Scott Carpenter, Randy Brisson, Rich Germeau and others came up with over 130 DNA samples from around the globe and in a very short time.

For those confused, DNA isn't a vitamin or a rap group. "DNA, short for deoxyribonucleic acid, is the molecule that contains the genetic code of organisms. This includes animals, plants, protists, archaea and bacteria. DNA is in each cell in the organism and tells what proteins to make". That would be the short-Googled version.

These brave determined men obtained these samples in numerous states and provinces. Each were delivered to a scientist of THEIR choice, (a scientist who never knew it was coming). This scientist was ultimately credible however, due to leaked info, a scientific community under strict orders to NOT accept these findings, her career was annihilated, the DNA study swept under the carpet, the "big names in the Bigfoot community" carry on keeping the topic and all of you going in circles, still today.

Hopefully this well-known successful and professional hunting guide 'coming out' is going to pave the way for many others by way of giving courage and as well delivering a "NO MORE BS" to the people stance. The time is well overdue.

This first book is only the beginning, an introductory if you will. First, we focus were we should all have been focussing from day 1, The People. That is the evidence we all 'should have' paid attention to. Next up, the foot prints, then the video examples, photos and finally the DNA.

Was/has there been Sasquatch beings killed? YES. Is there proof? YES. Will the owners of it finally cave in and share? They say they will, it's a waiting game. There is much at stake.

Governments, religion, business, deep state, its all factors.

Bottom line is we are being lied to and THAT is easily proven. From the very first day we all attend the public-school system, its done, we are lied to and mislead in one form or another.

Maybe you can, or maybe you can't tell that I didn't cherry-pick emails sent to me. Relaying honest people's experiences means every person counts. Every single word of every email sent to me means something and adds to something for someone who wants to read it.
Experiences vary however, every single item mentioned possibly helps someone somewhere. This book was not created to entertain. It was created to support while giving troubled souls a voice. These voices are much needed by literally thousands around the globe.

There are nearly 9000 emailed encounters in my inbox at this time. Soon the second book will be available for all to read and share.

As we move along, I will be inserting more knowledge I have as well as numerous others.

The time has come, it is time we all spoke out loud. Being afraid of each other is now a thing of the past. The truths cannot be stopped.

There is much more to come.

I will leave you with this, trust yourself, listen to your gut instincts. Never go against, you will lose. You are in the forest? Mountains? Bring a canine when possible, listen to their warnings. Listen to the wildlife, they will tell you when something isn't right.

Be aware, take note of your surroundings. NEVER go against your inner feelings. Something feels off? Feels like dread? Death is near? LEAVE immediately.

Gather up your friends, family, whoever and LEAVE. Get away from cover, get into the open, get back to safety. Go back another day, rely on your instincts as they are always accurate. This is what I do and have done for years, and I am still here.

The governments and or "mainstream science" are NOT going to assist you when it comes to this knowledge so drop them. Listen to those who lived this experience, listen to the First Nation people of the land, listen to your neighbour, learn and openly share the knowledge.

The endless circle has been spinning long enough, jump out.

Be safe, Steve Isdahl

Index

Printed in Germany
by Amazon Distribution
GmbH, Leipzig

18538350R00179